T·H·E
MOMMY GUIDE

Real-Life Advice and Tips from over 250 Moms and Other Experts

Susan Bernard

CONTEMPORARY
BOOKS

A TRIBUNE NEW MEDIA COMPANY

Library of Congress Cataloging-in-Publication Data

Bernard, Susan, 1950–
      The mommy guide : real-life advice and tips from over 250 moms
and other experts / Susan Bernard.
            p.   cm.
      Includes bibliographical references and index.
      ISBN 0-8092-3797-0
      1. Mother and child—United States.   2. Child rearing—United
States.   I. Title.
      HQ755.85.B475   1994
      649′.1—dc20   94-10974
                                                                                   CIP

Published by Contemporary Books, Inc.
Two Prudential Plaza, Chicago, Illinois 60601-6790
Manufactured in the United States of America
International Standard Book Number: 0-8092-3797-0
10   9   8   7   6

In memory of my father, Berny Schwartz
There never was a daughter who loved her father more

To my husband and best friend, Bernie Rotondo,
for his unwavering belief in and support of all my endeavors

To our son, Alexander Bernard Rotondo, my inspiration

To my mother, Marjorie Schwartz, the best "mommy" of all

And to the rest of my immediate family, Jane Schwartz Jaffe; Gib
and Samantha Jaffe; Tracy, Zachary,
and Jim Schwartz; with love

CONTENTS

ACKNOWLEDGMENTS

Throughout the course of writing a book there are so many people who make a difference and who help in so many different ways. They believe in you, they think you're a good writer, they like your material and let you know it, they tell you you're smart, funny, and talented (and you wish you could record it and play it back every day), they provide contacts when you need them, they offer words of encouragement when you're doubtful, they are generous with information, they provide technical support and assistance, they listen when you rage, they are jubilant when you're excited, they offer good advice, they ask how they can help you, and they baby-sit your child.

I extend my sincere gratitude to everyone who has helped along the way. I would particularly like to thank the following people:

Bernie Rotondo and Marjorie Schwartz for taking care of me and Alexander throughout the duration;

Jane Schwartz Jaffe, who helped tremendously with the mothers' quotes by interviewing a slew of additional moms in the final moments;

Ruth Kupers, who listened and provided great support;

Linda Castile, who generously shared information and advice at every turn;

Claudia Hudgens, who listened, commiserated, and took care of Alexander;

Gretchen Thompson for her friendship; Norman Kolpas for his advice;

Dan Hutson and Roberto San Luis for their respective editorial and design assistance with the first draft;

Ethel Salgarolo, who transcribed many of the interviews; Brenda Koplin for her copyediting expertise;

all the subject matter experts and moms who helped make this book what it is and who contributed so significantly;

Nancy Crossman, who believed in *The Mommy Guide* and gave me the time and space to finish it; and the people at Contemporary Books who worked on the manuscript and are doing their best to make the book a success.

INTRODUCTION

I was thirty-nine when I gave birth to my son, Alexander. The last baby I'd intimately known was my sister, who's five years younger than I am. So much for recent experience.

I'd worked for the last twenty years and had never had much interest in children. When I was in my early thirties and every woman I knew (and possibly every college-educated, upwardly mobile career woman in the northern hemisphere) was pregnant, I opted against trying.

"I don't think I like children," I declared unabashedly to my husband. "They seem to take all your time. They're messy. They turn formerly interesting, well-read, and highly educated adults into baby-talking blatherers."

He nodded. We'd recently had dinner with a couple we used to like and with whom we'd always had a lot in common. After the birth of their son all they could discuss was the quantity, color, and consistency of infant bowel movements.

My husband and I agreed when we left—at nine o'clock in the evening because they both were exhausted by the nightly feedings—that we didn't need to see them again, ever, or at least until their son entered college.

Eight years later, when we decided we wanted a child, we couldn't believe how much we'd changed. On June 11, 1989, with the birth of our son, Alexander, we instantly became the people we used to hate. Our voices went up three octaves, and we started talking in a manner that can properly be described only as baby-talking blather. As one of my MWOC (married without children) friends disdainfully observed the last time I saw her (which was ages ago because it now seems as though all our MWOC friends have dropped us from social gatherings), "Have you noticed how you simply gush when you talk about Alex?"

I hadn't, but it didn't surprise me. In the first six months of Alex's life we did almost everything we had vowed we wouldn't. We told anecdotes about our Lamaze class. We discussed my labor in great detail. I nursed the baby in public places. I leaked milk on my silk blouses. My husband and I showed baby pictures to anyone who mentioned Alex's name. We discussed his progress with pride. Visits to the pediatrician's office were recounted word for word.

We took Alex to restaurants, aggressively ignoring the glares of childless diners who were mouthing to each other, as we used to do, "I hope they don't sit next to us." We pretended we didn't notice when Alex began babbling loudly.

As the first year and part of the second of Alexander's life sped by, I realized my life was changing in almost every way, and I wanted information and advice—from experts and from other mothers. From the experts I wanted up-to-date information, solutions to problems that required a certain background and expertise, and pithy advice on subjects on which volumes had been written. From the mothers I wanted reassurance I wasn't alone. I wanted tried-and-true methods of dealing with everyday problems. I wanted practical tips that worked.

But there was no *one* book that dealt with all this. And thus *The Mommy Guide* was born. I came up with a list of more than fifty topics that interested me and the mothers I knew, ranging from major issues of concern including bedtime, childbirth, child care, newborns, and preschools to less weighty topics like bathing, housework, malls, and pets.

I interviewed some 125 experts, including educators, pediatricians, psychologists, lactation specialists, professional organizers, children's bookstore owners, nutritionists, reading specialists, family travel agents, catalog experts, and housecleaning mavens. Some are well-known personalities; some are not. Some are mothers; some are fathers. In every case I've selected the most knowledgeable people.

I've got advice on how to shop from catalogs, how to travel with kids, how to pick a preschool, what to look for when choosing child care, how to deal with laundry, and how to cope with sibling rivalry. I've got recommendations on how to pick an obstetrician-gynecologist, what to do when your children won't sleep at night, how to handle a noneater, and how to organize your life. And I've cut to the chase so that you can glean what you need from reading a few pages instead of having to find and read an entire book on the subject. But if you want additional information, I'll tell you where to get it.

I sent surveys to or talked with more than 125 mothers throughout the country. A large percentage have at least a bachelor's degree. Some have become stay-at-home moms; others are working full-time. Those who are working are teachers, lawyers, college professors, nurses, entrepreneurs, secretaries, and salespeople, and a host of other women with a breadth of experience in a wide variety of careers. Most have one or two children; a few have four or five. They live in Los Angeles, California; Charlotte, North Carolina; Pittsburgh, Pennsylvania; Lake Oswego, Oregon; and dozens of other cities and states. Everyone had tips and advice to give.

This book has been an absolute joy to write. I've learned more than I ever anticipated. I was heartened to find that many of my concerns are universal, that most of my problems and frustrations are common, and that the sense of abundant joy and fulfillment I am deriving from motherhood is widespread.

To the mothers and experts who participated, my heartfelt thanks. To the scores of mothers who are interested in what we have to say, we welcome you to the fold, and we look forward to hearing your suggestions, questions, and advice as we explore motherhood in the nineties.

A few final words: Where topics are controversial, I have tried to represent different points of view. In using the book as a resource guide, please realize that while every single telephone number and address was correct when we went to print, numbers change and people move. Finally, regarding the usage of gender pronouns, this is always a tricky issue. We have done our best to use feminine and masculine pronouns equally.

Susan Bernard
Los Angeles, California, 1993

ACTIVITIES

efore my son was born, I thought one of the greatest drawbacks of parenthood was that children's activities seemed to consume all of their mothers' waking hours. Friends and acquaintances were taking their three-year-olds to gym class, swimming lessons, music class, Mommy and Me classes, and art lessons.

A tennis-playing friend said that when her three-year-old came home from music class and she put on a CD, he turned to her and said, "Schumann." This was from a child who still wasn't toilet-trained and could barely speak clearly. I, having accomplished both of the former, couldn't identify Schumann to save my life.

So once I did decide to get pregnant, I resolved that since I wasn't by nature a group-oriented person, we wouldn't participate in a lot of group activities. In retrospect that wasn't a great idea. It would have been nice for both of us to have met other mothers and infants.

Once Alex entered his second year, and we were feeling a little isolated, I changed my mind and decided to expand our horizons. I found out about a Mommy and Me class [it's an opportunity to be in a group setting with your child, and music, movement, and age-appropriate play are the main activities] at the local park he and I frequented, and I signed us up.

At the first session both of us were dismal failures. In a class of six other children and their mothers he became inexplicably shy. He clung to my leg, barely participated in the activities, and withdrew when approached directly either by the other children or by the teacher. I, who am usually outgoing, friendly, curious, and competent, failed to introduce myself to the other mothers before class,

1

knew very few of the songs, and felt awful that my wonderful child whom I adore was wimping out.

When we returned home that afternoon, I poured my heart out to my husband, Bernie. "Alex and I failed our first class," I said mournfully.

"What was the problem?" Bernie asked with genuine surprise.

"I should have worn my Polo loafers; I was underdressed. Alex hardly let go of my leg. I knew only three of the twenty songs we sang," I confessed. "Most of the other children had been in classes like this before. This other little girl his age, Alana, knew every song [and supposedly the entire alphabet, according to her mother]. I guess I've been holding Alex back."

"So now you're participating," he reassured me. "I don't think you've lost that much ground that you can't recoup," he said sensibly. "He's only fifteen months old."

Of course, I knew he was right. Still, I was shocked by the strong emotions generated that day, alternating from guilt to concern. I felt guilty for not having had Alex participate in these types of activities earlier. I was concerned he seemed to like adults better than small children.

The second session was equally bad. Between working and writing, I didn't have the time to learn fifteen new children's songs. Between playing, napping, and eating, Alex must have strengthened his resolve not to like this class, and that myriad activities fifteen minutes in duration were not satisfying for someone with a much greater attention span. This time Alex totally ignored the other children and cried each time a new activity began and he had to relinquish his toys from the last one. He was the only child who cried; I felt inadequate as a mother.

I thought about it all week long and decided to drop out. I just couldn't see the value of participating in a class that didn't satisfy either his or my needs. I didn't make one new friend; Alex hated it. I decided the whole experience was a disaster.

Three months later I decided it was time to try again and signed us up for a Mommy and Me gym class at the local YMCA; Alex and I both loved it. Since then we have participated in art classes at our local museum, nursery nature walks, and a swimming class, all with great success. So perhaps the lesson to be learned from all this is that if you persist you will find activities you and your child will like. At least it worked for us.

SOURCES OF MOMMY AND ME ACTIVITIES

Art studios
Children's bookstores
Churches and temples
Community colleges
Exercise studios
Kids' gyms
Hospitals
Libraries

Museums
Parks
Play groups
Preschools
Swim clubs
Volunteering
YM/YWCAs
Zoos

THE MAGICAL WORLD OF GYMBOREE

More than a million people in the United States go to Gymboree classes every year. Their backgrounds vary, according to Laurie Kirschbaum, owner-director of three Gymboree franchises in Southern California. "We have a ton of working parents, and we try to accommodate them by having classes on weekends or during the evenings," Kirschbaum says. "There are also parents who stay at home. They participate because it's a special time for the mother, father, or caregiver and child—without phones and interruptions. It gives them a chance to meet other parents, and their kids love it. We stress parent and child interaction. We have discussion times that allow the parents not only to exchange information but also to get a sense of who's in the group that they're going to connect with."

Gymboree offers seven different age-appropriate classes for children who are newborns to those who are five years old. In every class there are lesson plans that have been designed by child development specialists and are provided through the corporate headquarters. The teachers give input as well. "In CradleGym, the program for infants through three months," says Kirschbaum, "we cover child-care issues, news, and trends and discuss the prevalent child development theories. Every week we have a different focus. We teach songs and lullabies. Parents learn about developmentally stimulating play, but we also give them permission to have fun. We also bring in guest speakers and do special projects."

Kirschbaum, who is the mother of three, got involved with Gymboree as a franchise owner after a high-powered career in

WHAT WE'VE DONE WITH OUR KIDS

∎

"Our Mommy and Me group (and we let Dads participate too!) came about after our Lamaze reunion. We all live near each other, and our children are within four months of each other. We started meeting in a park when our kids were about eight months old. Our children are now almost three, and we still get together once a week."

∎

"I did a Gymboree class with our first child, and it was great fun. With the second child it was fun but a bit of a hassle. With the third child it wasn't possible. A neighborhood play group is a *great* source of friendship between moms and tots."

∎

public relations. "I wanted something where I could spend more time with my children," she says. "It's been great. There are people like me all over the country who put a lot of our energy into our centers. We get great corporate support, and yet there's so much love on the local level."

Source: Laurie Kirschbaum is the owner-director of three Gymboree franchises in Southern California and the mother of three. For more information on Gymboree classes call 800-632-2122.

LIBRARIES

Many public libraries and some children's bookstores offer storytime activities for infants and toddlers and their parents. In Beverly Hills, California, children's librarian Pamela Greene has been doing a toddler storytime at the public library for almost ten years. "We offer storytime to children ages two and up and their parents or caregivers. It lasts forty minutes. We introduce the children to the classics of children's literature for that age group. We also sing songs, play records, show films, and do finger plays."

Greene says that classes for toddlers are particularly popular. "A lot of the feedback from the mothers is that it's one of the first things they can do to get out of the house that's a free program. It's a good way to introduce parents to children's literature. Some of the mothers are from other countries, so they don't know our childhood lore, and they get to learn the nursery rhymes along with their children."

An added benefit that moms like, Greene says, is that the program is more structured than some of the other Mommy and Me activities they attend. Mothers participate with their children by listening, singing, and reading. "We have a theme every week. We have a display of books that relate to the theme. We'll introduce parenting books, show them what's available in our collection, and make them aware of a lot of different resources." Greene says that a lot of moms form play groups that meet after the storytime is over, so the library also provides a good opportunity to meet other mothers with similar interests.

Source: Pamela Greene has a master's degree in library science and is a children's librarian at the Beverly Hills Public Library, Beverly Hills, California.

PLAY GROUPS

What they are. Play groups are informal groups of parents who come together to provide a play experience for their children. The groups usually last a year or two. You can start with very young children, but since they don't really play together until they're older, you might initially consider it more of a mothers' support group. When the children are ready to play together, the group can evolve into a true play group.

What the benefits are. Play groups are good support vehicles for mothers—and it is usually the mothers who participate—who feel isolated because much of their time is spent with young children. Nowadays there are so few extended families that most mothers really need to hook up with other moms for support and information, whether it's about discipline or toilet training. For the children there is the enormous benefit of socializing with other children. They begin to understand the social structures of sharing and playing together in a very informal atmosphere.

Finding other parents. You can begin networking by putting up notices in pediatricians' offices, community centers, and YM/YWCAs. You can talk to people at the park. If you have an older child, you can put up a notice at his or her school. Our group was started after I had spent a week indoors in Manhattan in the dead of winter with my toddler son, who was sick. I never felt more isolated in my life. We went out for a walk when he was well again, and I approached every mother with a child of similar age and asked if she was interested in being in a play group. Absolutely every mother said, "I'd love it."

Deciding the age range of your play group. It is best to keep the age range within a six- to eight-month span because there is an enormous difference between a two-and-a-half-year-old and a one-and-a-half-year-old.

Determining group size. The group's size is very important. It affects how secure the children feel, how easily they play together, and how much attention you can give them. The size will depend on the age range of the children. For an eighteen-month-old or two-year-old, you'll want to have a fairly small group: six or seven children maximum. The size will also depend on whether all the mothers are participating or some will leave.

Deciding where to meet. Sometimes parents rotate homes within the group. Some use community centers or community

"We took a Parent and Tot (crafts and stuff) class and a kindergym class (tumbling). They provided a fun way to meet other children and moms. As a result, when my daughter was two years old, a group of us started a play group that formally dissolved when the kids began school at five years. However, we [the moms] sort of became a support network for ourselves, which continues on."

■

"A friend organized our play group. She knew a lot of women with children around the same age. We started meeting in a park that had an enclosed play area, which made it very relaxing. Eventually we moved to her backyard, where we take turns providing snacks for kids and moms. It's pretty low-key, and everyone looks forward to Thursday morning."

■

"Several of the nursery schools in our area offer toddler play groups for children one and a half to two years of age. They meet once a week for two hours. I picked two different groups and two different schools. I like the loose structure and that they both had child playtime and mommy talk time. I've met some really nice people, and we've started to make play dates outside of the school. It also gave me a good look at the nursery schools so that when it comes time to choose one I'll know what to expect."

■

rooms within their apartment building; some rent space at a church or synagogue.

Parent meetings. Initially you should meet to discuss the expectations of the play group. What do you want from the play group? How do you want it to function? Some very important issues to discuss—before you even organize—are how parents feel philosophically about different concerns, like toilet training and discipline. How are things going to be handled? Bring up very specific instances so that you make sure all the parents feel the same way. Some parents will spank children if they bite or hit; if you oppose that approach, you might want to find another group.

Parental responsibilities. These will depend on how the group is organized. If there are just parents and all the parents come every week, then you would meet to discuss how the parents will interact with the children. If just a few parents are going to be there each day—or if there are caregivers and parents—the responsibilities will be different. In any case, you need to define all the participants' roles.

Setting up the space. No matter where you meet, you want to make sure that the space is childproof and safe. If it's in the home of one of the children, you might want to put away any of that child's special toys and discuss which toys may be shared. When a group comes to a child's home, that child can become very protective of the environment and may suddenly not want others to touch anything. Some play groups will even invest money in neutral toys that can travel with the group.

Helping your child adjust. If the group meets in your home and you plan to stay, it is important to help your child adjust by talking about the fact that other children will be coming to your house and playing with his or her toys. If the play group meets elsewhere and you plan to leave, you need to prepare your child very gradually; it could take as long as six to eight weeks. Your child will require time to get comfortable with the whole idea of being in a group situation, to become used to going to different homes, and to get to know and trust the other parents before you leave.

Source: Sheila Wolper, M.A., the author of Playgroups, *is the founder and director of Beginnings Nursery School in New York. She was a nursery school teacher for eighteen years and is the mother of a son who is the reason she initially started a play group.*

THE VOLUNTEER VENUE

The key to discovering a satisfying Mommy and Me experience is to find people you like who are engaged in the kind of activities you enjoy. A good source that is often overlooked is volunteer activity. While Nursery Nature Walks in Los Angeles is a somewhat unique program—geared to families with infants through eight-year-olds who learn to appreciate and preserve nature by going on walks throughout wildlife and parkland areas in Southern California—similar kinds of activities moms (and dads) can participate in can be found elsewhere.

"People can get involved in our organization by going on walks with their kids or by becoming docents and leading or helping with the walks," says Director Judy Burns. "We usually provide child care at the docent training sessions so that everyone who wants to can participate. Many mothers take their children to the monthly meetings. There is also an annual nature festival that more than four thousand people attend. Some work at the festival itself, others help out in the office, distribute information, work on publicity, or paint signs."

This kind of involvement allows mothers of young children to meet other moms, to participate in something they believe in, to utilize their skills, and to interact with other adults. "It's been great for me," says Linda Bodek, who oversaw the festival one year as well as handling the initial distribution for the Nursery Nature Walks book, *Trails, Tails & Tidepools in Pails*. "We've met some wonderful people. My son David and I have gone on hundreds of walks, and my husband Mick has genuinely enjoyed accompanying us on most of them. As a full-time mom, volunteering has helped me keep my sanity and utilize my work skills, and I have also had a chance to share my love of nature with other people."

Source: Judy Burns is the mother of two and the director of Nursery Nature Walks, 1440 Harvard Street, Santa Monica, CA 90404; 310-998-1151.

AMUSEMENT PARKS

Ever since 1970, when a good friend wasn't allowed to enter Disneyland because of the length of his hair and his generally slovenly (albeit very sixties) appearance, I have hated amusement parks, particularly Disneyland. It wasn't a rational hatred, but it had remained steadfast for twenty years.

As a child I loved Disneyland. My aunt and uncle from Texas used to take us on an annual basis. But things turned in the seventies; I suddenly felt a strong antipathy toward the very essence of what amusement parks stood for: frivolity. As a serious antiwar college student, I wondered how anyone in good conscience could seriously believe it was morally justifiable to spend an entire day with Mickey Mouse, Donald Duck, Goofy, and their friends.

In the eighties I lightened up a bit. With the birth of my niece and nephew and their subsequent desire to partake of Disneyland and Universal Studios, I found myself biting the proverbial bullet and once again standing in long lines with people in Bermuda shorts and black socks sporting hats with ears and wearing automatic cameras around their necks.

With the nineties the transformation is finally complete. When Alex was three years old, my husband's sister Sandy took us all to Disneyland. We prepared with great anticipation. The night before, I packed an entire backpack full of what I considered necessities: sunblock, juice boxes, Cheerios, film, hats, and diapers (no, he still wasn't potty-trained). I made Bernie charge the video camera. I brought our Disney audiotapes for the car. I suddenly remembered how thrilling it had been to go to Disneyland when we were children. I couldn't wait to show Alex my favorite rides—the Autopia and Pirates of the Caribbean.

As we approached the park, I marveled at how wondrous it all seemed. "Look, Alex," I gushed, "isn't it wonderful? Wait until you see what's inside," I said, pulling him through the turnstile.

Once inside, much to his amazement and my pleasure, stood life-sized versions of Mickey, Minnie, Donald, and Goofy. I was ecstatic; Alex was terrified. "Mom, I want to go home," he said with tears welling up in his eyes.

"Honey," I said gently, trying to mask my disappointment, "it's just Mickey, Goofy, and Donald—our friends. We read books about them. They're not real. It's just people inside costumes."

"I don't want them to touch me," he said, pulling back. "They're scary."

"Oh, no, they're not," I cajoled.

"Yes, they are," he said. "I want to go home," he repeated much louder and with more resolve. I frantically looked for Bernie, Sandy, and my mother. They were within shouting distance. I picked up Alex, and we all walked quickly toward New Orleans Square so we could go on the Pirates of the Caribbean.

What a mistake! Again he was terrified. I cursed myself for not knowing better. The ride was dark. The pirates are scary. There's a lot of shooting and loud music with lyrics that surely aren't intended for toddlers. I spent the entire ride explaining that the pirates are just mechanical dolls. By the time the ride was over, I was exhausted. We picked Alex up and ran toward Fantasyland, hoping to salvage what was quickly becoming a disastrous morning.

Thank goodness for small favors and Fantasyland. To tell the truth, I hadn't been on many rides in Fantasyland; when I was a child, we thought they were too boring and didn't want to waste our time there. Yet, as we started determining which rides were appropriate for a small child who was seemingly scared to death, Fantasyland suddenly took on a new dimension. There were lots of possibilities.

He was finally having fun; we got a few good photographs and some good video footage. He was ready to go home when we walked past the Autopia. It was closed, but there was an empty car out front. Alex pretended to drive it for a half hour. He was in heaven. Bernie, mother, Sandy, and I looked at each other in amazement. The kid was having the best time of all sitting on a ride that didn't move.

Finally, when we convinced him there was one last ride to go on that he would really enjoy, he was ready to go. We headed to It's a Small World. Everyone walked quickly ahead; I dragged along behind. I've hated that ride for years. It's sappy; that insipid song

HOW WE FEEL ABOUT AMUSEMENT PARKS

■

"We go to amusement parks a lot. We always go during the week, when it's not crowded, and we get there before it opens. We do a lot of fun stuff right off the bat so that by noon we all feel satisfied and know that, if we had to leave right then, we've had a great time. Of course, we always end up staying late."

■

"Before we took our son to Disneyland, we spent a lot of time talking about the difference between fantasy and reality. He had a great time! At one point he reached over, took my hand, and said, "Don't be afraid, Mom. This stuff isn't real; it's just pretend."

■

stays with you all day. I went on the boat grudgingly. The minute we got inside, Alex came alive. His eyes became as large as saucers; he was entranced.

"Isn't this great, Mom?" he said in awe. "It's so beautiful. Look at those kids. See all those kids," he gushed.

Tears came to my eyes. It was wonderful. He was floating on air as we left the park at 3:00 P.M., an unheard-of time to leave when I was a child. But Alex was tired; so were we. It had been a success. That night, as Bernie and I were going to bed, I said, "Maybe next year we should stay overnight at the Disneyland Hotel."

"What did you say?" he asked with amazement.

"Oh, nothing," I said humming the lyrics to "It's a Small World." I was thinking to myself how old Alex would have to be to go to Walt Disney World. I've never been there.

✄

AMUSEMENT/THEME PARKS— SOME OF THE BIGGEST

1. The Magic Kingdom at Walt Disney World, Lake Buena Vista, Florida
2. Disneyland, Anaheim, California
3. EPCOT at Walt Disney World, Lake Buena Vista, Florida
4. Disney-MGM Studios at Walt Disney World, Lake Buena Vista, Florida
5. Universal Studios Florida, Orlando
6. Universal Studios Hollywood, Universal City, California
7. Sea World of Florida, Orlando
8. Sea World of California, San Diego
9. Knott's Berry Farm, Buena Vista, California
10. Cedar Point, Sandusky, Ohio

Source: Amusement Business, *Nashville, Tennessee, 1993*

TIM O'BRIEN'S TEN
AMUSEMENT PARK TIPS

1. Pick up a guidebook and entertainment schedule. Whether you've got a child in a stroller or in a backpack, you'll want to save as many steps as possible and not do a lot of backtracking. It's very important to plan ahead, get a map, lay it out in front of you, and figure out when the show times are, where the restaurants are, and which rides you want to go on.

2. Beat the lunch rush by eating before noon or after 2:30 P.M. Since children get really fussy if they can't eat when they want to, you need to plan for meals in nonprime times. It seems that everyone at amusement parks gets hungry at the same time, and then there are long lines. If you do have to wait, you should definitely have snacks—like apples or crackers—with you.

3. Wear sunscreen and drink lots of liquids. The sunscreen seems obvious, but people forget. In the olden days we used to laugh that they never had drinking fountains in amusements parks so that you would drink more Coke. Now, wherever you find a big rest room area, you'll always find drinking fountains.

4. If you've got medication that needs refrigeration, go to the first-aid station or talk to the park manager. Most first-aid stations can handle medication. If you say, "I have to keep this medicine cool," they'll do it. They've got refrigerators, so it shouldn't be a problem. If it is, talk with the park manager.

5. Don't buy souvenirs until you're ready to leave. While souvenirs are enjoyable, I often see a little stroller being pushed with a kid in it and another stroller being pushed with a big teddy bear and a lot of other stuff in it. It's much easier to get around the park if you're not overloaded.

6. Use rental lockers. With most of the lockers now, unlike the kind that used to be at the old roller-skating rinks we went to, you can have unlimited access. You don't have to put in extra money to pull your key out and put it back in, so it makes sense to put in the stuff you don't want to haul around or leave in your car.

7. Take your child to the bathroom before standing in line for a ride. I see this happen all the time when I'm with my daughters. Someone has waited in line for twenty-five or forty-five minutes, and when they get to the front, the child has to go to the bathroom. It usually makes for a frustrated parent and an unhappy child.

8. Before putting your children on a ride, find out where the exit is. Most parents stand at the entrance to a ride. When it's

"Perhaps it is a bit of a memory-lane stroll. The crowds and cost are negatives. It's a very limited source of entertainment. We go once a year."

■

"There are no amusement parks here in Alaska. We travel to California to go to Disneyland, which, of course, makes a trip to an amusement park a big event. We love to see the excitement on our daughter's face!"

■

"We don't like the crowds of people. If we were the only ones to go (impossible), we would love them. I hate the monetary pressure of having to buy a ten-dollar toy worth fifty cents that lasts an hour."

■

TIPS FOR FIRST-TIMERS

■

"Take a stroller until your child is old enough that it would be embarrassing to use one."

■

"Don't feel as if you have to see and do everything to get your money's worth. If you cover a small portion of the park or the child wants to ride the same three rides the entire time, enjoy the 'memories in the making.' "

■

"Take plenty of energy and a childlike attitude. It makes for a better time."

■

"Get there just before the park opens, when the children are fresh."

■

"Pack a lunch and necessities in a backpack. Bring healthy snacks."

■

time for their children to get off the ride—if they're old enough to walk—that parent has to run frantically to get around the corner. By that time, the kids are scared to death because there was no one to meet them. If you wait at the exit, it's not a problem. For younger children, most parks will let a mother or father actually put the child on and take the child off the ride, and that's important.

9. Don't make your children go on rides when they don't want to. Take them off a ride when they're unhappy. These are the most important tips of all. Forcing kids to ride something they don't want to is terrible. Sometimes a child starts a ride—particularly in a kiddie area—and then wants to get off. Talk to the ride operator. They're trained to handle this and should be able to stop the ride for safety reasons as well as for customer relations.

10. Don't turn your visit into a marathon. Don't try to see everything when you're traveling with small children. At the big parks—just because you paid a lot to get in—you don't have to spend the whole day. You probably paid as much for your hotel room, and taking a nap and a break will do wonders for your kid. Children's expectations are so high and their adrenaline is pumping so much that initially it's kind of an overload. An amusement park should be the same as going to a science museum or on a field trip. Give it to them in small doses.

Source: Tim O'Brien, author of The Amusement Park Guide *and* Where The Animals Are, *is the southeast editor of* Amusement Business, *a trade publication that covers the mass-entertainment industries, including amusement parks. He's the father of two and lives in Franklin, Tennessee.*

HOW TO SEE
WALT DISNEY WORLD WITH KIDS

Kim Wright Wiley is the author of Walt Disney World with Kids *and* Disneyland and Southern California with Kids. *She's the mother of two and lives in North Carolina.*

SB: When should you visit Walt Disney World?
KWW: Spring and especially fall are the best times—if you avoid the holidays like Easter, Memorial Day, and Christmas—because it's less crowded and you don't have the heat and humidity. My family has enjoyed it the most in October, but right up through mid-December is a very good time. From Thanksgiving on, it's decorated for Christmas and it's really gorgeous.

SB: How long should you stay?

KWW: Four to five days would be pretty much a minimum visit now that they've got three major theme parks and four minor ones. If you do it in less than four days, you are just going to kill yourself.

SB: Where should you stay?

KWW: Probably the single biggest decision is whether you want to stay in a Disney-owned hotel or not. For a long time the only real difference between Disney hotels and those owned by others was that the Disney hotels were more expensive. But Disney has opened up three budget hotels—the Caribbean Beach, Port Orleans, and Dixie Landing—that are competitive in price. Because of that, I advise people to stay on-site. That way you don't have to keep moving your kids in and out of the car; you can just take the shuttles.

Another consideration for people with young children is child care. While price and location are always premier factors in choosing accommodations, the availability of child care is a wonderful option. Many hotels in Orlando have kids' clubs that provide on-site child care and special programs. They also offer free child care if the parents want to go out at night. Among the best off-site programs I've found are the ones at the Hyatt Regency and (if you don't want to spend that much money) the Holiday Inn Main Gate.

SB: What are the best attractions for parents with young children?

KWW: Go straight to Fantasyland in the Magic Kingdom, where the kiddie rides are concentrated. I think perennial favorites, even for very young kids, are Dumbo, Small World, and Peter Pan. Also try the Disney–MGM Studios Theme Park, which has become very kid oriented. It used to be viewed as an older person's park, but they've come up with three attractions that are major hits with young kids: the Voyage of the Little Mermaid, the Teenage Mutant Ninja Turtles show, and the Honey I Shrunk the Kids Adventure Zone—where the kids seem miniaturized because of the huge garden hoses and Cheerios. The last time I was there I noticed a lot of parents who had taken the toddlers in there and let them play as a break from passive attractions.

SB: What special advice do you have for parents with small children?

KWW: Hang on to your kids when you're in crowds of people. I once did a survey on where kids got "lost" most frequently.

"Go on a school day, when it's not so crowded."

■

"Be prepared for your child not to want to sit in the stroller and to carry him the majority of the time."

■

"Trust your child's instincts. Don't push your kids into rides if they're uncertain. If you as a parent don't like particular rides, don't go on them."

■

"Go slow and start small. Try a carousel or a merry-go-round before trying a whole day at a large park. It can be overwhelming for little ones all at once."

■

"If your children are grouchy or tired, rest in the first place you can find. If they're timid or frighten easily, don't go."

■

Parents mentioned Mickey's Starland because it's always crowded with small children. When you're at places like that, where there is lots of stuff that kids get excited about, be aware that you need to be especially cautious.

And one more thing . . . I've heard parents say, "Oh, children need to be seven or eight years old to really appreciate Walt Disney World." I personally consider that to be total bunk. I think that with necessary precautions, very young kids can enjoy it. I wouldn't go in July with a two-year-old, but with planning, two-year-olds can have a great time, and there's no reason not to take them.

AUTOMOBILES

Two years before Alexander was born, my Renault Le Car was on its last legs. It was the third vehicle I'd owned: my *first* new *car*. I was definitely ready for something more befitting my station in life.

Bernie, on the other hand, had owned more than a dozen cars. He is a certifiable car person. In fact, I am convinced he is the only male over twenty-one in the entire country who subscribes to both Road and Track *and* Car and Driver. He is also an avid fan of "The Car Show," a tedious call-in talk radio program whose listeners discuss such interesting topics as where to find a muffler replacement for a 1962 Plymouth Valiant. He tapes "Motor Trend" on PBS and plays it back late at night after I've gone to bed.

When we talked about the prospect of buying a new car for me, I kept on saying things like "Well, you know, my hatchback has such great trunk space, maybe we should buy a wagon. It would be great for trips. You know how we always use my car to cart plants and things back from the nursery. Yeah, I think we need a wagon."

Even at the time I knew I was really thinking that we needed a family car in case we were going to have a baby. Nevertheless, I continued, "It should probably have four doors so that when we take our parents places, it's easier to get in and out. I think I'm ready for an automatic. I'm tired of driving a stick shift. I want a big car."

What I meant was that I wanted a four-door in case I had to put a baby in the back seat. I thought that automatic transmission would be easier should there be distractions. I wanted the safety of a big automobile.

Bernie didn't take much convincing. Of all the cars he'd

owned, he had never had a wagon. He would drive it on fishing trips and to transport things. I'd take it to work.

When we went to buy the car and the salesman started his at-this-point-unnecessary spiel on the value of Volvo wagons for families with children, he was surprised when we said we didn't have any children. He paused, as if he was not sure how to proceed. He looked at us as if to say "Then what is the point of buying this particular model?" His attitude might have suggested that this was a harbinger of things to come. Yet we were not at all prepared for our friends' reactions.

"Why did you buy a wagon?" they asked rhetorically. "Are you thinking of starting a family?" Fellow workers and total strangers felt some odd need to comment on the appropriateness of a wagon for a childless couple and wondered what our intentions were. I was totally taken aback. It was just a car, not a lifetime commitment. It seemed as if everyone was waiting for the big announcement.

Thirty-six car payments later, when Alex was born, it was almost anticlimactic. People looked at us knowingly. It was a bit unusual having the car precede the kid, but we had evidently been transparent. As it turns out, the wagon has been a godsend. I not only feel safe driving my small son in the increasingly dangerous and frenetic traffic that typifies the Los Angeles freeway system, but I also love the car for all the reasons we bought it.

The trunk space is truly magical. We pack all of the usual stuff and are always amazed at just how easy it is to throw things in at the last minute. The four doors are truly wonderful for getting a small child in and out of a car seat. Automatic transmission is sublime for a forty-something mother whose left leg is tired of pressing a clutch pedal. This big car is not only safe and secure but is somehow the perfect vehicle for transporting our little threesome.

Every now and then, when I think about the day we signed the financing papers, I realize that we didn't just buy a car; we bought a lifestyle. And it's one that I am happier with than I ever would have imagined.

ॐ

CARS FOR KIDS

Jim Farley, M.B.A., is the product development manager at Toyota Motor Sales, U.S.A. His parents have always owned a station wagon and still do, even though their kids are grown.

SB: *What are the most popular automobiles for families?*

JF: If you're interested in buying something other than a sedan, you have three choices: a wagon, a sport utility vehicle, or a minivan. Three pretty distinct options. Wagons are for people who don't want to sacrifice the carlike parts of the utility vehicle. Wagon owners want good handling and control. They want to be able to carry cargo and passengers, but they don't want to give up the safety. Our research shows that wagon buyers tend to be more conservative; at least the Taurus wagon buyers are. They could easily have bought a sports utility vehicle, but they didn't want to take the risk. They don't want to be perceived as driving a "mommy" vehicle or as outdoorsy folk. They just want a little more cargo but with the same kind of sedan image.

SB: *What is a sport utility vehicle, and who buys it?*

JF: A sport utility is a trucklike vehicle that seats four comfortably but has room for enclosed cargo. The Jeep Cherokee was the first compact sport utility that brought family buyers to the sport utility market. The most popular sport utility vehicle right now is the Ford Explorer. The sales have been unbelievable because Ford did a couple of things that broadened its appeal. They lowered the vehicle so that it's easier to get in and out of. It's huge inside so that you can easily seat three adults and two children. And there's a lot of cargo space for all the kids' stuff. When we did a focus group with utility buyers a couple of years ago, we found that in this category the Explorer was the only vehicle that people could see themselves in forever.

SB: *What about minivans?*

JF: In the late eighties the minivan market was dying, and now it's booming. Part of the growth has been fueled by what we refer to as the "lead boomers." They're between thirty-five and forty-five years old, the wealthiest part of the boomer generation, the people you saw on "Thirtysomething." A lot of these people who grew up in the sixties and seventies—and whose parents drove wagons—are reacting against the image of the wagon.

They may also feel the minivan offers the passengers more comfort. When people get into a minivan, they've got a lot of

WHAT'S AVAILABLE WHEN WE DON'T WANT A WAGON OR A SEDAN

■

MINIVANS

Chevrolet Astro
Chevrolet Lumina APV
Chrysler Town & Country
Dodge Caravan/Grand Caravan
Ford Windstar
GMC Safari
Mazda MPV
Mercury Villager
Nissan Quest
Oldsmobile Silhouette
Plymouth Voyager/Grand Voyager
Pontiac Trans Sport
Toyota Previa
Volkswagen EuroVan

■

room, and the kids can sit separately. In a wagon, if you've got two kids and their friends, you've not only got to bring the third seat that fits in the trunk, but it's still cramped. In a minivan you can bring your friends and their kids and feel comfortable. Actually, though, there is less cargo space. But the real point is that people who buy minivans like the image it projects.

JIM FARLEY'S FAMILY CAR–BUYING CRITERIA

• **Basic utility needs.** You're probably going to keep this car for five to six years, so you've got to think about what's going to change in your lifestyle during that period. How much cargo do you usually carry? How many kids? What are your kids like? Do you have kids who fight all the time and need to be separated by bucket seats (which aren't available in all models)? Do you have one child, and do you use your car primarily for going to work? Do you drive car pools and take other people's kids? What do you use your vehicle for? Is it primarily for commuting and driving around town, or will you use it for long vacations? You'll want to assess your typical usage and what the other scenarios will be.

• **Drive train.** What kind of driving do you do? Is it very hilly where you live, or is it flat? If it's hilly, you may want to look at a V-6 or an upper-grade engine. If it's flat, a four-cylinder engine is fine.

• **Format.** Do you need a front-wheel drive or rear-wheel drive? If it were my family and I lived in a climate with inclement weather, I'd put them in front-wheel drive; no doubt about it. It's better traction than a rear-wheel drive, even one with a traction control system. In front-wheel drive most of the mechanical systems are over the front tires, and that gives you a lot of control. If you're living in Denver or Boulder and it's snowing all the time, you may want to look at four-wheel drive. They're heavy cars and expensive to maintain, but it may be worth it depending on where you live.

• **Budget.** Are you going to buy the car with cash or make monthly payments? You should have a good idea what payments you can afford before you go shopping.

• **Safety.** This is a critical factor for families, and I know it's covered elsewhere in this chapter. Briefly, I'd look at antilock brake systems, air bags, and seat belts. In addition to the equipment in the car, look at the engineering of the car itself, its crumple zone, how it's designed to absorb injury, how the engine responds to a crash and a lot of other data available in *Consumer Reports* or in the Department of Transportation National Crash Assessment Program.

• **Image.** It's the first consideration in people's minds, but they're never willing to admit it. You know, a Volvo says something a little different from the Taurus, and a Mercedes Benz station wagon says something else. The Ford Explorer buyer is looking for something different from the Toyota Land Cruiser buyer. I think a Volvo owner is an affluent person but very conscientious and pretty thoughtful. Taurus owners are conservative families from Cleveland, Ohio. And Benz owners are saying they can afford anything. An Explorer says family and rugged. Now a Grand Cherokee says luxury and sportiness. It's the luxury sport utility that people might use who are out in the middle of Africa on a safari with their children. It's a Range Rover image, but it's got that rugged twist to it that a Range Rover will never have. The Range Rover is more of a pure luxury image like the Benz station wagon. The Voyager or the Caravan says a big family from Cleveland. The Previa owners are progressive people who are also status oriented. They need the utility of a minivan, but they are not typical minivan buyers.

• **Making a decision.** Drive all the vehicles you're interested in and put your kids in them. Simulate your environment as much as you can. Visualize putting in all the cargo you'll need in the worst-case scenario. Think about driving to work or going to the gas station. Are things laid out conveniently? Is the cup holder in the right spot? Is it easy to read in at night? Narrow it down to two or three vehicles and spend more time on those. Drive them at night. Drive them when it's raining out. Simulate your environment as much as you can with the time that you're given.

SAFETY CONSIDERATIONS

• The first factor should be reliability. An unreliable car may leave you stranded in a dangerous place, some dark highway, in a bad neighborhood, or just on the road, all of which are unsafe. At Consumers Union, we send out annual questionnaires to our readers, and we get back about two-thirds of a million replies. We have a really large database, and I think we have been remarkably accurate in predicting the reliability of various cars. The results remain very consistent from year to year—one indication that we're doing a pretty good job there.

• Antilock brakes are very important. Whenever they're available,

SPORT UTILITY VEHICLES

Chevrolet CK Blazer/S10 Blazer

Chevrolet Suburban

Ford Bronco

Ford Explorer

GMC Jimmy/Typhoon

GMC Suburban

GMC Yukon

Honda Passport

Isuzu Rodeo

Isuzu Trooper

Jeep Cherokee/Grand Cherokee

Jeep Wrangler

Mazda Navajo

Mitsubishi Montero

Nissan Pathfinder

Oldsmobile Bravada

Range Rover

Toyota Land Cruiser

Toyota 4Runner

■

we recommend them. Unfortunately, in some cars they're available only in the high-line models, but we do believe they help a lot. They are most effective on slippery roads, but they can help on dry roads as well. They keep the wheels from locking up. They keep the wheels rolling so you still have steering control and won't slide. You can actually brake and steer at the same time, whereas if you make a panic stop without antilock brakes, you may skid; the car won't respond to the steering wheel, and you'll have no control at all.

• Air bags are another item we strongly favor. Their usefulness is pretty much restricted to front-end crashes. They're not useful in a rollover, for example, or in a rear-end crash or a side impact, but in a front-end crash they are more effective than safety belts because they spread the load over a wider area of the person's body.

• Obviously, safety belts are important too. Our position is that three-point belts are much better than lap belts, but a lap belt is certainly better than nothing. Incidentally, you should wear your safety belt even with an air bag. I think that's an important piece of information to give people. First of all, the safety belt keeps you in the proper position so the air bag can do its job, and second, if you're involved in anything other than a front-end crash, you still need the safety belt to keep from being thrown out of the car, especially in a rollover, where the air bag is virtually useless. A rollover is a benign accident if you're belted and a deadly one if you're not.

• I hate to comment about car size and weight because it is possible to design a small light car that's crashworthy. A small car may be more maneuverable than a larger car, so it might be better able to avoid an accident. On the other hand, the laws of physics would say that other factors being equal, a heavy car is safer than a light car in a crash. But many design factors enter into the equations, so it's hard to generalize.

• Good handling is important too. Read test reports and find out which cars handle safely. Some are tricky; we find that some spin out more easily than others. What that means is that if you skid, the tail end comes out and you lose your steering control. Some cars tend to slide straight while others start to spin. So the way a car loses control may be important too.

Source: Alex Markovich is assistant managing editor of Consumer Reports *and has been a car writer since 1958. He's the father of three.* Consumers Union, *publisher of* Consumer Reports, *is located at 101 Truman Avenue, Yonkers, NY 10703; 914-378-2000.*

NEW CAR ASSESSMENT PROGRAM

The National Highway Traffic Safety Administration conducts a New Car Assessment Program (NCAP) to determine how well various vehicles perform during a 35-mph frontal crash into a fixed barrier. This 35-mph crash test is equivalent to that of a head-on collision between two *identical* vehicles, each moving at 35 mph. The test is also equivalent to that of a car moving at 70 mph striking an identical parked car.

All new cars and light trucks sold in the United States must meet a stringent 30-mph frontal barrier safety compliance test standard to reduce the likelihood of head, chest, and upper leg injuries. This standard for frontal crash protection ensures that all new cars and light trucks sold in this country provide occupants with reasonable crash safety protection.

NCAP tests magnify the differences among vehicles so that consumers have additional information on the comparative frontal crash protection of various passenger cars and light trucks. For a copy of NCAP crash test results, call the auto safety hot line, 800-424-9393.

Source: U.S. Department of Transportation, National Highway Traffic Safety Administration.

BABY-SITTERS

When Alexander was two months old, my mother invited my entire family and Bernie and me to dinner and the theater. That meant we'd have to leave Alex home alone with someone who wasn't related to him. We had never done that, and I wasn't sure I was ready to start. I didn't know how to find a sitter. So I called a neighborhood friend.

"We're having a family celebration," I began enthusiastically. "Do you have a baby-sitter you *really* *trust*?" There was a long pause on the phone. I sensed great discomfort.

"Susan, I know you're new at this," she replied slowly. "But baby-sitters are worth their weight in gold. You just don't give them away."

"I'm really sorry," I said politely, trying to mask my annoyance. "Do you mind telling me how you found your sitter?"

"It takes a lot of time," she acknowledged. "I use the job boards at UCLA, interview a number of students, and I usually come up with one I really like. My first sitter sat with the boys for almost three years before she graduated. I just went through the entire process again and got a great replacement."

"How much do you pay?" I said with some hesitation.

"Well, I uh . . . ,"—she laughed a little, almost in embarrassment—"I pay top dollar, but she's so good, and the boys really like her."

"How much?" I pressed.

"Six dollars and twenty-five cents an hour plus mileage."

"An hour?" I repeated in shock. I couldn't believe it. I wasn't paying that much for my daytime child-care person, and Alex was awake *when she came*.

"Well, you can get people for less, but it's difficult to find someone you trust, that your kids like, and who's reliable."

I hung up and wanted to cry. What a major production! In the first place, I wasn't sure I was ready to leave Alexander, and I certainly hadn't anticipated the cost and the bother of setting this up. Yet I'd been so critical—before he was born—of friends who had stopped going out because of sitter problems.

If I didn't begin lining up some sitters, that would soon be us. Since I didn't feel comfortable hiring a stranger, once again I went to my Rolodex with a vengeance. I called everyone I had ever known for recommendations. I was looking for teenage children of friends, maiden ladies from the neighborhood (not a large target market segment), widows, child-care providers who moonlighted, and, if at all possible, baby-sitters of people I knew.

I was getting nowhere fast. Finally, when I was at the end of my rope, a colleague who lived in my neighborhood admitted she did have a sitter she liked. Hearing my tale of woe, she relented and gave me her phone number.

Over the telephone the woman seemed lovely. She said she loved babies. She had a warm voice. She had years of experience. I knew my friend thought highly of her. She was available the night I needed her. I hired her.

In person she was acceptable if not exciting. She was neat and clean. She brought some proofreading material to work on (a good sign) while Alex was asleep. She was capable when she held him, and so we left.

The evening was uneventful. I called three times. Alex was fine. When we returned home, she had taken notes on the evening. Alex had had three bowel movements at specifically noted times. He had had one bottle, and had slept most of the time.

As we got ready for bed that night, Bernie enthusiastically said, "Now aren't you relieved? She seems nice enough. She's competent. And reliable."

"I'm not using her again," I replied as I changed into my nightgown.

"You're not?" He was genuinely surprised.

"Did you see her eyebrows? She tweezes them and uses a pencil to draw in new ones."

"I don't think Alex noticed," he replied incredulously.

"Did you see the cross around her neck?" I mumbled while brushing my teeth.

"You're married to a Catholic, honey," he said, at a loss.

"Well, you don't wear a cross, and I don't wear a Star of

HOW WE FIND SITTERS

■

"The local high school in our neighborhood has a job board. I set up an appointment and introduced myself to the teacher in charge. She prescreened the kids for me, and it was great."

■

"Because my hours are flexible, when I hired a daytime child-care person for my son I told the agency I wanted someone who could work a few nights a week as well. On these days she doesn't arrive until the afternoon. We try to schedule most of our weekly events when we know she's coming. I use a teenage neighbor on weekends."

■

"Neighborhood churches. It's not that I'm so religious, but it's worked for us. I've had two wonderful women who have been like surrogate grandmothers to our daughters."

■

David," I retorted. "She's probably a religious zealot. You don't want a zealot taking care of your son, do you?"

"He's only two months old," he responded sensibly. "He won't notice."

"She's just not my kind of person," I mused as if trying to explain my feelings to myself. "I need someone around Alex who's more like I am." Bernie never did quite understand, but then finding baby-sitters has always been my responsibility anyway. Since that first experience I've gotten some terrific sitters through friends.

For the last year I've been courting a thirteen-year-old boy who lives across the street. I always smile and wave. We invited him, his brother, and his parents over for brunch a few times. Bernie thinks my behavior is shameless. Yet the day Jeffrey's father said he could begin baby-sitting for us almost immediately, I knew it had all paid off. I sang the Rocky theme song all evening long, and while Bernie hinted that perhaps I was overreacting, I smiled demurely and shrugged my shoulders before triumphantly raising my fist in the air.

ॐ

BABY-SITTING CO-OPS

One of the least expensive and convenient alternatives to hiring sitters is to start a baby-sitting cooperative with other moms. They'll baby-sit for you, and you'll do it for them. Some mothers prefer developing this arrangement with a few close friends whose children they know well. Others like the flexibility of a large group. The upside is that it's free, you know the other sitters and should feel confident in their child-care skills, and your child will have an opportunity to play with children he or she knows and likes. The downside is that you will have to pick up and drop off your child, you may not want to baby-sit for others on your "free nights," and if someone else's child gets sick at the last moment, you may be out of luck. Still, many mothers swear by this option, and it is surely one to explore.

SITTER SOURCES

The difficulty in finding sitters is a universal problem—and it does take time—but there are a variety of good resources. Everyone agrees that while the ultimate decision is intuitive, you should check references carefully. Here are the sources that mothers recommend:

Agencies
American Red Cross baby-sitting course graduates
Baby-sitting cooperatives
Churches, temples, and other religious organizations
Early childhood education classes
Friends, relatives, and neighbors
Help-wanted ads
Job boards at high schools, colleges, and universities
Neighborhood bulletin boards
Nursing schools
Pediatricians' offices
Scout troops
Senior citizen centers
Situation-wanted ads
YM/YWCA
Word of mouth

"Word of mouth. There are a number of kids in our neighborhood. Some have outgrown baby-sitting, but they know younger siblings of friends. When we've been desperate, my husband has asked everyone he works with whether their kids baby-sit. We've gotten some great sitters that way."

■

"Try nursing schools or the early childhood education department of local colleges. These students are going into related professions. I think they're much more responsible than teenagers. You may have to pay more, but it's worth it for the peace of mind."

■

MOMMY'S CHECKLIST

☐ Make sure the sitter has the important phone numbers and that these are listed under Baby-Sitter's Basics (the form that follows). When you leave the number of an available adult, make sure that person will be home. You don't want the sitter calling 911 in a nonemergency situation because you or the other designated adult are not available.

☐ You need to go over each child's routines, including feeding, bedtime, toilet, and entertainment. Be specific. Toilet procedures for a three-year-old are different from those for a one-year-old. In one case the sitter needs to know how to change diapers; in the other case she needs to remind the child to use the toilet.

Discuss the bedtime rituals in detail. If your toddler goes to

WHAT YOU SHOULD LOOK FOR

■

"Find out whether the baby-sitter has emergency training and experience with children of your children's ages."

■

"Interview them in person before you're going to have them sit for you. Let them hold your baby. One teenager told me she had lots of experience with infants. No way. She didn't even know how to hold my son. I found someone who had three younger brothers. It's been great."

■

"Think about using male sitters. Our boys originally responded well to them, and now our daughter loves them too."

■

bed at 8:00 P.M., with the lights on or off, the door open or closed, a bedtime story read in bed or a song sung, the baby-sitter needs to know that. When you're finished explaining each routine, ask, "Do you have any questions?" Sometimes there is so much information, the baby-sitter's eyes begin to blur.

☐ Allow time—with first-time sitters—for a house tour. Take them through your house so they will know the locations of the kids' rooms, where the phones are, where the first-aid supplies are, where the exits are, what the quickest route out is in case of fire, where the burglar alarms and fire alarms are, and which areas are off-limits.

☐ Make sure you leave first-aid supplies.

☐ Through the American Academy of Pediatrics you can order the First Aid Chart, which is a wonderful resource for identifying how to respond to first-aid problems. Send a check for $2.95 to the American Academy of Pediatrics Publications, Attention Publications Department, P.O. Box 927, Elk Grove Village, IL 60009-0927.

☐ Go over house rules, and those include snacking. If you leave healthful snacks for your children, be aware that most sitters— if they're teenagers—might want Coke and chips or cookies. It's nice to ask sitters what they like. They are usually very shy about their own needs, and it's nice to have options for them that are appropriate for their age level.

TV watching is another one of the house rules that need to be discussed. Teenagers are naturally attracted to MTV and horror movies, and those are two things you probably don't want your own kids to watch. But you have to be specific. You should say, "I do not want to have the MTV channel on when my child's awake, and while you're here I want you to be sure to do such-and-such." You have to make your desires clear and not be apologetic about them. After all, baby-sitting is a job, there are certain ground rules, and you need to establish them up front. Don't assume that sitters should have the common sense to know what you expect. Tell them.

☐ Talk about playmates and friends. When you hire sitters, I don't think it's a good idea to expect them to take responsibility for other people's children. One additional child might be entertainment for your own; two or three end up being an increased risk.

☐ Talk about the sitter's privileges with friends as well. Again, be very specific. I think it's important to say, "We don't want you to have your friends over while we're gone." These things don't have to be discussed over and over, but they should be said at some point. You also need to discuss the rules regarding telephone usage.

☐ If you have a pet, explain what the routines are.

☐ It is important to discuss discipline. If we are talking about a two- or three-year-old, you need to go over what to do if the child doesn't mind. Talk about setting limits. Explain how to handle potential problems. You need to give sitters enough information so that their methods for dealing with problems are consistent with your parenting style and are such that your child will respond.

☐ One last word of advice, which is really my first caveat: you must be very careful when you choose a sitter. Having a sitter with CPR training is nonnegotiable as far as I am concerned. I believe that child-care preparation and education in the areas of accident management are critical. I think it's tremendously important to have sitters come to your house so you can see how they are with your children before you hire them. That provides you with a good opportunity to go over all the rules and procedures before they baby-sit for the first time. If you feel someone isn't right for one reason or another, don't leave your children with that person. Be very thorough about checking references and trust your intuition.

Source: Patricia Keener, M.D., is the mother of three, professor of pediatrics at Indiana University School of Medicine, and the founder of Safe Sitter, an organization dedicated to training baby-sitters, 1500 North Ritter, Indianapolis, IN 46219; 317-355-4888.

"A knowledge of first aid is essential. There are classes for children through the YMCA, Scouts, and Red Cross. I'm more comfortable with sitters who have CPR experience. I also ask situational questions. "What would you do if my daughter hit her head . . . was crying uncontrollably? I'm a registered nurse, so maybe that's why all this is so important to me."

■

"The first time I hire new sitters, I have them baby-sit when I am going to be home. They get a chance to meet my kids. I'm able to see how well they interact and to show them our routine. My son's only three months old, so I like to show them how to feed, burp, and change him. I look for a certain comfort level, maturity, and sense of responsibility."

■

BABY-SITTER'S BASICS

In those first few months—and with new sitters—it's always nerve-wracking trying to remember what information to leave when you have to be away. If you fill out the following, it should cover most of the basics.

BABY-SITTER'S INFORMATION SHEET

_____ will be at _____

Your names, first and last   *Name*   *Phone number*

We plan to be home by ____ o'clock.

Things to Remember

Bedtimes _____

Feeding times _____

Favorite toys _____

Favorite books _____

Other instructions _____

_____

Emergency Phone Numbers

           Name   Number

Pediatrician _____

Neighbor _____

Relative _____

Preferred hospital _____

Police department _____

Fire department _____

Poison control _____

Ambulance _____

What to Say in an Emergency

This is _____
Sitter's name

The emergency is _____
Explain the problem

I'm calling from _____
Address   *City*   *Zip code*

My phone number is _____

The nearest cross streets are _____

These are the directions to the house. _____

_____

_____

The preceding information is good to discuss with your sitter in anticipation of an emergency. You might want to fill in all the information but the nature of the emergency in advance.

For your sitter:

The Babysitter's Handbook, by Barbara Benton. New York: Quill William Morrow, 1981.

Babysitting, Safety Bulletin No. 66, National Safety Council, 444 North Michigan Avenue, Chicago, IL 60611-3991; 312-527-4800.

BATHING

During one of Southern California's droughts that almost brought about a mayoral water-rationing decree, I thought briefly that we might have to move away from Los Angeles. For as long as I can remember, bubble baths have been my salvation. Some people commune with nature to find life's meaning. I soak in the tub until I'm as wrinkled as a prune.

As I look back on my bath-taking history, I realize that baths have also been a great source of adventure. One dreary Sunday morning in Istanbul, I went to a Turkish bathhouse where a two-hundred-pound bath attendant who didn't speak English gave me an entire body massage that was a peak life experience. In Tiberias, Israel, I bathed in water that had healed people for centuries. And in Glen Ivy, California, I immersed myself in a tepid, squishy mud bath that was surprisingly regenerating.

Still, nothing I'd experienced had prepared me for bathing with a small child. When my son, Alex, was tiny, I couldn't wait until he could come into the tub with me. Part of it was because I found that bathing him—first with a sponge bath, then in the kitchen sink, and later in the tub by himself—was extraordinarily stressful. I couldn't believe how many things I had to remember. There were seemingly dozens of necessary supplies. Between caring for his circumcised penis and his navel, I was a nervous wreck. The idea of shampooing his hair—when he had a soft spot on his head—made my knees weak.

Later, when Alex could bathe in the tub by himself—sitting inside one of those rings—it wasn't any more relaxing. He always flailed his arms and legs, and I was terrified he would drown. So I *sat sort of next to him in a hawklike fashion that was not the most relaxing posture.*

The climax of the bathing experience was always the hair washing. Alex's screams could be heard throughout the neighborhood. In an attempt to make the experience more pleasant, I scoured my catalogs for bath product aids. They had these wonderful pictures of little children in the tub who were wearing their little suds protectors—and smiling—while their moms shampooed their hair. My son wouldn't let me put any of these products—and I bought four different styles—on his head, so there was no way to know whether they would have worked.

Finally, when Alex reached nine months, I felt we were ready to bathe together. I was sure it had to be less stressful, and it was. Bubble baths for him were pure joy. He would try to blow the bubbles as hard as he could so that he could watch them flutter around the room. I bought bath paints so that we could draw pictures, and giant stickers of seaside scenes that we used as the basis of bathing stories. His boats, plastic books, toys, and bottles replaced my loofah sponge and mitt, cypress wood-handled bath brush, and terry bath pillow. I let him shampoo my hair—before I shampooed his—and it worked. He loved getting me all soapy and then didn't seem to mind when I got him soapy as well. Our baths were a pleasant—if non-relaxing—way of ending our day.

At the age of three, he began bathing alone, and so did I. The bath has now been transformed again. For him the tub has become another play area. He takes in all his soldiers and knights; they have battles. He pretends to cook meals and fills dozens of vessels with water. He explores his body—a fairly typical activity for a child his age, I'm told.

For me the tub is once again a sanctuary. After I bathe Alex, there's nothing I like better than to immerse myself in the tub, turn on the water until it's scalding, pick up a magazine, and soak until I wrinkle.

BATHING SUPPLY CHECKLIST

■

Be sure you have these things at hand, near the tub or sink *before* you begin bathing the baby.

☐ Mild soap

☐ Baby shampoo

☐ Rubbing alcohol

☐ Vaseline or A&D ointment for circumcised boys

☐ Cotton balls and cotton swabs

☐ Towels; one heavy one for the kitchen counter and one to dry the baby

☐ Washcloth

☐ Change of clothes

☐ Diapers

☐ Brush for hair

■

BATHING YOUR BABY

Until the umbilical cord has detached, which usually takes anywhere from five to twenty-one days, your baby should not be immersed in water because the umbilical cord needs to stay completely dry so that it can fall off. Therefore you need to give your baby a sponge bath. Babies can be bathed every day, every other day, or even every third day. Some infants like being bathed; others cry uncontrollably at first. For a new parent it's most nerve-wracking until you get a little bit of experience under your belt. Most hospitals offer prenatal classes where you can learn the basics. But still, the first time you do it at home by yourself, it will undoubtedly be a bit exhausting for you and your baby.

Each hospital has its own method for bathing your baby. Some will recommend that you start at the face, then wash the baby's hair and work your way down. Others recommend washing the hair last so that you can quickly put a hooded towel over the baby's head and prevent a chill. Ask your pediatrician for his or her preference.

The Sponge Bath

1. Make sure you have all your supplies ready (see "Bathing Supply Checklist"). Leave the diaper on and wrap the baby in a towel. Work from the cleanest area—the face—to the dirtiest—the bottom. Start with the eyes, using a damp cloth or a cotton ball to clean each eye, wiping from the inside corner to the outside corner.

2. Wipe the face with a damp cloth and plain water.

3. Using a cotton swab or a washcloth, clean the *outside* of the baby's ears and *behind* the ears. Never put cotton swabs *in* the baby's ear because it can damage the ear canal.

4. Holding the baby in the football hold (so she's facing you and your arm is supporting her upper back), wash the baby's hair by holding her over the wash basin or sink (whichever one you're using). With your free hand, put a little water on the head, a small amount of baby shampoo, and with a soft brush or your hand, gently scrub the baby's head. A lot of people are afraid of the soft spot, but it is actually quite tough and can handle a gentle massaging on top. Rinse well with water and dry the baby's head. You will need to shampoo your baby's hair only two to three times a week.

5. Unwrap the baby and, using a bar of soap (which I recommend because it tends to make the bath water less

soapy) or a liquid baby soap, wash under the neck, the armpits, the arms, and the chest. After you wash the top half, rinse and dry.

6. Turn the baby over and wash her back. Rinse and dry.

7. Putting the baby on her back on the towel on the sink counter, wash, rinse, and dry her legs.

8. Until now, you will have left the diaper on. Now you can take it off to wash the genital area. With an infant girl, you wash from front to back so that bacteria from the rectum doesn't get into the vagina.

    With a boy—if he has been circumcised—wash around the penis and scrotal area first with a little mild soapy water and rinse well. You can wash the rectal area after you've washed the penis and scrotal areas. If he's been circumcised, apply some vaseline or A&D ointment on the tip of the penis to keep it from sticking to the diaper. It usually takes about two weeks for the circumcision to heal. If a boy hasn't been circumcised, wash everything on the outside. Do not retract the foreskin. Sometimes little boys who aren't circumcised get a cheesy discharge. It's called *smegma* and is a lubricant, not an infection.

9. At this point, dry the baby, change the diaper, and dress him or her, because babies chill fairly quickly.

10. Cord care is the last task. The goal is to get alcohol to the base of the cord. It's the part that is attached to the navel at the skin level and is where babies tend to have problems with infection because no air reaches it. Take a cotton swab applicator that is soaked with alcohol and clean the base of the cord. You may need several swabs because it's kind of gooey down there. If you use cotton balls soaked with alcohol, drip them and use your finger to gently move the cord so that the alcohol gets down around the base. When the cord is ready to detach, there may be some dried blood.

    A lot of people think this hurts the baby, but it doesn't. There are no nerve endings in the cord. What children are responding to is that the alcohol is cold. Cord care is very important in preventing infection.

Source: Ann Meier, R.N., is the mother of three, an American Society for Psychoprophylaxis in Obstetrics (ASPO) Lamaze-certified childbirth educator, a certified lactation specialist, and the coordinator of the Childbirth Education Program at Huntington Hospital in Pasadena, California.

HOW WE MAKE BATHING ENJOYABLE FOR OUR CHILDREN

■

"Our son plays with bath toys, blows bubbles, and uses bubble bath. He gets to let the water out himself. After baths, we let him run around the house naked and shout 'Here comes the nudie boy.' He loves it."

■

"My husband enjoys bath time more than I do. That's usually the time I need space. He's great about getting the giggles going and thinks up a variety of games such as pick the towel, the shampoo, and the soap. He also shampoos their hair and shapes funny hairdos."

■

"Bath time at our house is teatime for all the waterproof dolls and animals. We keep our daughter's tea set and some of her play food in a basket on the tub ledge. If it's shampoo day, she washes their hair while I wash hers."

■

"My son loves to bathe and shower. In the bath, I give him spray bottles and bubbles. In the shower, I let him fingerpaint on the walls with nontoxic fingerpaints. We both have fun."

■

"I'm not one of those mothers who believes that children need to bathe every night. Perhaps because I've never insisted, she's never resisted."

■

"We keep the bathroom and bathtub adjoined to the baby's room filled with toys for him to play with, and we try to change and rotate the toys once a week."

■

THE TUB BATH

A tub can be defined as a baby tub, your kitchen sink, or one of those little sponges that fits into your sink or a plastic tub. You can begin giving your baby a tub bath once the umbilical cord has fallen off and is completely dry inside and/or the baby doesn't want to lie down flat any longer. You probably won't use an infant plastic tub much beyond two or three months because by then the baby wants to sit upright, which is not possible in the plastic tubs. The main value of the plastic tub is that you don't have to worry as much about slipping because the baby is lying on his or her back in a slanting position.

The primary difference between a sponge bath and a tub bath is that babies can be totally immersed in water in the tub. You can soap them all over, but you shouldn't wash their hair in the tub. The best way to wash their hair, still, is to have them lying flat with their head over the sink.

When your baby is three or four months old and can be put into the family tub, you will probably want to buy an infant safety ring—a wonderful device that suctions onto the tub bottom. The baby sits on a piece of foam in the middle with his or her arms hanging over. The ring gives the parents some security in that it holds the baby up so that at least one hand is free for washing. Another valuable and practical bathing device is an inflatable cover that fits over the water spigot to protect the child's forehead.

One critical word of advice when bathing your child: Never leave him or her in water alone, even for an instant. Children have drowned in one inch of water. People think this could never happen to their baby, but tubs are very dangerous. Children slip, they fall, and they can scald themselves if they are able to turn on the water.

The bath should be a pleasant experience for your child and you. When your child is older, there are lots of wonderful bath toys, boats, nontoxic bath paints, stick-on plastic characters for a great bath story, plastic books that can be immersed in water, and a host of other plastic toys that will make bathing a fun experience.

Source: Carole Miller, R.N., is a registered nurse and a nationally certified Lamaze childbirth educator. She is coordinator of Parent Education/Women's Health Services at Saint John's Hospital and Health Center in Santa Monica, California. She is the mother of four.

BEDTIME

During the first year of Alexander's life he didn't sleep through the night. He'd wake up three or four times. We tried patting him to sleep; that made it worse. The moment he saw us he would sit up (or stand up when he was older) and cry twice as hard. I tried letting him cry, and I couldn't. Alexander rarely cried during the day, and those plaintive sobs at night went right through me.

I talked with the pediatrician. He had given such good common-sense advice about everything else. "Just let him cry," he said. "It may last a half hour the first night, but it will be less the second night. By the end of the week he should sleep all the way through."

I went home determined to follow his advice. He had been a pediatrician for more than thirty years. He had seen thousands of children. Obviously he knew what he was talking about. My unwillingness to let Alex cry was irrational.

The next night, at about 11:00 P.M., Alexander woke up and began crying. I looked at the clock. I sat and listened. The small cries turned into genuine sobs. I lay in bed, clutching my chest, waiting. I looked at the clock again. They got louder and louder. He began a choking kind of sob. I bolted. It was 11:07.

I took him into bed with us. "I'll try harder tomorrow night," I said apologetically to Bernie. "I just can't stand listening to him cry at night."

We went through this for a week, one or the other of us ultimately giving in. On the worst night I let him cry for fourteen minutes. The volume never diminished. The sobs just got deeper and more penetrating. "I can't stand this," I said to Bernie. "Maybe he's having a nightmare.

"We said we'd let him cry," he reminded me. "I think he's too little to have nightmares. The pediatrician said he will stop doing this if we stop picking him up after a moment's tears. We discussed this last night."

We both stiffened our bodies to brave this out. Alex persisted. In his room down the hall, he must have sensed our conflict. After twenty minutes Bernie couldn't stand it. This time he picked him up. The moment Alex was in our bed, he stopped crying. The second his head touched the pillow, he smiled and went back to sleep.

I stopped discussing my problem with our pediatrician. Everything I'd ever read and heard suggested it was terrible to bring your child into your bed. Dr. Spock said no.

My sister had horror stories to tell me. One couple she knew who let their daughter come into their bed when she was an infant couldn't get rid of her at age six. Another, who tried to break their son of the habit after he was out of the crib, on the advice of their pediatrician had begun locking their bedroom door. In the morning they'd find him sleeping right outside the door, curled up on the floor.

I couldn't bear the thought. But in my weakness, what psychological trauma was I creating? And besides, I was getting really tired of never sleeping through the night. Alexander had become an absolute bed hog. He would sleep horizontally between his father and me. Sometime during the night one of us would leave and sleep in the guest bed because we were falling over the edge of ours.

In desperation I called a friend with four children. When I asked if she'd ever had this problem with any of her kids, she paused.

"With all of them," she finally said. "They've all slept in our bed at one time or another."

I was so relieved I almost cried. "What did you do?" I implored. "How did you solve it?"

"I guess each child instinctively understood that when a new child was born, the older one couldn't sleep with us anymore," she said comfortingly. Since I knew there was a three-year gap between all the kids, I was shocked and greatly relieved.

"You mean they would sleep with you for three whole years?" I asked in wonderment.

"Not for the whole time. Just when they needed to. It worked out all right."

I couldn't believe it. Her kids were great. They were so well adjusted. They were nice children.

The pressure was off. If she did it, so could I. I would just handle it.

A few months later, when Bernie was going out of town for a week on business, I decided now was the time. I wasn't obsessed with it the way I had been earlier. I didn't feel this great pressure to reform Alex because I was doing a bad thing. Rather, I just felt it was time to change his sleeping patterns.

The first night he cried for a half hour. The second night he cried for fifteen minutes. A week later he slept through the night. Our pediatrician had been right. It did take just a week. But this time I was ready. I'd stopped worrying about his nightmares. I knew he wasn't going to choke to death. I was ready for him to sleep through the night. And so he did.

᪥

THE FIRST YEAR OF LIFE

Newborn babies average sixteen to eighteen hours of sleep a day, spread out in about five sleep episodes. The hours they sleep are not random. Within just a few days of birth babies usually sleep longer at night than during the day. By two months of age nearly half stay asleep or rest quietly for at least five hours during the night, giving parents a chance to return to more normal sleep patterns. By the end of the first year most children are down to one long sleep period at night and a morning and afternoon nap, altogether about twelve to fourteen hours of sleep a day.

You can help your baby learn the ways of the world if you:

• Schedule night as "sleep time" and day as "wake time." Avoid play and entertainment at night. Confine those activities to the preferred waking hours.

• Teach your baby that the bed is for sleeping. Put the baby into bed when it's bedtime. Try to keep the baby from getting used to falling asleep in your arms or on the living room couch or needing a pacifier or bottle to fall asleep.

• Keep lights off or low at night.

• If the baby cries, go in, but don't make a fuss. Pat the baby; change a diaper, without taking the baby out of bed if possible. Don't turn on bright light. Keep noise and conversation to a minimum.

SOLVING BEDTIME PROBLEMS

■

"I nursed all four of my children to sleep for most of their first two years. Then we did the 'take the baby back to his or her bed twenty-five times the first night' routine for about a week, and that was that."

■

"When our twins woke up during the night, my husband (the non-breast-feeding parent) went into the room, didn't pick them up, but said he would stay. Then he slept on the floor until the child fell asleep."

■

"Our four children have had a variety of problems. When they wouldn't go to sleep in their beds, we let them fall asleep elsewhere and then moved them. When they came to our room during the night, we made a chart with stars and prizes for staying in bed. It was surprisingly effective, even for our two-year-old, but maybe that was because he had older siblings."

■

AGES ONE TO THREE

These are years of growing independence. Children learn to walk, talk, feed, and dress themselves and master toilet skills. Learning to fall asleep by themselves and to return to sleep quickly if they awaken during the night is an important accomplishment too. As with walking, the first steps often are shaky.

Bedtime crying and middle-of-the-night tearful awakenings are among the most common problems brought to pediatricians and specialists in children's sleep. Parents find these problems exasperating. They often report they've "tried everything." And they usually are surprised to learn that their best efforts to soothe may in fact be perpetuating the problem.

Parents often take a crying child out of bed. They rock the child, sing, offer food, read stories, even take the child into their bed. Sometimes they let the child fall asleep in front of the TV. All these measures establish conditions for falling asleep that require a parent's presence. The child doesn't learn how to fall asleep alone.

One good way to cope with bedtime protests:

1. Put your child into bed awake in a darkened, quiet room. Some children need a special blanket or favorite toy to fall asleep initially and to provide comfort on awakening during the night.
2. Say good night and leave the room.
3. If your child cries, wait five minutes before going back.
4. Stay in the room for two or three minutes so your child knows you're there, but don't pick the child up. Keep your conversation to a minimum. Then leave, even if the child is still crying.
5. If crying continues, wait ten minutes before returning. Stay briefly and leave again.
6. If crying continues, wait fifteen minutes before coming back.
7. Use the same routine during middle-of-the-night awakenings and at nap time. On subsequent nights, add five minutes to all waiting periods. The going and coming show your confidence in your child's ability to function independently. At the same time you provide reassurance that you are not going away forever. Crying during the learning process won't harm your child psychologically, the experts say. More likely, it will be harder on you.

Source: Sleep Problems in Children: A Parent's Guide, © *1992, American Sleep Disorders Association, 1610 14th Street N.W., Suite 300, Rochester, MN 55901.*

FOUR APPROACHES TO BEDTIME

The family bed. The basic philosophy is that parenting, nurturing, is a twenty-four-hour proposition. The family bed works especially well with high-need children whose needs continue strongly all night long. To determine whether it is working for you, ask yourself: Is everybody sleeping, or is somebody's sleep being disturbed? If someone is not sleeping or you are playing "musical beds," it may be time to look at other options. If everybody is sleeping, then don't be concerned with what your relatives or the neighbors say. The bottom line is not who is sleeping with whom but who is sleeping.

You should know, however, that when a child starts out sleeping in your bed, he or she may be with you for many years. So, when will your child leave your bed? Purists would wait until the child is ready. If you are ready before your child is, there are ways to get your child out of your bed and teach new sleep habits without a "cold turkey" approach that might be devastating to both of you.

Cry it out. This is a time-honored approach, the one that many pediatricians recommend. You simply let your child cry until he falls asleep and learns to sleep on his own. It is my personal belief that you need to give an infant up to six months to develop the neurological maturity it takes to be able to sleep through the night.

Crying it out is the shortest method; it usually takes four nights, and it *usually* works. It is easier with a younger child than an older one because you have more control when your child is in the crib than when in a bed. At bedtime, once you put the child down—after whatever your routine is—don't return to the room, whether or not your child is crying. In the middle of the night, either don't respond or, if you do, go in, check, make sure everything is OK, say good night, leave, and then don't come back. The child essentially is learning that waking in the middle of the night or needing a parent to help him go to sleep will not be reinforced.

Teaching in small steps. This method refers to any approach in which you employ a gradual teaching method. One "small step" method that may be helpful for moving the child out of the family bed is to begin by letting the child sleep in a sleeping bag next to the parents' bed. The next step might be for the child to begin the night in his or her own room with permission to move to the sleeping bag as needed. Another "small step" is to make the

"Our seven-month-old was waking up three times a night. We let him scream one night for one hour and an hour later for twenty minutes. This took a couple of nights. It works letting them cry, as hard as it may seem."

■

"All my children have their own blanket with satin trim that I would rub on their cheek as they nursed. The association was such a pleasurable one that each child used the blanket to settle themselves to sleep, which was my original intention."

■

HOW TO DEVELOP A BEDTIME ROUTINE

■

"Tell your kids what they are going to do tomorrow so they will be anxious to sleep and tomorrow will come quickly. We've developed a ritual. Every night when our children go to sleep, we talk about our day. Sometimes I do it in such detail that my children are almost asleep by the time I've finished."

■

"I've got five kids. From the very beginning we've always had a bedtime routine with a bath and reading. And my husband and I have always traded off so that the kids were used to each of us. The sooner your kids learn to be flexible (no easy task for a one- to three-year-old), the happier you'll all be."

■

child's room so attractive that the child finds it very enticing to be there. Then the parent can stay in the child's room until the child goes to sleep or gets used to the idea of staying in bed. Another way, with a child at least two and a half years old, is to use positive reinforcement so that the child is rewarded—with either stickers or inexpensive toys—for going to sleep or staying in his or her own bed at night. With small steps, the child is gradually getting more skilled at staying alone and you are weaning yourself out of the bedtime process.

Living with it. In some situations and with some personalities you will have to decide that for now there's nothing you can do or "choose to do" to work on a particular sleeping problem; for example, the child who is repeatedly ill or who is dealing with difficult life circumstances (you are going to be moving soon, there is a new baby, you are going through a divorce). Maybe the child is going through a developmental issue, like separation problems. You may want to wait a little bit for the issue to pass or simply for the child to learn independently.

A final word of advice: There is no single best approach to handling sleep problems. Just as each child is unique, each parent is unique—with different values, different tolerances and temperaments. The key to finding the best solution is to find the one that fits you, the one you can commit to enough to see it through until you reach your goal.

Source: Rebecca Huntley, author of The Sleep Book for Tired Parents, *is a family therapist from Seattle who is a consultant on sleep problems and a parent educator. She is the mother of three and has been through sleep issues with all her children.*

A FEW WORDS FROM A SLEEP GURU

Richard Ferber, M.D., author of Solve Your Child's Sleep Problems, *is director of the Sleep Lab and the Center for Pediatric Sleep Disorders at Children's Hospital in Boston, teaches at Harvard Medical School, and is a pediatrician. He's the father of two.*

SB: Why do so many children have sleep problems?
RF: Actually, what happens most often is that children show many variations of normal sleep. However, some variations may involve the parents more than others. It's usually the latter that people feel

are problems. So, for example, if the child wakes up a couple of times a night, which is normal and which we all do, and goes back to sleep on his or her own, it's usually not considered a problem. If the parents have to get the youngsters back to sleep, which may take as little as covering them, putting a pacifier in their mouth, and patting them on the back, or as much as walking them about and driving them in the car, it's a problem.

SB: How do you develop good sleeping patterns?

RF: The first thing is to have a good understanding of what normal sleep patterns are. The second is to have a good understanding of what a child should be doing at each age. You also have to realize that there's a give-and-take underlying all this. Not all youngsters are exactly the same in their development. Also, children usually can't establish a normal schedule themselves. It takes regular input from parents.

Children must have regular naps and regular mealtimes. You need to maintain the regularity of their schedule within reason. Take cues from your child according to his or her needs and capabilities. A child who needs thirteen hours of sleep shouldn't be on an eleven-hour sleep schedule. If he or she is ready to give up one of the naps, trying to force the child to nap may not work. Trying to cut out one of the naps before the child is ready, also may not work.

You should also pay attention to how your child is developing. A lot of issues don't need to be prevented as much as understood. Learn to know when things are settling into place and be ready to make changes if they're not happening on their own. Most youngsters are beginning to sleep through the night at four months and should have the capacity to do so at five or six months. If you're continuing to have problems with your child, you may want to step back and figure out if something you're doing is promoting the problem so you can make the appropriate changes.

SB: What advice do you have for moms "at the end of their rope"?

RB: Moms should just realize that most problems are solvable once they understand why they're there. Probably the most important message I can give is that there is no one approach that can solve all children's sleep problems. The best way is to try to understand what is happening with your child, figure out a program for dealing with it, and see how your child responds. If it continues, get outside help.

"Keep it consistent. If you rock and then sing, do it the same way every night. If you read special books at bedtime, always make time for those books. Children feel more secure if they can expect certain rituals and look forward to them. We stick with the rituals even when our kids say they are not tired."

■

RESOURCES

Organizations

National Sleep Foundation
122 South Robertson Blvd., 3rd Floor
Los Angeles, CA 90048

Further Reading for Children

The following books about bedtime are personal favorites recommended by Linda Dimitroff, mother of two and manager of Children's Book World in Los Angeles, California; 310-559-2665.

Goodnight Moon, by Margaret Wise Brown. New York: Harper & Row Publishers, 1947.
Sleepy Time, by Gyo Fujikawa. New York: JB Communications, Inc., 1983.
Ten, Nine, Eight, by Molly Bang. New York: Greenwillow Books, 1983.
Time for Bed, by Mem Fox. San Diego: Gulliver Books/Harcourt Brace & Co., 1993.

BIRTHDAYS

When I was pregnant, we were invited to the birthday party of a friend's one-year-old. Far be it from me to judge other parents—since postparenthood I've done everything I said I would never do—but I felt it was excessive. Aside from the fact the party cost more than my wedding—it was catered by a well-known "A-list" caterer—and there were twenty screaming one-year-olds and their overdressed parents in attendance, there were also ponies.

On a quiet residential street in Los Angeles, were three of the cutest ponies I've ever seen, giving rides to mostly terrified children. As Bernie and I walked through the maze of pony poop on the way to our car I said, "I will never overindulge our child to that degree for his birthday."

So, as Alexander's first birthday approached, I panicked. I would awaken in the middle of the night plagued by questions. How could I make his birthday special for him without going over the boundaries of good taste? Should we invite our friends and their children, or should it be a family affair? What kind of lunch should we provide for a child whose favorite food is a gruellike cereal? And more philosophically: Does a one-year-old even understand the concept of a birthday?

Bernie felt I was making a mountain out of a molehill. He couldn't believe that someone who, with her mother, had planned her own wedding in less than an hour was literally spending days worrying about a first birthday party. "You know this party is for us, not for Alexander," he sensibly reminded me after we'd talked about the party for the hundredth time. "You know Alex cannot conceptualize what a birthday means. The child can barely talk."

43

"But he'll see it on video when he gets older," I argued. "And if we don't do something thoughtful and special, he'll think we don't care," I said with tears in my voice.

Bernie, being the consummate diplomat and devoted husband, said gently, "Honey, we'll do whatever you want." I burst into tears. He went out for Time *magazine and came back four hours later.*

When he reappeared, I had regained my senses and planned the entire event. I had decided it would be for our immediate family at our house for a few reasons. First, birthday parties for babies are usually rather boring. The conversation—mostly about child rearing and child-care providers—is painfully dull. There are always great chasms between the people who bring children and those who don't. The childless guests can converse like adults. Those of us with children, however, continually have to excuse ourselves because our little angels, whom we adore, are fighting over a toy, running into dangerous objects, trying to open the presents of the birthday kid, or secretly helping themselves to the birthday cake.

Finally, if we're being honest, only family members are interested in seeing our children open the "gazillions" of presents they have bought them. In fact, since most one-year-olds are incapable of opening presents, the task becomes the mother's responsibility. (Personally, I'm not sure why mothers seem better suited to this task than fathers, except that inexplicably we have been bred to smile and come up with just the right response for an entire host of gifts that we not only wouldn't buy for our child but that we abhor.)

Suffice it to say that Alex's first birthday party was a great success. It was a low-key but love-filled affair. His grandparents, aunts, uncles, and cousins doted on him. The lunch was delicious: Bernie cooked, and I did the dishes. We all had tears in our eyes when we sang "Happy Birthday" to Alex. He had his first taste of birthday cake—ever—and put his face in it. A great photo opportunity.

While he may not have understood the concept of birthday and presents, he did seem to revel in the excitement of the event. Most important, when he gets older and looks at the video, he will know that we did something thoughtful and special because we cared.

BIRTHDAYS: A THERAPIST'S VIEW

Renee Schwartz has an M.S.W. in clinical social work and a Ph.D. in clinical psychology with postgraduate training in child psychotherapy. She is a child and adult therapist in private practice, a child development consultant to preschools and parents in Los Angeles (310-393-0947), and the mother of one.

SB: *Why are birthdays important?*
RS: It's not really until age three that children begin to understand that birthdays are for celebrating something special about their date of birth. Until then children feel something and enjoy a party, but they don't necessarily understand that it relates to their birthday. They know that people are admiring them, giving them attention, loving them in some way, and are excited to be with them, but they don't know it is a special acknowledgment of their birth. That is a fairly abstract idea and difficult to grasp at so young an age.

SB: *How do you feel about the trend of having a child's party for couples with their children?*
RS: From a personal perspective, my husband and I gave a big party for our son's first birthday, and we invited our friends and their children. Since I like to cook gourmet food, I developed a fancy menu, spent a lot of time cooking, and bought this great cake; by the time the party started, I was exhausted. In retrospect, I think the presence of a lot of grown-ups really takes away from your enjoyment of your child. The first birthday party may be the first time a child begins to develop a sense of community, when he begins to learn that there are friends who are like family and who love each other and him. But when you overdo it in terms of numbers, the child just feels overwhelmed. And it is overwhelming for the parents as well.

SB: *What should parents expect when planning a party for a one-year-old?*
RS: The party is more of a celebration for the adults in the family than for the child. For a one-year-old, you don't want the party to be too overwhelming and too stimulating, because he or she will get lost in that. If you want your child to enjoy it, there should be a few kids your child's age, a few toys to play with; the children should be able to go outside, to walk around and explore things. At one, children can't really open gifts, and there's too much pressure even to look at all the gifts that are given to them. Having

BIRTHDAY PARTIES: HOW WE DO IT

■

"We concentrate on location and food. For our daughter's second birthday we invited all our friends and family to bring their favorite dish and come to our favorite park. Everybody had a great time. Because it was potluck and people met over a picnic table, it was a relaxed atmosphere."

■

"We try to keep it simple and inexpensive. Our son loves pirates, so we did a treasure hunt in our backyard. We buried treats and gave each child a map. We had a ball, and the parents did too. We like to have our children's parties in the morning, when the kids are in good, happy moods. The whole thing cost about $50, including the treasures. Instead of a cake, use decorated waffles."

■

a few adults with their kids, a little cake, and just being together is enough. You want your child to feel a sense of connectedness with you, but you also want to open his world a bit to include other people who love him.

SB: *What about parties for two-year-olds?*
RS: If kids are in toddler groups or day care, they will be much more group oriented. If the party is for a child who is home with a mom and is in a group only occasionally, a party with a group of children might be overwhelming. In either case you should keep the number of kids to a minimum because the children will need supervision. At two a child can play more with other children. You should consider activities in the background like water play, a tub of bubbles, sandbox toys, and other avenues for parallel play. At this age the children have more of an awareness that the party is oriented toward them and the birthday song is being sung to them.

SB: *What about three?*
RS: At three, children usually know that their birthday party is a celebration of their birth. At this age I think the festivities really do become a birthday party. Children understand that people are excited, and they are excited, because it is their birthday. At this age they have probably entered preschool, and they have separated more from their parents, physically and emotionally. They are beginning to feel more competent. They see the birthday as a celebration of that. Still, the feeling of a community of people who are excited and happy and want to celebrate with this child is what the main point should be. As parents, if we worry too much about hiring "the snake lady" or whomever—while those things can be fun—we begin losing sight of why we are having the party. If we run around frenetically—because there are so many activities planned and so much to do—then we are not truly celebrating the day with our children.

SB: *As a mother and a therapist, what party tips do you have for parents?*
RS: Sometimes I will give two parties: one for friends and their children and one for relatives. That way everyone is included, but it is not overwhelming. I also think you need to remember that birthdays are times that you want to look back on as having enjoyed with your child. Parents need to communicate how wonderful it is to spend time with family and friends who care about each other.

MEREDITH BROKAW'S
BIRTHDAY-PARTY-PLANNING TIPS

• **Invitations.** If at all possible, do homemade invitations, simply because that little extra effort of putting yourself and your own creativity into the invitation says a great deal to the recipient. What you're likely to find is that everybody who gets a handmade creative invitation, and by that I do not mean something elaborate, will come to the party ready to participate. Try to let your child— even a young one—help by putting stickers on or coloring a section of the invitation. That act of participation may be as important and significant to the child as the party.

• **Guest list.** The rule of thumb, which is to invite the same number of children as your child is turning in years, seems to work the best. But some parents find it difficult to limit guests, particularly once children start school. To get around it, I often suggest to parents that it's more the ratio of parent and parent-helpers to children than it is the actual number of children who are invited. Having both parents and friends participate is very effective. You may even consider hiring the teenage baby-sitters you use when you go out.

• **The theme.** Children should always be involved in choosing the theme, even when they're little. Nobody knows your child better than you do, so an observant parent will know if a child is more interested in trucks or in Superman. At the younger ages teddy bears or balls or colors can dictate what the theme of the party is.

• **The decorations.** Decorations set the tone and the mood. They're part of the theme. But you don't necessarily have to buy decorations to make the theme come to life. One of my best examples is the safari party. Most little kids have a collection of stuffed animals; that seems to be part of the American culture at this point. You can use them—with all your plants—to create a jungle atmosphere, and you don't have to buy anything.

• **Games and activities.** You should have more than you need because young kids' attention spans are not long. Sometimes there are games that you think are foolproof, but they don't work; in that case you want to be able to move to something else. The classics like pin the tail on the donkey usually work well, and my experience is that treasure hunts and scavenger hunts are always winners. It doesn't matter whether the guests are two-year-olds searching for the hidden plastic animals in the sandbox or teenagers searching for exotic objects.

• **Entertainment.** I don't think you need it for infants and

"We let our daughter have only a few children over, and it's worked out well. For her second birthday she had four little girls to our house. I bought Play-Doh and stick-on earrings for them, and each child got a helium balloon. I made finger sandwiches for the kids and parents alike. It was very relaxing, and we had a great time."

◾

"Our son's nursery school can be rented for $35 on weekends for birthday parties. We had his third birthday party there, and it was great."

◾

"We waited until our daughter was three for a traditional party. We had it at the dance studio where she was taking lessons. We invited all the kids in her class. There was too much going on for them, although I think they all had a good time. It was pretty expensive, so we won't do that sort of a thing again."

◾

"We've had just family parties for our daughter's first and second birthdays. Her third birthday is coming up, and she wants a party. Not only that, but she's already picked out her birthday cake—vanilla ice cream with sprinkles. She's more interested in the cake than in planning the party. We're having a morning park picnic with ten children and their parents. We're all looking forward to it. The key is simplicity."

■

toddlers. Parties for which the parents have hired a magician, a clown, or an acrobat—unless parents have seen them and know they are excellent—are the riskiest. A lot of children at this age are afraid of strangers, particularly if they're dressed in funny clothes. And any type of activity in which the children are just onlookers rather than participants doesn't seem to work as well.

• **Gift opening.** The question of whether to open gifts during the party is certainly a personal one. I should preface this by saying that one of the reasons why I feel it is so important to have kids participate in activities and to have a theme is that all of a sudden the whole issue of gifts becomes secondary. So many birthday parties now are organized around the opening of presents that the spirit of the birthday party is lost. The essence of a party is to entertain your friends and for everybody to have a good time. It shouldn't be about presents. With that said, if you want to open gifts, one good idea for little kids is to do it as each child arrives. Their arrivals are usually staggered. Some mothers give the child who's giving the gift his or her party favor in return. It doesn't have to be something big, but it is a way of saying, "You've given me a present; I have something for you, too."

• **Food.** Again, if you've got a lot of fun activities, food doesn't seem to be that important, but it depends on what time of day you're doing the party. If you've gotten everybody up from nap time, you should have some juice or something to eat or you're going to have a lot of crying kids. In my experience over the years, more cake goes uneaten than eaten. But kids expect birthday cakes, you can work them in with your theme, and it's a nice part of the decoration.

• **One last thought.** I believe birthdays are really important for children and parents. It's a time when parents can teach some real values about including people and how to thank people. It's a time to allow your child to feel he or she is the center of the universe for one day of the year. It allows children to build their own self-esteem and confidence about who they are. It's an opportunity for parents to put some meaningful memories in the bank for their children's future years.

Source: Meredith Brokaw, former teacher, mother of three, and wife of TV anchorman Tom Brokaw, is the founder and owner of Penny Whistle Toy Stores and the coauthor of five books, including The Penny Whistle Birthday Party Book.

CAKE-BAKING TIPS

- If you like to plan ahead, do so. Your baked cake will stay up to three months wrapped in heavy-duty foil in the freezer. Always thaw cake completely before icing. You cake will still be fresh and easy to ice because it will be firm.
- Packaged two-layer cake mixes usually yield four to six cups of batter, but formulas change, so always measure. Here's a handy guide. One two-layer cake mix package will make any of the following: two eight-inch round layers, one ten-inch round layer, one nine- by thirteen- by two-inch sheet, or one character cake.
- If you're in doubt as to how many cups of batter you need to fill a pan, first measure the cups of water the pan will hold and use this number as a guide. Then, if you want a cake with high sides, fill the pan two-thirds full of batter. For slightly thinner cake layers, fill half full. Never fill cake pans more than two-thirds full. Even if the batter doesn't overflow, the cake will have a heavy texture.
- For three-inch-deep cakes, we recommend pound or pudding-added cake batters. Fill the pan half full only.
- To prevent a cake from sticking, once you grease the inside of a pan with solid vegetable shortening or a vegetable cooking spray, sprinkle flour inside the pan and shake the pan back and forth so the flour covers all the greased surface. Tap out excess flour; if any uncovered spots remain, touch up with more shortening and flour. Or, if you prefer, line the bottom of the pan with wax paper after greasing. This eliminates flouring the pan. Your cake will unmold easily but with more crumbs on the side.
- To unmold the cake, let it cool for ten to fifteen minutes. Place the cake rack against the cake and turn both the rack and the pan over. Remove the pan carefully. If the pan will not release, return it to a warm oven (250°F) for a few minutes, then repeat the procedure. Cool the cake completely for at least one hour. Brush off the crumbs and frost it.

Source: Cake Decorating, *Wilton Yearbook, annual. Wilton Enterprises, 2240 W. 75th Street, Woodridge, IL 60517. For a copy of the current yearbook, cake-decorating products, information on cake-decorating classes, or a cake-decorating video course, call 708-963-7100, extension 320.*

BREASTFEEDING

When I got pregnant, I was a bit concerned about how my breasts would survive the experience. For the last two decades, having showered publicly in dozens of gyms and having gone to a number of different spas, I have seen every type of breast imaginable. And if asked—although I can't imagine by whom—how my breasts compare with others, I would say, "Quite well. They're a nice size and well shaped."

So I was understandably concerned as to how my breasts would react to an infusion of milk and to being continuously sucked on in what I had heard was not a terribly delicate way.

It turned out to be a valid concern. From the moment Bernie's sperm penetrated my egg, I think my breasts began growing. They were tender from day one. None of my bras fit by the second month, and I had to buy maternity bras almost immediately. By the eighth month my bra size almost matched my age. And while there was something oddly appealing and natural about the entire process, I began to feel a little anxiety as well.

It bothered me when my nipples began turning brown and I got these raised bumps on them during the fifth month. I was concerned how anything that felt so tender could ultimately be sucked with such vehemence. A friend with a newborn had once confided in me that when her son began nursing she felt as if a vise had been permanently affixed to her nipples. This was not a positive mental image. I planned to breastfeed Alex because I knew how important the antibodies would be for him, but I was convinced that—given my nature—it wasn't going to be one of those peak life experiences.

As it turned out, I did enjoy breastfeeding, but it wasn't as easy as anticipated. Because Alexander developed a viral infection in *the hospital, I had to begin pumping milk from the second day he was born. The nursery nurses gave me a very expensive pump, and one of them showed me how to use it; the problem was she didn't tell me when to stop. On the fourth day, when I was sitting by the isolette touching Alex, one of the other nurses opened the refrigerator where the milk was kept and saw that I had produced twelve bottles. "My God, you could sell this," she shouted gleefully. "Have you ever considered becoming a wet nurse? Why are you pumping all this milk?"*

I, with due modesty, was mortified. "Because no one told me not to," I answered demurely. "I have been pumping as much as I can."

"Didn't you realize that the more you pump, the more milk you have?" she asked sardonically in a voice that could be heard across the country.

"Obviously not," I answered with a weak smile. Everyone (but me) laughed. And after this initial humiliation, that particular nurse took a liking to me and became my personal lactation consultant. Once Alex was out of the isolette and I could begin nursing him, the other nurses would gently but rather ineffectually try to help me.

The first time I had a problem breastfeeding Alex on this nurse's shift, she grabbed hold of my breast and positioned Alex onto it in one deft movement. Later, when he was having difficulty affixing himself to my breast, she pinched my nipple, and within moments he was happily sucking away. If it was time for his feeding and he seemed unable to glom on, she would stroke him, and his mouth would open as large as a basketball. When I held him and the standard nursing position didn't seem to work, she showed me a few variations. After a few days I was a pro, and Alexander was breastfeeding with abandon.

By the time we left the hospital, after seven days, Alex and I were poetry in motion. After total humiliation, personal embarrassment, and a complete loss of modesty, I had become as competent as a wet nurse. Thank goodness, I don't have to make my living this way. But if my love of writing ever diminishes, who knows? There are plenty of careers that are far less fulfilling.

OUR BREASTFEEDING EXPERIENCES

■

"I find nursing to be very natural and enjoyable. With my first child I sought the help and advice of various lactation specialists. My daughter latched on with great ease, which made the whole thing more relaxing. I am a little more rushed with her than I was with my son, but I think that's always the case with a second child. What I love about the whole experience is that it forces you to stop and just enjoy the moment with your child."

■

"My son and I both enjoyed nursing, physically and emotionally. He seemed to get a good immune system going. The hardest part is weaning."

■

BREASTFEEDING BENEFITS

For Babies

- Breastfed babies have fewer allergies, fewer gastrointestinal and respiratory tract infections. Human milk contains antibodies to everything to which the mother has ever been exposed and protects the baby in that way. If the baby is exposed to something to which the mother has not been exposed, the baby introduces that virus or bacteria into the breast, and the breast will automatically manufacture antibodies against that particular organism.
- Human milk contains all the essential lipids, fats, and fatty acids that the baby needs for optimal brain and central nervous system development.
- Human milk contains everything a full-term baby needs in just the right proportions for healthy growth and development in those first months of life, so it is a complete food and a perfect food for babies.
- Breastfeeding builds a close attachment between mother and baby.
- Breastfeeding aids in dental development.

For Moms

- There is lower incidence of breast cancer and osteoporosis.
- There is less bleeding after birth, so there is a lower risk of hemorrhage after childbirth.
- There is a lower incidence of urinary tract infection in the breastfed baby and the mother.
- Breastfeeding tends to promote weight loss in the majority of mothers.
- Breastfeeding is a natural contraceptive. Called the Lactational Amenorrhea Method (LAM), it is successful 98 percent of the time with a few caveats. First, the baby must not be older than six months. Second, the mother must not have resumed menstruating. Third, the baby must be breastfeeding full-time or almost full-time without any supplements.

Source: Betty Crase is the mother of four and the manager of the breastfeeding reference library and database for La Leche League International, P.O. Box 1209, Franklin Park, IL 60131-8209; 708-455-7730 or 800-La Leche (525-3243).

BREASTFEEDING BASICS

Find a terrific chair, a straight one with arms, rather than a couch, which is usually too deep. Put a pillow on your lap and position your baby on his side facing you in the tummy-to-tummy position. For beginning breastfeeding, the best hold is the crossover hold. If the baby is feeding on your left breast, you will be holding him with your right arm. If you hold the baby behind the neck and support your breast with your left hand, you will have excellent visibility and control when the baby roots. You can assist the baby with his weak little neck muscles by putting him on the breast when his mouth is open exceptionally wide, a gaping wide mouth, and then pull him on. Once you've accomplished a latch-on in that position, you can then reverse your arms and go back to a standard cuddle hold.

The average infant wants to nurse for anywhere between fifteen and forty-five minutes. Many infants will simply let go of their own accord when they're finished. You need to pay attention and learn about your baby's sucking and swallowing pattern. By watching, you can figure out when he's done. We're getting away from telling mothers to nurse for ten minutes on each side. For some infants that's too much, and for some it's not enough. You need to watch your own child, and when he looks as if he's asleep at the wheel and he's barely sucking, there's no swallowing going on, he's been lying like that for several minutes, and nothing's happening, you can probably take him off your breast. But my hunch is, left to their own devices, most infants will end the feeding on their own.

Source: Kathleen Huggins, R.N., M.S., author of The Nursing Mother's Companion, *is a nurse and lactation consultant and runs a breastfeeding clinic in San Luis Obispo, California. She is the mother of two.*

TEN TIPS FOR BREASTFEEDING

1. It's not supposed to hurt to breastfeed. Use pain as your guide: if it hurts, you need help. Most of all you need to get your baby on your breast better.
2. Don't put your baby on your breast until his or her mouth is completely open. A common mistake is to start the baby nursing the minute he opens his mouth. "Wait until his mouth is as wide as when he cries or yawns." Then bring him quickly

"I breastfed my first child for thirteen months, my second for fifteen months, my third for twelve months, and my fourth for nine months. With the first one it seemed like a year was the right amount of time. The second one never drank from a bottle for her entire life, so I continued nursing her. But one morning she got up and, instead of wanting to be nursed, she went off to play. It just about broke my heart; I went into a total postpartum depression. My third child started waking up a few times a night. I erroneously decided that maybe if I stopped nursing him he'd stop waking up. I had planned to let my last child nurse as long as he wanted to, thinking it would be between fifteen and eighteen months. He broke my heart when he quit after nine months."

■

"I nursed my daughter for two and a half years. That felt right for both of us. When the issue of weaning came up, I found that it wasn't until I absolutely couldn't get up one more time in the middle of the night that suddenly it was easy to say no. She didn't seem to mind. I realized that taking care of my needs was also taking care of hers."

■

"I nursed my oldest for fourteen months and my youngest for a year. I loved the closeness and the convenience, although it did get tiring at night. We went to Australia for three months when our older son was a baby. Nursing was great in terms of traveling, not having to worry about formula when you're in a foreign country. It made me feel so good that I could provide my child with the perfect food. Since my husband's family and mine have allergy problems, I wanted to give my children that extra protection."

■

to your breast, nose touching. Don't worry about suffocating him. Babies don't suffocate at your breast. If they can't breathe, they let go and breathe with their mouth.

3. You can put your finger underneath the breast and your thumb on top, but keep them back of the areola. If your fingers cover your areola, your baby has no choice but to suck on your nipple. That's what causes scabs and bleeding and makes the process painful.

4. If you're planning on breastfeeding, don't let the hospital nurses feed your baby sugar water or formula from a bottle unless there is a medical reason. Some hospitals give it routinely when there is no medical need. A mother really needs to be on top of that and say "Unless I have information to the contrary, I don't want my baby to receive sugar water or formula." Not only does it undermine breastfeeding, but foreign protein may trigger allergies.

5. Start your baby on your breast as soon as possible, because milk supply depends on suckling. The more you nurse, the sooner your milk is going to come, and the more quickly you'll move into mature milk with higher quantity. If you don't have good suckling, then you won't have a good milk supply. If your baby is not latching onto the breast at all within forty-eight hours, you should start pumping so that your milk will come.

6. Don't worry about your milk flow those first few days, because your baby won't starve. Full-term babies are born with seven days of food and water in their bodies, so although the milk flow doesn't begin immediately after birth, there is colostrum which is loaded with protein and antibodies to fight disease. The baby will be in fine shape until your milk supply starts, between two and five days after birth.

7. Don't stop nursing when you're engorged. Even if your breasts are tender or you feel as if "you've got boulders on your chest," keep nursing. What decreases engorgement is a good milk flow, so the more you nurse, the sooner the engorgement will decrease.

8. Don't worry if your baby loses a little weight in the hospital. That's normal. Babies actually can lose up to 10 percent of their birth weight in those first few days. A bottlefed baby is not going to lose quite as much because he's fed a large quantity from the very onset, but you shouldn't worry—when you're nursing—if your baby does lose weight.

9. Don't take your baby off your breast too soon. Milk isn't

sucked out of your breast; it's released by a physiological response. When your baby sucks, it sends a message to the brain for the pituitary gland to release the hormones oxytocin and prolactin. The prolactin causes us to produce milk, and the oxytocin causes us to release it (the let-down reflex). If you take a baby off your breast too soon, you aren't giving that let-down a chance to happen.

10. Don't stop breastfeeding just because you're having problems. Get help. Most hospitals have classes in breastfeeding. Some pediatricians employ lactation specialists. The La Leche League has offices throughout the country. Whether you breastfeed for a few days or a few years, it can benefit your child. So don't stop just because things aren't going well right away.

Source: Corky Harvey, R.N., M.S., is a registered nurse and a certified lactation consultant. She has taught Lamaze classes for nineteen years and is in private practice as a lactation consultant in Los Angeles; 310-826-5774. She's the mother of three breastfed kids.

"I nursed my daughter for four months, which was what my pediatrician said was the least amount of time with the most amount of benefits. It wasn't a prime life experience. Getting her to take a bottle was easy, and that gave my husband the opportunity to experience the intimacy that comes from feeding your infant. It worked out well for all three of us."

■

MATERNITY AND NURSING BRAS

- Nursing bras and maternity bras are essentially the same except that nursing bras feature a top or center flap cup opening to make nursing more convenient.
- For optimum comfort, purchase your maternity bras as soon as your fashion bra is uncomfortable. The wider bra sides and underbust band will increase support. The additional fabric over the breast area can make heightened sensitivity less bothersome. The extra rows of hooks and eyes allow for adjustability throughout pregnancy.
- Because of the fit, a nursing bra should be purchased no earlier than the eighth month, preferably a few weeks before birth. Bras that are too tight can cause breastfeeding complications and lead to plugged ducts.
- When buying a maternity or nursing bra, you should be professionally fitted or know the criteria, which include the following: Do the cups fit smoothly? Does the center seam lie against the breastbone without gaps between the cups? Is the bra band straight around or slightly lower in the back?
- The average bra size in the United States among women who aren't pregnant is a 36C, and since pregnancy can increase band

size by at least one and cup size by one to three, the "average" size now becomes a 38D.

Source: Julie Neskey is director of public relations for Leading Lady Companies. For a copy of their free guide for the proper fitting of maternity and nursing bras, call 800-321-4804 or write to Leading Lady Companies, 24050 Commerce Park Road, Beachwood, OH 44122.

THE BREAST PUMP: A MOM'S BEST FRIEND

Breast pumps allow moms to continue breastfeeding even when they aren't at home. Indispensable for working women, they also give full-time moms flexibility and allow mothers whose children are sick or premature to provide breast milk for their babies in the hospital.

There are hand pumps, battery-operated pumps, small electric pumps, and very powerful electric pumps. If the pump you choose doesn't work for you, move up to a more sophisticated one. Many women fail when using breastfeeding pumps because they think they don't have adequate milk. Usually the problem is with the pump. Some women will do well on the smaller and cheaper pumps. Others don't have the patience or the ability to use them. Many times their immediate reaction when their pump isn't supplying the milk their child needs is to stop breastfeeding and begin using formula. They never think about buying a better pump or renting one, yet rental pumps are available throughout the country. And in the long run, buying formula over an extended period is much more expensive than renting a pump.

In any case, and whatever pump you choose, you'll need to be patient. Try using it for a few days during relaxed times and between feedings. If you're working full-time and need to produce enough milk for an entire day, give yourself time to increase your milk supply. The main point to remember when you're having problems with pumping milk is that most problems can be resolved with good equipment and proper instruction.

Source: The Pump Station, 12012 Wilshire Blvd., Suite 105, Los Angeles, CA 90025; 310-826-5774.

CATALOGS

While I hate shopping in person, I had never bought anything from a catalog until I got married. I couldn't imagine buying things I couldn't try on. I knew the savings could be significant, but still I wondered why people like us who live in large cities—where everything is available—would choose to shop by catalog.

Bernie, who loves to shop, had been buying from catalogs for years. He was on everyone's mailing list, and ordered dozens of items every year. He bought everything from fly-fishing supplies to khaki pants. I knew he was a discriminating shopper, but still I was surprised each time a new item appeared on the doorstep.

"How can you buy slacks without trying them on?" I asked skeptically as he opened a box containing a pair of corduroy jeans.

"I know the waist size and the pant length, and after all, it's not a life-threatening decision." he patiently explained. "If you buy from a reputable company, the quality should be good: People who have been in business for years sell good merchandise, or they wouldn't survive. Besides, you can send everything back."

Of course he was right. So little by little, I began buying catalog products; a nightgown here, a T-shirt there. But never more than a few items a year and never a pair of slacks.

When Alex was born, everything changed. Suddenly I was on every child-related product mailing list in the country. We received catalogs for clothes, toys, shoes, cotton clothes, diaper wraps, musical instruments, safety equipment, books, and breastfeeding supplies.

The products were wonderfully enticing. It was exciting to enter the world of catalog shopping: I quickly developed a workable *schedule. Mornings were spent dialing the 800 numbers. After-noons, while Alex slept, I pored over the catalogs. Did he need new sleeping gowns? Yes, we were washing his three times a day. Was a sheet with Velcro more practical than fitted sheets that needed to be removed under the bumper pads? Oh, I thought so. Does an infant need a wide array of colored socks? Well, it's still cold in Los Angeles in June, I reasoned, and socks weren't that expensive.*

Every day some new little gift would arrive. It was great fun waiting for the UPS courier. Since Alex couldn't have visitors dur-ing the first month, because he'd been ill in the hospital, the gifts were a welcome addition to our day.

A month later when my MasterCard bill arrived, I was flabber-gasted. A sock here and a sheet there could certainly add up. Of course I was also paying for shipping charges. Still, I wasn't at all prepared for the cost of my overindulgences, and since I was unemployed, I couldn't take the money out of my paycheck either. How humiliating to have to go to Bernie and confess.

"I need you to pay my MasterCard bill this month," I casually said one evening after dinner. Since Bernie knew I was not a big shopper, he nodded, hardly listening. That was easy enough, I thought to myself.

A few days later I heard a shout when he sat down at his desk to pay his bills. I came running in. I thought he'd hurt himself. "Three hundred and fifty dollars!" he yelled. "What in the world have you been buying?"

"Oh, a few things here and there."

"A hundred dollars is a few things here and there. Three hun-dred and fifty dollars is something more substantial," he responded firmly.

"Well," I answered as I looked through the bill, "I've bought socks, sleeping gowns, and an educational toy." I paused. He waited. I continued. "Diaper wraps, a comforter—which was quite a savings, I might add—a hat, his first shoes, a few blankets, a gate for when he starts walking, some books [actually you might refer to it as a small collection], and a pair of slacks for me."

"Slacks. You bought slacks? I can't believe it," he said. "You said you'd never buy slacks through a catalog."

"I just measured my waist and pant length. It was easy. They look nice," I replied quietly.

"Well, I think we need to cut back a little," he responded, regaining his composure. "With you not working, we just can't have these unexpected expenses."

"You're right, honey," I said and kissed him on the cheek as I blithely went into the other room to look at some catalogs. "I think I'll get a part-time job," I mumbled under my breath as I checked the few items we absolutely needed.

෨

SUE GOLDSTEIN'S MAIL-ORDER TIPS

- Never send cash; order by check, money order, or credit card.
- Find out the company's policy about returns and exchanges; sometimes there is a restocking charge, and they will assess you a percentage of the value of the merchandise for accepting it back. You won't be out the entire dollar amount, but you may be out 10 to 25 percent of it.
- Never order strictly from a post office box without checking with the local Better Business Bureau in the state in which the post office box is listed. If you have a dispute, you can't sue a post office box.
- Make sure when you are looking at a catalog or getting a price quote from a company that the amount quoted includes the shipping charges and any applicable sales tax.
- Know ahead of time—either by reading the catalog or by calling—how the company will deal with a return: if it's not what you ordered, it's the wrong size or color, it doesn't fit, it's broken, or it isn't anything like what you thought it would be based on the picture. Sometimes the company will ask for a specific reason for the return. Generally mail-order companies are very service oriented, so they will want to make you happy. Lots of companies today that want your business are offering unconditional guarantees so that you can return merchandise you're not satisfied with no matter how long you've owned it.
- There's a federal rule that orders must be shipped within thirty days of receipt of your order. If there's going to be a delay, the company must notify you and be willing to give you the option of canceling the order. It also must provide you a toll-free way of communicating if you have something to return.
- Keep track of your orders. Use a written record. If you pay by check, indicate on the check stub or on the back of the check what it is for and what the address and phone number of the company are. If you use your credit card, keep a record of the

CATALOGS WE USE

■

After the Stork
800-333-5437

**Biobottoms Fresh Air Wear
for Kids**
800-766-1254

Brights Creek
800-285-4300

ChildCraft
800-631-5657

Chinaberry Book Service
800-777-5205

Constructive Playthings
800-832-0572

Discovery Toys
800-426-4777

Hanna Andersson
800-222-0544

**Lakeshore Learning
Materials**
800-421-5354

Lands' End
800-356-4444

Lilly's Kids
800-285-5555

Music for Little People
800-727-2233

Patagonia for Kids
800-638-6464

Perfectly Safe
800-837-KIDS

The Right Start Catalog
800-548-8531

TC Toy (all wooden toys)
800-359-6144

Toys to Grow On
800-542-8338

transaction on a calendar so that you have a way of keeping track if it's not delivered. It is preferable to pay by credit card because if there's a problem you can have the credit card company intercede. With checks, many companies will wait until your check clears before they ship.

Source: Sue Goldstein, author of Great Buys for Kids, *is called "America's diva of discounts." She has appeared on hundreds of talk shows—"Donahue," "Oprah," and "Good Morning America," to name a few. She is the mother of one and lives in Dallas, Texas.*

STAN FRIDSTEIN'S MAIL-ORDER ADVICE

- Make sure the catalogs are accurately representing their products. Buy relatively small from a catalog the first time you shop them because a lot of catalogers are famous for photographing products that look beautiful and are of great value, but when you see the product, you're disappointed. So first, check that you're buying from a catalog that gives you all the necessary specifications.

- See if they have an 800 number. Why should you have to pay for the honor of giving business to someone? Also, make sure they have a toll-free number for customer service issues. Anyone who doesn't have an 800 customer service number is telling you, "We'll take your order for free, but if you've got a problem, we don't really want to hear from you."

- Find out what kind of guarantee they have. If a catalog doesn't offer a full guarantee of satisfaction with no caveats and no time limits, don't buy from them.

- Evaluate whether their pricing is competitive. There are catalogers who still believe that you should pay extra to shop through the mail. I absolutely disagree. I think that we offer convenience, and it costs us more to get that catalog into a customer's hands. At the same time, we don't have to pay rent for stores on Fifth Avenue, Michigan Avenue, and Rodeo Drive.

- Find out if they are members of the Direct Marketing Association (see page 61). Membership in the DMA means they are probably legitimate and they adhere to DMA rules and regulations. It means that you, as a consumer, have an independent organization you can contact if you're having a problem.

- Finally, take your friends' recommendations. If you talk to people who have had bad experiences with a catalog, you should probably at least give it a second thought. It's one of the reasons that the good catalogers know a happy customer will tell ten other people about you and an unhappy customer will tell one hundred; it's human nature. Therefore, good catalogers bend over backwards to keep buyers happy. Maybe that's your best defense!

Source: Stan Fridstein is the president and cofounder of The Right Start Catalog, *a market leader in the juvenile products industry. He's the father of one.*

THE DIRECT MARKETING ASSOCIATION

To help educate consumers on the variety of shopping methods available to them and to ensure a smooth transaction, the Direct Marketing Association offers a variety of free informational booklets. *Tips for Telephone Shopping* includes a checklist of steps for consumers when they shop by phone, tells how consumers are protected, and gives information about 900 numbers and computerized calls. *How Did They Get My Name?* is a guide to understanding direct marketing mailing lists. *DMA's Great Catalog Guide,* Seventh Edition, offers consumers almost 200 catalogs in 50 product categories.

To receive any of these booklets or the *Great Catalog Guide* ($3 check or money order), send your request, name, and address to Consumer Affairs, Direct Marketing Association, 1101 17th Street NW, Suite 705, Washington, DC 20036-4704.

The DMA is also your resource if a problem arises. The Mail Order Action Line (MOAL) was established in 1981 to help people who are having a problem with a particular mail-order transaction and have not been able to resolve it themselves. Consumers can request assistance from MOAL by writing to the DMA at the address listed above. Clearly state the details of the problem, the name and address of the company, the item or service ordered, and the date of the order. Photocopies of material that substantiate the complaint should be included.

Source: Direct Marketing Association, Inc., 11 West 42nd Street, New York, NY 10036-8096; 212-768-7277.

CHILDBIRTH

My pregnancy was so easy, I figured childbirth would be a snap. I didn't really have any preconceived notions; I'd never been very interested in hearing other people's stories. I was sure it was like everything else in life; it was a question of mind over matter. If you expected it to be tolerable, it would be. If you expected it to be the most painful experience of your life, that was possible too. I think a comedian on a cable show put it best: "If you think too much about how it feels to squeeze something the size of a watermelon out of something the size of a grape, you'd never get pregnant."

She was obviously right, and so I hardly thought about it at all. I was too busy glowing and thinking about the life that was growing inside me. If that sounds cornball and somewhat naive for an urban-dwelling, college-educated career woman, you're right. My attitude surprised even me. While a pregnant colleague was reading everything ever written about birthing, I chose to ignore the issue. I knew that for centuries women had given birth without scholarly research. They seemed to survive, and so would I.

Maybe it was hormones. Perhaps the baby needed too many of my brain cells. In any event, I'd barely read a thing when we attended our first Lamaze class—my sole attempt at prenatal education. And despite everything Bernie and I had heard to the contrary about "the new breed of older women who were having children," we were by far the oldest people in the class.

The teacher was a wonderful kind of sixties person who believed that natural childbirth was optimal, drugs were not good, and doctors were doing too many cesareans. We passed the class with flying colors. I learned how to breathe; Bernie learned how to *coach. We decided we were interested in natural childbirth. We were model students. I knew this birthing thing was going to be easier than I had even anticipated.*

Wrong! It was not only the most painful experience of my life, but it also helped convince me—once and for all—that God is clearly not female. Otherwise, why would this wondrous experience of giving life be so painful, exhausting, and downright humiliating?

I was in labor—on and off—for three days. I checked in and out of the hospital three different times. Absolute strangers saw more of my body than I had seen during my entire lifetime. I was poked, prodded, pushed, and pried at. I had to lie in positions that not only lacked modesty but also defied all sense of propriety.

I developed a ligament pain that was so intense I was unable to feel my contractions.

Finally the decision was made to break my water Sunday, June 11, at 10:30 A.M., and Alexander wasn't born until 11:14 that night. Babies were popping out all around me. Other women pushed for ten minutes and heard that wonderful cry of birth. Their Lamaze methods worked. Their breathing exercises diminished the pain. The moment of birth was climactic. Their faces glowed as they cradled their babies.

By the time Alex was taken by cesarean section, I looked like a dishrag. My hair was matted to my head. I felt twice my thirty-nine years. My entire body hurt. I had never felt such excruciating pain. Once I was assured he had the appropriate number of fingers and toes, I went to sleep. I vaguely remember seeing him. I have no memory of holding him.

I think I woke up two days later. Once I was feeling better and more composed, I was able to evaluate the experience a bit more objectively. I decided that the entire natural childbirth movement was a crock. I felt evangelical in my praise for epidurals. I liked the support of my husband beside me, but I thought Lamaze breathing techniques as a method of diminishing pain were highly overrated. I was also convinced that giving birth was unequivocally a peak life experience, if only I could remember it.

A brief note: *There are almost as many opinions on "how to have a baby" as there are doctors, nurses, midwives, and researchers in the field. Some people push for natural childbirth; others swear by epidurals. New research has shown that* doulas *(birth assistants who are described in "Childbirth: A Nurse/Midwife's View") aid the birthing process; some hospitals won't allow them in the birthing room. My essay reflects how I felt when I gave birth. If I had it to do*

OUR BIRTHING EXPERIENCES

■

"It was the most marvelous feeling in the world except for the excruciating pain! All three were vaginal deliveries, yet so very different."

■

"It was no picnic. Labor lasted thirty-six hours only to be followed by a C-section, which was the best part and the only way to have a baby as far as I'm concerned."

■

"My son was born in a freestanding birth center in Los Angeles. I had a long (thirty-six-hour) labor, but it was a wonderful experience thanks to the midwives and the atmosphere of the birth center. My daughter was born in a birth center attached to a hospital in Illinois. This time I had a short labor (six hours), and she was born two hours after I arrived. Her birth was equally exciting but much less strenuous. The midwives were wonderful on every level."

■

over again, I would probably use a doula, take childbirth classes early in my pregnancy, walk in the early stages of pregnancy, opt for a massage for relief of discomfort, and try a number of alternative methods for pain control before resorting to medication. But it's a very personal decision and one that you'll need to make for yourself once you talk with other moms, read the literature that's available, and consult with your OB-GYN.

⤳

APPROACHING CHILDBIRTH: A MOTHER/LAMAZE INSTRUCTOR'S VIEW

Labor and delivery will be different for every woman, and usually a woman who has several children will describe each labor as a different and unique experience. Before it is actually time for the baby to come, changes in the mom's body will tell her that labor is approaching. Not all women will notice all of these signs, but usually every mom will have some signs of approaching labor.

Four weeks before a first-time mom is due—at thirty-six weeks—the baby is likely to "drop" or engage in the mom's pelvis. With the baby in a lower position, there is slightly more room for the mom's lungs and stomach to spread out, and with this comes relief. If the mom has been quite short of breath, she may notice that she is able to breathe more easily. Also, heartburn is somewhat relieved. The other side effect of the lowering is that even though the mom thought she was rushing to the bathroom all the time already, the need to urinate seems ever greater now. She will not have volumes of urine, but the capacity of her bladder is now so small that it always feels full.

During the last eight weeks, when the baby is growing half a pound a week, pressures increase in all directions. Moms who have felt a mild backache throughout pregnancy may notice increased backache pain. Others may feel a backache for the first time.

Hormones are causing muscle relaxation for the baby to have as much room as possible when he or she comes through the birth canal. This can cause the hip joints to feel loose. Combined with late weight gain and increased backache, this gives many pregnant women the wide-stanced posture (waddle).

Many women will notice an increased vaginal discharge. This accompanies changes in the cervix that the caregiver will note during the vaginal exam. Some doctors and midwives do vaginal exams weekly from thirty-six weeks on. This provides information about dilation and effacement of the cervix. Other caregivers, however, do not do these exams, since this information frequently creates a false assurance that labor will not begin during a certain period or, more frequently, false encouragement that labor *will* be starting during the next day or so. When it doesn't, it can be very disappointing.

One of the difficulties for first-time moms is the question of how they will know when labor has begun. Many women have weeks of prelabor contractions, commonly called "false labor." Contractions, whether they are true labor or prelabor contractions, are uncomfortable sensations in the lower abdomen. For some they feel like menstrual cramps. For others they feel more like indigestion, and with this there is often diarrhea as the contractions occur and there is pressure on the bowels. Other women feel early contractions as a backache.

In all these situations the contraction has a beginning and an ending, and in early labor the contractions may last forty-five seconds. The difficulty is determining whether these feelings are true labor. Unfortunately, there's no way to know without having your cervix checked, although one way to reassure yourself is to get up and move around. With prelabor contractions will usually go away. With true labor they will intensify.

In either event, walking around is a good idea. With true labor, being in an upright position, rather than lying down with the pressure on your back helps. If you have walked around for a while, and the contractions are getting stronger and closer together, you can be fairly confident that this is "the real thing." Many first-time moms go to the hospital, are checked, and are advised to go home or walk around the hospital for an hour or so before they are rechecked.

Most women will feel more relaxed if they stay home for this early part of labor. Starting labor can be quite thrilling. The baby is finally coming after months of planning, waiting, and hoping. Moms and coaches are full of excitement, apprehension, expectations, elation, fear, and exhilaration. No wonder they're nervous! Contractions are not too uncomfortable, and all Mom and the coach really need is a little help in relaxation. Unplugging the phone is a good start. Quiet music often helps. Back rubs and massage will help both people at this point. Moms should probably not eat, but they should drink a lot of clear fluids—apple juice, 7UP, ginger ale. Walking around the neighborhood or a park that

"I had back labor for one hour with my first. My second was a perfect two-push delivery of an over-nine-pound son. My third was a C-section for a footling breech, and I had an induced VBAC [vaginal birth after cesarean] for my fourth. I never had any medicine except for the cesarean."

■

"Both of mine were natural, vaginal births. No drugs or major interventions. Labor lasted about a day, heavy labor about six hours. I was very happy. Very exhausted."

■

"My first was thirty-six hours of labor at a birth center, and then I was transferred to a hospital. It was not a pleasant experience to say the least. But I did have my son as 'naturally' as possible; no hard drugs. My second pregnancy was breech and I had to have an external version [externally turning the baby into a head-down position] and pitocin and nisentil. Again, not at all pleasant; about twelve hours of hard labor. No C-section, thank goodness."

■

"My first child was a C-section because the doctor was in a hurry. For the next two deliveries I insisted and fought for vaginal births. My daughter's birth was a glorious experience where I actually felt high."

■

is close to your house will help calm you and help with the progress of your labor as well.

Fifteen percent of moms will have their amniotic membrane rupture as a first sign of labor. These women should notify their caregiver, and most are advised to go to the hospital and consider this the beginning of their labor. That's when the real excitement begins!

Source: Linda Castile is a Lamaze instructor in Del Mar, California, and the mother of four.

CHILDBIRTH: AN OBSTETRICIAN'S VIEW

The First Signs

The first signs of labor are variable. The most common thing that happens first is that you will lose your mucous plug, which is a little bit of blood with mucus. Associated with that will be some uterine contraction that you may interpret as cramping or as lower back pain. Some women will be sure they're having uterine contractions. They can tell it's happening because they feel their abdomen getting hard and they're getting some pelvic pressure at the same time. When the contractions begin, they're usually mild and spaced far apart—maybe every fifteen, twenty, or thirty minutes. Sometimes that part of the early labor is not noticeable, but gradually over time the contractions get a bit stronger, last a bit longer, and get a bit closer together. That's one of the phrases we use: *longer, stronger, and closer together.*

Once you know you are in labor, you don't automatically have to come to the hospital. What we usually look for, when you're having your first baby, is if your contractions are about five minutes apart, last about a minute, and are strong enough so that you find it difficult to walk and talk during one. That's a common way to figure out if you are ready to be admitted to the hospital.

By then, assuming things are normal, you will usually be dilated to about three or four centimeters, sometimes more, sometimes less. We also admit someone to the hospital if her water breaks, and it may break even if she's not in labor. In that case we have to watch her and wait for labor to start. Sometimes women can stay at home after their water breaks. It depends on the obstetrician.

Active Labor

The active phase of labor is usually diagnosed when the cervical dilation reaches about three or four centimeters. The reason for having the distinction of an "active phase" is that the first part of labor is very long, and the length of time of that part of labor, which is called the *latent phase*, is variable. For some women it can last one or two days; for others it might be a few hours. Typically, once you're about three or four centimeters dilated, you usually have the baby within, on average, about eight to twelve more hours.

The active phase of labor is often when an obstetrician will decide to admit you to the hospital. The rate of progress of cervical dilation is usually about one or two centimeters of dilation per hour. The contractions occur about every three minutes during the active phase. They're generally very strong and very intense. This is when you need to pursue whatever method you're choosing to deal with your labor pain, whether it's Lamaze, Bradley, an epidural, or nothing.

That will continue until you reach around eight or nine centimeters of cervical dilation. Then the stage of labor known as *transition* begins. Transition is even more uncomfortable, but it's also brief. The contractions can be every two to three minutes apart, and they can last as long as one and a half minutes, which is very little time between contractions. At this point the cervix is very thin, it's almost completely open, and the baby starts to descend farther down the birth canal. Up until now the mother has not been required to do anything actively other than deal with the discomfort of contractions.

Once the cervix reaches ten centimeters of dilation, we say the patient is "complete." This means that the cervix cannot be felt by the obstetrician, it is fully dilated, and the second stage of labor has begun. At this point only the baby's head can be felt during the vaginal exam.

The Second Stage

In the second stage you use your own muscular effort to help bring the baby out. This is a very active part of labor in terms of the participation of the mother and the coach. Depending on your degree of concentration, you may need a great deal of encouragement from the people around you to focus because the contractions are so strong. Some women are actually relieved when they

FOREWARNED IS FOREARMED

■

"Decide what you want and find a doctor who will give it to you. Interview doctors to determine if they really share your views or are just telling you what you want to hear."

■

"Your health and the baby's are most important. Let this direct your decisions about how to proceed. Also, you deserve to reflect fondly on the birth experience. Great pain is not going to make for a better experience."

■

"Go to midwives and have your baby at a birth center unless you are high-risk. Don't even consider doing anything else. I knew labor and delivery nurses in a regular hospital setting, and I would avoid it by any means possible."

■

"Take a childbirth preparation class. Don't panic at the first signs of labor. Conserve your energy. Have a supportive partner or friend present throughout the labor and delivery. Talk about the options before: medication, what if a cesarean is necessary, episiotomy, circumcision. Have support at home—someone to clean, cook, and wash."

■

"Stay calm and relaxed. Remember to breathe. Study yoga and other relaxation techniques. The human body is designed to function appropriately; just let it do its thing and you'll do fine."

■

"Don't be scared. I think people emphasize the horror stories. Listen to your doctor, not your relatives or friends who say they know what is best; you're not paying them."

■

reach the second stage, though, because their ability to push can help diminish the intensity of what they are feeling somewhat.

With the first baby this phase lasts—on average—about one to one and a half hours. It can be as short as ten minutes, and it can last up to three hours or even longer. This is also the part of labor the baby is under more stress, so fetal monitoring is crucial. The second stage will end when the baby is born.

The Third Stage

The final stage is devoted to the expulsion of the placenta. Basically, there is a variable length of time after the baby is born before the placenta will naturally be expelled. Most obstetricians help the placenta come out, because there is a concern that it could get trapped inside the uterus if the uterus contracts down. Another concern is that the mother could lose too much blood if there is a long delay before the placenta is delivered. So they help by pulling a little bit on the placenta, on the umbilical cord, or by massaging the uterus a little bit.

Immediately after the placenta is delivered, the standard practice in most institutions is to give the mother pitocin so that the uterus contracts. Then once the uterus is firm and the bleeding is reasonable, the next step is to check for tears or lacerations, place any sutures (stitches) if needed (to repair an episiotomy—an incision made in the perineum, between the vagina and the anus—if one was performed), and then the delivery is over, and the fun begins.

Source: Bryan S. Jick, M.D., is a board-certified obstetrician-gynecologist in private practice in Pasadena, California, and the father of two.

CHILDBIRTH: A NURSE/MIDWIFE'S VIEW

Childbirth can be one of the most empowering times in a woman's life. The strength, courage, and self-esteem needed for an expectant mother to create such an experience can be developed by means of the following two essential factors: early prenatal education and proper support from those around her during labor and the actual birth.

By early education I mean more than just attending the traditional series of childbirth classes with which most couples are familiar. While the information provided is quite beneficial, I find that for the most part it is presented rather late in the pregnancy—usually in the eighth month. By this time many women are already experiencing fear of the approaching task ahead.

At my Family Educational Center, I encourage women to take early prenatal classes. These sessions usually begin from the third to the fifth month of pregnancy. This is the time when most expectant mothers are experiencing the greatest sense of well-being. Since the birth is still a few months away, the expectant parents tend to be less fearful, more attentive, and have a longer period of time to practice the necessary skills.

Among other topics, we cover proper nutrition, which is vitally important for the expectant mother's own well-being and is essential for the normal growth and development of the fetus. In addition, women are made aware of the physiological and psychological changes they are and will be experiencing. They learn about relief of discomforts and relaxation techniques that can significantly diminish their anticipatory anxiety. We show them which exercises can strengthen and tone muscles, thus adding to a positive self-image and trust in their body's ability to meet the challenges of the birth process.

Once a woman begins active labor, the people she has chosen to be with her at the birth play an important role in the outcome of her experience. In childbirth education classes, expectant fathers and/or partners are taught useful techniques to help comfort and support the woman during her labor. As a labor and delivery nurse and a midwife, I have frequently observed these support people becoming quite emotionally involved, often to the point of feeling overwhelmed by the whole birth process and thereby unable to provide all the support that is needed.

To rectify this situation, I recommend having birth assistants—people whose job it is to guide and oversee the process. They usually fall into two categories. They are either family members and friends or specially trained women, known as *doulas*. Their job is to focus on the needs of both the expectant mother and father, offering support and encouragement as needed.

The crucial evidence that supports the use of doulas comes from six controlled studies carried out independently in five countries around the world. The studies have been analyzed by precise statistical methods separately published in the *New England Journal of Medicine*, *Journal of the American Medical Association*, and many other notable publications, including the text

Mothering the Mother, by Marshall H. Klaus, M.D., a distinguished neonatalist and researcher.

When the results of these six studies are calculated together, the presence of a doula reduces the overall cesarean rate by 50 percent, length of labor by 25 percent, oxytocin use by 40 percent, pain medication by 30 percent, the need for forceps by 40 percent, and requests for epidurals by 60 percent.

With over thirty years in the field of labor and delivery, I have come to the conclusion that preparation of mind and body throughout the pregnancy combined with a continuous strong support system during the birthing process enables the woman in labor to access her own inner strength. The empowerment that comes out of this strenuous and demanding experience lays the groundwork for her to meet future challenging life experiences with a greater sense of self.

Source: Judy Chapman, R.N., CNM, is a registered nurse, certified nurse midwife, and ASPO-certified Lamaze childbirth instructor. She is the director of the Chapman Family Center in Santa Monica, California, 310-453-5144, and the mother of three.

***A brief note:** The most frightening part of childbirth for many moms is contemplating the pain. Everyone knows someone who has had the most horrific birth experience in the history of the world, witness my own. And those are the people who tend to relate these stories in great detail when you're newly pregnant and throwing up every morning. (I wonder if we should have had a disclaimer before my essay: Harmful if read during morning sickness.)*

Still, it's not unexpected. Somehow, from the time girls begin menstruating, they instinctively know that giving birth is painful. Once you've given birth, of course, you inevitably feel it's not nearly as bad as they said it would be—or it's far worse than you could ever imagine. So what's a mom to do? The American College of Obstetricians and Gynecologists describes the following options.

PAIN RELIEF

Behavior Techniques. Many women take childbirth preparation classes to learn what to expect during labor and delivery, as well as breathing methods, relaxation techniques, and other ways of coping with pain and discomfort during childbirth. These classes can be quite valuable, and some women are able to use these techniques to get through childbirth without the need for pain medication. Other women find that using these techniques combined with some medication is helpful in relieving the discomfort of labor and birth. It is up to you and your doctor to weigh the risks and benefits of each method of pain relief.

Pain-Relief Medications. Pain-relieving medications fall into two general categories: Analgesia is the relief of pain without total loss of sensation. A person receiving an analgesic medication usually remains conscious. While analgesics don't completely stop pain, they do lessen it. *Anesthesia* refers to the loss of sensation. With some forms of anesthesia you will lose consciousness, while with others you won't.

Systemic analgesics (like Demerol) provide pain relief over the entire body without causing loss of consciousness. They act on the whole nervous system rather than on one particular area. They are often given as an injection into a muscle or vein. Because these drugs can slow the baby's reflexes and breathing at birth, as a rule they are avoided just before delivery.

Local anesthetics usually affect a small area and so are especially useful when the doctor has to make an episiotomy. One advantage of local anesthesia is that it rarely affects the baby. The main limitation of these drugs is that they do not relieve the pain of contraction during labor.

Pudendal block is given as an injection to block pain in the perineum, but it does not lessen the pain of uterine contractions. It is especially helpful for numbing the perineum before an episiotomy is performed. It also relieves the pain you may have around the vagina and rectum as the baby descends through the birth canal. It is considered one of the safest forms of anesthesia, and serious side effects are rare.

Paracervical block is a form of local anesthesia that involves injecting an anesthetic into the tissues around the cervix (opening of the uterus). It relieves the pain you may experience as the cervix dilates (widens) to allow the baby's head to descend into the birth canal. While paracervical block provides good pain relief, it wears off quickly. Sometimes it causes the baby's heart rate to slow; this is usually temporary. In rare cases it persists and means that the doctor needs to deliver the baby quickly.

Epidural block, another form of local anesthesia, affects a much larger area than any of the methods described so far. It numbs the lower half of the body to varying extents, based on the drug and dose used. It is injected into the lower back, where the nerves that receive sensations from the lower body meet the spinal cord. It is helpful for easing the pain of uterine contractions, the pain in the vagina and rectum as the baby descends, and the pain of an episiotomy. While the drug is working, though, you may lose some muscle control in these areas, making it harder to "bear down" during delivery or to move your legs.

Epidural block can have some side effects. It may cause the mother's blood pressure to drop, which in turn may slow the baby's heartbeat. Usually steps are taken to prevent this problem: before the mother receives the medication, fluids are given through an intravenous, or IV, line in her arm, and she is positioned on her side to help circulation.

A spinal block, like an epidural block, is given as an injection in the lower back. However, a spinal block has to be injected into the spinal fluid, so the needle is injected a little deeper. Because the effects of the drug do not last long, and because it is usually given only once during labor, it is best suited for pain relief during delivery, particularly if forceps or vacuum extraction is needed. It is the pain method most often used for cesarean birth. It can cause some of the same side effects as epidural block.

General anesthetics are medications that cause you to lose consciousness. When general anesthesia is used during childbirth, the mother will not be awake or feel any pain during delivery. It is not used to relieve the pain of labor. It is rarely used for routine vaginal deliveries. It is often used for cesarean delivery or other urgent situations.

Source: The American College of Obstetricians and Gynecologists. Pain Relief During Labor and Delivery. ACOG Patient Education Pamphlet #AP086. Washington, DC © 1989.

FURTHER READING

The Complete Book of Pregnancy and Childbirth, by Sheila Kitzinger. New York: Alfred A. Knopf, 1989.

The Complete Mothercare Manual, by consultants Rosalind Y. Ting and Herbert Brant. New York: Prentice Hall Press, 1987.

Pregnancy & Childbirth, by Tracie Hotchner. New York: Avon Books, 1990.

What to Expect When You're Expecting, by Arlene Eisenberg, Heidi Eisenberg Murkoff, and Sandee Eisenberg Hathaway. New York: Workman Publishing, 1991.

CHILD CARE

Before Alexander was born, I chose not to think too much about child care. Midway through my pregnancy I decided I was going back to work only part-time. I figured it just wouldn't be that difficult to find someone to take care of him three days a week.

While a pregnant friend was comparing the costs and benefits of hiring a nanny or a baby-sitter as opposed to family day care, I decided to go a different route. I would ignore the entire issue until after Alex was born. The thicker my friend's research folder became, the more I retreated. I didn't even want to discuss the subject; not with her, not with Bernie, not at all.

My rationale was that I didn't know how I was going to feel about child care until after I saw my baby. The truth was that I hadn't really come to grips with how I felt about someone else caring for my child. My own mother hadn't worked outside the home when I was growing up. I had strong feelings about latchkey kids and strong prejudices about "quality time" replacing "quantity time."

Child care was a very emotional issue for me. I felt my choices were critical decisions that would affect Alex's upbringing in a major way, and yet I also felt the verdict wasn't yet in on the effects of child care for infants. I realized that a lot of women had little flexibility in making these determinations because of economic considerations. But I did have options; I knew I could afford to quit work altogether. And while it would be a tight squeeze, we could still pay for the basics: the mortgage, insurance, car payments, food, and clothing.

Once Alex was born and I was a bit more knowledgeable about what kind of care we were talking about, the decision was still not *easy. I had all sorts of preconceived ideas about what was right and wrong for me, and I never broke through those barriers. But I was able to sort out the problem in a semirational way and easily deal with the variables over which I had no control.*

The first was that our house was too small for a live-in. That eliminated the possibility of a nanny, an au pair, or a housekeeper—from what I'd heard, the most convenient and reliable type of child care available.

Second, I knew I wasn't willing to take Alex to either a center-based program or a family day care arrangement. Neither appealed to me, although I had heard wonderful success stories about the latter. Still, rightly or wrongly, center-based care appeared too institutional, and family care worried me. I couldn't imagine how one person could take care of three to six infants or toddlers when I could hardly manage one. The physical act of changing, feeding, holding, and caring for a gaggle of children seemed overwhelming.

So the only situation that was viable for me was that of a baby-sitter coming to my house. But I had anxieties about that as well. I worried about hiring a stranger, no matter how superlative the recommendations. My criteria, other than the basic quality of care, were plentiful. I wanted someone who was loving. I wanted someone who would read to Alex, play with him, take him on walks, watch him play in the yard or in the family room, talk and sing to him, hug him when he cried and even when he didn't, be patient with him when he started walking and talking, and protect him if he were ever in danger.

I didn't want someone who would watch television during the day because I don't approve of it. I didn't want someone who would yell at him if he didn't eat or force him to eat when he didn't want to. I didn't want someone who would put him into his crib if he were naughty or, worse yet, spank him. I wanted someone who was patient, affectionate, responsible, inquisitive, friendly, thoughtful, energetic, and kind.

In short, I wanted what every parent wants in a caregiver: a saint.

The first few people I interviewed had been recommended by caregivers of friends. I didn't feel comfortable with any of them. It was a gut-level decision. In one case I didn't like the way the woman held Alexander; in another she seemed very sweet but not too bright. I quickly eliminated the entire list. I ruminated about child care night and day. I panicked. I was supposed to start work in a month, and I didn't have anyone lined up.

"Maybe God is sending me a message," I said to Bernie. "Per-

OUR GREATEST DIFFICULTIES WITH CHILD CARE

∎

"Being forced to look for someone to take care of your child is a big problem by itself. I panicked. I cried. I wanted to quit my job. But once I found quality, stable, loving people, I felt much better about it. Other people can take care of our babies!"

∎

"In many cases, if you work full-time and have a commute, the hours are too limited. If you find a place you really like, it costs a fortune. I spent weeks visiting all kinds of different centers—near work and near home—before finding one I felt good about. I wish my company or my husband's provided child care."

∎

haps I'm just not supposed to leave Alex with a stranger."

He looked at me as if I'd finally gone round the bend. He knew I was not used to getting messages from God with any regularity. He also knew that I was not handling these interviews very well because I had told him I wasn't. And that I wasn't generating enough interviews because I had told him I wasn't. Once again he responded to the situation with great sensitivity. "You don't have to go back to work if you don't want to," he reaffirmed. Somehow, I needed to hear that for the hundredth time.

Now that the pressure was off, I suddenly came up with the perfect solution. A few months earlier Vilma, the housekeeper/companion of an older friend of mine, left her employ to have a baby. She is quite a wonderful person and certainly someone I would trust without a moment's hesitation. I called her to see if she wanted to bring her son, Tomas, who is two months younger than Alex, with her and baby-sit with Alex. I'd need her three days a week, from 9:00 A.M. to 5:00 P.M. She was willing and able; thus began our child-care arrangement.

The first period of our relationship brought highs and lows. As I had suspected, Vilma was terrific with Alexander and Tomas. She was everything I'd hoped she'd be, and she orchestrated this dual baby-sitting relationship with aplomb. She was also habitually late, which not only made me crazy but also made me late for work. Then she became more prompt, and I quit my job because I couldn't handle Alex, my work, and my life. Without the extra income I couldn't afford to keep her.

Two months later I went back to work when I was offered a more flexible freelance situation, and Vilma came back to work for me. Everything worked out terrifically well. It was fun watching Alexander and Tomas grow up together. Alex is a head taller, and Tomas is a size larger. As they grew older, they played together, chased each other, and generally made a mess of everything. The house vibrated with laughter, shouting, and tears. But the tears were quickly kissed away, and the laughter was always near. Vilma was the saint I was seeking. I know I wouldn't have had the patience to care for two babies.

All in all, things have worked out better, but certainly differently, than I thought they would. My concerns about someone else taking care of my child were unfounded. I think Vilma did a better job than I would have on a daily basis. I learned that I needed to get out of the house and work at least three days a week for my own sanity. I also needed time to write.

I learned that no child care situation is ideal. Your needs

change, and you do the best you can. Once I had the capability of working more at home, it was impossible for me to do it on the days Vilma and Tomas were there because I didn't have a room of my own, and I couldn't work with two children scurrying about. So I rented an office.

I spend a lot of time with Alex, but not as much as I thought I would. I alternate between feeling like I'm doing what I need to do for him and for me and feeling guilty that I'm as selfish and self-oriented after giving birth as I was before. I still worry about "quality time" versus "quantity time," but not as much.

What I don't worry about at all is Alexander. He's a wonderful child: happy, enthusiastic, curious, and loving. There's no doubt that his childhood is different from what mine was. He's got an older mother. He is spending more time with caregivers and less time with me. But it's all working out. Maybe God was listening.

༄

TYPES OF CHILD CARE

In-Home Care

This category includes nannies, housekeepers, au pairs, and baby-sitters—anyone who comes into your home to take care of your child. With infant care, while it may be difficult, I would advise parents to try to postpone making a definite arrangement until after they've had some time to get to know their baby. Learn a bit about your baby's personality: some babies are calmer, some get agitated more easily; some sleep easily, some have problems sleeping. Try to think in terms of hiring someone who will continue to be good with your baby as he or she grows. Some caregivers adore newborns but may not respond as well to the more active baby who is crawling or to the mobile toddler. Ask questions that will cover issues that come up later on.

Whomever you consider choosing, checking references carefully is critical. It is equally important to spend time with the caregiver before you leave your baby with her. No matter how good the references are, how good the interviews are, and how good the caregiver seems to be, the best way to judge how a person is with your child is to see her with your child. Plan to spend a week—if possible—when you pay the person and stay home with her and your baby. Gradually let her take over what you do when you are there. Once she takes over, drop by unexpectedly or have a friend or relative visit to check on them.

"It was impossible for me to find a facility that had openings at the same time for a three-and-a-half-year-old and a two-year-old who's not yet potty trained. We finally found someone to come to our house. It's expensive. I would have liked my older son to have had the opportunity to be with other children his own age, but it just didn't work out."

■

"I visited a number of different family day-care houses before finding one I liked. In some, the television was on during my entire visit and the children were sitting zombielike around it. In others, I didn't feel good about the child-care provider. It was more of a gut-level reaction. Finally, I found a woman I loved, and the children seemed so happy. She and her helper care for four to eight children. They are warm and loving. There are a lot of developmentally appropriate toys. I've sent both my girls there and couldn't be happier."

■

"What I learned is that the person who may be great with an infant is not necessarily right for your toddler. In my case, my initial child-care provider, who came to the house, didn't speak English although she was very loving with my son. When he started talking, he became frustrated when he couldn't communicate. After much soul-searching I switched him to a family day-care setting. Within days he became a much happier child."

■

Family Day Care

This is an arrangement in which your child is taken care of in someone else's home. First, you'll want to know the caregiver's feelings about children. You want to know her experience. With very young children, it's going to be necessary to talk over so many things, from the practical matters of timing of feedings to the more complex developmental issues, so it's very important that you feel comfortable talking with the caregiver and telling her how you feel. If there are other children in the home, find out how the caregiver will balance the needs of all the children.

Again, you should spend some time observing in the setting before you select it. Be there with your child to observe how things work, rather than how they are supposed to work, and to help your child adjust to the new situation. Licensing standards governing group size, safety, etc., vary from state to state. Certainly you should check to make sure the program is licensed, but keep in mind this guarantees only that minimum standards are being met. Think in terms of the age range of the children and how many children a person can safely manage.

You must also check very carefully on safety and cleanliness. If all seems in order, the most important issue is how the caregiver reacts to your child and how your child reacts to the caregiver. There are people who can cause tension even in very young infants as well as toddlers. Trust your instincts. Try to match your child's needs to the caregiver's personality and style. Some children need a very calm and gentle person; some respond very well to someone who's more boisterous. What kind of person will be best for your child?

Infant/Toddler Centers

The single most important consideration is the caregiver. Pay less attention to glitz and fancy surroundings. There should be a safe, comfortable, and clean environment with appropriate materials and equipment for infants and toddlers. Again, licensing is a basic, but do not assume that licensing in and of itself means that the place is a good one for your child. The standards vary, and some are minimal.

You want to see a small enough group so that children receive individual attention. You don't want to see twelve infants in a room. You want to see enough caregivers. You want to see caregivers interacting with babies rather than talking with each other. You don't want to see babies spending undue amounts of time in high chairs, slings, cribs, and playpens as opposed to being able to crawl, being held on laps, interacting with people, and exploring. You want to make sure that you'll be able to talk to the director or caregivers about your baby, that their approach is to have you involved and to work with you, and that you'll always be welcome. *Never* put your children in a family day-care home or a center where you cannot visit whenever you want to.

Source: Judith Berezin, author of The Complete Guide to Choosing Child Care, *has spent twenty years in the child-care field working with children and parents, as well as training family day-care providers and teachers. She has a master's degree in early childhood education, is the mother of two, and lives in New York.*

CHILD CARE ISSUES

Carollee Howes, Ph.D., is a professor of developmental psychology at UCLA and the author of a substantial amount of research on child care. She is the mother of a daughter who has spent a significant part of her life in quality child-care situations.

SB: Is child care good for children?
CH: Child care can be terrific for children *if* you consider these important variables: if it's a high-quality arrangement; if the teacher-child relationship is a nurturing and secure one; if the provider is well educated, well trained, and well compensated to do a good job of nurturing and teaching children. If these elements are all in place, then you start looking for the kind of relationship that the child and caregiver build with each other.

SB: Are there any studies that have shown how child care affects kids in terms of social development, IQ, and language development?
CN: There's a large body of research literature on each of these topics. Given the preceding caveats, which is to say that we're talking about high-quality child care, you can expect the following:

• In terms of social development, look for a child who is competent and skillful in social interactions with peers; a child who builds stable, important friendship relationships with peers; a child who trusts that adults will take care of him or her and that he or she can use them as resources for learning and for support.

TIPS FOR FINDING GOOD CHILD CARE

■

"Make sure they have a 'drop in on us any time' policy."

■

"If you plan to hire someone to work in your home, ask for references and check all of them. Develop a list of questions. Find out why the person left the previous situations. Prioritize your needs and wants. Have the person come to your house when you're there. Go with your instincts."

■

"Check the kitchens and the bathrooms of a child-care center! They tell you a lot. Everybody's classrooms look great."

■

"Run a newspaper ad and prescreen people on the telephone before 'in-person' interviews. We did that and got dozens of responses."

■

"Check with other mothers. I found my day care by word-of-mouth. The child-care provider interviewed me as much as I did her."

■

"Look for kind people and playmates that are close to the age of your child. What works best for me are small sitting arrangements in another mother's home."

■

"Visit potential sites for more than a short period of time. Come unannounced and at different times during the day. Watch the staff interaction with the kids. Do the kids seem happy? Is there enough for them to do? Are they properly supervised? Is the parenting philosophy of the day-care provider similar to yours?"

■

- IQ is probably one of those things that is least affected by child care. First, we don't have great ways to measure little kids' IQs. Second, when we do, it seems to be most influenced by maternal education, which is probably a proxy for genes as well as education.

- Language development is definitely affected. Look for a child who uses language adeptly; is very adaptive in the kind of language used; a child who can use language to communicate ideas, needs, and wants. One of the potential benefits of child care is that often children who are learning language are in child-care arrangements with others who speak a different language. When there is both their home language and another language, the children tend to become quite good at both, which is an advantage. If your child is in a child-care arrangement in which the adults and children do not speak his or her home language, I think you have some potential problems.

SB: *What do infants need in a child-care setting?*
CN: They need physical safety. They also need the opportunity for what we call floor freedom—the ability to explore on their own locomotion. They shouldn't be cooped up in playpens or cribs all day long. They need a stimulating environment; one where people are talking to them and there are things to see, to touch, and to mouth. They need nurturance and cuddling.

SB: *What do toddlers need in a child-care setting?*
CN: Toddlers need all of that plus a little more space. By the time the child has his or her first birthday, I think peers become increasingly important. Children really need same age mates to try out things with.

SB: *What advice do you have for parents who are looking for child care?*
CN: Spend as much time as you possibly can in the prospective setting. If it's someone in your home, pay the person to be there while you're there until you feel comfortable leaving. If you are sending your child to a family day care or to a center, spend hours there on different days—so that people forget you're there but so that you can see what a normal day is like.

CHILD CARE AWARE CHECKLIST

Caregivers/Teachers

☐ Do the caregivers/teachers seem to really like children?

☐ Do the caregivers/teachers get down to each child's level and speak to the child?

☐ Are children greeted when they arrive?

☐ Are children's needs quickly met even when things get busy?

☐ Are the caregivers/teachers trained in CPR, first aid, and early childhood education?

☐ Does the program keep up with children's changing interests?

☐ Will the caregivers/teachers tell parents what their child is doing every day?

☐ Are parents' ideas welcomed? Are there ways for them to get involved?

☐ Do the caregivers/teachers and children enjoy being together?

☐ Is there enough staff to serve the children? (Ask local experts about the best staff-child ratios for different age groups.)

☐ Are caregivers/teachers trained and experienced?

☐ Have they participated in early childhood development classes?

Setting

☐ Is the atmosphere bright and pleasant?

☐ Is there a fenced-in outdoor play area with a variety of safe equipment? Can the caregivers/teachers see the entire playground at all times?

☐ Are there different areas for resting, quiet play, and active play?

☐ Is there enough space for the children in all these areas?

Activities

☐ Is there a daily balance of playtime, storytime, activity time, and nap time?

☐ Are the activities right for each age group?

☐ Are there enough toys and learning materials for the number of children?

☐ Are toys clean, safe, and within reach of the children?

In General

☐ Do you agree with the discipline practices?

☐ Do you hear the sounds of happy children?

☐ Are children comforted when necessary?

☐ Is the program licensed or regulated?

☐ Are surprise visits by parents encouraged?

☐ Will your child be happy there?

Source: Child Care Aware is a partnership for quality child care sponsored by Dayton Hudson Corporation and its divisions, Target, Mervyn's, Dayton Hudson's, and Marshall Field's in cooperation with Child Care Action Campaign, National Association of Child Care Resource and Referral Agencies, National Association for the Education of Young Children, and National Association for Family Day Care.

CHILDREN'S BOOKS

When I was pregnant, a well-meaning friend asked what I was reading. "Mostly mysteries," I replied. "I just can't read enough of the female hard-boiled detective genre."

"No, I mean to the baby," she countered.

I looked at her quizzically. "I don't read aloud, if that's what you mean. I don't think the baby is ready for murder mysteries yet."

"Of course not," she patiently explained. "But you should read books to him so that he'll like reading when he's born. You know, studies have shown it makes a difference."

She never provided the studies. I never read aloud to my unborn son. I didn't feel I needed to. I knew he would like reading because his father and I love to read and our house is full of books. We started a library for him before he was born. There were thirty books waiting for Alex when he arrived home that first day.

Some of them were gifts. A friend from work bought him Animalia, *with its spectacular illustrations, by Graeme Base. My sister periodically bought him books and added an illustrated Mother Goose to his collection. My mother brought* The World of Christopher Robin *home to him from London. Our favorite books of all are the ones Mother has made him about our family. She writes the poems and uses family snapshots for graphics. They're quite special.*

Both Bernie and I have added to Alex's library. When he was a month old, I started his Dr. Seuss and Babar the Elephant collections. Bernie bought him Curious George. *Bernie's mother has bought Alex different series of books that she buys in her neighborhood grocery store, and they are surprisingly good.*

When Alex was an infant, I used to hold him on my lap and

read him the books I enjoyed reading most. Horton Hears a Who *was one of the best. I've always loved the poetry, have admired Horton's loyalty, and am a real pushover for happy endings. Alex tolerated the book for months before he started pushing it away with his hands and feet when he was a year old. I'm hoping his taste level improves.*

Curiously enough, at eighteen months, he seemed to have clearly defined preferences. His favorite books were the one-word chunky books about mommies, daddies, farm animals, toys, and the like. While the concept of teaching him words this way was great, and I thought it was lovely that he liked looking at photographs of other small children, these books are so boring you want to tear out your hair and scream.

I just cannot find the attraction here. There are worlds out there to be discovered—funny make-believe animals to encounter. Enough of all this reality reading.

I vividly remember warm summer afternoons, sitting beneath a big leafy shade tree sipping lemonade, in the backyard of my childhood friend, Lenka. Her mother, Elva, would read aloud a chapter from Winnie-the-Pooh. *We were suddenly transported into A. A. Milne's world of make-believe, and it was glorious. Once I had Alex and we began reading together, I fervently hoped to re-create that special feeling. And I'm sure I will. But for a brief moment, it mostly seemed as though I were stuck in a mire of one-word nouns.*

ॐ

WHY READING ALOUD MATTERS

Bernice E. Cullinan, author of Read to Me: Raising Kids Who Love to Read, *is a reading specialist, professor of early childhood and elementary education at New York University, and the mother of two.*

SB: Why does reading aloud matter?
BC: It's the single most important thing that parents can do to assure success in reading. First off, it provides a model for children's language by providing a foundation for language development. Children hear new vocabulary words. They hear the sounds of book language, which is different from spoken language. Being read to expands their experience and their knowledge about how the world works. It helps them make sense of their world. Besides, it's fun. There's a whole emotional bonding when sitting beside a

child or holding him or her on your lap. The feeling of warmth and emotional support that results is very strong, and it remains with a child. For some reason or another, we remember our book experiences throughout our adulthood.

SB: *What are some ideas for getting started?*

BC: Start with something short and sweet and fun. Poems and verse are excellent places to begin. The child doesn't have to sit still for a long time, but what you're saying is "Hey, listen to this." Find out what your child is interested in and then find books that are central to that interest. Words are all around us, and there are other ways to stimulate reading as well. While a child is at the breakfast table, you can read off the cereal box. The bathtub is a good place. You should have books in the car. Bedtime is a superb time to read, and reading is the perfect transition from a wild, active day to sleep.

SB: *What reading activities do infants like?*

BC: Mother Goose, singsong lullabies, "This little piggie went to market," all the folklore. Infants love melodic, rhythmic lullabies. A child understands the rhythm of his mother's heartbeat when he's in the womb. When a child is in his mother's or a caregiver's arms and feels the rhythm of the rocking chair and the melody of a song, it is very satisfying. It certainly is for me: my vision of heaven is singing lullabies while rocking with a baby.

SB: *What reading activities do toddlers like?*

BC: You have to catch them on the run. Toddlers like board books, cloth books, plastic books, and bathtub books. Find ones that are attractive, durable; ones that can stand little hands turning pages. The books should have bright pictures, vivid colors, and strong graphic design; not a lot of print. Toddlers really go for the pointing and labeling books, ABC, and counting books.

SB: *What are your tips for making readers out of your preschoolers?*

BC: Help them to see all the wonderful things that are in books. Let them know how much fun it is to read from books. Preschoolers are innately curious. They want to know how things work. They have that fascination with details, so when they see what's inside books, they're just enchanted. We talk about children having a short attention span because of television. But they will sit for a half an hour or an hour just looking at books when you read to them. Relate what you see in their life to the book. Build beyond what the books say. Ask them questions. Listen to their

A BASIC BOOKLIST

■

A Child's Garden of Verses
Robert Louis Stevenson

Big Red Barn
Margaret Wise Brown

Curious George
H. A. Rey

Goodnight Moon
Margaret Wise Brown

I Went Walking
Sue Williams

The Little Engine That Could
Watty Piper

Madeline
Ludwig Bemelmans

*The Orchard Book of
   Nursery Rhymes*
Zena Sutherland

The Story of Babar
Jean de Brunhoff

answers. Let them know that what they think counts. Invite them to join you in the repetitive phrases. That's called readinglike behavior. It's a very important step in the process of learning to read. If children act like readers, they eventually become readers.

JIM TRELEASE'S ADVICE ON READING ALOUD

Parents often complain that when they read aloud their children won't pay attention for any length of time. They tell me, "I'm reading the story. Why isn't the child paying attention?" First of all, most toddlers and infants don't understand the words you're using, so what you need to do is talk the book, not read it. Look at the pictures, because we all become visually literate before we become print literate. Before the child can understand the meaning of the word *ball*, he can recognize a ball. He's got this image in his head from the ball that was in his playpen or in his crib, and he knows what that is. Then he sees a picture of a ball on a page, and the parent's objective should be to make the connection between that ball he has seen and the ball on the page.

Second, research shows that for a twelve- to eighteen-month-old child, the average attention span is about three minutes. At this point, if your child becomes restless and has reached an age where he is able to crawl away, let him go. Wait a couple of hours, corral him again, read another three minutes, and let him crawl away. These periods are separated by long segments of time when a child is doing what a child is supposed to do—that is, explore and play, which is the business of childhood. But you're eventually liable to accumulate twenty to thirty minutes of reading time and develop your child's attention span, which is what it's all about.

The earlier you start this process, the easier it is. Many parents say to me, "I try reading to my child, and he won't sit still at all." When I ask them when they started reading to their child, it's usually when he is older, say three or four.

My response is "If you waited until this child was four years old to try to give him a bath, don't you think you'd have a hard time getting him into the tub?"

Of course the analogy to reading is obvious: the sooner you start reading to a child, the easier it is to acclimate the child to the sound of the reading voice (which is really different from a speaking voice) and to the idea of books and connecting books with pleasure.

One of the universal questions you get from people from all cultures and in all languages is "Why do children want the same book over and over and over again?" My response is very simple. "Do you have a favorite CD or audiocassette that you play over and over? Why do you keep playing it when you know all the words to the songs?"

Usually people respond that they like the music; it's satisfying; it evokes memories. In fact it's the comforter we all need in some form or shape in our lives. Well, reading the same book over and over at night is the same kind of security blanket for that child. Maybe it's an intellectual security blanket. All the child knows is that he has spent the day with his mother, father, or a caregiver, and now it's the end of the day, and what is going to happen to him? He is going to be left in a dark room by himself. But last night, the parent read that child a story, and that was the last thing he remembers before the parent turned off the light. It was almost an insurance policy. That story got him through the night. So he wants it again tonight, and the next night, and the next.

Bruno Bettelheim once suggested: "We should be asking not why a child wants the same story, but what exactly is in that story that brings so much solace or consolation to that child at that troubled hour?"

And by the way, there is no accounting for taste. At least 50 percent of the time a child will pick the most rotten children's book in the history of the world and adopt it as a favorite. That's OK. Make sure you nurture the interest. If you keep that book around, you keep feeding that child's interest in that story, but what you also want to do is broaden the palate. So you don't just read one book a night to a child; whoever said one story is enough? When your child's got a favorite, and you're a little tired of it, you expand the repertoire to two or three books a night. Eventually he will develop a new favorite as he is exposed to other stories.

There are also going to be sections of a book that a child doesn't understand. He likes the story but can't figure out why he likes it, and he may even find it confusing. A wonderful case comes to mind. A young history teacher in New York City once told me about his favorite book, *A Visit from St. Nicholas* (The Night Before Christmas), when he was three and a half. He would badger everyone in the family to read to him night after night, day after day. They always did, but what they couldn't figure out was why he called it the book about the man who got sick. One night

The Tale of Peter Rabbit
Beatrix Potter

Tomie de Paola's Favorite Nursery Tales
Tomie de Paola

The Very Hungry Caterpillar
Eric Carle

We're Going on a Bear Hunt
Michael Rosen

Where the Wild Things Are
Maurice Sendak

Winnie-the-Pooh
A. A. Milne

Source: Lynn Kelly, mother of three and manager of The White Rabbit, Children's Books, 7755 Girard Avenue, La Jolla, CA 92037; 619-454-3518.

■

it became clear when his grandmother was reading the story to him and came to one particular page, "When out on the lawn there arose such a clatter, I sprang from the bed to see what was the matter. Away to the window I flew like a flash, tore open the shutter, and *threw up* the sash." Twenty-five years later this history teacher could still remember how confused he had been by that story. "They never told you," he said, "why the guy threw up and whether he got better or worse."

There are many reasons why a child wants the same book night after night, but if your child is asking for books you should feel good. There are a lot of parents of nine- and ten-year-olds who would gladly change places with you because their children *hate* books. Maybe if they'd nurtured their children's interest—no matter what the book—when they were toddlers, these children would still love to read.

Source: Jim Trelease is the author of The New Read-Aloud Handbook *and* Hey! Listen to This. *He works full-time lecturing on the subjects of children, literature, and television. He lives in Springfield, Massachusetts, and is the father of two.*

A USER'S GUIDE

• **Picture books.** Look for pictures that intrigue the child and tell the story. For very young children the story must be told without a lot of details because the children aren't able to distinguish among them. The wonderful part about wordless books is to engage your child and have him or her tell you what's happening in the stories by asking questions: "What do you see here?" "What's going on?" "Tell me what happened to this character." "What do you think is going to happen next?" Try to involve the child in making predictions about what the activities for the next pages will be.
• **Nursery rhymes.** Purchase books that have an illustration for every rhyme. Sometimes you'll find that nursery rhyme books will have five or six nursery rhymes on a page but only one illustration. You'll want to be able to point to something in a picture when you're reading the rhyme. Books like Tomie de Paola's or Wendy Watson's *Mother Goose* are good because they have been designed so that every rhyme has an accompanying illustration.

- **Folk and fairy tales.** With very small children you need to look at what I call the "beast tales" and not "Snow White and the Seven Dwarfs" and "Cinderella" or some of the others that include emotions like greed and jealousy that these children have not yet been exposed to. Look for stories like "The Little Red Hen," where there are very simple rules and if they're broken, consequences ensue. "The Three Billy Goats Gruff" and "The Three Little Pigs" are good because they deliciously scare children but don't involve all those other emotions.

- **ABC books.** Be careful with ABC books. They have gotten more and more sophisticated so look for ABC books that are simple. The one that I love is *The Guinea Pigs ABC.* When you look at an ABC book, find what age group it's directed toward. Bruno Munari has some wonderful ABC books that give parents an opportunity to point at each thing and talk about it; there's an illustration and a word that goes together, so it's an opportunity to increase vocabulary and just have fun with words.

- **Factual books.** It used to be thought that young children could respond only to stories, but there's been some interesting new research showing that little children are very much ready for books about the world around them. Increasingly we're seeing that publishers are responding to this. A good example is the Dorling Kindersley Eyewitness Juniors books. They have remarkable graphics with photographs. Small segments of information on each page are arranged simply to arouse childen's curiosity, designed to lead them through the book.

- **Point-and-say books.** These are the books in which lots of items are arranged on a page. The Ahlbergs have a wonderful one, *The Baby Catalog,* and so does Jan Ormerod. Richard Scarry's books are like that. As adults we might say, "Yuck, there's too much," but small children love that sort of thing. Word books are another part of this category. As a parent you can point at different words and ask questions like "Which things go together on this page?" "Which things don't go together?" That's always fun.

Source: Marilyn Carpenter is the mother of three, works with school districts on staff development issues, writes curriculum materials, and consults with parents on book-related issues.

BUYING BOOKS
FOR INFANTS AND TODDLERS

The key to choosing the right book for your child, according to Dr. Betsy Hearne, editor of the *Bulletin of the Center for Children's Books*, is your own enjoyment. When you pick up the picture book and read it, is it clever or cloying? Engaging or boring? Original or clichéd? Look at the illustrations carefully—the way a child will. Can you live with them? If you like the book, your children will soak it up.

Some guidelines you should look for when buying books for infants and toddlers are a sturdy format that a child can chew on; clear, uncluttered pictures; a text that involves the child with physical movement or dramatic action; rhythmic patterns of art and language; a broad range of selection from books about familiar everyday experience to simple folklore and fantasy; and books with many uses from identification to storytelling.

Picture books should have illustrations on every page and very little text. They are meant to be read aloud and the pictures pored over. When your child grows older, look for books with durable stories and illustrations. What's important to remember is that every child is an individual and will gravitate to different styles of both art and story. To some extent what you like and what they like are matters of taste. People furnish their minds the way they furnish their rooms, with words and pictures that appeal to them.'

Source: Betsy Hearne, Ph.D., author of Choosing Books for Children, *is the editor of the* Bulletin of the Center for Children's Books *and is on the faculty of the University of Illinois, Urbana. She is the mother of four.*

CLASSES

In anticipation of Alexander's birth we received information on classes for the Lamaze method, preparation for breastfeeding, nutrition, infant CPR, and baby care. Having not been a group person for the last twenty years, I took the path of least resistance and attended only the Lamaze class.

It turned out to be better than I had anticipated. The five couples who participated were all patients of my doctor. We had widely divergent backgrounds and absolutely nothing in common except that we, of the feminine gender, were all pregnant. That seemed to be enough for the women. The men had other reasons for attending.

When the teacher asked the husbands why they were there that first night, the answers were quite telling. One man said he was there because he knew this would be a peak life experience for him and his wife and he wanted to participate actively. Another said he knew how painful childbirth was and he wanted to be supportive.

My husband said he was there because I was making him be there. I had no problem with Bernie's honesty. He had said a number of times during the nine-month period that he wished it were the old days, when all he would have had to do was show up in the waiting room with a box of cigars. After what we were to experience later, I certainly think that would have been preferable—for both of us.

Be that as it may, we attended every class, and Bernie was a supportive participant, as I knew he would be. After the third week it seemed as if someone dropped out every time to deliver a baby. So each session became a kind of success story. The first woman's water broke at work. They drove to the hospital. She walked around *the block for forty-five minutes. She gave birth in a few hours.*

The second woman's water broke in the middle of the night. Her husband told her to go back to sleep. By the time they reached the hospital she was fully dilated and gave birth within the hour. It was a snap, and she had been the person in class who kept on asking about which drugs she might take for pain.

The other stories were equally motivational. On the one hand we were learning all these interesting breathing techniques. On the other hand you couldn't pay for better birthing stories. I figured it was a tribute to our teacher. I was sure that since we had paid attention, practiced, and done as we were told, all of our babies would pop out somewhat easily in a reasonable period of time.

Of course my entire theory bit the dust when my delivery was my worst nightmare. Still, the value of the class was not diminished. We had learned a lot. In retrospect, I wish I had taken more classes earlier in my pregnancy. In talking with mothers who did, they seemed more confident and more prepared. They were able to share concerns with people in the same situation. They said that the sense of camaraderie was uplifting. They developed a coterie of excellent resource people to call on for support.

I've subsequently learned there are also a number of courses one can take after your baby is born and they, too, are a great source of information and support. For someone with a nongroup orientation, my enthusiasm for these kinds of classes surprises me. As a person for whom everything has undergone a major transformation, it's just what I might expect.

CLASSES TO LOOK FOR

Baby care	Lamaze childbirth
Breastfeeding	Mommy and Me
Cesarean birth	Parenting
Child care	Prenatal and postnatal
Expectant parents'	exercise
orientation	Sibling preparation
Grandparenting	Stress strategies
Infant CPR	Twin expectations

MOMMY AND ME CLASSES

Stephanie Hayutin, R.N., M.A., is a registered nurse with a master's degree in clinical child psychology. She is pursuing a Ph.D. and leads weekly support groups for new mothers and infants. She is the mother of two.

SB: *Who attends Mommy and Me classes?*
SH: In my classes the moms tend to be a bit older, between thirty-five and forty-five rather than twenty-five to thirty-five, which is what you might expect. They are, in general, upper-middle-class career women who have been very successful and have been high achievers. They tend to have been married for a long time; a good percentage of them have had fertility problems, so these are much-anticipated pregnancies.

For the most part they are mothers of first children. They are used to having had a lot of control over their professional lives and have had very organized home lives as well. As you know, nothing undoes all that as quickly as the arrival of a newborn baby. The moms come to the classes as soon as they're ready. Their babies are anywhere from one week to several months. The moms tend to stay a minimum of a month; they come once a week for an hour and a half. Some stay as long as six months, and they form play groups with the other moms once they leave.

SB: *Why do women attend Mommy and Me classes?*
SH: They're basically support groups. Our intention is for mothers to be able to meet other new mothers with new babies so moms can get a sense of how different babies are. Many women, at least on the west side of Los Angeles—and I suspect throughout the country—have very little sense of what newborn babies are like unless they happen to have friends who are having babies. They find the experience to be a searing one and are staggered by how difficult it is.

By the time they're ready to leave the classes and I ask them, "Looking back now, what do you most wish someone would have told you or talked about with you before the baby came?" they almost uniformly answer, "No one ever told me how painful it would be to go through the birth process, and no one ever said being a mother could be this difficult."

SB: *What kind of support do you offer?*
SH: It's individualized according to the group, but in many cases we talk about who the moms were before they had these babies—

93

WHAT WE'VE TAKEN AND HOW WE FEEL ABOUT IT

■

"I liked my infant child-care class. It was good, sound advice in a no-pressure situation. I enjoyed observing other babies and their parents."

■

"Our local hospital offers a program of classes for pregnant women. I had already been around babies a lot, so the only class I took was CPR. I learned a lot. In fact, when my daughter was a year and a half old, she choked on a piece of cantaloupe. I was so glad that I had taken the class. The instruction sheet was on the refrigerator door, and I grabbed it and went to work. It's a year later, my daughter is fine, and the sheet is still there. I'm trying to get pregnant, and I'm planning on taking a refresher course. This time I'd like my husband to come too."

■

what parameters they are dealing with in terms of their leaves of absence or jobs. Many are economically locked in to working and have to stay with their jobs. Most of those who have to go back to work do so anywhere from six weeks to five months after their babies are born and often have a very difficult time with that step. So we spend a good deal of time talking about child care, what the advantages and disadvantages of in-home and out-of-home care are. What can make it emotionally easier for the mom? Is the baby going to survive this? Of course the baby is going to survive this, but these are very emotional issues.

We also talk about infant development—what babies are supposed to do at given ages, what the developmental milestones are, although in the zero-to-three-month bracket, there aren't too many. Nonetheless, in terms of infant development, probably in the earliest months we focus on feeding and sleeping and soothing. Many new moms worry whether their babies are eating too much or too little, whether they are sleeping too much or too little during the day, and whether they are holding them more than they should and spoiling them. These are the most common questions.

We work on the couple's relationship a lot, how it has changed, how it was affected by the pregnancy, if it was, how it is affected afterward. I'd say the majority of mothers are upset at the degree of one-sidedness that is inherent in caring for newborns, and a lot of what I do is to normalize their experiences. Once moms begin to focus on the fact that whether you are breastfeeding or bottlefeeding, newborns tend to be in a one-to-one system of caretaking, things become more understandable. It isn't that they have a crummy husband or that they are failing somehow to engage their husbands or to make a space for them; it's just that infant care requires a one-on-one relationship. A lot of couples—prebaby—have talked about the concept of shared parenting but find the reality to be quite different.

Another issue we work on is the delay in returning to normal sexuality. While many obstetricians give the go-ahead for a full sexual relationship after six to eight weeks, most mothers are not ready then. Many say they have lost their sense of sexual excitement or arousal altogether and have no idea where it went or if it will ever return. That, again, is a normal part of the postpartum phase and may last up to six months, but it comes as a complete surprise to most people.

SB: What about the dads?
SH: We started a Dads and Babes class, but the dads rarely came.

Some of them said via their wives, "No, I'm not interested." "Dumbest idea I ever heard of." "Why would I ever want to sit around with a group of men I don't even know with a baby I don't much enjoy taking care of right now and talk about anything?" Others said they were too busy with work.

So we changed the format to include the whole family. Now the moms and dads come with the baby. We spend an hour together in which I lead a discussion of what it's like to have a baby—which is usually something the moms have already gone over. I lecture on infant development, and then the moms go off with another leader, and the dads, babies, and I work together. Many times the moms find it difficult to leave, and there is always a flurry of last-minute instructions: "Don't forget this bottle of water." "Don't forget that I just changed her."

But once the moms leave, there is almost a sense of an enormous collective sigh. The babies stop crying, the dads relax, and they really do have a lot to say. For the most part they seem to be thrilled with fatherhood, but they do universally complain about fatigue. They also say that they don't know how to help their wives. On the one hand the wives seem to want help; on the other they often feel the husbands are not doing the necessary task well enough. It ends up being a really eventful day.

LAMAZE CLASSES

"The Lamaze method is a combination of techniques and information to help a woman prepare for and get through her labor and delivery," according to Diana Simkin, coauthor of *Preparation for Birth, the Complete Guide to the Lamaze Method.* "It's so popular because the alternative is pretty frightening, yet it is what a lot of our mothers, mothers-in-law, and grandmothers went through. They basically had no idea of what was physiologically going on. They did not know the terminology: cervix, effacement, dilation. They were examined without knowing why they were being examined or what the doctor was looking for. They didn't know what to expect. They were separated from their spouses and everyone else who loved them. So they were totally alone in a hospital room, they were medicated, and it was a terrifying experience."

Today more than 150,000 Lamaze classes are offered annually in the United States, attended by more than two million parents, according to the American Society for Psychoprophylaxis in Ob-

"My obstetrician insists that all of her patients take a breastfeeding class. I thought it was great. They taught us that everyone can be successful and that it's just a matter of finding the technique that works for you and your baby. It was a very positive experience."

■

"I took an infant preparation and a Lamaze class. Both were sort of helpful, but I wished they had prepared me more—told me more about breastfeeding, first aid, ways to calm a crying baby. I wish I had known about offering a baby water the first few days, especially if it's hot. We didn't know, and our son cried and cried. I wish they had told us how to organize things better so that when the baby came our whole life didn't feel turned upside down."

■

"In my recovery yoga class you are allowed to bring babies until they crawl. It offers a great sense of belonging, a forum for information, and I've met new friends."

■

"My husband and I took baby care, infant CPR, breastfeeding, and the psychology of parenting classes. They significantly lessened my anxieties. When I got pregnant with my second child, we took our two-year-old back to the same hospital for a sibling class."

■

stetrics (ASPO/Lamaze) headquarters in Washington, D.C. "Some attend the classes because they want to experience birth without medication," Simkin says. "Others come to class because they want to be able to deal with labor until they receive medication."

Whatever the reason women take the classes, the Lamaze techniques include a series of breathing patterns in which ". . . the breathing is a comfortable pace for the mother. The breaths are even," Simkin says, "the mind is focused, and the body is relaxed."

Still, Simkin cautions against mothers feeling that by learning Lamaze breathing they will be in control of labor. She says, "The Lamaze technique helps a woman cope with labor and deal with the pain. It teaches women how to focus and how to accept rather than fight the pain."

Simkin recommends that if you're interested in finding a Lamaze teacher you look for an ASPO-certified childbirth educator because of the rigorous training they go through. You can call 800-368-4404, which is the national ASPO/Lamaze office, for referrals in your area. She also suggests you talk to the instructor before enrolling in the class. "Instructors vary, and you want to make sure you have one you can relate to and who is going to teach a good class."

Source: Diana Simkin, coauthor of Preparation for Birth, *is an ASPO/Lamaze-certified childbirth educator in private practice in New York City; 212-348-0208.*

DECORATING

*W*e live in a small house, and we've always enjoyed its simplicity. The walls are mostly white, the carpet is an industrial gray, and little by little, we've added furniture as we could afford it. Had it been left to me, our house would have remained more austere. Prior to marrying Bernie, I had never owned too many things. I had once lived in an apartment for three years, and everyone who visited assumed that I'd just moved in because there was so little furniture.

So needless to say, I was as shocked as any of my friends when, six months into my pregnancy, I became obsessed about how we should decorate Alex's nursery. Discussions on wall coverings, furniture, sheets and comforters, and window treatments became pivotal.

We spent weekends looking through wallpaper books, taking home samples, and evaluating our choices at different times during the day and night as the light changed. We pondered decorating questions as if we were determining Alexander's entire future. Was blue the right color for a boy's room or too stereotypical? Were Laura Ashley prints—even in blue—too feminine for a boy? (At the time these questions embarrassed even me.) Was a border a necessary complement or an unnecessary expense? Should we paint the room to save money, or was a painted room too sterile?

One would hope that our country's leaders spend as much time evaluating our foreign policy as we spent picking a wall covering. And it got worse—if that's possible—once we started looking at furniture. We literally spent hours comparing cribs. In more sane moments I wondered whether it was morally justifiable to spend as much on a crib as some families paid for a month's *rent. Were the more expensive cribs safer, or did it just seem that way? Should the slats be close together so that he wouldn't get his head caught, or were all the slats positioned suitably? Did he need an oversized, Italian-designed, state-of-the-art crib, or would a "made in America" plainer version suffice? Would Alex like white, or should we go for bleached wood? It was slightly easier evaluating changing tables and rocking chairs. The primary concern with the changing table was whether we wanted a combined changing table/chest of drawers or two separate items. The rocking chair was purely a matter of comfort.*

Two months before Alex's birth we bit the bullet and made our choices so that everything would be ready. Yes, we picked a blue-patterned wallpaper with a border, and it looks great. We finally chose a middle-of-the-line crib and a matching changing table/ chest of drawers, and they've worked out wonderfully. We ended up with white Levolor blinds because the entire house has them. The comforter and sheets are a plain light blue to blend in with the wallpaper. The rocking chair is a hand-me-down from a friend.

It's a fine room. I felt great about it before Alex was born, and it still makes me smile. The best addition has been an original "work on paper" that a good friend made for Alex. It hangs proudly on the wall.

Now that Alex is older, I can't imagine how or why the importance of these decorating decisions became so overblown. It was obviously the "nesting syndrome" gone awry. Maybe if I knew more about nature, I'd find a flock of upwardly mobile birds who spend an inordinate amount of time discussing the composition of their nests. It sure would make me feel better.

꩜

NURSERY BASICS

• **Crib.** Most of the cribs currently on the market—if they are not backstocked—should meet American Society for Testing and Materials/Juvenile Manufacturing Products Association (ASTM/JMPA) voluntary guidelines. They should have nontoxic finishes. They generally have a dual-drop or one-drop side, meaning that one side of the crib will drop down so you can put the baby in and take the baby out, change the baby in the crib, or change the linen.

• **Crib mattress.** You want something firm and constructed to ensure your child's correct bone, skeletal, and spinal development.

Most mattresses come with a triple laminate vinyl topper so that technically no moisture will go through. Most are standard size.

• **Mattress pad.** This protects your mattress from staining. Pads that are waterproof and quilted are available. In case of an accident—which is not infrequent with infants—you may want to have an additional pad on hand.

• **Bumpers.** These are used mainly to prevent babies from bumping their heads or getting their arms or legs stuck between the slats. As soon as your child is old enough to use the pad as a step, remove it from the crib.

• **Sheets.** Most people look for sheets that are 100 percent cotton knit. They need to fit the mattress securely.

• **Small moisture-proof pads or lap pads.** These are generally used in a strategic area of the crib when the child is small. Many moms place them under the area where their child drools, spits up, or poops. One pack of two should be sufficient.

• **Blankets.** Generally when your baby first comes home, he is swaddled in a receiving blanket. Later on, he will need a couple of crib blankets. The cotton thermals are great because they are good for summer and winter.

• **Quilts.** Most parents buy them primarily for decoration; they aren't used to cover infants because they're too heavy.

• **Changing tables.** There are many choices. You can have a traditional changing table with two drawers below. There are also flip-kits or dresser kits that you can put on top of a dresser. Your choice depends on how much space you have. There is a vinyl foam piece that is very economical; it can also go on the dresser, and you can secure it. They are all about thirty-two inches high.

• **Chest of drawers.** Think about the height if you plan to use the chest for a changing table as well. A three-drawer chest is usually just right. Look for something that has stops on the drawers so that a toddler can't pull them out. Since a chest is a fairly substantial investment, consider buying one that your child won't outgrow.

• **Rocking chair.** We sell primarily gliders. The traditional rocking chairs tend to scoot along the floor, but a lot of women have heirlooms and are pleased to use them. The gliders are exceptionally comfortable. You can place them right against the wall because they won't move.

• **Diaper pail.** They are pretty basic. Some have deodorizing charcoal tops, but most of them come with a compartment in the lid where you can put the deodorizing disks.

• **Lamp.** There are two schools of thought: Either get one that

OUR FAVORITE NURSERY ITEMS

■

"When my son was born, we went all out. We wallpapered his room in a sailboat theme because that's what my husband loves. We recently had a baby girl, and we've moved both kids into a bigger room that they will share. We chose a 'Sesame Street' theme, because our two-year-old loves it. He picked out his own sheets and helped put the character stickers on the wall."

■

"At first I was fixed on water beds. I had a water bed canopy crib for my daughter. I've just repainted her room pink, and I got an easy-to-do stick-on border with a circus design that my daughter did herself. She enjoyed helping, and it looks great. Now she wants bunk beds and a sister!"

■

matches your bedding and is very babyish or get a transitional lamp that might be a spindle or a ginger jar; then you can just change the shade, and the child can use the lamp as a toddler too.

Source: Karole Romer is a salesperson at Sid's Discount Baby Furniture, 8338 Lincoln Blvd., Los Angeles, CA 90045; 310-670-5550.

DECORATING THE NURSERY

• **Color.** Many mothers of girls still tend to go toward pink. They like that frilly, floral look. A lot of vintage drapery panels like the old rose pattern are being used. For a boy the cowboy theme is always popular; you can mix it with cow-printed fabrics and bandannas. Checks and stripes are popular, as is red and white ticking. When mothers don't know what the sex of the baby will be, they tend to go with a multicolored stripe in pastel tones.

• **Lighting.** A ceiling-mounted fixture can bring the theme into the room. For example, if a wall muralist has painted clouds on the ceiling, she can incorporate the ceiling fixture into the design. If the theme is cowboys, a lantern or a ceiling fixture with horse-shoes might be appropriate. A standing lamp or a tabletop lamp is always a good idea so that you don't disturb the baby at night if you have to go into the room.

• **Walls and ceilings.** A wall mural is a wonderful addition. It is something a child can relate to and is designed specifically for that child. A chair railing molding going around the room also works well. You can paint above it and paper below. If you're on a budget, consider a wallpaper border; you can paint one color above and one below it.

If you choose wallpaper, make it simple. Pick something like a stripe or a scattered pattern. The problem with wallpaper for nurseries is that it tends to be very juvenile, and once you've put it up you're stuck with it. Eventually your child is going to want something else. It's much easier and less expensive to change paint color or even wallpaper borders than it is to repaper.

• **Window treatments.** Babies are not light sensitive, so you don't need to block out light; you just need some sort of light limitation. For little girls I like balloon shades. They're feminine and poofy. If you're working within a budget, consider a nonmovable window treatment that acts like a valence rather than one that goes up and down and requires a lot of fabric. You can incorporate window treatments with Levolor blinds, Duettes, or soft shades.

For boys I recommend natural wood poles with the balls at the end and big rings with drapes. Soft pleated Roman shades that incorporate one or two fabrics are always a good choice.

• **Flooring.** I recently had a wall muralist paint a lasso on a bleached wood floor for a boy with his name spelled out in it. It was terrific. If you have a wood floor—and want to keep it—consider painted stains. Area rugs on wooden floors will allow you to play with your baby on something soft. If you want to use wall-to-wall carpeting, use nylon—rather than wool—because it is stain resistant and long lasting.

• **Furniture.** Aside from the basics, don't hang anything over the crib. If you do any type of framing, use Plexiglas for safety purposes. Round edges are safer than hard edges. If you have tall bookcases or other pieces of furniture, consider having a baby safety company (often listed in the phone book) come out to secure them and to baby-proof the room as well.

• **Storage.** Toy chests are fabulous. If there is a bay window or any type of window area, consider a built-in window seat with a pull-up top or doors on the front that you can use for toy storage. High shelves going across the perimeter of the room work for displaying collectibles, stuffed animals, or toy trains. Recently I've used old trunks with fabric lacquered on them or handpainted for storage, but they need a lot of baby-proofing. Finally, closet organizers can be a big help in finding ways to hide all the toys you don't want to see.

Source: Debra J. Dressner is the owner of Dresco Design, 2345 Century Hill, Los Angeles, CA 90067; 310-286-9483.

TEN SAFETY TIPS FOR CRIBS

Every year more than thirteen thousand children are injured in crib accidents that are serious enough to require hospital treatment. Consider the following guidelines when buying a new or used crib:

1. Corner posts should be the same height as the end panels and should not extend above them.
2. Space between slats must be less than 2⅜ inches and no slats should be missing.
3. All screws, bolts, and hardware must be in place and tight to prevent the crib's collapse.

"We lived in a garden apartment and could not paint. I sewed a set of crib bumpers (and I don't sew), and I hung a small stuffed pickle (called Super Pickle) over the changing area so that our daughter could swing this pickle while I changed her diapers."

■

"My sister-in-law painted a mural in my oldest daughter's room before she was born. It was called a tree of life, but it had a lot of animals in it. There was a lion, a raccoon, and a sloth. It was quite wonderful. Since my daughters shared a room then, they both were able to spend their childhoods with it. One son had a cars and trucks theme, and the other had a spaceman theme with glow-in-the-dark stars."

■

"The first two children were in a used crib with a crib mobile. There was no room and no money. Number three has a very small room but with a lot of light from French doors. I also bought a lovely used wicker crib with built-in drawers and a chest of drawers to match. There's a tropical fish and a planets mobile. I like things simple."

■

"Before our daughter was born, I bought crystals that I hung in her window so that they would create rainbows on her walls and ceiling. I would lie on the floor where I planned to place her crib to gain some perspective on how the room would look to her. It was admittedly a rather nutty thing to do, but it's how I came upon the idea of the crystals. The rainbows delighted her."

■

4. The mattress must fit snugly so that two adult fingers cannot fit between the mattress and the crib side.

5. The mattress must not be easily dislodged at any point of the crib. A 1988 standard states that the mattress support must be able to withstand a 25-pound upward force from underneath the crib. It is meant to keep all four mattress support hangers securely attached to the headboard and the baseboard of the crib. Failure of even one hanger can cause the mattress to sag in the corner and pose an entrapment hazard.

6. Bumper pads should be attached securely to all sides of the crib with at least six straps. Excess lengths of strap should be cut off. The bumper must fit snugly in all four corners of the crib. There should be no gaps between the bumper and the crib sides.

7. Pillows are not recommended for use in a crib.

8. Crib gyms and mobiles must be removed when a baby is able to push up on hands and knees.

9. A child who can climb out of the crib or is thirty-two to thirty-five inches tall has outgrown the crib.

10. The crib should be located with safety in mind. Avoid placing it near any lamps, dangling cords, ribbons, windows, fans, heaters, or climbable furniture.

Source: The Danny Foundation, 3158 Danville Boulevard, P.O. Box 680, Alamo, CA 94507; 800-833-2669.

FURTHER READING

Children's Rooms & Play Yards, by the Editors of Sunset Books. Menlo Park, CA: Lane Publishing, 1988.

The Childwise Catalog: A Consumer Guide to Buying the Safest and Best Products and Services for Your Children, by Jack Gillis and Mary Ellen R. Fise. New York: Harper Collins, 1993.

Designing Rooms for Children, by Mary Gilliatt. Boston: Little Brown and Company, 1984.

Guide to Baby Products, by Sandy Jones with Werner Freitag et al. 3rd ed. Yonkers, NY: Consumer Reports Books, 1991.

The Perfectly Safe Home, by Jeanne Miller. New York: Simon & Schuster, 1991.

DIAPERS

*P*rior to Alex's birth, I decided unequivocally that I would use cloth diapers instead of disposable ones. As a philosophical environmentalist—someone who thinks a lot about the environment rather than doing anything about it—I knew that disposable diapers were a nightmare. I had seen pictures of barges that were seemingly composed solely of disposable diapers.

Intellectually, it made sense that if each person were willing to assume responsibility for cutting back on waste, the planet would be in better shape. In the sixties we used to say that if you weren't part of the solution you were part of the problem. While there wasn't much about the sixties I liked, I felt that this was a great way of encouraging personal responsibility. Besides, my younger sister, who has become a recycling advocate and moralist, kept anonymously sending me articles in the mail about waste and put me on a diaper-service mailing list.

So, with a few weeks to go, I called the cloth diaper company that services our area. They were very informative on the telephone. I learned that there were diapers designed particularly for newborns. You no longer had to fasten diapers with safety pins; they now had Velcro diaper wraps. I could determine how many diapers I thought I'd need weekly, but I could change the order if I had underestimated. They'd deliver half the diapers before Alex was born so that we'd be ready for him. They would pick up twice a week. They would provide a diaper pail, and best of all, I wouldn't even have to empty the dirty diapers in the toilet. I could put them in the pail, mess and all. If this weren't enough, cloth diapers were less expensive than disposable ones.

The first order of diapers was delivered before Alex was. In the *hospital, though, where I learned to diaper Alex, they used Pampers. Although I didn't ask, I'm sure there are sanitary reasons for using disposable diapers in hospitals. I must admit that they were certainly easy and convenient to use.*

When I got home, I had Bernie buy a big package of Pampers, justifying the purchase as a way to make things as simple as possible when everything else was so new and overwhelming. Disposable diapers were quite simple. They were more absorbent and easier to dispose of when we took Alex out.

Those first few weeks, I make a few halfhearted attempts to use the cloth diapers. But the first time I put them on Alex, he peed within moments and was sopping wet. I tried again, but soon after, when I decided to take him on a walk, I didn't relish the thought of changing him in the ladies' lounge at Nordstrom and carting around a wet and heavy diaper for the next hour or so.

Still, when people asked if I was using disposable diapers or cloth, I said, "I have a diaper service." That was, of course, true if a bit deceitful. What I really used the cloth diapers for were rags; they were great for spit-up. But at each diaper pickup our loads were getting smaller and smaller. And our diaper bills were getting bigger and bigger because we were paying for cloth diapers we didn't use and disposable diapers we did.

I think I may have gone on with the charade for months if Bernie hadn't finally asked one day, "Why are we still having the cloth diaper service delivery when we use Pampers?"

"Well," I answered thoughtfully, "morally, I believe in using cloth diapers. It's something we should all do for the environment." I showed him the picture of the barge that was composed of disposable diapers. I read the statistics on how disposables contribute to overall waste in landfills. "I firmly believe in cloth diapers."

"But you're not using them," he logically replied. "They sit in Alex's drawer. They are very expensive rags. Our diaper bills are high enough without paying for something we're not using. I know you're embarrassed to tell your friends that you use disposable diapers, but just think about it."

Of course he was right. We canceled the service the next week. In retrospect, I still feel guilty about my inability to follow through on something I morally believe in. In this case the sixties seem very long ago. Of course, back then they also said that you should never trust anyone over thirty, and I'm now forty-something. Perhaps they were right.

THE CASE FOR CLOTH

- Diapers are the first—and most intimate—garment your baby will wear. From day one you should be teaching your baby about the good things in life, what to value, and what's good for his or her body. Let your baby experience soft, natural fibers and the feelings and comforts they give versus plastic and cellulose throwaways. It's a value choice; disposables don't reflect well on good taste.
- Cloth diapers provide a breathable, healthful environment where fresh air prevents diaper rash from irritating your baby's skin.
- Cloth diapers are versatile. Depending on your baby's needs, you can single-, double-, triple-diaper or just fold more thickness and absorbency into the appropriate location.
- Cloth diapers are reusable and better for the environment. Eighteen billion plastic diapers are buried in U.S. landfills each year. Cloth diapers eliminate this unnecessary garbage. Parents are becoming aware that a throwaway society is a wasteful society. Our babies will develop into ecologically responsible citizens provided we parents start them out with a good example.
- Paper and plastic diapers cause up to five times more skin irritations than cotton diapers. No doubt the flame-retardant chemicals, perfumes, and deodorants that disposables may contain contribute to these skin irritations.
- Parents tend to change cloth diapers more often because they are so economical—rather than trying to make an expensive disposable last a little longer—so baby's skin stays healthier and baby stays generally happier.
- Cloth diapers save you money. Whether you choose to use a diaper-laundering service or wash your own diapers at home, the savings are considerable over disposable diaper use.
- Babies who wear cloth diapers toilet-train more easily. According to each baby's timetable, toilet training is accomplished by having a clear sense of when there is a wetness present. Disposables mask this sensation.
- Cloth diapers feel comfortable. As babies grow, there are longer and longer periods when the diaper area stays dry. Why encase your baby in a shower-cap-like environment? Wearing cloth diapers is wearing a natural fiber garment.
- Cloth diapers are healthier. Disposables can pose a health hazard. They are filled with wood pulp. Chemical deodorants are added to mask the wood pulp mill smell. Splinters and other sharp objects have been found within the stuffing. There are

WHY WE USED WHAT WE DID

∎

"I used cloth diapers for the first eleven months. It was important to me that my son have cotton against his skin. I have to say I never was very good at fastening them, so when my son became too squirmy at eleven months I lost patience and switched to disposables. They were a whole lot easier and much more absorbent."

∎

"We used a diaper service. I wanted to use cloth diapers, and it was incredibly convenient. I never had to worry about running out. The biggest plus for me was that they didn't smell in the diaper pail. I'm very sensitive to smell. The plastic diapers always smelled."

∎

"I would never consider washing diapers. They're the 'dark ages.' I used disposables because of convenience. They were drier and neater."

∎

known cases of suffocation due to a disposable's plastic outer layer blocking the breathing area. Other babies have pulled out the filling of disposables and blocked their airways. The Consumer Product Safety Commission has hundreds of complaints against disposables on its computer files that may be available through the Freedom of Information Act.

Source: Joan Cooper is the mother of two and the founder and executive vice president of Biobottoms Fresh Air Wear for Kids, P.O. Box 6009, Petaluma, CA 94953; 800-766-1254. She is committed to socially responsible business.

THE ARGUMENT FOR DISPOSABLES

• **Skin care.** Disposable diapers that incorporate absorbent gelling materials are better than cloth in helping to keep the baby's skin drier and helping maintain a stable pH level, which is important to maintaining healthy skin. These findings were published in 1987 editions of the peer-reviewed journals: *Pediatrician, Pediatric Dermatology*, the *Journal of Pediatric Health Care*, and the *Journal of the American Academy of Dermatology*. Keeping the skin dry can help minimize the potential for a rash to occur. With cloth diapers it's like sitting on a sponge.

• **Infection control.** According to the 1990 U.S. Census Bureau, nearly three million children, or 60 percent of children under the age of three with working mothers, are in group care. Feces and urine are better contained in disposable diapers, resulting in reduced fecal contamination of a child's environment. Kids in group care settings share toys. They sit on toys. They always have their hands in their mouths. You want to see that environment kept as clean as possible. You want to see diaper contents remain in the diaper. A panel of the American Academy of Pediatrics and the American Public Health Association recently developed standards on the use of diapers in child-care programs.

• **Health.** A new report issued by the nation's leading pediatrician and public health organizations recognizes the benefit of disposable diapers in day-care centers. Titled *Caring for Our Children–National Health and Safety Performance Standards: Guidelines for Out-of-Home Care Programs*, the report is the culmination of four years' work by a joint committee of the American Academy of Pediatrics and the American Public Health Association. The report notes that modern disposable diapers meet the criteria outlined in the standards, while reusable cloth diapers—worn alone or with pull-on pants—are not recommended. Some cloth products, which can be changed as a single unit, do meet the physical requirements, but they have not been shown to help contain feces and urine sufficiently.

• **Environment.** The environment includes more than solid waste. It also is air and water quality, water consumption, and use of nonrenewable resources, such as oil, gas, and coal. Both cloth and disposable diaper use have an effect on the environment.

While there are many factors to consider, studies of the environmental effects of cloth and disposable diaper use conclude that both have an impact on the environment—but it is different. According to a study conducted by Franklin Associates for the American Forest and Paper Association, Diaper Manufacturers Group, the use of cloth requires more energy, water, and wastewater resources, while disposable diapers contribute to solid waste.

An independent peer review of the Franklin findings was conducted in 1991. The peer review panel consisted of professionals from academia, the U.S. Environmental Protection Agency, the Society of Environmental Toxicology and Chemistry, and a consulting firm. It is important to note that the EPA did not participate as an agency.

• **Convenience.** Disposables are easier to use. They are convenient for travel, for day care, when laundry facilities aren't available. Because they contain better, overclothes and bed linens are changed less frequently. The diaper change can be faster.

Source: Elaine Matthews, a registered nurse, is a public relations manager and spokesperson for Procter and Gamble in Cincinnati, Ohio. She is the mother of three.

DIAPER SERVICE BENEFITS

• Convenience is the key. A diaper service gives you the convenience of once- or twice-a-week delivery of diapers that are left on your doorstep. We provide a hamper, a net liner (which the driver picks up), and a deodorant disk. Deliveries and pickups can be made in your absence.

• We use cotton diapers that are 100 percent reusable. Unlike disposables, cotton diapers breathe to prevent a skin-stressing buildup of heat under the diaper.

• We are environmentally sound. We use less water and energy than you can use in home washing. We use less water than

"I used cloth in the very beginning, but they seemed so huge on my daughter. They didn't hold anything, and she got a terrible diaper rash. I switched to disposables, and I never looked back. It made my daughter very portable."

■

"I used disposables with my older daughter. I didn't want to deal with smelly, messy diapers. When my son was born, I was more conscious of the environment. I went to a friend's house who used cloth, and the diapers didn't smell. So I signed up for a diaper service, and I'd do it again. I didn't stop using cloth until my son was potty trained."

■

"For my oldest, I used disposables. I never thought about it. When my younger son was born, I switched to cloth. My guilt over the environment was too much, and I'd already messed up with my older son. I used the disposables only for going out."

■

"We use cloth for our son in his Montessori program. They believe that when a child wets, he needs to feel the wetness so that he can understand that urinating makes you wet. Of course, they change him right away, but it still helps with potty training."

■

"I used disposables when we were out of the house and at night. There was less leaking, and the moisture was drawn away from the skin."

■

manufacturers use in manufacturing disposable diapers. We recycle our waste water, which contains no industrial chemicals, and is then treated by county sanitation processing.

- Our ten-step multiprocess washing gets the diapers really clean. Each step of this protective process is under the National Association of Diaper Services' laboratory control.
- There is no rinsing or soaking with Dy-Dee's diapers. They are equipped with an antibacterial agent that retards the growth of bacteria and the odor. You deposit the soiled diapers in the container and leave the rest to us.
- Our diapers are pH balanced to be most compatible with the normal skin conditions of your baby. Our research shows that 54 percent of babies who wear cotton-diaper-service diapers never have a skin rash at all.
- We provide five different sizes of diapers, so you can go all the way from preemie diapers to toddler pants. When the fit gets snug, you can move to the next size.
- We're cost-effective. Our service costs less than disposable diapers do but more than home use does, unless you factor in the cost of your time, which is certainly significant.
- The billing process keeps you informed of diaper expenses on a monthly basis.
- A diaper service with cloth diapers makes it easier to potty-train your child because he or she knows she's wet.

Source: Lisa Anne Ganguin is the public relations/marketing coordinator of Dy-Dee Diaper Service, 40 East California Blvd., Pasadena, CA 91105; 818-792-6183.

DINNER

When I was growing up, dinner was my favorite meal. The five of us always ate together in the breakfast room, and the dinner hour was a time to talk about the highlights of our day. It was "The Donna Reed Show" and "Father Knows Best" rolled into one.

The dinner hour was a time of education as well as animated conversation. We learned the art of storytelling; I still cringe when I hear people rambling on endlessly without getting to the punch line of a story. We learned how to cut to the chase. We also learned good table manners. The position of my father's left eyebrow was an indicator of how well we were doing. Letitia Baldridge would have been proud.

For years when I was single, I went out to dinner every night. Once I got married, dinner once again became a family affair. Bernie and I ate together most nights. When we returned home from our busy days, our meal together enabled us to catch up on daily events, gossip about friends and colleagues, and spend uninterrupted time together before we bathed, read, caught up on work, listened to music, or watched TV.

When Alexander was able to join us at dinner, the dynamics changed drastically. As soon as he was old enough to sit through an entire meal, we realized that he had not inherited either of our eating genes; he alternates between being a noneater and a picky eater, much to our chagrin. And I alternate between being a reasonable adult who intellectually understands that the dinner table should not be a battleground and that a missed or unbalanced meal will not cause a nutritional deficiency and being a raving *maniac who can't stand to see her small child wreak havoc with a hallowed tradition.*

After a particularly grueling meal in which I made Alexander three different entrees, I finally stopped the craziness. I sent Alex into the family room with his father while I cleaned up the dishes. I reread Dr. Spock's advice on feeding problems and came up with a revised plan. I decided that Alex's unwillingness to try new foods was not a reflection on me.

Most important, I decided to reclaim the dinner hour. I told Bernie that once again we needed this to be our time to talk about our day with each other. I said that we should obviously try feeding Alex, and if he ate, fine, but that we should stop focusing our entire meal on him. If he wanted to get down from the high chair and play with his toys, that would be OK, but we shouldn't keep ministering to his every need.

He agreed, and dinner once again become a pleasant respite from the tensions of the day. It was more relaxing for us, and Alex was eating better without the fuss. As the months progressed, I looked forward to the time when he would be able to participate more fully.

Recently I began explaining—on a very simple level—how you cut to the chase of a story and what a punch line is. Bernie began practicing raising his left eyebrow, although we think it may be a bit premature to teach Alex table manners. We both agreed that before we can teach Alex how to refrain from talking with his mouth full he needs to learn how to talk in general. For two college-educated adults, we feel we've come a long way.

ॐ

A BALANCED DIET

Roberta R. Henry, R.D., is the director of nutrition and food service at Children's Hospital, Boston, and the coauthor of the Parent's Guide to Nutrition.

SB: What is proper nutrition for toddlers?
RH: Somehow "proper" nutrition and toddlers seems incongruous! Even balancing a toddler's diet can be a challenge. But toddlers should be offered a variety of foods from the major food groups (milk, meat, fruits/vegetables, breads). Parents, on the other hand, should not despair if their toddler eats erratically.

Most healthy toddlers will receive the nourishment they need over time—even though their approach is rather unconventional.

SB: Do children really need three meals a day?
RH: There is nothing magical about three meals a day. Many feel that providing children with four or more meals a day is the best approach. Three meals a day seems more traditional than necessary.

SB: Should every meal be balanced?
RH: Whether each meal is "balanced" is not as important as whether a variety of foods, chosen from all the food groups, is eaten during the day.

SB: What are some suggestions of foods you should encourage? Allow? Avoid?
RH: Breads, cereals, rice, pasta (the bread group) should be the mainstay of the diet, followed by vegetables, fruits, milk, meats, poultry, fish. Fats, oils, and sweets should be eaten sparingly. Parents of children under the age of two should generally not restrict their child's diet and should consult a pediatrician and/or registered dietitian if questions arise.

DEALING WITH FOOD FUSSINESS

Ellyn Satter, R.D., M.S., M.S.S.W., author of Child of Mine: Feeding With Love and Good Sense, *is a therapist at the Family Therapy Center of Madison, Wisconsin, and the mother of three.*

SB: Why is food fussiness such a big problem for infants and toddlers?
ES: It's really not. The problem is that parents have difficulty knowing what's normal behavior for children. They expect children to emerge from the womb knowing how to eat a variety of food and a variety of textures of food, and they tend to get pretty excited when children don't. But in reality eating is a skill that children learn gradually over time. They push themselves along, learning to like new foods. They will put food in their mouth and take it back out again. They will sample it for taste and texture and not swallow it. For most parents that looks like food rejection, but it's really not. It's a child's way of getting accustomed to the food and learning to like it.

SB: We still all know children who are picky eaters even though their parents cook nutritional family meals. Why is that?

ES: One of two things can happen. One is that the child is extremely sensitive to taste and texture, and it takes him a long time to learn to like new foods. The other is that parents will then get excited and upset about their child's eating habits and put pressure on him or her to try the food, and then the child will tend to like the new food less, not more. Even if you don't get into a struggle, if you put pressure on children to eat, they are less likely to enjoy whatever it is that you're pressuring them about.

SB: How do you establish a positive feeding relationship?

ES: You establish a division of responsibility in feeding. The parents are responsible for what, when, and where. The child is responsible for how much and whether. That means that the parent is responsible primarily for the menu, for the shopping list, for seeing that a meal gets put on the table and that a reasonable assortment of food is included in a menu. This includes making some judicious decisions—matching a less favorite vegetable with a more popular meat so that a child can find something at the table that he can be successful with, which makes mealtime pleasant and enjoyable.

Then it's up to the child to pick and choose from what's available and to eat or not eat what is presented to him. The child, probably from trial and error, will learn that if he leaves the table and immediately wants something else, his parents are going to say, "No, you've had your meal. Nothing else now until snack time." Snack is part of the structure of feeding children. There should be regular meals and planned snacks. But other than these opportunities to eat, a child should not be allowed to panhandle for other food because it will take away his motivation to learn to like the nutritious food his parents are providing him.

SB: How does parental behavior affect children's eating habits?

ES: If parents enjoy good food and are positive about good food, then children are going to be inclined to grow up and be very much like them. If, on the other hand, parents are tremendously finicky or parents are dieters and don't trust their body's ability to regulate eating, then children are likely to be mistrusting of their own hunger, their own appetite, and their own ability to eat the right amount of food. We're talking amounts as well as types of food. Children know how much they need to eat, and once parents have provided the appropriate amount, they can trust them to eat the right amount.

SB: *What feeding tips can you give to new moms and dads?*
ES: From birth on, children know how much they need to eat. With infants you work to calm them and feed them in a smooth and continuous way, paying attention to information coming from them as to how much they want to eat, how fast they want to eat, and in what fashion they can manage to eat.

The big shift is toward the end of the first year and into the second year, when rather than feeding the child on demand you gradually make the shift to the structured feeding of the family meal. That's really important and appropriate because toddlers require structure to feel secure. Parents need to provide the limits that are inherent in the structure, or their toddlers are just going to push them around.

SB: *All of this seems so rational, but what do you do if your child refuses to eat what you provide for him and you worry whether he is going to develop a nutritional deficiency?*
ES: What you're talking about is very typical, and it leads to a type of feeding that was described by Jean Ann Anliker in a study that was done at the University of Massachusetts. Parents of preschoolers put meals on the table, they urged their children to eat certain amounts and types of food, but when the children left the table, they were allowed to eat what they wanted to.

What you end up with is a real crossing of the lines of division of responsibility. While it is understandable because you do worry when a child won't eat anything, in the long run your child will do better if you refrain from pressuring him to eat and you're firm about setting limits on panhandling food from others.

Again, you need to have realistic expectations and an understanding of how children operate with food. They do not eat some of everything at a meal as adults do. Typically they eat only one or two food items. They do not always like the same food. They are fickle about what tastes good to them on a particular day. So you can't possibly predict what they are going to eat. You have to keep doing your menu planning, offering them a variety of food, and letting them eat a partial meal—which is very typical of children. If you average out the nutritional content of these partial meals over a week or two, you find that children get what they need.

HOW WE DO IT

■

"My husband works late, but we do try to sit down together. The eating part isn't bad, though making dinner is horrible. My two-and-a-half-year-old can entertain herself for a period of time, but the baby cries the whole time I'm trying to cook."

■

"I feed my son early, at about five, and my husband and I eat later. I usually sit with my son while he eats. He watches a video while we eat. When the video is over, he'll join us at the table and sometimes eat a bit more. That's our main family time."

■

"We all sit down together and eat. It gets a bit hectic because everybody eats something different, so I'm making at least two and sometimes three different meals. But I feel that we're setting an example for our children and it will only get easier as they get older. The hardest part is that our girls aren't very good eaters."

■

LAWRENCE BALTER'S ADVICE

Lawrence Balter, Ph.D., is the coauthor of Who's in Control? Dr. Balter's Guide to Discipline Without Combat *and* "Not in Front of the Children . . ." Helping Your Child Handle Tough Family Matters. *He is a professor of applied psychology at New York University and the father of three.*

SB: How important is the family meal?

LB: It's very important to have some family meal. Obviously with today's lifestyle it's not possible to have a family meal every day, nor is that necessarily vital. But I think there should be some effort—on at least some occasions—for a family to eat together. It provides the family with an opportunity to develop a tradition. It's a chance for people to get caught up with what's going on. For infants and toddlers it's the very beginning of socializing children to routines that are part of civil society.

SB: What is acceptable mealtime behavior for infants and toddlers?

LB: There is very little you can impose as far as discipline and decorum go. Certainly, for infants, having them sit in their high chair at the table—for a little while—is important, just so they can feel they are part of the family and they can partake in the group activity. Obviously you shouldn't expect much more of them than that. The main objective for parents of infants is to feed them properly and nutritionally in a pleasant way rather than to impose a bunch of standards on them. It's a mistake to overdo neatness with an infant; they should just enjoy the eating experience.

I'm not too keen on restricting toddlers either. If they come to the table and sit for a couple of minutes, that's OK. You can't expect them to "dine" and have a lengthy conversation. They are there for business: they sit down, they eat, they get up, and they leave. Sometimes they stand up and eat; that's OK too.

SB: What advice do you have for parents who are much more rigid and just cringe when you say "Let them stand up and eat" or for other moms and dads whose own parents would never have tolerated that kind of behavior?

LB: Not everything that our parents did with us was necessarily a good idea. Sometimes you impose discipline on kids when they're too young, and it becomes a struggle, while if you wait for six months or a year it wouldn't be. By the time children are in preschool they actually enjoy the little rituals of having the table set, they like the order, they have more control over the utensils, and they take pleasure in the routine. Parents need to be patient, because toddlers want to move around and keep going, and that's part of the developmental stage.

SB: When and how should you teach your child table manners? And by table manners, I mean sitting through a meal, eating one's food in a fairly neat way, not throwing food on the floor, and allowing adults to speak to each other and to the child—the "Father Knows Best" model.

LB: What you're talking about is unrealistic, but children *do* need to practice appropriate behavior, and parents have to understand what the norms are for different ages. When a nine-month-old keeps dropping or throwing things off the tray, you have to expect that. It's part of experimenting, like dropping the fork and watching you pick it up. It's age-appropriate, so to get worked up over it is a mistake for you and for your child. However, at fifteen months, if your child is still throwing food, you need to figure out that he or she is finished eating, and you take it away. Gradually, children learn that after they've finished eating they shouldn't throw food or mash it in their hair.

With toddlers, once they've eaten with you, if you want to sit and talk, why can't they be given an area nearby where they are safe and where they can do something on the floor like working on a puzzle or playing a game? You can't expect them to be seated with you for the rest of the hour; it's not something they can physically do.

All children need practice (if you are going to take them out) eating in a place outside the home. Obviously, manners are different in different places. It helps to take a young child to a place that is very tolerant of children, where you can have a quick meal. Don't expect to have a leisurely meal yourself. Don't take them out to eat with you because you're hungry. Take them so that they can learn how to eat in a public place. If you expect them to know how to behave the first few times, you will be frustrated and get angry. Once you do go out with them and teach them what kind of behavior is expected, they will do better.

SB: How does your advice on eating relate to your basic philosophy of discipline?

LB: My philosophy is that there are short-term and long-term goals. Very often the short-term goals counter what our long-term efforts are. So if you invoke expedience for the short-term benefit, you are going to mess up your long-term goals. Imposing rules that

"We cook simple meals, and my husband and I trade off responsibilities. One night I cook and he watches the kids, and the next night he cooks and I watch them. Sometimes I feed my two-year-old earlier, and my husband and I eat after he goes to bed. But the baby cries as soon as I sit down, no matter what the time."

■

"Dinnertime was chaos, but now we've gotten into a routine. We make sure that we eat by seven, and we try to sit down together as a family."

■

"My husband works late, so usually it's me and my daughter. When she was younger, we sat in the kitchen, but now that she's two-and-a-half we sit in the dining room and talk. I give myself one night off a week when I have a baby-sitter who feeds her dinner. On weekends we sit together as a family. I think eating together is a nice habit to get into. You can teach your children socialization skills and manners. We never watch TV or read when we eat."

■

children are not ready for, probably means having uncooperative children as they get older. If family dining is a pleasant experience while they are young, then the table will be a place they gravitate to and enjoy being part of when they are older.

SB: *What are some tips for maintaining discipline during mealtime?*

LB: • Make it short and sweet.

• Don't insist on decorum that is beyond your child's limits.

• Try to make mealtime as pleasant as possible.

DISCIPLINE

One night, when I was three months pregnant, I turned to Bernie as he was watching a Chuck Norris video on TV and said, "What is your theory on disciplining children?" Without missing a karate kick he said, "Corporal punishment."

"Hmm," I murmured, as he turned up the volume to preclude any further discussion. Despite what he'd said, I wasn't worried. He's an artist. He wears glasses. He fishes with barbless hooks and gently places the little critters back in the water. Besides, I knew our son-to-be would have his father's wonderful disposition and not need any major discipline.

The wonder of being pregnant—and not being around many small children—is that you end up astounded at how much you have to learn. As it turned out, Alex did have Bernie's nice disposition until he reached the "terrible twos." And overnight Bernie and I began disagreeing about almost every aspect of disciplining a small child. I wished we'd resolved things earlier. He thought I was too strict. I accused him of being a "wuss." We were both firmly entrenched in our roles.

My voice immediately assumed a new tone of authority when Alex's behavior offended my sensibilities. I sternly talked with him when he drew on the wall with crayons, turned his milk glass over to see the patterns it would make on the carpet, sat on the drier door and broke it, put his cars in the toilet to see if they would float, purposely and continuously turned off the TV set when we were watching it, kicked his cousin, and broke my favorite lamp from Gump's.

Although neither of us believe in corporal punishment, I did spank Alex a few times: when he bolted into the street, persisted in *drawing on the wall, once bit me so hard it brought tears to my eyes, and ran away in a department store so that I couldn't find him for at least a few minutes (although it seemed like a lifetime).*

Inexplicably, when Alex turned three, he suddenly became a holy terror for a few months. After a few days of the worst behavior I could recall, I frantically called my pediatrician. "I thought the terrible twos were over," I groaned.

"It's actually a misnomer," he responded. "He's just testing you. It will pass."

"I've become shrewish," I moaned to a friend. "It seems as if I am constantly talking to Alex about the same things over and over, and he doesn't respond. Either he's got a hearing loss—and we should check it—or, worse, he's ignoring me."

"He'll get over it," she responded calmly.

"Easy for you to say," I responded sarcastically. Her children were in their twenties.

Alex's behavior persisted. Bernie and I began screaming at each other in frustration. "He's only three," he would say. "You're expecting too much."

"That's undoubtedly what Al Capone's father said when he was little," I sneered. "And probably if Al's mother had disciplined him more strictly, he wouldn't have become a mob boss."

"I don't like it when you make fun of my Italian heritage," he quietly responded.

"This is not an ethnic slur," I said with clenched teeth. "I could have said Bugsy Siegel's mom."

"But you didn't."

Needless to say, the conversation degenerated from here. Alex seemed to sense our conflict and began playing us against each other. When I said no—no matter what about—he would say that his father had said yes. In our defense, we never openly contradicted each other, but it was getting out of hand.

So again I called my pediatrician. He explained how important it was for Bernie and me to work together to establish a philosophy of discipline that we could both live with. He repeated what my mother had told me, which is that "consistency between parents is essential and that you should not disagree or contradict each other about discipline in front of your child."

Then the pediatrician suggested that Bernie and I sit down and prioritize all of Alex's antics that bothered us and pick the few infractions we couldn't live with. When these took place, Bernie and I should firmly say no. If Alex persisted, he should then be put on a chair in a room by himself (with the door open so he wouldn't get frightened). The doctor informed me that this wasn't cruel and inhuman punishment but that children dislike isolation. He also cautioned that it should be reserved for those indiscretions we had repeatedly warned him about.

After implementing some of the good doctor's recommendations, things improved almost immediately. And while we continued to have lengthy philosophical discussions late at night about discipline, Alex suddenly outgrew this rather unappealing stage, and he once again became the well-behaved little boy we adore.

What's extraordinary is that a few weeks later, when our little angel threw what can be described only as a full-fledged tantrum in the clothing section of a department store, I heard his father say in a very stern voice, "Alex, cut it out right now." Alex looked at him incredulously, got up off the floor, and smiled agreeably.

Will wonders never cease!

FIRST DISCIPLINE TECHNIQUES

• **Teach limits.** This means setting limits for children, making sure they understand rules and how the family environment is structured so that they know what's expected of them. You sometimes enforce these limits with consequences.

• **Use distraction.** Distraction is a way of helping to avoid battles with the child by offering something that is more appealing than what he's doing. For example, if you have a child who has just come in from outdoors and didn't want to or won't take off his coat and hat and is having a bit of a temper tantrum, you might distract him by looking outside and talking about what a squirrel is doing. Once he gets engaged, you start helping him take his clothes off, and he's forgotten all about the issue.

• **Offer substitutes.** In offering substitutes, you are really making sure that you give your child an attractive alternative. If a child is playing with the knobs on the television—and you've asked her to stop—you might say, "I'm going to read a story to some lucky girl in this room. Do you know who that might be?" You then offer the reading of the book as a substitute for the playing with the knobs on the TV.

• **Making a game out of discipline.** This strategy attempts to enlist the cooperation and participation of your child and often sets up a challenge or gives her a task that is more appealing than the one she's resisting. It works well with chores or tasks like

HOW WE DISCIPLINE OUR CHILDREN

■

"My husband and I are both disciplinarians. Time-out seems to work pretty well; actually just the threat of it works. We try to avoid spanking our daughter but have done it when she runs into the street."

■

"Boy, this is a hard one. What you need to be is calm and consistent, and I'm neither. I tend to fly off the handle, so I try to set clear limits. I use time-out and sometimes take away privileges, like television."

■

"I lock myself in the closet. Just kidding! I make my kids be by themselves if they are being difficult. I give one warning before I send them to their room. Mostly I use a very stern voice when I want them to listen. I rarely yell unless I'm in another room. They're still so little that we haven't come up with a list of serious problems."

■

picking up toys. If you make the task more fun, you don't really have to discipline in the narrower sense of the term. You can avoid a battle of wills, the use of a threat, or some other technique when, in fact, you can get your child to do what you want in a different kind of way.

• **Limit access to objects and activities.** Often parents need to remove toys or games that may cause frustration. You need to limit children's access to things that are going to cause problems. If you don't want children playing with the salt and pepper at the restaurant, you move the items to another table.

• **Child-proof your home.** In a sense you are creating an environment that's going to reduce conflict and problems. In child-proofing, you are usually removing more seductive objects or temptations—ones that can be dangerous—again, a wiser strategy than the alternative, which is using too many *no*s or allowing a dangerous situation to exist.

• **Criticize the behavior, not the child.** Starting when the child is very young, make sure that if you attack something, it's the behavior and the actions of the child rather than the child's character. Saying, "I don't like it when you throw a temper tantrum" is much better than telling your child he or she is headstrong, stubborn, or unmanageable.

• **Repeat rules often.** When you have a young child who is just beginning to learn the ways of the world, and certainly of the family, you cannot expect her to know and remember rules encountered for the first time. You can't assume that because you said something yesterday your child is going to remember it today.

• **Use rhyming rules.** This is a creative way of helping a child learn rules. A catchy phrase like "A fight's not right" or, "End of the day—time to put your toys away" is certainly easier to remember than an ordinary rule.

• **Avoid abrupt changes.** This is very important, particularly because many young children don't handle change very well. When you say to a child, "It's time to leave now," you need to remember that children aren't always on our schedule, and they don't necessarily like to change from one activity to another. So you generally have to give them warnings and announcements ahead of time so that they have an idea of what kind of change is needed, and they can adjust to that change.

• **Offer help through frustrating situations.** When children get frustrated, they shouldn't be scolded or attacked in some way. They do need help and support, and that is a very important role of parents. As children approach the age of three, they want to be more independent. They want to try things themselves. They can't always succeed very well, so we, as parents, have to help them succeed without taking over from them and subverting their independence.

• **Anticipate and avert problems.** This relates to limiting access, discussed earlier. Try to anticipate problems, because it is so much easier to anticipate them than to deal with them afterward. If you're going on a car trip and you haven't brought things for your children to play with, you can anticipate that siblings will fight because they don't have anything better to occupy their time. If you prepare by bringing toys or materials to play with and by explaining the kind of behavior you expect in the car, you might be able to avert the problem.

• **Offer choices.** Some types of parent training offer this as a very important aspect of discipline. Giving children choices helps them grow and become independent and make their own decisions. They also respond better when parents are not giving them orders or directing their behavior.

• **Give leeway to make mistakes.** This technique reminds parents to maintain realistic expectations for children. We want to allow children the leeway to try new behaviors. That means that parents know that children's efforts will be imperfect and give them this extra margin for error; by doing so you exempt them from punishment, scolding, or criticism.

Source: James Windell, author of Discipline, A Sourcebook of 50 Failsafe Techniques for Parents, *is a psychotherapist who works with children, adolescents, and families. He is the father of two and lives in Bloomfield Hills, Michigan.*

THE "TIME-OUT" METHOD

What it does. The "time-out" method is a way of providing corrective feedback to children. When a child engages in behavior that is inappropriate, instead of punishing him or her to change the behavior, it's important simply to realize that part of parenting is socialization. And in socialization we need to give kids positive feedback when they engage in appropriate behavior as well as let them know they've done something wrong by giving them corrective feedback. Time-out is a very effective means of providing corrective feedback to children without hurting their self-esteem

"I guess we mostly removed them from the setting. One time, when one of my children was just awful, we left the grocery store because it was unmanageable. Our kids got spanked when they did something dangerous like running in the street."

■

"Discipline? What's that? These days, at almost three, my daughter is starting to have major tantrums. I try to talk to her about them, but if she's unreachable I put her in her room and tell her she has to stay there until she's calmer. She was perfect until about two, and then her sister was born. It's hard to tell what caused the problems, being two or having a sibling. It was probably a combination."

■

1417232426272831323338394041424344454647484950515253545556575859606162636465666768697071727374757677787980818283848586878889909192939495969798991001011021031041051061071081091101111121131141151161171181191201211221231241251261271281291301311321331341351361371381391401411421431441451461471481491501511521531541551561571581591601611621631641651661671681691701711721731741751761771781791801811821831841851861871881891901911921931941951961971981992002012022032042052062072082092102112122132142152162172182192202212222232242252262272282292302312322332342352362372382392402412422432442452462472482492502512522532542552562572582592602612622632642652662672682692702712722732742752762772782792802812822832842852862872882892902912922932942952962972982993003013023033043053063073083093103113123133143153163173183193203213223233243253263273283293303313323333343353363373383393403413423433443453463473483493503513523533543553563573583593603613623633643653663673683693703713723733743753763773783793803813823833843853863873883893903913923933943953963973983994004014024034044054064074084094104114124134144154164174184194204214224234244254264274284294304314324334344354364374384394404414424434444454464474484494504514524534544554564574584594604614624634644654664674684694704714724734744754764774784794804814824834844854864874884894904914924934944954964974984995005015025035045055065075085095105115125135145155165175185195205215225235245255265275285295305315325335345355365375385395405415425435445455465475485495505515525535545555565575585595605615625635645655665675685695705715725735745755765775785795805815825835845855865875885895905915925935945955965975985996006016026036046056066076086096106116126136146156166176186196206216226236246256266276286296306316326336346356366376386396406416426436446456466476486496506516526536546556566576586596606616626636646656666676686696706716726736746756766776786796806816826836846856866876886896906916926936946956966976986997007017027037047057067077087097107117127137147157167177187197207217227237247257267277287297307317327337347357367377387397407417427437447457467477487497507517527537547557567577587597607617627637647657667677687697707717727737747757767777787797807817827837847857867877887897907917927937947957967977987998008018028038048058068078088098108118128138148158168178188198208218228238248258268278288298308318328338348358368378388398408418428438448458468478488498508518528538548558568578588598608618628638648658668678688698708718728738748758768778788798808818828838848858868878888898908918928938948958968978988999009019029039049059069079089099109119129139149159169179189199209219229239249259269279289299309319329339349359369379389399409419429439449459469479489499509519529539549559569579589599609619629639649659669679689699709719729739749759769779789799809819829839849859869879889899909919929939949959969979989991000

"Whatever I'm doing, it's not working. Each week I try something new. This week I'm giving my son choices. It seems to be helping. We're starting to do time-outs in his room, and I'm learning to be more strict. He's been biting lately—not other kids, just me and my husband. For that kind of behavior I take away privileges. It made him unhappy when I tried to put him to bed without the usual storytime. He then told me that he knew it wasn't good to bite and asked me to read to him, which I did. It's hard to be consistent."

■

or making them feel bad about themselves, because it doesn't involve yelling and it doesn't involve hitting.

How to structure it. You designate a chair in the corner of a room someplace that is easy to monitor yet is not in the flow of traffic so that the child won't be disturbed during the time-out period. You have the chair facing the corner of the wall. You practice the time-out method with the child before you ever have to use it. You let the child know that from now on when he does something inappropriate, he is going to have to sit in the time-out chair. The time-out period is not prolonged; it's one minute per year of age of the child. (I've used it for children as young as two years old, but it's not appropriate for someone who's younger.) So, for a three-year-old, it's three minutes. Any longer than that doesn't serve any purpose other than making your child want to get out of the chair and encouraging him to leave the chair before the period is over.

The basic technique is to set a kitchen timer for the amount of time the child is in the chair. That way you and your child know when the time-out is over. When the child engages in inappropriate behavior, you catch that behavior as soon as possible. You don't find yourself repeating a request to do something. You initiate time-out immediately. You try not to get visibly angry at the child. You simply take the child to the chair. You have the child sit in the chair, and you go and set the timer. The child has to be quiet until the timer goes off. If he's not, you reset the timer. Otherwise you're accidentally reinforcing the child's behavior of acting out in the chair.

Catch them being good. What is really important for time-out to work is that you also catch kids being good. The phrase "catch them being good" is very important. Children will often act out for parental attention because being ignored is one of the worst things for a child. Your interacting with them, even in an angry way, when they are acting out is preferable to the child than being ignored. Appropriate behavior should be reinforced. You must always combine time-out for inappropriate behavior with a lot of positive attention and love for appropriate behavior. It's that combination that really makes time-out work.

Source: James W. Varni, M.D., coauthor of Time-Out for Toddlers, *is a professor of psychiatry at the University of California, San Diego, School of Medicine, and director of the psychosocial and the behavioral sciences program in the division of hematology-oncology, Children's Hospital and Health Center, San Diego.*

ALTERNATIVES TO USING POWER

The following techniques are ways to influence rather than control your child.

• **Find out what your child needs.** When your child was an infant, you spent most of your time trying to find out what his or her needs were and how you could meet them. You need to continue this when your child gets older. Find out why the child is behaving in some unacceptable way—whether it's crying, not going to sleep, or wanting to come into your bed. Invariably the child is trying to meet some need. Once you determine what the need is and help the child find a way to meet it, the unacceptable behavior will probably disappear.

• **Let's make a trade.** If a child is behaving in an unacceptable way—for example, playing with some expensive pottery or a sharp knife—you substitute something that is less valuable or less dangerous. In effect you make a trade. You're saying "You can play with this, but you can't play with that, because . . ."

• **Modify the environment.** When you bring someone new into your house, there are many ways to modify the environment to prevent behavior that will be unacceptable. That means moving valuables out of the toddler's reach until the child is old enough to understand they are valuable. It means being sensitive to whether your child has too much or too little in the surroundings to capture his or her interests. Most of all, the principle is to limit the environment rather than the child.

• **The confrontive I-message.** This is different from the evaluative and blaming You-messages that parents usually send when a child is behaving in some unacceptable way. "You're being a bad boy." "You shouldn't do that." "You're being thoughtless." "You know better than that." Those are the kind of messages we want to avoid. While you have every right to confront your child, the best way to influence the child is to say specifically: (1) what behavior is unacceptable, (2) what feelings you have about it, and (3) the effect of the unacceptable behavior on you. A good example of a three-part-message is "When you throw food on the floor I get angry because I don't enjoy cleaning it up."

• **The preventive I-message.** It's just like the confrontive I-message except that the unacceptable behavior hasn't yet occurred. So you are sending a preventive message in anticipation of problems. "We are going on a trip together in the car, and I would like us to make some rules now to prevent any problems." The preventive I-message reduces future conflicts by letting your child

123

know what your needs are and giving the child a chance to cooperate before being told what to do.

• **Shifting gears to reduce resistance.** Even when you send a really good three-part confrontive I-message, your child will often react with resistance, defensiveness, guilt, denial, discomfort, or hurt feelings. Rather than responding by sending another I-message, that is the time to do some active listening. What you're doing is acknowledging your child's feelings and shifting gears to communicate that you are not trying to get your own needs met at the child's expense. Children find it easier to change if they feel the adult understands how hard changing behavior might be.

Situation: A mother and her two-and-half-year-old toddler are at the table eating lunch together. The toddler is throwing his food on the floor.

Mother: When you throw your food on the floor I get angry because I don't enjoy cleaning it up. (Confrontive I-Message.)

Child: I don't like my lunch. I don't want scrambled eggs for my lunch. (Child states his or her need.)

Mother: You don't like the scrambled eggs and you threw them on the floor because you don't want to eat them. (Shifting gears with active listening.)

Child: I don't like scrambled eggs. I like peanut butter sandwiches. I want a peanut butter sandwich for lunch. (Child offers solution.)

Mother: You would like to have a peanut butter sandwich instead of scrambled eggs. (Active listening.)

Child: Yeah.

Mother: Well, it is OK with me if you have a peanut butter sandwich today. But when I feed you food you don't like, I need you to *tell* me that you don't like it instead of throwing it on the floor. Throwing food on the floor makes an extra mess that I have to clean up and I get really frustrated because I have a lot of work to do already. (Mother re-sends confrontive I-message.)

Child: I won't throw my food on the floor. I'll tell you when I don't like my food. OK, Mommy?

• **Problem solving.** Sometimes you reach an impasse. You've explained what behavior is unacceptable, but the child doesn't want to give up that behavior. Even with someone as young as three, you can problem solve together to find some solution acceptable to both.

• **When angry, find the primary feeling.** Most often when parents are angry they send You-messages. They may angrily say "Look at the trouble you caused me. You're always running around at the grocery store." Obviously, that is a blaming, angry You-message. Almost invariably, however, anger is not your primary feeling; it's your secondary feeling. When your child has acted up in the supermarket and you are angry, you are probably just using anger to get your child to stop. What you're really feeling is embarrassment. It's important to try to find out what the primary or basic feeling is and send *that* message. If you do, you might find yourself getting angry at your child much less frequently.

Source: Thomas Gordon, Ph.D., the founder of P.E.T. (Parent Effectiveness Training), is a clinical psychologist, the author of Discipline That Works, *and the father of two.*

EATING OUT

When I was single, I went out for breakfast every day; I had lunch and dinner out five days a week. By the time I married Bernie I was already eating out much less frequently, but we both genuinely enjoyed going to restaurants. At night we usually sought out local ethnic restaurants or relatively reasonable trendy ones. Every once in a while—usually for a celebration or with friends—we'd go to one of Los Angeles's finest and blow our entertainment budget for the month.

When I was pregnant, we vowed we'd never go to nice restaurants with Alex until he was old enough to remain quiet at the table. In the last few years we'd seen enough noisy small children and their seemingly oblivious parents to make us wonder if there were an entire generation of people with a hearing loss so significant as to render them incapable of knowing that they were ruining other people's meals.

Six weeks after Alex was born, we broke our promise and took him out to dinner. Our resolution to the moral dilemma of whether severe cabin fever was justification to upset an entire restaurant of contented diners was that we'd go early—thus ensuring we wouldn't see anyone we knew—and pick a lesser restaurant. We both agreed this was a reasonable solution and bolted from the house before we could think better of it.

Despite the glares we received as we walked to our table, Alex remained asleep during the entire meal. We scarfed down our food so quickly (in anticipation of an incident) that we were home before real people (those who eat at a reasonable hour as opposed to 5:30 P.M.) arrived.

This arrangement continued to work for eight or nine months.

Alex didn't always sleep through the meal, but he was usually quiet. When he wasn't, I popped a bottle into his mouth, which generally worked. He was content drinking; we were thrilled to be able to eat out on those nights when we couldn't get a baby-sitter. Our friends with children couldn't believe our luck; their children had always been disruptive in restaurants. They kept on telling us it wouldn't last.

Just when we were getting smug—developing one of those "our child is better than your child" attitudes—the roof caved in. From one day to the next it seemed that Alex had become a terror in public eating facilities. My mother, who is intensely loyal, would disagree and say that he was better than most children his age. Unfortunately that didn't help. No matter what age a person is, it is less than relaxing to eat with someone who bangs his spoon on the table, throws food on the floor, and stands up on his chair.

Three weeks later, after Alex had behaved particularly poorly at our neighborhood Chinese restaurant, I told Bernie that if we couldn't get a sitter, we weren't going out to eat—ever again. He agreed. The next Saturday night, after having called every sitter I knew, we reassessed our decision.

"He's not that bad," Bernie relented. "Let's just go out early."

"It depends on your definition of 'that bad,'" I retorted. "I think that trying to pull the tablecloth off the table is a qualifier."

"You're right, of course," he responded dejectedly. "I just wanted to go out."

"So did I," I said sadly. "Maybe if we went where there are other kids," I suggested hopefully. "That would probably work."

"We hate those kinds of places," he reminded me. I knew he was right. I suspected that the only thing worse than eating in a public place with your own small child who was misbehaving was eating with an entire roomful of children engaged in a similar behavioral pattern.

"I am philosophically opposed to eating fast food for dinner, and I won't consider being seen in one of those kinds of restaurants at night," I said vehemently.

Bernie looked knowingly at me. We burst into laughter and bolted to the local McDonald's. It was heaven. We were surrounded by kids. No one cared when Alex threw his Chicken McNuggets on the floor. He seemed thrilled that they actually gave him a toy for eating there. We had a wonderful time.

Since then we have eaten at dozens of McDonald's and had other fast food at family restaurants throughout the United States. On a recent trip to Santa Fe, when Bernie had a business meeting

127

HOW EATING OUT HAS CHANGED WITH KIDS

■

"Does Carl's Jr. and Der Wienerschnitzel ring a bell? Fortunately for us, we live in a popular area with a wide variety of family restaurants. If my daughter does not like the menu, we grab a 'meal deal' to go and take it out. People understand."

■

"It's decreased to two times a week. We have a sitter routinely on Wednesdays and Sundays so we can go out alone. Eating in a restaurant with a toddler is not my idea of a relaxing meal."

■

"It hasn't changed very much. We didn't eat expensive meals preparenthood. But I've worked hard to train restaurant-acceptable-behavior kids (as much as possible) because I refuse to eat in family-style restaurants."

■

one night, Alex and I went to the McDonald's near our hotel, and I read The New Yorker *while he played on the outdoor equipment. I may have changed in many other ways, but I still have good taste in reading material.*

༄

FAST-FOOD RESTAURANTS

Jayne Hurley is a registered dietitian and associate nutritionist at the Center for Science in the Public Interest in Washington, D.C., where she writes for its Nutrition Action Healthletter.

SB: *Why do so many kids beg their parents to take them to fast-food restaurants?*
JH: Probably because the ads are directed at kids, not their parents. For example, we did a survey a few years ago and taped twenty hours of Saturday morning television on all the major networks and Nickelodeon. What we found was that 96 percent of the ads were for junky, salty, fatty, sugary foods. Only 4 percent of the ads were for food you would consider healthful. What's happening is that companies are spending an enormous amount of money targeting kids and the kids don't have a chance.

SB: *Should kids eat fast food?*
JH: Despite the improvements in fast food—and there have been a lot of them in the past five years—the average fast-food menu is still a minefield of fat, salt, and sugar. It also typically consists of foods that are lacking vitamins A and C and fiber. This is the total opposite of what the nutrition recommendations are from the surgeon general, the National Academy of Sciences, and just about every health authority in this country, all of whom are saying we should be eating more fruit and vegetables, more grains, and fewer meat and dairy products. In fact that's very hard to do at a fast-food restaurant. The long-term problem is that we're setting kids up for health problems down the road, including everything from heart disease and cancer to tooth decay and obesity.

SB: *What is the worst type of fast food?*
JH: Absolutely those double- and triple-stacked hamburgers. Every restaurant seems to have its own version. I don't think people can even imagine how bad they are. Just one of these sandwiches may supply all of the fat—or more—than you should eat in an entire day. We can't forget that the number-one source of fat and artery-

clogging saturated fat in the average American's diet is ground beef, and the reason for that is probably the popularity of fast-food restaurants.

SB: If we do take our kids to fast-food restaurants, what tips do you have for maximizing the nutritional value of the food we order?

JH: If they are going to have hamburgers, buy the smallest ones available. At McDonald's, that would be the small burger or the McLean Deluxe, which is made with lean meat. Skip the cheese. Hold the sauces. The grilled chicken sandwiches from Burger King and Hardee's are pretty good, but skip the fatty mayonnaise-type dressing and you slash the fat content by one-third. Substitute a side salad with light dressing for the fries. Order 1 percent milk or juice instead of soda.

If your kids are in the mood for chicken, Chicken Tenders from Burger King and Chicken Stix from Hardee's are the lowest in fat; Wendy's Crispy Nuggets are the worst. If you're talking about milk shakes, the only place to go is McDonald's. They put out a really low-fat milk shake. If your kids will eat it, a baked potato with a small amount of cheese and broccoli is a good choice too. On any given day, only 9 percent of Americans are eating the five or more servings of fruits and vegetables that are recommended as a daily requirement, so the potato may be an important addition to their diet.

THE FAST-FOOD DIET

Mary Donkersloot, author of The Fast Food Diet, Quick and Healthy Eating at Home and on the Go, *is a registered dietitian in private practice in Beverly Hills, CA; 310-843-9090.*

SB: How can fast foods be healthful foods?

MD: The good news about fast-food restaurants is that there are many more options these days. You can go to fast-food restaurants where there are new lower fat choices—a grilled chicken sandwich that isn't breaded and deep-fried—with three to four hundred calories and ten to fifteen grams of fat. Burger King has its BK Broiler, which is its number-one seller. McDonald's has its McLean Deluxe; it also has packages of celery and carrot sticks. Carl's Jr. has a Santa Fe Chicken sandwich, a baked potato, and a salad bar. Jack in the Box has the Chicken Fajita Pita, which is very tasty, and

"We've just begun to eat out again in moderate restaurants. Our child has always been restless, and, short of fast-food places, Chinese restaurants were all we could manage. Also, our daughter is a picky eater, so why spend the money if she doesn't eat?"

■

"We prefer taking our son out to lunch because he gets tired at dinnertime and is less patient."

■

"With the first child, eating out was nonexistent. With the second, we were into fast foods. Now my husband and I can go out to a nice place with or without the kids."

■

HOW WE KEEP OUR CHILDREN QUIET

■

"We find the worst table in the restaurant, the one near the kitchen. No one in their right mind would want to sit there, but our toddler son loves it. There is plenty of activity to keep him amused. The waiters and waitresses talk to him and bring him special snacks. If he makes a little noise, no one ever seems to hear him."

■

"Bring finger foods for infants and crayons and coloring books or small toys for toddlers. It works for a while, but inevitably the moment your food arrives your child will say, 'Mommy, I have to go potty.' "

■

a teriyaki chicken bowl with rice—only six grams of fat. Around the country there are fast-food chains that flame-broil chicken, which is very healthful. These places have expanded their choice of side dishes so that you can find a lentil dish, an all-cucumber salad, a variety of beans, and steamed vegetables; the options are unlimited.

SB: How can one eat healthfully?
MD: • **Lower the fat in your diet.** Fat is a dense source of calories, and it leads to being overweight and to other health problems. In addition, for a busy mom, that makes her tired, and that's a big motivator. You can't just fill kids up on fruits and vegetables, because their stomachs are smaller, and children as well as adults need a wide variety of food. By establishing healthy eating habits, they won't develop a palate for rich, high-fat foods.
• **Eat less saturated fat.** Saturated fat raises cholesterol in the blood two and a half times more than cholesterol itself. So saturated fat is a major cause of clogged arteries.
• **Limit cholesterol.** Our bodies can handle only so much cholesterol a day. Thereafter, it builds up in the arteries.
• **Have adequate but not excessive protein.** High-protein foods are usually high-fat foods. I encourage people to shift toward a vegetarian diet, which will increase the intake of vitamins, minerals, and fiber and decrease the fat. Trim meats of the visible fat, use skinless poultry, and cook legumes with minimal salt and fat. The low-fat or nonfat dairy products are best.
• **Eat more complex carbohydrates.** The caveat is not to eat more complex carbohydrates *until* you've decreased the amount of meat you're eating. Otherwise you'll just increase your calories. The grains, legumes, vegetables, and fruits should be the mainstay of your diet because they are high in fiber, vitamins, and minerals and low in fat. We know that cultures that eat in this manner have much less incidence of heart disease, obesity, diabetes, and certain forms of cancer.
• **Increase your fiber intake.** Fiber maintains the normal functioning of the gastrointestinal tract to alleviate constipation, which is a common problem. Fiber can also decrease the incidence of colon cancer. We're all exposed to carcinogens from time to time, and if you eat a high-fiber diet those carcinogens have less time to remain in your system and cause a problem.
• **Limit sodium.** Your sodium intake will decrease naturally as you eat fewer processed foods and more fresh fruits, vegetables, and legumes. Limited sodium doesn't need to be a focal point.

• **Maintain your ideal body weight.** I see a lot of overweight people who focus on all these different things, but then they overeat, and that wipes out all the other good things they are doing. Ironically, the binge type of overeating stems from restricting foods. It is important to help people bridge the gap between ideal and practical—so they can prioritize and balance their food intake. One of my clients lost 40 pounds, partly by making room for 250 calories worth of dessert each day.

• **Get an adequate amount of vitamins and minerals.** The definition of *adequate* continues to change, and the perceived health benefits of certain vitamins continue to evolve. For years we have been looking at vitamin E in relation to cancer, and now we're looking at it in relation to heart disease as an antioxidant. I recommend that adults take a multivitamin and mineral supplement. Children get an adequate amount of vitamins and minerals by eating a variety of foods. Since that may not always happen, you may consider a vitamin supplement. Just make sure they are not recognized as "candy" by kids—too many vitamins could cause problems.

SB: What tips do you have for parents who want to teach their kids healthful eating habits?

MD: The best tip is for them to be role models and to recognize the importance of the family meal, because I see it disappearing. I discourage parents from teaching kids, by example, that to lose weight you have to eat "special" foods, because this sets up a pattern of good foods and bad foods. The best way to lose weight *and* establish healthy eating habits in children is to make wise food choices and exercise regularly.

FURTHER READING

Kids Dine Out, by Susan Gilleran. New York: John Wiley & Sons, 1993.

"I nurse my baby. Ugh!"

■

"Go to dinner early. Sit outside if possible, even in winter; we bring sweaters. Bring crackers for the waiting time."

■

"We bring all kinds of gadgets to keep them quiet and go for a walk if the food is slow in coming. Paper-scissors-rock is a good table game."

■

ENTERTAINING

efore we were married, Bernie used to tease me about the scarcity of my dowry. I owned one pot and pan, cheap table settings for four, a few bowls, a coffeepot, and mismatched flatware.

He, on the other hand, had a kitchen that was so fully stocked I mistakenly assumed the first time I saw it that he had been married before and that his wife had died, leaving him everything. When I finally summoned up the courage to ask him why one person who was living alone needed so many things, he simply said, "For entertaining."

The more I got to know him, the more I understood how and why he'd accumulated so much. It seemed as if every time we went shopping he bought another piece of kitchenware that was "absolutely essential." The pasta pot was obvious; the demitasse cups a little less so; the jelly roll pan, casserole dish, steamed pudding pan, electric mixer, barbecue, champagne flutes, and tortilla and guacamole dish have all come in handy.

They were used with great frequency when we entertained. When we had friends over, we really went all out. Our handwritten menus on which Bernie carefully listed every course, including the wines (often plural), were studies in gastronomic delight and excess. There were years when we cooked mightily, entertained elegantly, and charmed and delighted our friends.

These days our patterns have changed dramatically. Our parental status does not allow us the luxury of leisurely Saturday morning shopping sprees, day-long cooking extravaganzas, and volatile late-night parties with merry revelers who can sleep late the next morning.

Entertaining has taken on a new meaning. We're interested in dishes that can be cooked tastefully but quickly, menus that are interesting but not expensive, beverages that are refreshing but not hangover-producing, and desserts that elicit "wow" but are not drop-dead ecstasies.

We now entertain couples with children. We eat before it gets dark. The china is getting dusty from lack of use in the cupboard, and finger food has taken on a new meaning. Recently, after we served brunch on the patio to some neighborhood friends and their children, I said to Bernie with surprise, "You know, I had a very nice time."

"So did I," he agreed as if in disbelief. Bagels, danishes, cold cereal, bacon, juice, milk, and coffee seemed a lifetime away from asparagus frittatas, homemade sausage, potatoes in their skins with onions, homemade scones, and espresso.

When they left and Bernie asked me how old the boys were, I knew why. For preteenagers, they were actually delightful company. We talked about their school, their soccer teams, and their favorite classes. Their antics were extraordinarily entertaining to Alex, who giggled with glee. Their preoccupation with him allowed us to talk to their parents without interruption.

When they left, we were sorry to see them go. We suddenly realized we were more than ready to entertain families. Adult conversations on real estate, films, politics, religion, and culture seem highly overrated after all these years. A little "Teenage Mutant Ninja Turtles" talk is somehow a welcome relief.

৯〉

ENTERTAINING BEAUTIFULLY TOGETHER

Alexandra Stoddard is the author of twelve books, including Living Beautifully Together *and* Making Choices: The Joy of a Courageous Life. *She is the mother of two and lives with her husband, in Connecticut and New York City.*

SB: When your children were little, what were some of the most successful ways you and your husband entertained other families with children?

AS: Holiday parties. All our parties were family parties. We got to know the moms, the dads, and the sisters and brothers of the children. The dads would help with pitch the pennies, and the moms would help with the cooking and serving of the food. We all

OUR CHANGING ENTERTAINING PATTERNS

■

"We entertained a lot more before we had kids. Now we do more potlucks or eat out with friends. We seem to hang out with people who have children, and we try to avoid doing the holiday dinners at our house. When we see friends who don't have kids, we'll often invite them over later at night, not necessarily for a meal."

■

"I've always entertained a lot. My daughter goes to bed at eight, so I often invite people over for a late dinner. Sometimes we include her in dinner and then put her to bed before we have coffee and dessert so we can talk. I'm really lucky; she goes to bed most times without a fuss. In fact I made a very conscious decision when she was born that I wouldn't get quiet when I put her down to sleep. I wanted her to be accustomed to a certain noise level. It's worked out really well."

■

slipped into patterns and gender roles without meaning to, but the dads loved to do the games and the moms loved to cook. Those were wonderful times, and now that my daughters are grown, their friends still come to the house for parties.

SB: How did you adapt menus to kids? How did you think of the games? How much planning did all this take?
AS: The process is the reality, as Dr. Samuel Johnson often said. I love planning; I love the anticipation. The children will tell you which games they like best. Pin the tail on the donkey was always a favorite. You can pitch pennies into a basket; the children always giggled when their dads missed. It's also fun to get shelf paper and tape it all over the walls in your hall, provide felt-tip markers, and let the children make a mural. You keep those forever; they're a slice of life.

Let the children know it's *their* party as well. I don't ever remember a child breaking anything in my house. When parents say not to do "this and that," it makes children petrified. If you just embrace them—and let them be—they do so very well. I always let my children entertain in their own rooms. If we were having a family party, we would set up the table in their bedrooms and let the children have the food and drinks there. They could play house, and that was fun. Children are usually very fastidious, so if they spill something, they will clean it up or they will call their mom.

As far as the food is concerned, everybody likes finger food. All that formality and pretension of the eighties was so silly. People spent all this money having their flowers arranged and the food cooked by someone else. The process is what's fun, and you do that with your children. You let them make a mess in your kitchen. Everyone loves sandwiches. Pink lemonade is always a favorite. Use paper plates; there's always time for the porcelain later.

SB: How did you teach your children to behave in social situations?
AS: I don't like any form of criticism; I don't learn from it. I actually shudder when I'm criticized. I embrace confirmation and affirmation, and so do my children. Recently in church, there was a little four-year-old who screamed out, "Hi, Alexandra," and the entire church heard it. I was so touched, I had goose bumps all over my body. She went up to the altar and said, "Hi, Dad" (to her father who is the minister), and it was so *sweet*; so endearing.

She had come over for tea a few weeks earlier. She and her sister ended up with chocolate ice cream all over their pinafores. We were in the garden, so we took their dresses off to wash them, I gave them my bathing suits and fastened them with ribbons in the back, and they went home in a red wagon. We never had a better time. I think children *instinctively* know how to behave if you let them be themselves.

I have only daughters; I know nothing about boys. But I've always incorporated my children into everything I've done. I've taken them on business trips; to ranches in Texas. They're the loves of my life, and I've loved every minute I've been with them. I have loved the whole idea of being part of the process of their growing up and exploring. I feel very blessed, and I'm absolutely sure that the reason I have such a happy professional life now that they're out of the nest is that I can look back and say "Golly, what *fun* we had."

SB: What practical tips on entertaining can you give to new moms?

AS: The word *entertaining* is daunting to me because I've never entertained in my life. I have people over, and we enjoy each other's company. Some practical tips might be to sit down and plan the invitation with your children. A written invitation is something they can press in their memory book. Children love memorabilia; in fact, if moms can have a pretty little box for their children's memorabilia it's a wonderful way to preserve memories. Listen to your children and *involve* them.

Perhaps my best tip is not about entertaining but just about being with your children. When my girls were little, they used to have a half day at school on Tuesdays. I would pick them up and bring balloons or a party bag, and we would go on an excursion. I'd never plan it in advance. I'd ask "Where should we go today?" And I think that one of the things children relate to is when a parent takes them seriously and listens to them. Kids are always so programmed between their schools and after-school sports, and it seems as if parents are always trying to farm them out. But what's really quite wonderful is just to *spend time* with them.

Listen to their answers when you ask "What should we do?" Their requests are usually so reasonable. Many times we would go to Paley Park and just sit and watch the waterfall together. As I look back on it, because the rest of my life was so busy, I feel grateful that every Tuesday afternoon was a special one for us. It didn't matter what we did, as long we were together.

"More ordering in; less complicated menus. Less alcohol. Evenings end earlier."

■

"We rarely invite childless friends. They don't understand what is 'normal' behavior for infants and toddlers. Meals are rarely relaxing at our house. When we entertain at home, we like to include our children, so we invite other moms and dads with kids. We go out to eat with our friends who don't have children."

■

TIPS ON ENTERTAINING

■

"Keep it simple. Don't try to do more than you have time to do, or you'll exhaust yourself."

■

"Make the children very much a part of the festivities and start your own family rituals that they will cherish for life."

■

"Plan simple meals that you can cook ahead. Casseroles are great. Lasagna and chili are great crowd pleasers at our house. Plan something else for the kids. Turkey dogs, pasta, macaroni and cheese, and peanut butter sandwiches—as a last resort for any meal—always work for us."

■

"Rent a movie. Provide a small group of toys near you for the kids."

■

"Do afternoon barbecues. Ship the kids out if you're doing serious entertaining."

■

FAMILYFUN ENTERTAINING TIPS

- Let your children help you plan the party. They are sure to contribute ideas for food and games that your kid-guests will enjoy, and the more your children feel like hosts, the more successful the event will be.
- Plan an ice-breaking activity that the kids can all do together as soon as guests arrive. Make it something simple that does not need much adult supervision—a kids' tour of the house and yard, for example, or a group mural (hang butcher paper and put out markers). This enables the kids to get to know each other (or become reacquainted) on their own time, and adults then get a chance to greet each other.
- Be sure to have ready a few structured activities, such as playing games or making crafts, but don't interrupt the kids to participate in these if they are getting along well and devising their own entertainment.
- If you have a big group, suggest that each parent take a half-hour shift supervising the kids. That way the children get to know each adult (and vice versa), and each adult is likely to have enough enthusiasm and energy for one short shift. (The other advantage, of course, is that the adults all get time to talk among themselves.)
- Plan a meal that encourages everyone to move around and get to know each other. Barbecues are successful for just this reason, as are picnics. You can also try an ice cream sundae bar or a cookie-decorating party. (And no matter what is on the menu, be sure to have peanut butter and jelly and other kid staples on hand so your adult guests don't have to spend the meal imploring their children to eat unfamiliar food.)
- Have in mind a few activities that adults and children can do together as a group. Charades, softball, touch football, and group walks through the neighborhood are all tried and true. For older children—if you want to be more creative—you can try something more unusual, such as a game of group portraits: write everyone's name on a piece of paper and put the pieces into a hat; each person then pulls the name of another and draws his or her portrait; in the end, everyone must guess whose portrait is whose.
- In the event some kids tire out before their parents (or just in case one or two children need some quiet time), put out a few children's books or comics and have on hand a couple of children's videos.

- At the end of the party, take group pictures so that you can send copies to your guests later. With older children you can encourage the kids to exchange phone numbers or, if your guests are from out of town, addresses. This ensures that the kids will feel that their party was only the beginning of an on-going friendship and exchange.

Source: Alexandra Kennedy is the editor of FamilyFun. *For subscription information, call 800-289-4849.*

PARENTS ENTERTAINING TIPS

- Change your expectations. You can't expect young children to be happily entertained for very long. Children don't play on their own together very effectively until they are four or five.
- Think about hiring a baby-sitter and sharing the expense with the other parents. As long as you are able to supervise, a mother's helper—a youngster of eleven or more—who enjoys playing with children is always a good choice.
- Limit the number of children. Keep the ratio of caregiver to kids small enough so that you feel confident the children will be supervised adequately if they are in another room.
- Entertain in the summer. It's obviously more difficult when children are all cooped up inside.
- Brunch is preferable to dinner because of children's schedules.
- Rent a video that all the children can enjoy. Before the children come over, make sure the other parents approve of the video.
- Include the children in the activities. You can't expect them—at that age—to be by themselves and not interrupt the adults.
- Explain to the parents what kind of evening or day it is going to be. If you want a fairly formal evening, explain that you are going to have baby-sitters who are great with kids but if they don't think their child will be comfortable, they may want to bring their own baby-sitter.
- A kids' table is a good idea. If it is the right size for the children to sit at comfortably, and it is decorated in a special way, it's usually more appealing. Let the children help with the decorations. Construction paper and stickers and clear contact paper make it easy to design place mats, which is a fun way to keep the children busy before the meal.
- Ask the parents in advance if there is something special their children like to eat. If you expect kids of different ages, make sure the food is appropriate for the youngest ones. You don't

"If you have friends with children, that's great. Trips to see Disney movies and walks to the nearest park can be worked into the day, leaving the adults to share some time together."

■

"Have friends bring in food. Ask what each person would like to bring. There is always tons of food. Everyone gets to try new dishes. It's a good way to entertain without getting exhausted."

■

"Find a way to have your child help you with ideas and preparation. Try out games ahead of time and ask your child for suggestions to modify the games."

■

"If you're entertaining couples without children, have dinner after your children's bedtime. If you're entertaining with children, do early dinners or brunches so you won't cut into their sleeping times."

■

"Set realistic goals. Concentrate on gathering with friends, not impressing them."

■

want to serve hot dogs to kids who can't chew them or give older kids foods a toddler might choke on were he to pick off the older children's plates.

- Don't turn the evening into "restaurant for a day." Frankly, there are certain kid-friendly foods you can't miss with. It's perfectly fine to order a pizza for the kids. If you want the food to be part of the party, having people make their own pizzas is fun.

- Another obvious choice for food is pasta. Kids love it. You can reserve some pasta without sauce for those who won't eat it. Children also love food you can dip. If you are serving a dish with sauce, consider putting the sauce on the side and letting the kids dip their food into it.

- Don't worry if the kids don't eat; they won't starve if they miss one meal.

- Casual entertaining is the only way to go. Try to make dishes that won't taste awful if they are not piping hot. Everyone with small children spends part of the meal away from the table because of interruptions. It's nicer if you don't have to come back and face cold, congealed food.

Source: Ann Pleshette Murphy, the mother of two, is the editor-in-chief of Parents *magazine. For subscription information, call 800-727-3682.*

EXERCISE

*A*t my peak, I awoke every morning at 5:30 A.M., jogged a few miles before work, played tennis three days a week, bicycled twice a week, and went to the gym in my free time. Throughout the years I have always been engaged in one form of exercise or another. Every couple of years I take up a new sport, buy all the requisite equipment, and pursue it until something else strikes my fancy.

A number of years ago, when roller skating was the rage, I bought a pair of $100 skates, went down to the beach in Venice, California, where everyone was skating, and promptly skated into a tree. I had been doing well all day except that I hadn't learned how to stop. That night I came home, put an ice compress on my hands to ease the swelling, and arranged for skating lessons. I had to drive forty miles after work and pay $25 for a thirty-minute lesson to watch the six-year-olds in my class make me look foolish. The skates were quickly retired to the garage—my sports equipment cemetery.

Every once in a while I look in the garage to see reminders of sports past. There is a Boogie board, a baseball glove (the Johnny Carson players, a softball team), tap-dancing shoes (which have inexplicably disappeared), swimming goggles and fins, a few golf clubs, a leather jump rope and a how-to jump rope book, and a ten-speed bicycle.

While some might say that all this sporting equipment represents a certain dilettantism, I would disagree. To me they all represent failed exercise programs. Every time I took up a new sport, I figured it was a new way of making exercise more enjoyable. And they were, for a brief period of time. The difficulty was that I could *never summon up enough enthusiasm to sustain interest in them.*

My other habitual—and costly—stab at exercise is my periodical gym joining. I have joined gyms at least ten times in my life. I have joined the well-known ones that celebrities advertise in the newspaper, a lesser-known one that was geared to women only, and a neighborhood one that had less equipment but more serious clients. At my worst moments I have signed yearly contracts and have gone ten times or less. In the best of times I have been considered "a regular."

My most costly gym-joining experiment preceded my pregnancy by a few months. Just before I entered a diet clinic, I joined a gym and paid for ten sessions with a personal trainer. I figured that if this commitment didn't shame me into dieting and getting into shape, nothing would. I hoped that my trainer would be not only an exercise specialist but a personal motivator as well.

As it turned out, my personal trainer was a recently washed-out minor-league baseball player who was interested in breaking into commercials. He was so busy primping and flexing (because you never knew who would see you in the gym) that he barely noticed when I fell asleep on the Exercycle. When my program was over, I had gained three pounds and my arms were an inch thicker. I washed my three new pairs of tights and leggings and threw them into the garage.

Since Alexander's birth, I've turned into a slug. I am so tired in the morning I cannot make myself wake up a half hour early and walk. I can't bear to see myself in my tennis clothes, so I've stopped playing. And since I can't afford any new sports equipment or clothing, there is no incentive for coming up with new sports that might appeal to me.

Still, I have promised myself that I'll start some new exercise program before my next birthday. The only thing worse than being an "old" mother of a small child is being an out-of-shape one.

Bernie has recently promised to finance this exercise program. So lately I have been looking in the paper to see what gyms are offering discount memberships. The one thing about habitual gym joiners is that we always feel better when we join a gym—even if we don't go.

EXERCISE DURING PREGNANCY

Dr. Raul Artal has a dual professorship in obstetrics and gynecology and exercise science at the University of Southern California. He is the coauthor of Pregnancy & Exercise *and the father of three.*

SB: *Should pregnant women exercise?*
RA: My answer is a qualified yes. Pregnancy should not be a state of confinement. Women should continue to lead normal lives. However, one has to take into account that a variety of changes occur in pregnancy, women may have to modify their exercise routines. Some women will have to consider eliminating exercise altogether, depending on whether their pregnancy is proceeding normally.

SB: *What are the effects of exercise on the mother? The fetus?*
RA: A mother can continue to derive cardiovascular benefits if exercising on a regular basis. Exercise may also affect her psychological well-being, her ability to conduct a normal life, to maintain balance, and to perform certain physical tasks. So there are certainly positive effects.

In terms of potential risk, one has to keep in mind that the most significant changes that occur in pregnancy are anatomical changes. There is a change in the center of gravity that can lead to lower back pain. Some may experience a softening of ligaments, and a loosening of joints, precluding them from engaging in certain types of exercise. Because of these changes, pregnant women who exercise may be exposed to the risks of musculo-skeletal injuries. The other risk that is always mentioned is that women who are already at risk for premature labor—*and only those women*—may have premature labor precipitated by an exercise routine. Another concern, which may be caused by some of the physiological changes in pregnancy—a faster heart rate, higher blood volume, and higher incidence of anemia—is that pregnant women, at least theoretically, are at risk for cardiac complications. But that has never been proved. It is open to investigation.

In terms of the fetus, and this was always the fear we had, any benefit the mother may gain from exercise may be outweighed by potential fetal risk, the most significant risk being fetal distress. Of course, if there are obstetrical or medical complications, there is a higher risk for fetal distress. There are also other potential problems in the early stages of labor as well as later. The best

WHAT WE DO

■

"I still exercise every other day. We have a treadmill and a stationary bike. I also have hand weights. I do forty-five minutes at a time. It's great!"

■

"I finally quit the gym after not going for one whole year. I swam every day when I was pregnant, but I hate paying for a baby-sitter so I can exercise. Now I walk every morning and take my baby with me. Pushing the stroller is a good workout."

■

"I worked out before I had a child, all through my pregnancy, and I continue to work out. I exercise at home two days a week, and the other three days I stroll my daughter to the park and do the track."

■

advice for any woman who wants to get involved in an exercise program is to discuss it with her doctor, thus ensuring that there are no problems.

SB: What are the best types of exercise during pregnancy?
RA: Because of the changes in joints and ligaments, exercise that exerts the least stress on these areas—like swimming and aquatic exercises—are probably a good choice if one can afford them. If not, walking and stationary bikes are a nice alternative. All types of exercises that engage large muscles but at the same time do not exert undue stress on the joints and ligaments are preferable.

SB: You're conducting a study in which women ride a stationary bike during the early stages of labor. What is the impact of exercise during labor?
RA: As a result of exercise in the early stages of labor, the body will produce its own pain killers, the endorphins, and by doing so, a woman will not experience the initial pain of labor.

EXERCISE PROGRAM GUIDELINES: PREGNANCY AND POSTPARTUM

- Regular exercise (at least three times per week) is preferable to intermittent activity. Competitive activities should be discouraged.
- Vigorous exercise should not be performed in hot, humid weather or during a period of febrile illness.
- Ballistic movements (jerky, bouncy motions) should be avoided. Exercise should be done on a wooden floor or a tightly carpeted surface to reduce shock and provide a sure footing.
- Deep flexion or extension of joints should be avoided because of connective tissue laxity. Activities that require jumping, jarring motions, or rapid changes in direction should be avoided because of joint instability.
- Vigorous exercise should be preceded by a five-minute period of muscle warm-up. This can be accomplished by slow walking or stationary cycling with low resistance.
- Vigorous exercise should be followed by a period of gradually declining activity that includes gentle stationary stretching. Because connective tissue laxity increases the risk of joint injury, stretches should not be taken to the point of maximum resistance.

- Care should be taken to rise gradually from the floor to avoid orthostatic hypotension. Some form of activity involving the legs should be continued for a brief period.
- Liquids should be taken liberally before and after exercise to prevent dehydration. If necessary, activity should be interrupted to replenish fluids.
- Women who have led sedentary lifestyles should begin with physical activity of very low intensity and advance activity levels very gradually.
- Activity should be stopped and the physician consulted if any unusual symptoms appear.

Source: American College of Obstetricians and Gynecologists. Exercise During Pregnancy and the Postnatal Period *(ACOG Home Exercise Programs). Washington, DC. © 1985. 409 12th Street S.W., Washington, DC 20024-2188; 202-638-5577.*

EXERCISE CLASSES

"It used to be that doctors would say that if you haven't been exercising, once you get pregnant is not the time to begin," according to Lauri Reimer Mihailov, a fitness consultant who specializes in pre- and postnatal exercise at Saint John's Hospital in Santa Monica, California. "Primarily, the reason was that women weren't participating in exercise programs that were geared for pregnancy, delivery, and preparation for postpartum," Mihailov explains. "But courses geared specifically for pregnant women are different. They are more gentle and nurturing. We follow ACOG [American College of Obstetricians and Gynecologists] guidelines. And many women who exercise for the duration of their pregnancy feel better throughout their pregnancy, have a quicker recovery, and get their stamina back sooner." Mihailov offers the following advice on what you can expect from prenatal and postnatal classes.

Prenatal classes

- Stretching and limbering are an important component of exercise because in pregnancy your ligaments and joints start to get looser and more unstable. Stretching and limbering not only build stability but also decrease the tightness and tension that can occur during pregnancy.
- Cardiovascular exercises are important too. Using the ACOG

"I've always exercised, although I have less time now with two kids. When they were very little I had them in part-time day care three mornings a week. That's when I went to the gym. Now that my son is in preschool, I go to the gym three mornings a week and do a full workout, cardiovascular and weights."

■

"I've always exercised. When I was pregnant, I switched to swimming. After my son was born, I went to a postpartum class with him. That was great because you could stop and nurse if you had to, and it was social. When my son was five months old, I went back to my gym, where they offered baby-sitting and I could do a more strenuous workout."

■

guidelines, which set your target heart rate for cardiovascular training at no higher than 140 beats per minute, you should learn to monitor your heart rate to ensure you aren't working out at too high an intensity. This is important because your unborn baby cannot dissipate heat in the form of sweating.

- Strengthening is the third element. You will want to strengthen all the major muscles in the body, but you may need to choose alternative positions for some muscles. Strengthening the muscles in the upper body, specifically the upper back, arms, chest, and shoulders, is very important because as the size of your belly grows, your center of gravity changes, thus altering your posture and sense of balance.

- Exercises for the lower body should include strengthening the buttocks, hips, thighs, and calves. Calf-strengthening exercises help prevent leg cramps, which are a common symptom during pregnancy.

- The abdominal muscles should be strengthened as well. There are several recommended alternative positions for pregnant women. One of the best ones is the pelvic tilt, which can be done on all fours (hands and knees), a good position for exercise because it eliminates a lot of the stress on the back. Other alternative postures for abdominal strengthening include side lying and seated and standing positions.

- Pelvic-floor strengthening exercises, or Kegels, are important pre- and postnatal exercises. These muscles, which are normally underutilized, should be conditioned and prepared for the trauma of childbirth. Conditioning the pelvic floor (perineum) during pregnancy will allow it to stretch more during delivery without tearing and will help to prevent sagging and displacement of the pelvic organs.

Postnatal classes

- Key elements of postnatal exercise include stretching, rhythmic movements, continued strengthening work, total body muscle conditioning, and cardiovascular exercises.

- The midsection is usually the primary area of concern in addition to general fitness and the return of your endurance. It is a good idea to do some general abdominal work right from the beginning, when you are still in bed; contract-and-release, and pelvic tilts are a good way to start. Abdominal work will vary depending on whether you have had a C-section or a vaginal delivery.

- Cardiovascular workouts can be more vigorous; most of the time it's still low impact.
- Kegels should be continued immediately in postpartum.
- Once your energy level is high enough so that you feel you can do more than what a postnatal class offers, you're probably ready to assimilate back into a regular exercise program. Look for classes where you can bring your baby with you.

Source: Lauri Reimer Mihailov is a fitness consultant, teacher of pre- and postnatal exercise classes, and the owner of Body Physics Studio in Playa del Rey, California; 310-453-2380.

EXTENDED FAMILIES

hen I was eleven, all of my grandparents were not only still living but also lived within a few miles of us. What a wonderful way to grow up!

My maternal grandparents introduced us to a world of elegance, grace, and celebrity. When they were young, they were friends of the stars; George Burns and Gracie Allen, Jack and Mary Benny, Ed and Sylvia Sullivan, Al Jolson and Ruby Keeler, and Groucho Marx were names I grew up with.

Sunday buffets at Hillcrest Country Club, lunch and an afternoon on the pitch-and-putt golf course, hardcover books, funny stories, bridge, homemade strawberry shortcake, elegant table settings, handmade sweaters, Cadillacs, Vitalis hair ointment, and Chanel No. 5 perfume are all part of my legacy.

My paternal grandparents represented the values and struggles of European immigrants. At their apartment for a weekly dinner of Old World delicacies—knishes, noodle kugel, and fricassee—my gentle, cigar-smoking union foreman grandfather spun tales of his early life in the sweatshops of Chicago. My quiet grandmother, who would more often cook than talk, occasionally told stories of what it was like to have come alone by ship to this country from Russia. They both had the stability, endurance, and fortitude of people who had worked hard to raise a family during difficult times.

With all four of my grandparents and what I knew of their lives, I felt that my background encompassed a richness of heritage and experience that made me special. I never tired of hearing their stories; I longingly remember family holidays and all the times we spent together. I grew up embraced by the kind of love and support that most kids only dream about.

By the time I had Alexander, all my grandparents had died, and my father had as well. Their absence in his life is one of the greatest sorrows in my own. Still, Alex does know how wonderful it is to have family members participate in his life; he sees them all the time.

Bernie and I both feel that family is extraordinarily important. While friends can enrich your life in many ways, it is through family members that you see glimpses of your history and your heritage. Families can offer a kind of love and support that is unequaled by others. There is, after all, nothing so dear as a grandparent's love. I should know. All these years later, I am still sustained and fortified by my own.

ॐ

GUIDELINES FOR PARENTS AND GRANDPARENTS

Glenn Austin, M.D., coauthor of Grandparenting for the 90s, *has been a practicing pediatrician in the San Francisco Bay Area for over thirty years and has served as president of the American Academy of Pediatrics. He is the father of four children and the grandfather of nine.*

SB: In what ways can grandparents establish positive relationships with their grandchildren?

GA: The first and most important thing for grandparents to do is to establish good relations with the grandchildren's parents. If they work on that well enough, their relationship with their grandchildren generally falls into line fairly easily. And the best way to do that is to respect their own children as parents whether they agree or disagree with the way they raise their children.

There are at least a thousand ways of raising kids, and almost all of the time the kids turn out OK, although that's sometimes a result more of chance than of the way we do things. What's important to remember is that parents have the responsibility and the legal and moral right to take care of their own children and raise them as they wish. We, as grandparents, do not always agree. In fact, I think we frequently disagree, but if we want to maintain relationships with our children and grandchildren, we learn to be diplomatic—to bite our tongues, so to speak, and we're sometimes biting so hard it seems as though we may need a transfusion.

147

HOW EXTENDED FAMILIES PARTICIPATE IN OUR CHILDREN'S LIVES

■

"My in-laws are the most wonderful people. They are both retired, and they took care of our children at least one to two days a week when we lived in the same state. Now that we've moved, they miss our children desperately but visit us at least every four to six weeks. They take the kids everywhere, even on long car rides to visit great grandparents in nursing homes. They are very loving and giving and are a very positive influence in their lives—and ours. They do everything together and share equally in the responsibility of caring for the children."

■

SB: *Why is there so much disagreement on child rearing?*
GA: First, the public has been bombarded with "expert" advice on raising children. You can buy a book that will validate almost any theory you have. Second, each of us has a reaction to the way we were raised. Nowadays it's fairly common to blame your parents for all your own problems. In fact there was a book called just that, *Blame Your Parents*. It's funny and a little pathetic. But there is a big dysfunctional movement, and if you see and hear enough about it, you almost become convinced that all parents are dysfunctional.

Of course that's nonsense, but it does have an effect. A lot of young people who are having their own kids hear this, remember some of the things their parents did, and say, "I'll never do that." So the pendulum goes swinging back the other way, and they end up becoming either very authoritarian (if they had permissive parents) or very permissive (if they had authoritarian parents).

SB: *How do grandparents' relationships enhance their grandchildren's lives?*
GA: The fragmentation of the American family is a very unhealthy thing. I think the whole issue of whether grandparents are needed hasn't been given enough thought. There's no question that children need grandparents; they need roots. They need to know where they come from. Having someone who says "You're important enough to warrant my spending a good amount of time with you" makes children feel loved. Even if grandparents are not physically there, they can call and talk to their grandchildren on the telephone. They can send postcards or letters. Too many children are treated like modular products; they're put in day care or in public schools and shuffled from place to place. They need someone who recognizes them as unique individuals who count and are important.

SB: *What tips do you have for new moms who are having trouble with their parents or in-laws?*
GA: Sometimes you should just agree with your parents or in-laws and do things your own way when they are gone.
• **Communicate on a continuing basis rather than when you're angry.** You may need to say "You know, I know this is the way you do it, but I'd like to do it my way. It doesn't mean you're wrong or I'm wrong. There are many ways of raising kids, and I may need to make my own mistakes to find out what's right for me."

• **Express your needs.** In my practice—when I used to go on house calls and visit mothers with newborns—I'd sometimes find the grandmother would be playing with the baby while the mother was on her hands and knees scrubbing the floor. You may need to tell your mother or mother-in-law what you need even when it seems obvious. You may want to say "It's great that you're playing with the baby, but I also need your help."

• **Listen.** Recognize that your parents and in-laws are trying to be helpful. They may not always be right, and their advice may not always be good, but it represents their life experiences. Sometimes you just need to listen without arguing and ultimately make your own decision about what to do.

• **Give your parents and in-laws a hug when they leave.** You may disagree about everything, but remember that your parents and in-laws undoubtedly love you and your children and are usually trying their best.

A THERAPIST'S TIPS FOR DEALING WITH FAMILY MEMBERS

• When I was a new mom, I was nervous and kept my relatives away, and finally after six weeks my mother said, "I can't stand it any more, I'm coming over," and she came. I regret that she missed those weeks, but that was the time my husband and I needed for the adjustment. So my advice to new moms is to do what you need to do to feel confident. Read books and magazines. Talk to your pediatrician. Take courses. Have family members participate after you feel comfortable with your baby.

• Ask your own mother about the feeding, diapering, and crying philosophies in her day. You don't have to do child care the same way, but this is a time when you can connect with those who knew you when you were born.

• Whatever extended family members are doing that bothers you, talk about it; don't withhold and don't explode. Learn to say things like "We need some time and a chance to develop our own experience" or "You're making me feel inadequate."

• Expect differences among family members and talk about them. It's up to you to take a stand and explain your values when you know grandparents and other family members are going to stuff your child with objectionable foods, let her cry when you would pick her up, or, especially, when their behavior violates safety or health issues or a deeply felt value. While everyone may not

"My mother lives ten minutes away, visits several times a week, and is our official baby-sitter. She adores the kids and offers lots of good advice. My husband's father lives an hour away and visits once a month. He likes to talk with the kids and thinks they're wonderful."

■

"My mom and dad live a half hour away. They're both retired, we see them often, and they actively participate in our children's lives. The kids sleep overnight, they take them on outings, and we spend holidays together. The proximity has been a godsend when our kids are sick and can't go to the child-care provider. My husband and I both work full-time, and I don't know what we would have done other than take vacation days."

■

"My in-laws live a few blocks away, and my mother and stepfather live about a half hour away. My kids' grandparents have helped raise them. My oldest daughter spent ten days with my mother when she was fifteen months old so my husband and I could go on a camping trip. When my youngest son was three, I couldn't have gone back to work if it hadn't been for my in-laws. They took care of him all day Thursday and Friday afternoon."

■

interact with your baby the way you would—nor should they have to—there must be open lines of communication.

- Realize that there is more than one way to raise a child, so diversity is probably positive. Extended family members provide alternative role models for children. Diverse experiences are undoubtedly better than isolation.
- Ask relatives to cooperate with your routine, but remain flexible. Don't worry if your extended family gives your child too many sweets, lets him or her watch too much TV, or has different rules. Your child needs you much more than your relatives, and you're going to have the main impact on your baby.
- If you feel competition over the baby's affection, chances are there is a long-standing problem, and the baby isn't the issue. Get outside help.
- Whatever problems you have with family members, infants should have an opportunity to form their own relationships. Extended family members offer additional love, and there can never be too much of that for a child.

Source: Marjorie Slavin, M.S.W. is a family therapist with a private practice in Riverdale, New York, and a consultant to the Group for Grandparents in Divided Families at the Scarsdale Family Counseling Service. She is the mother of one.

CRITICISM WITHIN FAMILIES

Deborah Bright, Ph.D., author of The Official Criticism Manual *and* Criticism in Your Life: How to Give It, How to Take It, How to Make It Work for You, *is an adjunct professor at New York University and president of Bright Enterprises. She lives in New York.*

SB: Unasked-for advice and criticism can be among the primary causes of deteriorating family relationships. How should one handle criticism within families?
DB: Carefully. One of the things that makes criticism within families difficult is that there is a tremendous emotional investment. Often we try to be on good behavior and polite among friends and among people in the workplace. When we get home, we change. We say "Take me the way I am; we're family," suggesting that it is OK to be "sloppy" within one's family. But it's not. If we took as much care in trying to communicate with family members as we do with colleagues at work, there would undoubtedly be fewer family feuds.

We also need to look at family members the way they are, not the way they were. We have phrases like "I know her like a book," "He's always late," "Mom is the way she is, so forget trying to change her." Sometimes people have changed significantly, but family members don't realize it.

In either event, before we criticize family members we need to understand the power of criticism. No matter how you soften it, when you criticize you are communicating some degree of negativity. If mishandled, it can be very destructive. Words are piercing. Criticism can have life-lasting effects. It can destroy people's self-esteem and their self-confidence.

SB: What are the guidelines for giving criticism?

DB: First, you need to recognize that there are two types of criticism: in-bounds and out-of-bounds. In-bounds criticism is acceptable in a relationship. Its purpose is to change undesired behavior. How in-bounds criticism is received has to do with timing and content and whether the criticism fits within mutual expectations. There are times when criticism is rejected because the receiver is simply not in the proper frame of mind to listen. Or rejection of the criticism can occur because the receiver perceives the giver as being out of line for reasons of content.

Out-of-bounds criticism is never OK. An out-of-bounds criticism may be that a man's mother is always criticizing the way his wife takes care of their children. The mother-in-law doesn't like the way the daughter-in-law diapers the baby, feeds him, or bathes him. That's out-of-bounds, and it's up to the son to tell his mother.

Public criticism of a family member is always out-of-bounds. When you criticize someone in front of others, you are inevitably going to hurt feelings, tarnish the relationship, and ultimately get paid back in some way. Holidays are the worst times for this kind of criticism to surface. People hear the same stories again and again, and many of them are rooted in criticism.

Before criticizing members of your family, you need to ask yourself "Can they benefit from the criticism? Are they capable of changing? Will they accept criticism from me?" If they can't benefit and they're not capable of changing, you need to reconsider your position. If they are open to criticism, you need to focus on what the purpose of your criticism is and what the desired action will be.

SB: What are some tips for accepting criticism?

DB: The most important tip is that the receiver of criticism is the one who is in control. If, for example, your in-laws are visiting

"My side of the family doesn't participate at all. My husband's family has always been very involved. My husband owns a florist shop and greenhouse. His parents live on the property, so my children go to work and visit their grandparents at the same time. Now that the children are older, one uncle plays sports with them; another uncle works there after his regular job and shows them how to make Christmas wreaths or ride a bike. Also, other family members are always dropping by the business, so there is a lot of contact. My kids love to go there."

■

"My mother is my Sunday relief. This allows my husband and me to be able to do brunch or an afternoon movie. We have no other relatives in St. Louis."

■

from out of town and your mother-in-law wants to rearrange your dishes, you have two options. You can take a defensive stance, feel the criticism is out-of-bounds, and say "How dare you come into my kitchen and rearrange things? This is my house. I will run it the way I want to." Or you can let her rearrange things and then change them back when she leaves. You need to ask yourself "In the big picture, how important is this action? Why is my mother-in-law doing it? Is she being critical, or is she trying to show she cares but is expressing it in the wrong way?" The receiver has to look at the intent rather than just the actions. It is within the receiver's control to depersonalize the information.

Finally, the receiver needs to know from the giver of the criticism what the desired behavior is. So, using another example, if your mother is complaining that you never listen to her, one way to respond is to say "You're telling me that I'm not listening to you. What is it that I need to do that would indicate that I am listening to you?"

SB: *What are some alternatives to criticism when you disagree with family members?*

DB: Take the time to clarify expectations. If you were to build a list of everything family members criticize one another for, it's usually rooted in unclear expectations. There are so many unspokens. At work we clarify who is supposed to do what, when, and what quality we expect of them. In families we don't. We clarify things through criticism.

Make sure you think before you speak, because once you've opened your mouth, you cannot recover the words. When you start to say something, ask yourself "Do I know what I really want from that person?" Do you know the desired behavior? Sometimes, when you know that behavior, there is no reason to criticize.

Finally, if you know what you want, sometimes you need to ask for it. In many relationships, whether they are between parents and adult children, husbands and wives, or siblings, we need to ask for what we want rather than becoming angry because we're not getting it.

FATHERHOOD

In the years when I vacillated over whether I wanted children or not, I periodically asked Bernie how he felt about fatherhood. Since he was in his mid-forties when we married, I knew that having children obviously wasn't a top priority. Still, I wondered whether he felt his life would be any less full without them.

He said that he didn't think a lot about it, but every once in a while he wondered what it might be like to be a father. It certainly wasn't a pressing need on his part, and he said that ultimately the decision was mine. He thought it would be far worse for me if I decided that I really wanted a child and he didn't.

As I continued to contemplate the relative merits of motherhood, our biological clocks ticked on. By the time I gave birth to Alexander, Bernie was a first-time father at fifty-one. The upside of this was that he had traveled the world over, advanced to the top ranks of his profession, and was ready for the responsibility of fatherhood.

"The downside," as my sister put it so very bluntly one afternoon when we were holding a "Should we or shouldn't we have children?" session, "is that by the time your child is a teenager Bernie will be dead. But given how awful teenagers can be, that's not really such a bad thing, is it?"

All tasteless humor aside, it is true that by the time Alex is a teenager Bernie will be a senior citizen. Touch football and pickup basketball probably will not be real possibilities. But then they probably wouldn't have been fifteen years earlier. Bernie is not the most athletic person; rather, he's sensitive, artistic, and perhaps one *of the nicest men I've ever known. All this seemed like a fine legacy for any child.*

And it has been. As fathers go, older and younger ones included, Bernie is a gem. He's patient, caring, and loving. He changes diapers, baby-sits, feeds Alex, and roughhouses with him. He's willing to read him the same book over and over upon request although my limit is two times in a row no matter what the demand. He takes him to the park and will push him endlessly on the swing and patiently follow him around the sandbox, taking away cigarette butts as fast as Alex finds them and puts them in his mouth.

Bernie can't wait to teach Alex how to cook and how to paint—two areas that hold no interest for me. He's already planning their first fishing trip. He wonders at what age Alex will enjoy going to Europe, attending a concert at Carnegie Hall, and visiting art museums. My sense is that what Bernie lacks in youth and perhaps ultimately in the years he's able to spend with Alex, he'll make up for by his interest and enthusiasm.

It used to be that as a younger (by twelve years) wife of an older husband, I was able to reap the benefits of his maturity, experience, and perspective. I must admit, without a pang of jealousy, that Alex has replaced me as the object of Bernie's desire to share his interests and hobbies.

Still, when I mentioned to Bernie that I'd never been to a concert at Carnegie Hall myself and he said that the two of them would tell me all about it, I sobbed.

ॐ

A LOOK AT FATHERHOOD

"When I first wrote *The Father's Almanac* in 1980, there seemed to be more excitement among young men about the notion of close involvement with their children than there actually is now," says S. Adams Sullivan. "In the early eighties, 'involved fatherhood' was a really fresh idea, and women—having recently returned to work—certainly needed the help of another parent. A great deal of goodwill was generated on both sides of the question of bringing the father in and having him be a major influence in his children's lives. I'm not saying that there is a huge backsliding—or that men are turned off to male parenting," he continues, "but more recently a lot of sociologists and psychologists are saying that it is difficult for a man and a woman to cooperate in bringing up children.

"I strongly disagree with this notion," Sullivan says. "The men I've interviewed—for the first edition and the revision in 1992—are enthusiastic fathers. I talk with guys who really want to share their kids' lives. Having been involved in an important way with my own two boys—who are now grown—has been a wonderful part of my life."

Sullivan recommends that the best way for dads to get involved with their children is to participate from the very beginning. He says that researchers have found that the most active, satisfied and interested fathers are those who are right there in the delivery room, who learn baby care, who read the books about infant care, and who help with the day-to-day care. He feels that the most important qualities a father can bring to the relationship are love and excitement. "It's a two-way street," he says, "and that's what I wanted to get across in my book. If you make a big contribution to your family, you will get a great deal of pleasure in return."

So what is his advice for new dads? "With an infant, the day-to-day care is where it's at. It actually is fun to diaper a child," he says. "It's a little bit messy, but the child is getting a great deal of relief from what you're doing. The gurgles, the interplay are fun. Throughout infancy what you do with a child is to meet his or her needs and get the same pleasure that mothers have always gotten from meeting the needs of babies." Being with a toddler, of course, is different. "From this point on," Sullivan says, "you're in the lovely position of being a teacher to this very open, accepting, and interested student. You've got the whole world to explore. You've got someone you can turn on to everything."

Source: S. Adams Sullivan is the author of The Father's Almanac. *When his two sons were young, he worked at home as a freelance editor, which allowed him to spend long hours with his kids sharing the pleasures of fatherhood. He lives with his family in an old farmhouse in rural western New Jersey.*

HOW WE SHARE PARENTING

■

"My husband assumes all of the responsibilities one could possibly hope for except for breastfeeding."

■

"I do primary care, although usually my husband can be counted on to fill in gaps. We don't divide things fifty-fifty because it seems to set up turf wars. Sometimes he does 100 percent, and other times I do. We're comfortable with it."

■

"I'm home full-time now, and the majority of responsibilities fall to me. I understand and accept this. On weekends we share things more."

■

"My husband works at night, and his off-days are Sunday and Monday. He realistically has one day (Sunday) to be responsible. I feel I'm raising a child by myself with financial support."

■

JAMES LEVINE'S PERSPECTIVE

James A. Levine is the director of the Fatherhood Project for the Families and Work Institute, 330 Seventh Avenue, 14th Floor, New York, NY 10001; 212-465-2044. He is the father of two.

SB: *In what ways are fathers different from mothers?*
JL: At the risk of making gross generalizations and resorting to gender stereotypes, there certainly are differences. If you ask children, they are aware that dads tend to play more physically; they tend to roughhouse more. Dads are more active, even with very young infants. They might pick them up and throw them in the air, which is different from the containing or cuddling behavior of moms. So it's really a difference in style of nurturing rather than a difference in capacity for nurturing.

SB: *How does fatherhood change men's lives?*
JL: It's rare to meet a man who doesn't think that having a child is the most important experience in his life. You find this again and again with dads who attend childbirth. They are awed by the reality of becoming a father and by the experience of seeing their wives or partners give birth. All of a sudden there is a little person they are responsible for. Most men are very emotionally affected by the sheer act of childbirth.

SB: *How are today's fathers different from their predecessors?*
JL: In a study I did for *Child* magazine we found that today's dads are more hands-on. Many are very aware of wanting to have a different experience with their kids than they had with their own fathers. That is evidenced in the slow, gradual, but increasing involvement men are having with their children. I have to be careful about the way I categorize this. We're in the midst of an evolution, not an revolution. The failure of men to participate in child rearing is still one of married women's major complaints. They say, "My husband is not involved enough with the kids; the burden is all on me." They're right, but it's also accurate to say that men are doing more than they used to do. This is not a seismic shift, but it's a gradual change, and if you compare what is going on today with what went on thirty years ago, there really is a difference.

The main shift is that we've redefined fatherhood. It used to be that the good father was essentially a provider. We haven't given that up, but we've added to it that the good father is also a nurturer and that he is more involved with the day-to-day care of the kids. Again—this is not all men—more dads have the responsibility for dropping the child off at day care or picking the child up. Even if they're not actually participating in all the things that moms are doing, they're feeling a tug like "I should be doing that." Before, that wasn't part of the role; that was just what women did.

SB: What issues do you cover in your DaddyStress seminars that are applicable to fathers of infants and toddlers?
JL: • **The relationship with one's spouse.** The key issue here is that most dads in the seminar think we're going to focus on the relationship with the child, but the most important issue is to make sure that dads have time to have a relationship with their spouses. Since we're addressing the issue of stress—with both parents off and running in so many directions—what I see is that parents are working so hard to make a living and to make sure they have time for their kids that they end up not having any time for their relationship.

The major tip we give dads is to make a date—every week—with their spouses. Set aside some time that you're going to get out as a couple. Also try to build in time to connect together every day. It doesn't have to be an hour. If you have a ritual of sitting down together for fifteen minutes after you finally get the kids tucked in, just to catch up on what happened during the day, that may be enough. It's really important to remember you're connected.

• **The relationship with one's child.** We cover a lot of issues, including communication, discipline, the definition of quality time, and what to do in that time. For infants we recommend—even if mom is breastfeeding—that one of the ways to help start off the relationship is for mom to express her milk into a bottle and freeze it so that dad can do some of those middle-of-the-night feedings. That helps both parents. The advantage is that the mom gets more sleep and the dad gets the joy of having that kind of physical closeness with his child, which is really a very special experience. It makes a difference, particularly with infants who don't communicate except by looking at you and gurgling. When women are breastfeeding, they are having this kind of connection all the time, and dads are cut off from it unless they feed the baby as well. When they do feed the baby a bottle, they find it is a very powerful experience.

• **The relationship with one's work.** The issue is how to nego-

"When he's gone through a busy period at work and isn't home much, he'll do something intense with our daughter. It doesn't seem to be the quantity of time she needs with him; it's the quality. With me she gets quantity time, and I have to make sure it's not *only* quantity."

■

"We used to have something called the 'tag system'—when one parent lost control, he or she would 'tag' the other to take over. Now my husband puts in more hours at work and sometimes doesn't arrive home until the kids are in bed. I have no one to 'tag,' and it's very frustrating."

■

HOW OUR HUSBANDS HAVE CHANGED

■

"My husband is still a workaholic. He has less patience than I would have thought, but fatherhood seems to have brought out his more sensitive side. He's incredibly gentle with our daughter. He used to be more even-tempered and slower to anger. That's changed, but I think it's healthier just to scream and be done with it. It's more human."

■

"I don't know that he's changed, but I see the sweet, nurturing side more often. He's always been affectionate with me, and I love watching him with our kids. He worries more. He's always been a worrier, but now he has new things to worry about in terms of the kids getting hurt. He's more anxious about money because I stopped working. I think that makes him feel more vulnerable. We're older, and it's a concern that we'll be even older when our kids are still relatively young."

■

tiate or renegotiate your role at work so people understand you're no longer just a worker but also a parent. A lot of problems have to do with understanding your boss isn't a mind reader who will automatically make allowances for you now that you have a child. It also means learning how to speak up in a way that is not going to jeopardize your job status. Lots of men are afraid that if they show more commitment to their family they will be perceived as being less committed to work.

It's a real fear, but it's something we find that people don't talk about enough so that the fear becomes exaggerated. When they raise this issue with supervisors, there is often more room for movement or negotiation than they think. Of course, this is not always the case. Everyone has horror stories of the "boss from hell" who says, "I have to treat people fairly, so I can't make any special allowances." We have found, in the majority of cases, that there is room for accommodation, but it doesn't happen unless you speak up.

DR. MARTIN GREENBERG'S TEN TIPS FOR FATHERS

1. Anticipate engrossment. Engrossment is the preoccupation, absorption, and interest in the baby that fathers have when they first see the baby. This can occur at the birth and later, when the baby smiles and coos. It can happen much after the birth when the father sees his child crawl, sit, stand, or walk. It consists of a visual awareness of the newborn (the baby is seen as attractive), a tactile awareness of the newborn (a desire to touch and hold him), an awareness of the distinct features of the newborn, a perception of the baby as perfect, a strong attraction to the baby, a feeling of elation, and an increased sense of self-esteem (fathers describe feeling older, stronger, and more powerful). Engrossment is thus the development of the father-child bond.

2. Spend time with your wife and your child. A lot of times women feel exhausted and tired after the birth, and they need support. When a father is caring and loving with his children, it gives something special to his wife because she feels an increased sense of support. But most important of all, when a father spends time with his child he will invariably feel special, enthused, and included in the family. So his involvement with the child will give something back to him. The first two hours with a newborn are important because behavioral studies note this is when the child is looking about, his eyes are open, and he will be more responsive.

3. Assert your needs. Nowadays parents really have an opportunity to choose the care they want. They can choose the hospital, the care provider, or an alternative birth experience. Once they're in the hospital, they can choose rooming in or having the baby in the room part of the day and in the nursery part of the day so the mother can rest. An innovation that I think will be very helpful (which Marshall Klaus, John Kennell, and Phyllis Klaus have researched) is the doula—who is a support companion for the mother and the father (see "Childbirth: A Nurse/Midwife's View" in the "Childbirth" chapter for details).

4. Find your anchor at home. It's very important that the father build his own relationship with the baby—independent of the mother—and feel competent and connected to the baby. I feel the father should stay home at least the first week so that he can develop a sense of how he will participate in the life of the baby. A father can also become involved by taking pictures at the hospital, helping with the scrapbook, taking pictures of his wife, sending out the baby announcements, helping with the feedings, holding the baby, cuddling, singing to the baby, walking with the baby, and diapering.

5. Recognize your new responsibilities. Many fathers feel overwhelmed by their added responsibilities. They often talk about needing to go to work when they first see their baby. That is not because they want to distance themselves from the baby; rather it is a part of the whole feeling of nurturing and protection. Where it sometimes goes wrong is when the father feels he must work harder and longer because he now has so much responsibility; it can then seem as if he's disconnecting from his wife and child rather than trying to provide for them.

6. Face your child's crying bouts. Any parent who deals effectively with a crying baby feels an increased sense of competence and confidence. There are a number of things the father can do. He can hold or rock the baby. Babies respond to your voice, to movement; some respond well to the sound of a vacuum cleaner; others cry. Some like to be driven in the car. Men tend to defer to women on many issues relating to their babies. But women can help out by encouraging their husbands to handle the challenges as well as the pleasures.

7. Deal with your jealousy. There are two things men usually feel jealous about: first that they are going to lose their special

"He's aged quite a bit! I don't mean physically; he's still got that boyish look. His attitudes have changed. He's worried about financial stuff all the time. He's gotten more serious. He's very sweet with the children, but that's his nature. He has always been sweet to me."

■

"My husband is a great guy, always has been, and continues to be. His estimation of me has gone up. I think he's surprised at how much I love being a mom. He worries about providing for us. He feels more driven to succeed."

■

159

place with their wife; second, they are envious of the wife's special relationship with the baby. The way a father can deal with these feelings is by developing a close relationship with his baby. If the father becomes engrossed with his child, he, too, will want to spend time with the baby.

8. Keep your sense of humor. It's very important that you don't take yourself too seriously. Being a parent is hard work. If you're too serious, it's like a deadly potion that dulls and stultifies the nerves. When you laugh, you feel an increased sense of energy, and parenting becomes fun. Children are affected positively by hearing their parents laugh. Laughter is joy, and it has a healing effect on children and parents as well.

9. Recharge your batteries. The baby is so important and so powerful that parents need time for themselves to focus on their own relationship. When the child is always present, the mother and father tend to look at the baby and lose track of each other. The couple relationship is part of the family relationship. The couple needs time for themselves—to take walks together, to talk, to see their friends, to feel a sense of the spontaneity that they had before the baby was born. They need to recognize that they still have a relationship together that's independent of the baby.

10. Share yourself with your child. The father needs to be alone with the child. My preference is that the father take the child in a front carrier or a backpack and walk with the baby. As he does this, he gets away from the house, from the telephone, from distractions and interruptions. The rhythmic movement between father and child to some degree begins to bring him into a closer relationship with the baby. There's nobody else there; at that moment in time the father is the most important person in that baby's life. As he feels a sense of this closeness, there is a sense of incredible joy and companionship. It's almost as if the father and baby discover the world together as they go off alone. Patterns of relationships are set up early. You want to give fathers an emotional connection from the start so that they will continue to develop in a positive way.

Source: Martin Greenberg, M.D., is a psychiatrist and the author of The Birth of a Father. *He has developed a program for teenagers in which he teaches fathering. He lives in San Diego with his wife and is the father of two.*

FILMS AND VIDEOS

*F*ilms have always played a significant role in my life. While *I don't remember seeing a lot of films as a child, I could sing all the sound tracks from at least ten musicals, in-cluding* My Fair Lady, Flower Drum Song, *and* The Sound of Music.

Films have also been a barometer for friendships and an indicator of shared values. In 1968, when I went away to college at the University of California at Berkeley, I should have known during the first quarter that I had picked the wrong school when, at a screening of West Side Story, *the audience and my date jeered. I dropped the boy immediately and left the school a year later.*

On my second movie date with Bernie, an experience at a theater was a sign of how loyal, tolerant, and forgiving he would be in our relationship. Before the film started, they ran a short adver-tisement for a facility for emphysema patients. The pitch was bad enough, but when they started collecting money row by row, I balked, yelled to the usher that I hadn't paid my admission to be solicited, and nearly caused a riot. Bernie crouched in his seat but didn't abandon me.

Months later, when he could finally laugh at the "incident," we agreed that going to a movie together was a favorite date for both of us. We enjoyed similar fare most of the time, agreed that shared popcorn did not taste as good as individually bought cartons, and were willing to trade off films when necessary; a Terminator *was worth two "women's films." Over ten years, during our courtship and marriage, we saw at least 120 films, maybe closer to 200. Neither of us could imagine a life without movies—until we had Alex.*

When he was an infant and we were on a vacation in the

OUR CHANGING VIEWING HABITS

■

"We used to see films weekly. Now we see a film every three months or so."

■

"We go to 9:30 shows after the baby is asleep. We go almost exclusively to screenings where we can arrive just before the movie starts. We don't have time for lines."

■

"Disney and more Disney. We see lots of children's videos; they are entertaining and colorful. I am almost neurotic about violence."

■

"We love films and go at least once a week by ourselves. We began allowing our daughter to watch carefully selected children's videos with us. She started getting a zombielike look on her face whenever they came on and was totally transfixed. We decided it wasn't a healthy pastime, and so we rarely watch them anymore."

■

mountains, we took him to see the only movie playing in town at the only theater. It featured a dog. More experienced friends had convinced us that all small babies sleep during films. In a packed movie theater on a Saturday night, our small baby began crying. What was a mother to do? I decided that between the dog's barking and slobbering noises, nobody would hear the sounds of an infant nursing. And thus my son survived his first and last film experience as an infant.

Once we returned home, we vowed to maintain our film-viewing schedule. We didn't want to become video rental club members like every other parent we knew. We liked the big screen. We enjoyed seeing films with other adults (maybe this is an overstatement). We wanted to support the actors and directors whose work we admired.

About six months later, after a particularly expensive movie date, we looked at the financial ramifications of our purist attitude. It had just cost us $65, which included money for parking, the baby-sitter, and an inexpensive dinner, to see two of my favorite actresses in a mediocre film.

The next weekend we joined a video rental club. Over a six-month span we saw more than twenty-five films for the cost of that one evening. Now that Alex is older—and we don't feel that "our" choices are appropriate for him—we end up making our video selections in the children's section.

When Alex gets much older and can stay home by himself, perhaps we'll schedule regular movie dates once again. But by then we'll probably be on a fixed income. I wonder if they offer senior citizens' discounts at Blockbuster Video.

∾

CHOOSING FAMILY VIDEOS

Terry Catchpole is the coauthor with his wife, Catherine, of The Family Video Guide. *He contributes regularly to* Entertainment Weekly *and* Video Business. *He's the father of two and lives in Wellesley, Massachusetts.*

SB: *What are the criteria parents should consider when choosing videos for infants and toddlers?*
TC: At these ages one plus is that the kids will sit down for anything you show them. They might not stick with it, but they'll

begin watching. So it's a good time to discuss what you like with your children. You can begin the process of sharing your values. You can talk back to the screen—something you should always do, because it's an excellent way of communicating values at "every stage" of a child's growth. As you watch a video, you can comment on what the characters are doing and how you feel about it. Say, "Now why did he do that? Wasn't that a silly thing to do?" Or "Wasn't that a great thing to do? Look how nice he is. Look how bad she is."

Involve yourself and your child. One of the great things about video is that it can be so interactive. The viewer has total control, even more so than with television. You control what you see, when you see it, and how you see it. You can stop, you can pause, you can fast-forward, you can rewind. No other medium allows you quite so much flexibility.

SB: Why is it so important to choose wisely?
TC: A lot of parents don't think through the whole pop culture entertainment aspect of parenting. As we discussed earlier, when kids are little, they'll sit through almost anything you show them. In fact many parents use video as an electronic baby-sitter. Then, when kids get to be seven, eight, nine years old, they begin shaping their own opinions about what they like and don't like. These judgments to a great extent are formed by their peers. And suddenly parents realize that their kids are listening and watching things—or at least want to—that the parents object to. Parents aren't prepared for this or haven't thought it through. Either that or they shrug their shoulders and say, "Culture clashes are inevitable. There's nothing I can do about it." So they wash their hands of it and go their separate ways.

None of this needs to be the case. What parents should do first of all is expose their children to quality when they are little. For each family, quality is what you define it to be. You determine what has value, and you articulate that value. So when you sit down with your toddler and say, "Wasn't that person admirable for what he/she just did or said?" you are sharing your value system. When you talk about why a song is good or why you like a movie, you are communicating what are acceptable standards for entertainment. Later, when your children are older and come to experiment and spread their wings, the values you have shared will endure in surprising ways.

"We rarely go to first-run movies. We usually rent a videotape. The reason is the expense; between the cost of the movie and the sitter, it's outrageous. Also, an early show is hard to get to, and at a 9:30 show we'd fall asleep because we get up so early."

■

"We go out to the movies less but enjoy them more. (Or is it the time away from home that makes the film seem better than it is?)"

■

"We watch children's videos with our children. My two-year-old son loves videos with music. He likes Disney, 'Sesame Street,' and Raffi. The key is music. Raffi was his introduction to videos. He's just now starting to show interest in Thomas the Tank Engine. I say, 'Thank God for Walt Disney.' "

■

TERRY AND CATHERINE CATCHPOLE'S BEST BETS FOR KIDS

Feature Films

Duck Soup (1933). If you are two or ninety-two, the Marx Brothers are irresistible.

Born Free (1966). The ultimate animal/nature flick.

Yellow Submarine (1968). Gorgeous imagery, classic rock tune, and the Beatles!

2001 (1968). Youngsters won't understand it? Heck, adults don't understand it. The point is to relax and enjoy the majestic sweep of the heavenscapes.

Lady and the Tramp (1955). Everyone has a favorite animated Disney classic. This may be the best for small fry.

Animated and Specialty Films

Nonsense and Lullabies (1992). Best animated collection of nursery rhymes on video. Eighteen children's favorites, with brilliant animation to entertain parents.

The Little Engine That Could (1993). A children's classic, captured in sumptuous animation and enhanced with original musical tunes.

PreSchool Power! (1992). How-to tape based on Montessori methods, showing little ones more than fifteen skills (washing hands, feeding pets, etc.) alternated with skits and songs.

See How They Grow: Pets (1993). Great way to educate youngsters on animal growth cycles, with charming photography of puppies, kittens, fish, and birds from birth to one year. Nicely novel nature video.

Shelley Duvall's Bedtime Stories, Volumes I–VI (various years). Outstanding anthologies of classic children's literature, brought to life with gorgeous animation and celebrity narrators—from Ringo Starr to Bonnie Raitt.

PARENTS' CHOICE GUIDELINES
Questions to Ask Yourself

- Do the characters, music, plot, and photography come together to make a lively production?
- Does the theme promote values I believe in?
- Does the content provoke thought? Does it encourage questions?
- Is the length suitable for my child's attention span?
- Is the film based on a book? Is it the kind of story I would want my child to read? Is it a story that may appeal to people of different ages?

Good Videos . . .

- entertain and teach,
- stimulate imagination,
- may lead a child to reading. For many children, seeing a story on the screen is an incentive to reading it. When you can, offer the film and the book together.

Tips for Video Selection

- Select stories you liked as a child. If you find more than one version, look for first-rate talent—an actor, animator, or film company whose work you admire.
- Choose by author or musician. Writers or singers you or your child already know—Raffi, Leo and Diane Dillon, Mother Goose, Katherine Peterson—will seldom let you down.
- Consider movies you enjoyed as a child. Be aware, however, that minorities' and women's roles were narrow and often stereotyped. If you see that, talk about it.
- Ask advice from your child's teachers and from children's librarians. If you are having a special problem in your family—you're moving, the child is going to the hospital, you're getting divorced—request a tape that may help with those situations.
- Ask advice from other adults whose taste and standards mesh with yours.

Source: Portions of this text are reprinted from Parents' Choice: A Sourcebook of the Very Best Products to Educate, Inform and Entertain Children of All Ages *by Diana Huss Green, editor-in-chief.* Parents' Choice, *Box 185, Waban, MA 02168; 617-965-5913.*

THE BLOCKBUSTER VIDEO VENUE

Who we are. We're the biggest video chain in the world. Rental-wise, no one competes with us. Our system revenue is larger than our next 373 competitors combined. We're in 48 states; we have more than 2,200 stores nationwide, 3,258 in the world. Kids under five are a significant portion of our children's rental business and a major portion of our kids sell-through business.

Our buying criteria. The first thing we do is to watch the video. We're making a judgment on the content and quality. Is it meant for young kids? Is it nonviolent? Is there some socially redeeming value to it? Is there something the child can learn from watching it, whether it is simply learning colors, songs, good manners, or good behavior? Does the video provide good role models? Is it entertaining? Is it innovative? How large is the audience? Does it have a mass-market appeal, or does it have a special audience? Is it cross-merchandised with other products? Does it have a marketing budget? If it doesn't—but it is a terrific product—how will our audience learn about it so that it doesn't just sit on the shelf? Is it part of a series? If so, how did the series do? How is it priced for the sell-through market? Does it fill a hole in our product line? Is it what our audience wants, what they like, and what they'll rent?

Our advice for parents who are renting videos for their kids. Read as many parenting publications as possible. Read the packaging. See if there's an age range on it. Look for material you're familiar with. If at all possible, watch the video before your child watches it or at least watch it with him or her. If you find a particular tape your child likes and you feel comfortable with, and if it's part of a series, stick with that series. A lot of sing-along series for young kids are consistent and based on different themes. In our stores, look in the categories that are appropriate for your children in terms of their interests and age level. We have a section labeled "preschool" that's meant specifically for children five and younger. There are classic cartoons—which are more appropriate for six- or seven-year-olds. Ask questions of people in the video store. The more that parents request information, the more it will appear that there's a need that should be catered to. We try to be as responsive as possible to our customers.

Source: David Pulda is the children's and family buyer for Blockbuster Video, which is located in Ft. Lauderdale, Florida. He is the father of two.

GROCERY SHOPPING

I hate grocery shopping. I always have. When I was single my cupboards were bare. When I started dating Bernie, I was shocked by the amount of food he stored in his pantry. I had never seen so many canned goods outside of a market. Later I was to learn that he not only enjoyed a well-stocked kitchen but didn't mind marketing. For seven years Bernie shopped on Saturday mornings, and I played tennis.

But once Alex was born and I started working part-time, grocery shopping reverted to my list of weekly chores, and I detested it. One might have thought I would have been grateful to go shopping on a weekday morning when the market was nearly empty, but that didn't cut it. It is only fitting that since I really don't like cooking, I wouldn't like marketing either. I find it extraordinarily boring. And because I have never been interested in menu planning, not being able to decide in advance what I might feel like eating on any given night, marketing has never been a terribly creative endeavor for me.

There was also the additional problem of determining what to do with Alex while I shopped. In the first few months of his life, I worried that he would get chilled in the market so I left him with Mother. But even to me, that seemed overly protective, and it quickly became inconvenient.

Then I decided that since the market was a nice walk for us, I would shop more frequently, buy less, and put the groceries in his stroller. We tried it once but as I was only able to bring four items home—and had to return the rest—it didn't seem like a terribly effective way to spend my time.

So one morning Alex and I bit the bullet and drove to the

market like all the other stay-at-home moms in my neighborhood. I put his car seat in the grocery cart and we started shopping in earnest. But the first moment I had to turn my back on him, I literally freaked out. As I leaned over to pick out some apples and realized he was out of my line of sight, if only for a minute, I froze. What if somebody had tried to "steal" him while I wasn't paying attention? We quickly went home.

I called a friend who suggested that perhaps I was overreacting but that maybe I would initially feel more comfortable if I put Alex in one of those front carriers, which was a perfect solution. Once my hormones had subsided a bit, I was able to market while Alex sat in the grocery cart but I must admit that I always kept a careful eye on him.

Surprisingly, after the first year of my shopping for our family, Bernie volunteered to reclaim the chore. It seemed that he had been getting increasingly annoyed by the monotony of my shopping patterns. I consistently bought the same items. I wrote lists and never deviated from them. If we ran out of something, I would replace it, but I never thought of buying something new unless he asked me to.

He finally couldn't stand it any longer. For someone who loves to cook and to eat, the dreariness of my shopping and cooking patterns had caught up with him.

The following Sunday morning, as I was reading the paper, watching Alexander, and listening to Mozart, I did feel a little bit guilty as Bernie trudged off to the market; but as soon as I heard his car go down the driveway, I called my tennis partners and told them I thought I'd be back on the courts in a few weeks. I just wasn't sure how to break the news to Bernie. I hoped it wouldn't destroy the delicate balance of our new grocery shopping alliance.

And so far, it hasn't.

RONNI EISENBERG'S
TEN GROCERY SHOPPING TIPS

1. Have a good marketing list that your family learns to keep up with on a day-to-day basis. Keep track of everything you need. Have family members write down items when you're low but not out.

2. If you shop at the same market every week, make up a chart according to your supermarket's layout. For example, if aisle one is fruits, vegetables, and baked goods, you make up your list accordingly in the proper sequence.

3. Make shopping routine by doing it on the same day every week. Pick a day that is least crowded and when the shelves are well stocked, but don't go at 8:30 A.M. if that is when the staff is taking everything out of the cartons.

4. Plan your meals in advance. If you know what you are going to serve that week, make up the menus, list the items you are going to need, and shop for them.

5. Buy in bulk. Take advantage of sales. You'll save money, and it will allow you to shop less frequently.

6. File your coupons by date and by category. You want to use them before they expire. If you know what items you need, you can take out the appropriate coupons in advance. If you don't, take the whole folder or envelope.

7. Leave your children at home if you can. If you must take them, try to make it fun or instructional: older children can learn to pick fruits and vegetables, or you can teach them how to compare prices—it's a fun way to improve math skills. (I've got toddler twins and an eight-year-old, and if I take them along, I try to bring a baby-sitter as well.)

8. When you go through the checkout aisle, request that all like items be put together; you can even help pack the bags. If your fruits and vegetables are together, and your dairy products and frozen foods are in one bag, unpacking at home takes less time.

9. When you arrive home, organize everything immediately. Wash your fruits and vegetables so that they're fresh and ready to be eaten. Presort lunch extras and snacks like graham crackers or Cheerios into baggies or put them in airtight containers to save shelf space. If you have a baby, fill up bottles with milk so that you don't have to do it later.

10. If your menus are planned in advance, you can parcel out the

OUR FAVORITE SHOPPING TIPS

■

"Shop the clubs like Price Club, Osco, and Pace. Buy in bulk. Split with friends and neighbors. You'll save from 20 to 70 percent."

■

"Don't buy canned formula. Buy powdered formula and mix your own. You save 30 to 50 percent and won't waste all the cans."

■

"Diaper manufacturers test the market religiously. Make friends with someone who lives elsewhere and share coupons."

■

"Just because the price is right, don't buy quantities you don't need."

■

"If turkey is on special, cook a whole turkey and use it for leftovers whether it's sandwiches, turkey tetrazzini, or turkey soup."

■

"Buy a whole chicken and cut it up yourself. Save wings, necks, and backs for chicken soup."

∎

"Shop at stores in expensive neighborhoods because it's more enjoyable or shop at bargain stores and save money."

∎

"Buy generic brands. Brand loyalty is an extravagant anachronism. Most products are comparable. But don't buy cheap dishtowels, toilet paper, or plastic wrap because it's not worth the savings."

∎

"Use coupons. You can save at least 25 percent of your grocery bill."

∎

"You don't need to go to the discounts. Some grocery stores now have quantity sizes in enough categories that it's not worth going elsewhere."

∎

meats: store some of them, labeled and dated; marinate the rest for the evening meal. As you unpack tuna, you can make tuna salad for the next day. If you ever need single servings, wash chicken and wrap it in individual portions.

Source: Ronni Eisenberg is the coauthor, with Kate Kelly, of Organize Your Children *and* Organize Your Home. *She is the mother of three and lives in New York.*

DENIECE SCHOFIELD'S TEN GROCERY-SHOPPING TIPS

1. Arrange your list according to categories, including breads and cereals, canned goods; convenience foods; dairy products and eggs; frozen foods; health and beauty aids; household and miscellaneous; meat; produce; staples and condiments.

2. Make up a master shopping list. Compose a list of all the things you could ever buy in a grocery store. The list will serve as a wonderful memory jogger. A quick glance at the columns should remind you of items you might otherwise forget.

3. Plan menus. That's the best way to save time and money in the grocery store. When you begin shopping, and you're armed with a list of all the food you'll need for the next week or two, you can zero in on specific items and get out quickly. When you take the ingredients home from the store, take a few seconds to mark all the items you'll need for an upcoming meal. You can use a colorful self-adhesive signal dot or a permanent felt marker. Family members who see one of those marks on an item will then know not to eat it because it's needed for an upcoming meal.

4. Avoid shopping during peak periods, from 5:00 to 6:30 P.M. and on weekends. These early evening hours are when the folks who've been wondering all day what to fix for dinner do their shopping. They are a highly disorganized lot, so steer clear of them.

5. Be aware of regular prices so you'll be able to recognize bona fide sales and price reductions.

6. Whatever is done to food before you buy it (whether it's slicing, cooking, premeasuring, prepackaging, or flavoring) costs you money. Unless the product proves to be a great time-saving convenience, you may want to do those tasks yourself.

Remember, you always pay more for individual portions—boxes of cereal, bags of chips, drink-mix packets and so on.

7. If the price difference between egg sizes is less than seven cents, the larger eggs are the better buy.

8. Always weigh any produce sold by the piece and buy the heaviest piece.

9. If you travel a distance to reach a grocery store, an insulated beach bag or Styrofoam ice chest keeps frozen foods cold until you get home.

10. Using a collapsible shopping cart is a convenient way to get the groceries from the car to the kitchen in one trip.

Source: Deniece Schofield is the author of Confessions of a Happily Organized Family *and the mother of five. She lives with her family in Cedar Rapids, Iowa.*

COUPONS

Deborah Bozsa is a vice president of D'Arcy, Masius, Benton & Bowles advertising agency in St. Louis, Missouri, which publishes a reference book—mostly for professional use—titled Couponing as a Marketing Tool.

SB: *What is the status of the coupon industry?*
DB: In the past year coupon distribution has gone up, although coupon redemption has flattened out. That's probably due to several factors. Consumers know that every Sunday the coupons will be in their newspaper, so the coupons have become less special. It takes time to clip and sort them and an effort to remember to take them to the store. Yet the economy is still uncertain, consumer confidence may be eroding, and consumers' brand loyalty may be slipping, so people are still willing to use coupons.

SB: *Other than to save money, why do people use coupons?*
DB: According to a study done by professor Ambuj Jain, from Southern Methodist University in Dallas, people use coupons because it makes them feel smart, like they're beating the system or getting something for nothing. It also helps relieve the boredom of shopping. And it absolutely does reduce the risk of trying a new product. It decreases the amount of money that would be wasted if the product turns out to be unsatisfactory.

SB: *What are the major problems with coupon usage?*
DB: It's a problem for retailers because they have to collect them,

"Plan menus on at least a weekly basis. With four kids I plan them on a monthly basis even if I don't follow the plan entirely."

■

"Shop after dinner. Let your husband baby-sit for the kids. When you return home with all your groceries, he can help you put them away."

■

"If you've got a lot of kids, consider bakery thrift stores."

■

"Plan your meals around weekly specials. Double or triple the recipe and freeze the rest."

■

"A local grocery store claims to grind hamburger meat three times a day. The next morning they sell whatever is left over for half-price. It's a considerable savings."

■

make sure they've not expired, and ensure they are for the right product. So it holds up the checkout line. Also, since it takes three weeks for the retailers to get their money back from the coupon clearinghouses, they are, in essence, loaning money to manufacturers. And now, with double couponing, grocery stores must cover the cost of the doubled value.

SB: Why doesn't the industry eliminate coupons and reduce product prices?

DB: For two reasons: Coupons are still a relatively cost-effective advertising vehicle. Although a 5 percent redemption rate is considered high, coupons do provide significant advertising exposure. They are offered through a freestanding insert that features an appealing product shot, and a lot more people will clip the coupons than use them, which helps the manufacturer develop audience awareness of his or her product. Second, the savings that coupons generate for the 5 percent that are redeemed amounts to only pennies per product when spread among all purchasers of the brand.

HOBBIES

As I approached my fortieth birthday and evaluated various elements of my life, I decided I was becoming too one-dimensional; I used to have more interests.

I longingly reflected on hobbies past. There were tap dancing classes at UCLA. I knew I would never be a threat to Gregory Hines, but I loved the black patent leather shoes and delighted at hearing myself tapping down the halls of my dormitory. One year I played the banjo. I think it was when Country Joe and the Fish were big, but I can hardly remember. I do know that it was the year I wore overalls and a work shirt, carried banjo picks in my pockets, and fingered them like rosary beads.

Over time there were other passions: tennis, black-and-white photography, roller skating, poetry writing, guitar lessons, interpretive dance, bicycling, fencing, horseback riding, ballroom dancing, jogging, volleyball, Ping-Pong, and more recently, gardening. I used to pride myself on being a Renaissance woman.

Through disinterest, laziness, lack of time, or lack of skill, all these hobbies except tennis fell by the wayside. I can't remember how or why it happened, but suddenly I found the thought of all these abandoned hobbies very disturbing. It suggests a certain squandered potential that while possibly true is not what role models are made of.

It bothers me most these days when I read articles about famous people and learn that so-and-so is not only a well-known educator, journalist, entrepreneur, or scientist but also an accomplished concert pianist, a scratch golfer, and raises prize-winning orchids.

As I contemplate what I want to teach Alexander, I've decided

WHAT WE DO

■

"Without gardening I would probably be in a loony bin. It's extraordinarily relaxing. I've got an enclosed area in the yard. There's nothing like working in the soil with your hands and watching vegetables grow from seeds."

■

"Before my son was born, I worked ten- to twelve-hour days. I didn't have time for hobbies. Now, mothering is a twenty-four-hour-a-day job, but I find time to cook, sew, and read."

■

"Washing the dog once a week has become my greatest hobby."

■

"I play tennis twice a week. I've played since I was a child, and I promised myself that I'd continue playing after my kids were born. Often, when I have a million errands to run and think I should cancel, I make myself play, and I always feel better. It takes only an hour."

■

I need to broaden my interests and become a more accomplished hobbyist. Tennis is still the best prospect. While my sister and brother are convinced that I could have been as good as Martina if only my parents had pushed me, I think I would have been hard-pressed to beat Tracy Austin after her injury. Still, I do have a natural talent, and I know that with practice I can once again become an A club player. Maybe Alex and I will play mixed doubles when he's older. I want to be in shape just in case.

Banjo lessons are another possibility. I've always thought that family music sessions had a Norman Rockwell quality that bespoke more wholesome times. My fantasy would be to play Brahms piano duets with Alex, but since my childhood piano teacher said I was one of the worst pupils he'd ever taught, I think I'll have better luck with the banjo—an instrument mastered by rural people who marry close relatives. I don't think that's too much to ask.

I'd like to pursue one more hobby—preferably something in the arts—but I have no talent in that area, and it would undoubtedly take too long for me to become proficient. As it is, I'm working on a tight time schedule. I figure that by the time Alex is five years old, he'll be discriminating enough to know whether I'm a real contender or just a dabbler.

I'd like him to be able to say with pride to his friends that his mother has got a wide variety of interests and some hobbies in which she excels. I'd like to be able to say that myself these days. Time will tell.

ॐ

LEISURE TIME

Why leisure time is important. It's time during which one experiences freedom, unfettered by rules and roles and expectations of the world. It's an opportunity for self-expression, creativity, pleasure, socialization, fitness, and learning. It's a time to recuperate from demands, discouragements, and disappointments—all those things over which we have no control. And it's time for refilling our inner strengths and our inner resources.

How leisure time relieves stress and fosters good health. Physiologically, leisure provides an opportunity to use our bodies actively. Research indicates that physical activity directly impacts things like strength, endurance, and cardiovascular health. It helps to reduce depression and increase self-esteem. Emotionally, leisure is an opportunity to sort things out in our own mind, to share experiences with others, and to learn coping strategies. Freedom—the notion of perceiving control—is an important theme. Leisure is an opportunity to take control of our life, which in turn decreases stress and increases the functioning ability. In other words, leisure promotes health.

How most American women spend their leisure time. There is certainly not enough research, but what literature there is tends to indicate that in spite of the changing definition of family, women appear to spend the majority of their leisure time with family and often are the individuals who play the major role in meeting the family members' leisure needs. Women tend to focus more on the social benefits of leisure than on personal benefits. Their leisure often reflects the family's leisure. Next to family, visiting with friends appears to be the most important leisure experience of women.

More and more women are becoming involved in sports and fitness. Volunteer activities and community service continue to be popular and certainly are important in difficult economic times. For many, hobbies and homebound activities are a significant part of their lives, and these are often integrated with the necessary tasks of the home—for example, folding clothes and watching television. Things like sewing, cooking, entertaining, gardening—all types of activities that once might have been duties—can often become leisure activities as the woman becomes skilled and enjoys doing them.

We're seeing more and more women involved in outdoor leisure experiences, and increasing numbers of women are showing a preference for using leisure time for self-enrichment, for both formal education and learning skills. And we do know that the greater number of roles a woman accumulates, the less likely she is to have leisure time.

Advice on leisure for new moms. Leisure is necessary to balance one's life. If a woman doesn't take the time to renew and reenergize herself, she may reach the point at which there is nothing to give her family. It is also important for one's family members for the mom to be a positive role model in leisure. If Mom neglects herself, then the messages could be very negative: Adulthood is drudgery. It's not OK to have fun. Mom is not important. Parents must respect themselves if they want their children to

"I have a lot of hobbies, but I don't have time to do them. I haven't quite worked them into the schedule yet, but I haven't given up trying."

■

"I do aerobics when my husband comes home from work. I sew during nap time and play the piano when the children are awake."

■

"I schedule tap dancing once a week. I always come home smiling."

■

"I sew a lot. I smock. I have sewed all four kids' Halloween costumes. This year I sewed a Halloween costume for our school principal."

■

respect them, and children will learn from their parents how to use leisure intelligently.

Bertrand Russell once said that the intelligent use of leisure was the final test of civilization.

Source: Jan Tolan, Ph.D., is an associate professor in the Department of Leisure Studies and Recreation at California State University at Northridge. She is the mother of one.

TWENTY MOST POPULAR PARTICIPATION SPORTS*

SPORT	PARTICIPANTS (in millions)
1. Exercise walking	67.8
2. Swimming	63.1
3. Bicycle riding	54.6
4. Fishing	47.6
5. Camping	47.3
6. Bowling	42.5
7. Exercising with equipment	39.4
8. Billiards/pool	29.3
9. Basketball	28.2
10. Aerobic exercising	27.8
11. Golf	24.0
12. Boating (motor)	22.3
13. Volleyball	22.1
14. Running/jogging	21.9
15. Hiking	21.6
16. Softball	19.2
17. Dart throwing	18.8
18. Hunting with firearms	17.8
19. Tennis	17.3
20. Roller skating	16.8

*Seven years of age and older

Source: National Sporting Goods Association, 1992, Mt. Prospect, Illinois; 708-439-4000.

CRATS

Judith Bossart, the mother of two, is the editor-in-chief of Crafts *magazine, P.O. Box 3117, Harlan, IA 51593-2183; 309-682-6626.*

SB: *How do you define crafts for the purposes of your magazine?*

JB: How-to projects that can be made with materials purchased in a crafts store, in a needlework store, or in a fabric store. We do not do any crafts that we consider artisan, such as pottery, ceramics, or weaving. Except for a sewing machine, we rule out any expensive pieces of equipment.

SB: *What are the most popular crafts for your readership?*

JB: • Wearables, particularly sweatshirts on which people have painted using the squeeze bottle paint or iron-on transfers that they can then fill in with a color-book type of painting;

• sweatshirts that are embellished with pieces of old buttons, lace, and ribbons; and

• cross-stitch, which is no longer gaining in popularity but has leveled off to a high interest among those who do it.

• Quilting, in all of its forms, is popular today; not only traditional quilting but what we call "quick quilts" or "mock quilts," where you get a quilted look without sewing. You use fusible web, which is a thin fiber with a glue or adhesive on both sides that you sandwich between two pieces of fabric. When you apply heat, the glue or adhesive melts, bonding the material together. It is an easy way to get that quilted look, and you can put it on a wall hanging, a sweatshirt, a jacket, or even make a Christmas ornament with it.

• Crafters are very keen on dolls today. There's been a growing interest in cloth dolls for several years. Cloth dolls cover the full spectrum; there are baby dolls for little girls as well as very sophisticated ones designed for women. There is also interest in dolls that have wood blocks for bodies. We are seeing the beginnings of plunger dolls, which use a plunger as an armature for the body. Crafters are also using molds and oven-bake polymer clays to make faces, hands, and feet for dolls that have cloth bodies and clothes.

• Florals in all of their glory—whether we're arranging them in silk flowers, a wreath, a centerpiece or we're decorating hats with them. Ones made from ribbon—particularly the wire-edged ribbon—are popular, and they make bow making easy.

• Home-decorating items are always big, whether we are cross-stitching a pillow to use as an accent, stenciling a border around a room, or using a stencil on a small wood shelf or other piece of wood furniture.

SB: *What advice do you have for moms who want to begin learning new crafts but aren't sure where to begin?*

JB: In addition to my magazine, there are lots of books and videos out where you can learn the basics of crafting. And you can't forget television. There are some wonderful programs on PBS and on some of the cable networks. Moms can check their local listings, because all the programs are not available all over the country. Carol Duvall, who writes a monthly column for us, can be found on the "Home Show," where she demonstrates a variety of basic quick crafts that can pique your interest.

Nothing can beat a visit to a good craft shop in your local area. Many of them provide classes. Park districts across the country have a very heavy schedule of craft classes, and many of those classes are offered in the evening.

HOUSEWORK

There is a scene in the film Kramer vs. Kramer *in which Meryl Streep tells Dustin Hoffman that one of the reasons she's divorcing him is that he stacks his sweaters by color in the closet. He replies that he's an art director, suggesting that his obsessively neat and finicky behavior is endemic in the profession.*

In a theater packed with moviegoers, I was the only person who laughed aloud in a somewhat inappropriate manner. My art director husband glared at me. Suffice it to say we define neatness in different ways.

When Bernie and I got married and I moved into his house, forsaking my own abode, he told me there were a few house rules: Dishes could never be left in the sink overnight. The bed must be made every morning. Dusting should be done before you could write your name on the picture frames.

This wasn't to say he expected me to do these chores on a regular basis. He just anticipated some sort of shared participation. He would do housework one week; I would do it the next.

After the first week I realized that I had made a major mistake in agreeing so quickly to this arrangement. I had no idea what the term housework *meant to him. I watched in horror as he not only dusted and vacuumed but also scrubbed the toilet, shower, and bathtub, mopped the kitchen floor, polished selected pieces of furniture, cleaned the refrigerator (not a weekly task, he assured me), dusted some of the miniblinds (this was a rotating chore, and the entire house could be done in a month), and washed some of the windows (another rotating task).*

To some people, perhaps most people, this might not have seemed overwhelming. To me it was a nightmare. Saturdays were meant for sports, long bike rides, walks at the beach, and museum field trips. Between grocery shopping and housework, I'd never have to worry about skin cancer because my face and body would never see the light of day again.

First I panicked; then I called my friend Claudia Hudgens. She had worked for my grandmother and my mother and is the best housekeeper I've ever met. She takes great pride in her work, and she is a special friend. I asked her if she had a free day every week. She did, and I was in luck.

Bernie, who had never had a housekeeper, was overwhelmed by her ability and professionalism. When she finished, the entire house sparkled. She not only did the tasks we disliked most but even knew how to do things people just didn't do anymore. She made a special soap that could get any stain out; she washed Bernie's socks by hand; applied paste wax to the dining room table; dusted, polished, cleaned, and washed things in a way that the house smelled of sunlight and fresh air rather than detergent and cleaning fluids.

Now that Alex has joined our family, Claudia not only cleans the house every week but also takes care of him. He worships her. He is the only child we've heard of who knows how to vacuum like a pro, whose first word was broom, *who enjoys sweeping up the food he throws on the floor, and who cries when we won't let him sponge off the table after dinner.*

Bernie sometimes worries that Alex will be the only child in his preschool whose career goal is to clean houses. I'm not concerned in the least. He couldn't pick a better role model if he tried.

~

THE SPEED-CLEANING SYSTEM

We need to explain up front that the speed-cleaning system has nothing to do with liking or disliking cleaning. It has to do with getting cleaning over with so that we can get on to better things. We're all working these days, and the weekends shouldn't be bogged down with cleaning the house. It should be spent going to the park with the kids. To do that, you need a cleaning system so that you know where to start, what to do first, what to have in your right hand, what to have in your left hand—those kinds of things—so you will finish cleaning as quickly as possible. Cleaning fast doesn't mean killing yourself doing it. It means doing it in the most efficient way and using less energy because you're making fewer trips back and forth, up and down, and around and through the house.

The key tips:

• **Make every move count.** That means to work your way around the room once.

• **Carry everything with you.** Use a cleaning apron. In my mind, that's not different from the carpenter wearing a carpenter's belt. You certainly wouldn't hire a carpenter who didn't wear a belt and had to run up and down the ladder every time he or she needed a nail. Yet that's the way a lot of us go about cleaning the house, in the same haphazard way. The apron we use is designed to carry everything we need; it's got seven pockets and loops. Once you put your cleaning products in the particular pocket or loop in your apron, don't change them. You will be able to reach for everything you need without looking.

• **Make sure you have the right basic supplies.** You need a heavy-duty liquid cleaner, like 409 or Fantastik; a light-duty liquid cleaner like Windex; a toothbrush (which is great because it gets into the corners of anything and is great for knobs on stoves, around thermostats, the corners of molding, light switches, and dozens of other places); a scraper (for crud that gets stuck to your countertops), a razor blade in a razor blade holder (for spots of paint that have been on the mirror in the bathroom ever since you bought the house); cleaning cloths (we recommend 100 percent cotton ones because they are the most absorbent and lint free). If you have products we don't use that you like, put them into the apron in the same way. However, we have found that it's smarter to have one product that does ten things than ten products that do one thing each. You have fewer things to carry around with you.

• **Have a starting place in each room.** Work from top to bottom. Work toward your right. Never backtrack. If you backtrack, you're doing something wrong. If there is a cleaner you must have when you clean a room—and you have to go out and get it—that's fine, but work it into your system so that the next time you start cleaning that room you carry the supply with you.

• **Clean in a team.** If there's more than one person getting the house dirty, there should be more than one person cleaning it. There are a lot of somewhat liberated husbands out there who agree they should help with the housecleaning. But basically what they do is take out the garbage—which takes ten seconds—and the woman does everything else. That's not a very even distribu-

WHAT OUR HUSBANDS DO AND HOW WE FEEL ABOUT IT

■

"He does the laundry and the cooking. We have a woman clean once a week. My husband does 50 percent of the child care and half of the household responsibilities."

■

"My husband does outdoor maintenance, dishes, grocery shopping, laundry, vacuuming, and takes out the garbage. He has definitely increased his participation in the last six months because he realized things were not getting done."

■

"My husband helps pick up sometimes and will clean if I'm away. He works full-time; I work eight hours a week. The house is really my responsibility. My husband does all the repairs and special cleanup projects."

■

tion of the work. Housecleaning should be a team effort. Do it Thursday night when there's nothing on television so you don't have to waste the weekend.

Source: Jeff Campbell is the author of Speed Cleaning. *He is the owner of the Clean Team in San Francisco, California. For a free catalog of their products, call 800-238-2996.*

TIPS ON CONQUERING CLUTTER

- Organize clutter in one complete area. You can't go in and say "I'm going to do an hour here and an hour there"; that doesn't work. You need to devote at least half a day of uninterrupted time (a full day would be ideal) to the task. Get a sitter. Don't take phone calls. Don't have visitors. Don't leave the room and go into another room until you're finished.
- Set up cardboard boxes, including ones labeled "toss," "elsewhere," and "charity." As you come across items that go in another room, stick them in the "elsewhere" box, and at the end of the day put those items away. "Charity" should be bagged and taken to charity that very day, before you start recovering items. "Toss" should be bagged and tossed at the end of the day.
- Take all of the clutter out of the area. If you have a closet, take everything out of the closet and put it on the bed. Now you have an empty closet. Pick up items one at a time and decide whether you're keeping them. If you're keeping them, put them back in the closet in an organized fashion.
- Keep things close to their point of first use; use duplicates where it's justified. For example, you might have a pair of scissors in the bathroom and also a pair in your desk.
- Groups items together. In your closet, all the blouses go together; so do all the skirts and all the pants. In the cupboard, all the spices are grouped together; likewise for canned goods and boxed goods. All the knives go in one drawer; all the silverware in another.
- Reward yourself. When you're finished, go to a movie, take a leisurely bath, spend the entire evening reading.
- When things get out of hand, take ten or fifteen minutes and pick up the clutter in the room. The reason people don't do this is they tell themselves "I've got to clean up this entire room, and I don't have time to do it completely." You may not have time, but if you just pick up the clutter and put it away, the room will look much better and you will feel much better. You can always

vacuum and dust later. If you ignore the clutter, it builds on itself.

- Buy effective storage containers. Look for what you have around the house that's useful. Shoe boxes are great for everything, including the kids' crayons, craft supplies, and hosiery.
- Observe the in-and-out inventory rule. If something new comes in, something old goes out. That works for kids' toys, clothes, and fancy kitchen gadgets. For every new item you buy, there is probably something else you stopped using a long time ago.
- Watch out for the following common clutter traps:

   Catalogs. People keep them forever. Discipline yourself; once the next season comes, get rid of the previous catalog. Do the same with magazines.

   Children's papers and artwork. Keep a selection, not every piece of paper. It's one thing to keep that big piece of macaroni art; it's another to hang on to the mimeographed papers.

   Greeting cards. People tend to keep all the holiday cards and birthday cards their family members ever received. Just keep a special selection.

   Photographs. Everybody says, "I am going to put those photographs in an album when I get the time." Yet photographs tend to multiply throughout the house. If you don't do anything else, at least write who's in the picture and the date. If you don't have time to put them in an album, get plastic shoe boxes and label them in generic categories: vacations, pets, the kids, the family. When you do put them in albums, at least they'll be organized.

Source: Stephanie Culp, author of How to Conquer Clutter *and* How to Get Organized When You Don't Have the Time, *is an organization and time management consultant. She lives in Oconomowoc, Wisconsin.*

TEN HOUSEWORK AND LIFE TIPS

1. Put a couple of drops of Ivory dish soap in your bathtub when you're bathing yourself and your children. That will eliminate bathtub rings. When you're through using the shower, the sink, or the bathtub, wipe it down with a terry cloth towel or a squeegee, and you won't have to use cleansers to clean hard-water buildup.

2. Teach your children from the age of three to pick up after themselves. In their rooms, have open wastepaper baskets

"My husband doesn't do anything, really. Actually, unless he did stuff 'my way' it's probably OK. He maintains his own style, and that's just fine."

■

"My husband does laundry, a few meals, and some child care. Of course I would like more, but since he works seventy hours per week in his own business and I don't work outside the home, I wouldn't ask him to do more."

■

"My husband cooks or does the dishes on nights I do the other. He helps straighten, bathes the kids, and puts them to bed. I'm home more. He works long hours with little discretionary time. He encourages me to bring in as much help as I need. He is supportive. He works in the yard."

■

"He irons, takes out the garbage, cuts the grass, rakes, occasionally vacuums, and bathes the kids. No way is this enough participation. We both work, and I do most of the housework and child care. He is just like all the studies you've ever read, and it's our biggest source of arguments. If I could afford cleaning help, I certainly would."

■

"My husband was out of work for six months. During that time he took over all the household chores, including grocery shopping, cooking, laundry, cleaning, and driving our son to and from preschool. I felt like I'd died and gone to heaven."

■

and open dirty clothes containers, because kids usually don't like to open lids.

3. With some regularity, use your best china for your own children. It provides an opportunity to teach them table manners and how to behave.

4. By the age of three or four, teach your children how to vacuum spots, furniture, and the middle of the room. They love to help out. By the age of ten, your children should be able to help you cook, help plan the menus, and help chop ingredients.

5. Whoever cooks should do the dishes. It's a great way to learn how to cut back on the quantity of dishes you use.

6. The most efficient thing you can have in your house is a phone you can walk around with so you can unload the dishwasher, clean up the drawers, and pick up things while you're talking so you don't waste time.

7. Spend an hour each day tidying your house. If rooms are uncluttered, if the front entry looks nice, if the dishes are in the dishwasher, if the counters are clean and the tables are dusted, you won't feel embarrassed when people come to visit.

8. For in-depth cleaning—including drawers, closets, windows, under the beds, furniture—tackle a room a month thoroughly. By the time you get through each room, it will be time to start over again.

9. During the summer, play, garden, or clean out the shed in your garage.

10. Always leave time to spend with your children, especially when they come home from school. Listen to their side of the story. Do not judge them. Somehow make them learn what is right and what is wrong. Most of all, be consistent in punishment and money matters.

Source: Eugenia Chapman, coauthor of Clean Your House & Everything in It, *was formerly the head housekeeper at the Lion House, one of the great mansions that Brigham Young built for his many wives. She is the mother of eleven and the grandmother of fifty-six. She lives in Utah and frequently lectures on housecleaning.*

MORE HOUSEKEEPING TIPS

- Start with the washing. Do it at least a few days a week. Wash, dry, fold, and put the clothes away each time. That way the laundry never piles up.
- The first rooms to clean are the kitchen and the bathrooms. They are the most difficult and time-consuming.
- On a weekly basis, do the following chores. Keep the kitchen tile clean. Most people wash the top of the counter, but it's important to wash the tile in front because that's what people see when they walk into your kitchen. Clean the cooktop or stove. Wash the hand marks off the walls. Mop the floor every week with cold water; hot water will take the wax off. If you use soap, you'll dull the wax. Mop it as dry as you can. Wax it once a month.
- With the oven, you need to be very careful with oven cleaners. They can take paint off. Warm the oven a bit and use 409 or bathroom tub and tile cleaner. They're fairly mild, and if you clean with regularity, you never have to use the really abrasive cleaners.
- In the bathroom, wash the bath and shower tile on a weekly basis. Use Clorox or bleach mixed with water because it won't eat the grout out. If the shower doors are left open, they won't mold. Use glass polish to clean the doors. Mop the floor on a weekly basis with soap.
- In the living room, dining room, and family room, on a monthly basis you should do the following. Use a Dustbuster to clean all the pillows and chairs. Take the cushions out and do a thorough job. Wax the dining room table.
- On a weekly basis, use lemon oil to clean all the wooden furniture. Check for cobwebs. Dust. Vacuum.
- In the bedrooms, clean under the beds once a month and turn the mattresses. On a weekly basis, dust and vacuum. Change the sheets every week or every two weeks.
- Do windows every two or three months. Clean the window sills every week.

Source: Claudia Hudgens, mother of three, grandmother of five, and great-grandmother of five, has been a professional housekeeper for more than sixty years.

INDISPENSABLE ADVICE

When I was pregnant, I harbored the hope that a friend of mine or perhaps of my mother's would take me aside and, with Margaret Mead-like wisdom, tell me something about child rearing that would put it all in perspective. It never happened.

I also hoped that before my father died—in the fifth month of my pregnancy—he would call me to his bedside and tell me what he had learned while he was dying, and how I should raise my son in an increasingly violent and frightening world. That never happened either. I don't think Daddy ever knew he was dying, and perhaps those kinds of scenes take place only in films.

So it was a fairly uninsightful pregnancy, I'm afraid. The best advice I got was less global and more incident-specific. As things came up, I turned to the three people who have raised children more successfully than anyone else I know: my mother, my housekeeper, Claudia, and my friend Linda.

I talked to Linda all through my pregnancy because she not only gave birth to four children but also taught Lamaze classes for years. I called to find out what to anticipate from the amniocentesis and the sonograms. I called when I thought I was getting too fat and when I was worried I wasn't drinking enough milk. After Alex was born, I called almost every time he had a bowel movement for the first month and it was a different color from the one that preceded it. After Bernie looked at the phone bill and suggested that I install an 800 number at Linda's house, I decided that perhaps I was overdoing it.

For everyday kinds of questions and advice, I talk to Claudia and Mother. Claudia has raised three of her own children and five stepchildren in addition to many and assorted others during her *seventy-plus years. Mother has raised just us three, but we're all relatively well adjusted and happy, and that seems to be a unique combination these days.*

Much of what both Claudia and Mother tell me is just good common sense. If Alex won't eat, they say not to force him; he won't starve to death. When he hated the Mommy and Me class, they both told me not to push him. They said he was good with other children and suggested that maybe he just had a discriminating personality and didn't like the class.

They are his greatest defenders and his most beloved companions. They have been supportive and instructive—when asked—which is the most you can hope for. I know they try hard not to give me unsolicited advice, and for that I am deeply grateful.

I must say that after almost eighteen months of motherhood I had no Margaret Mead–like wisdom to share with my sister when she was pregnant. Of all the things I've learned to do in life, mothering is among the most difficult. Just when you think you've got it all figured out, your child enters a new stage or backslides into an old one.

I guess if I could tell my sister Jane anything about mothering, it would be to "watch the ball, anticipate, and follow through." That's what my father always told me when we played tennis. It's had great application in all aspects of my life. I find that whenever I "watch, anticipate, and follow through," I can accomplish anything. The same goes for mothering.

ɔ

DR. T. BERRY BRAZELTON'S ADVICE

T. Berry Brazelton, M.D., is founder of the Child Development Unit at Boston Children's Hospital and clinical professor emeritus of pediatrics at Harvard Medical School. He has been a practicing pediatrician for over forty years and is the author of more than two hundred scholarly papers and twenty-four books, including Touchpoints. *He is the father of four and the grandfather of three.*

SB: How do you define touchpoints of development, and why are they important?
TBB: Touchpoints are those predictable times that occur just before a surge of rapid growth—whether it's motor, cognitive, or

WHAT WE WERE TOLD

■

"Children are not appliances with warranties. Life is messy. (It's from the film *Parenthood*. I just loved that movie.)"

■

"Put cereal in that baby's bottle. Don't listen to that doctor. He's never had a baby, and he won't be the one who's up all night."

■

"Force yourself to take naps. When your baby is cranky, you're doing the dishes, and all else fails, give him your fingertip to suck on. Dishes can be done with one hand."

■

"My pediatrician advised me to get some help for at least several hours a week. At first I used the time to sleep, and later I saw friends or got a manicure. I took care of myself."

■

emotional. Our research has proved that in the first few years you can predict when touchpoints are going to happen. A touchpoint is the period that precedes a spurt in the child's development when the child falls apart—starts wetting the bed, sucking his thumb, throwing tantrums—and the parents fall apart with him. They think, Oh my God, we've been failures. If parents understand that this regression is a time for reorganization for the child to make the big spurt, they will not only feel less uptight and put less pressure on the child but will also realize the next spurt is theirs as well as the child's. And the pediatrician, nurse-practitioner, or family physician can be there to support the parents and to help interpret the regressions and predict the spurts of development so that the parents feel better about themselves.

SB: Since there are so many individual differences in babies, how can moms (and dads) learn to parent their own child effectively while allowing for the child's uniqueness?
TBB: This is really the focus of my television show, "What Every Baby Knows." It's an attempt to show parents, by modeling, how to look at their child's behavior and to interpret what the child does rather than what the child says. Children are very clear about what works for them and what doesn't. Adults are the ones who are complicated. I show parents how to watch their baby. You need to know that a baby who is laid-back, quiet, and watchful is more sensitive than a more active, constantly searching, driving, intense child. If you can interpret the kind of temperament your child has, it's easier to determine what kind of response will work for your baby as well as for you.

Parenting is not a one-sided relationship. It revolves around the parent and the child. The parents' history, their temperament, their occupation, and their lifestyle are part of the equation. In successful parenting you integrate who you are with who your child is, and that's a difficult job. I always say to parents, "You don't learn from successes; you learn from mistakes." When you make a mistake, you need to pull back and say "Uh-oh, that didn't work. What was I doing wrong? Was it the child, or was it the ghost in my own nursery?" Parenting isn't all that intuitive; there are elements of intuition, but you can learn a lot from the clues your child gives you.

SB: What are the most common parenting problems new parents face and how can they resolve them?
TBB: The most common problem, which we just discussed, is learning how to listen to your child. Another common problem is

learning how to put up with a child's fussing, to understand that a baby has six different cries right from the first, and how to work with each one. Crying can mean boredom, hunger, discomfort, pain, tension, and discharge (which is really just letting off steam at the end of the day). At least that's the way I interpret that colicky period that comes at the end of every day for most children. All these cries are different and mean different things. If a parent can stand back, wait, and see what the child is trying to do for himself or herself and then interpret the behavior, it makes it a lot easier.

Feeding is another common problem, particularly for mothers, but for fathers as well. Parents feel, Oh, God, I've got to get the right amount of food into the baby, because all parents feel that feeding is a key responsibility, and of course it is. When feeding becomes difficult is when a child becomes autonomous in the feeding process.

The three touchpoints for feeding are all in the first year, the times when the child is undergoing a new spurt in cognitive development. The first spurt is at four and a half months, when the baby won't stay at the breast and wants to look around the room. Every time something happens, the baby will pull away and won't go back to the breast. Mothers worry whether they have enough milk or if the baby is teething. They are looking for rational explanations for the behavior, but it's really just a developmental spurt. The way to handle it is to live through it, feed your baby in a dark quiet room to keep your milk coming, and not worry about it.

At seven or eight months, when the baby is able to master the pincer grasp—the separation of the thumb and forefinger—and wants to pick up food and feed herself, she is going to resist if you keep on trying to poke food into her. So give her two or three bits of soft food that she can manage herself and then go ahead and feed her the rest of the food. At twelve months the same sort of thing happens. A baby wants to be autonomous; he doesn't want to be fed any longer. A parent who hasn't learned to let the baby feed himself is already in trouble unless the parent adapts.

SB: After forty years as a pediatrician, during which you have participated in the parenting of more than 25,000 children, what is the most important advice you can give new parents?
TBB: Learn the child's language—his or her behavior. As you try things out, let the baby tell you whether you are on the right track. If what you're doing is right, you can tell by looking at the baby's

"My mom said, 'It's tough to be a child because adults watch your every move, scrutinizing everything you do. Think about what it would be like if someone watched and commented on you to that degree. Ignore what you can.' "

■

"My mother gave me the most important advice that got me through the baby problems. She said, 'Do what you have to do to make things okay.' "

■

"Don't make eating or cleanliness an issue."

■

189

WHAT WE HAVE LEARNED

■

"Don't judge other people's parenting of children, and there's less chance they'll judge you."

■

"Life can't be perfect; things don't always go just as you want them to. So it's futile to try to force your children to conform to your ideas of how things should be. Children have their own personalities, their own likes and dislikes, and their own ways of doing things. It's important to let them experiment and give them some slack."

■

"Enjoy all stages of childhood. Don't rush to get to the next stage, because it will come in due time. Remind your children often that they are special and you love them."

■

face, his body, and his responses. He will be happy and placid. When you're on the wrong track, the baby will be unhappy; he'll thrash and cry, his limbs may stiffen, and he may avert his face from you. It won't take long to learn what his behavior is trying to tell you.

A final word: Relax and enjoy yourself. I know that's sometimes difficult to remember, but it's really the most important advice I've got.

DR. MOM'S PARENTING ADVICE

Marianne Egeland Neifert, M.D., author of Dr. Mom's Parenting Guide *and coauthor of* Dr. Mom: A Guide to Baby and Child Care, *is a practicing pediatrician affiliated with the Presbyterian/ Saint Luke's Medical Center in Denver, Colorado. She is married and the mother of five.*

SB: *What are the greatest challenges of parenting today?*
MN: One of the key challenges has to do with the change in role stereotypes. In a way our parent's model was more simplistic. People had an idea of what it meant to be a mother and a father. Today it's so exciting to see expanded opportunities for everybody, but there are also problems because we may not have had models. We look to our mother's model, and if she was an at-home mother and we're out having a career, we don't know what that's supposed to look like. It's the same for our husbands, who may be more involved as fathers. So there's a trade-off; all this excitement with expanded role opportunities is coupled with anxiety about relinquishing former stereotypes.

A spin-off of all this is periodic role overload. Today parents feel like they have too little time; they feel overcommitted and overwhelmed, and this sometimes robs them of the joys of parenting. We have a new societal norm in which the majority of mothers are in the workforce. The result is that you get some great new opportunities, but you're just plain tired. You wonder, How can I meet everybody's needs and take care of myself?

Another change is the huge number of divorces—40 percent of children will experience parental divorce—and what that means for raising children today. Many single mothers don't have the benefit of a helpmate or a father figure for their children; there are many divorced people who are stepparents, or who are dealing with blended families, shared custody, or being noncustodial parents. All these relationships present attendant challenges.

It will always be a challenge to instill a positive self-concept in your children. Parents need to see this as a very important role beyond the fiscal care of the child: to be able to raise a child who feels like a person of enormous intrinsic worth. This has always been a big challenge, and it takes a lot of time. It's terribly important—and difficult—to value your children apart from their behavior, to transmit to your children that they are loved unconditionally so that they can go out and weather the storms of life.

SB: *What are some of the best ways to instill values in your children?*

MN: A lot of it is modeling and setting an example; nothing will ever be more important than what we do in our actions and say in our words. One of the main messages we want to impart to our child—by age three—is to respect others and their place in the world. You want to raise a child who appreciates and accepts differences in other people, who has an appreciation of sharing, and who has a concern for others. Maybe, even by age three, we can achieve some kind of consequence training where children learn "I'm not just a pawn in the world, but I am the result of my actions."

SB: *As a pediatrician, professor of pediatrics, wife, mother of five, and author, how have you managed to balance your life, set priorities, and integrate your professional life with your family life?*

MN: I would be dishonest if I didn't start out by saying I think I have been very lucky. I certainly have worked very hard, but I've had a lot of breaks. I had—and still do have—a wonderful husband, which is a miracle in itself. I had healthy, relatively easy children. I found many sources of support in my immediate family and my extended family.

I have a strong faith in God, and I feel that for me it is the power of God that lets ordinary people sometimes do more extraordinary things. I don't think I would have tried to do any of this if I didn't feel that there is a God, that He cares about me, this is part of His plan, and He's going to get me through.

In terms of work, when I look back on those early days of medical school, I don't know how I did it. I remember being on call for a period of months every other night when I was pregnant with my fourth child. What I learned from this experience is to look at what you can do under duress. During those years, and

"Do the best you can and let it go. Motherhood is a wonderful, emotional roller coaster that has tested me in ways I could never have anticipated. I feel stronger because of my experiences."

■

"Take care of yourself first, and you will be able to properly take care of your children."

■

"Don't ask for advice unless you intend to use it. 'Advisers' can sometimes get ticked if you don't do what they told you they did. Don't be afraid to try something new or different from the norm as long as it's reasonable. My third child refused to be breastfed, so I pumped the milk and gave it to him in a bottle. A lot of mothers might be offended by that, but it worked for me."

■

there were about seven of them, I literally couldn't have done it without saying "I'll take one day at a time." Maybe what's important is to realize that—whatever your circumstances—the difficulties you are experiencing don't have to be there forever. I used to joke when things were really bad and say "Well, this is better than labor" (although labor ends and has a wonderful outcome). But in a tough situation I would say to myself, "This, too, will end."

SB: How did you ever find time for yourself and for your husband?

MN: My husband is an exceptional person, and I do have great respect and appreciation for what he tolerated. We were really young when we got married; I was eighteen, and he was twenty-one. We just didn't know what we were getting into or what would be required. Probably what was hardest for us was renegotiating the traditional roles. People would assume he was the doctor-in-training, and no one commended him for being "Mr. Mom."

My advice for younger folks coming up is that you need to make your relationship a top priority. If there is one thing that I'd do differently, it would be to make the marriage and my own needs a higher priority. Now that my husband and I have sent our youngest child to college, we feel so lucky we survived it all, we still have one another, and we're still in love. One of the things we *did* do was to carve out minivacations, like an overnight at a local hotel. We had no qualms about asking people to sit for us. It took us twenty-five years to get the big second honeymoon in Hawaii, but we did have a lot of shorter vacations.

SB: What are the most important tips you can give to new moms?

MN: • **Diversity in families is their greatest strength.** Feel good about whatever constitutes your family and don't start off by saying "There's something imperfect here." Celebrate your family, whatever it looks like and whatever the circumstances.

• **Become informed.** Read books, look at videos, take classes. The more knowledge you have, the better off you are.

• **Be flexible.** Know from the start that it isn't going to go the way you expected it to go. The more rigid and controlling you are, the more difficult it is to be a parent.

• **Be kind to yourself.** Say, "It's OK to make mistakes as long as I promise to learn from them." Try not to waste energy beating yourself up over the mistakes. Apologize to your child when you're wrong.

• **Be willing to accept the disappointments of parenthood.** We all want parenthood to be better for our children than it ever was for us. We want our children to be the embodiment of everything that is good and perfect. But the truth is that all children are different; there are children who are hyperactive, who have learning disabilities or birth defects. That's part of the challenge of being a parent as well. Accepting the unexpected is how you grow and learn. In the end, learning to love your child—whatever he or she turns out to be like—is when you realize your strength.

• **Keep in mind that nothing is more important than the relationship with your child.** Don't lock horns with your older children. Always think about coming out in the end with a good relationship that will last a lifetime.

INTELLECTUAL PURSUITS

When I was in college, I was the kind of person who habitually changed her major. If I took a class I liked, I fantasized what it might be like to pursue the discipline in earnest. At varying times I envisioned myself as an anthropologist, a psychologist, and an art historian. Then I would take a second class, find it less than stimulating, and wonder what I could possibly have been thinking to consider the field as a career prospect.

The value of this type of educational background is that I knew enough about a wide variety of subjects that I have always been an excellent dinner table conversationalist—until I became a mother. At one of our first post-Alex dinner parties, when I talked with people who had older children or none at all, I felt as if I'd fallen off a potato truck. Not only had it been ages since I'd read a somewhat educational book, but I wasn't even reading the newspaper with regularity.

So when my dinner companion turned to me and said, "What do you think about the situation in the Middle East?" I didn't know what situation he was referring to. Was it the same situation, or had something changed during the week that I'd missed?

I smiled at my inquisitor and gave it my best shot: "Pretty frightening, isn't it?" That seemed to be all he needed to launch into a monologue on Middle Eastern politics and his perception of the changing U.S. position toward the region.

I breathed a sigh of relief. He was in a lecturing mode and didn't require my participation. All the pressure was off. He didn't care what I'd read or hadn't read that week. He couldn't tell by looking at me that my greatest concern at the moment was the quality, color, and consistency of Alex's bowel movements. It was *not obvious to him that I had become an intellectual slug.*

After dinner I told Bernie and our hosts that we needed to leave early because the baby-sitter had an early morning engagement. It was a lie, but it had taken all my intellectual prowess to get through dinner; I didn't have any energy left for a lengthy after-dinner conversation.

As we drove home in the car, I asked Bernie whether he thought I was much less intellectually oriented than I had been when we'd met. He said, "Absolutely not. You've just got other interests."

That, of course, was what I wanted to hear, and we'd been married long enough for him to know that. Still, I wondered what had happened to the young student who had read thirty difficult books in a ten-week quarter. I missed the enthusiasm of the young editor who had become a specialist in art and antiques by poring through books and magazines. I wondered when the seasoned business professional had stopped reading the UCLA Extension catalog in the hope of finding courses that promised to open up new worlds of knowledge and passion.

That night, as I peered lovingly at my sleeping child, I knew it wasn't his fault that I wasn't exploring intellectual pursuits the way I used to. Part of it was the daily grind of the workaday world. Part of it was the time limitation of trying to work, raise a family, and take care of a household. Part of it was inertia.

And much of it could be corrected. It was time to remember how to pursue learning for learning's sake. It was time to reclaim my earlier passions. It was time to salvage my reputation as a talented dinner conversationalist.

ᕬ

SOURCES

Alumni programs
Books on tape
Community college courses
High school night school programs
Museum programs/classes
Professional association annual conferences
Reading clubs
University extension programs

EXTENDING WITH EXTENSION

Michael Bley is the assistant dean of UCLA Extension in Los Angeles, one of the largest university extension programs in the country. He is the father of one.

SB: Who takes university extension courses?

MB: Our audience ranges in age from their early twenties to their sixties and seventies. On average they are in their early to mid-thirties. Currently they are 60 percent women. Two-thirds of the students take courses for career enhancement. Fifteen percent are taking degree credit courses. The other 15 percent or so are taking courses for personal development or cultural enrichment.

SB: Why take an extension course instead of going else-where?

MB: People like being with their peers. Our program in particular is targeted to people who already have a degree. In fact 70 percent of our students have an undergraduate degree, and a percentage of those have graduate degrees as well. We run current and topical programs. The university offers a certain prestige and quality. In a city like Los Angeles we are also able to offer exciting speakers for special programs. In broadcast journalism we've had Jack Anderson, Linda Ellerbee, and Walter Cronkite. We had a course on American humor that Whoopi Goldberg participated in. We've had Gary Larson and Victor Borge. It's the same in the more unique fields. We had someone from the Smithsonian fly out for a course to discuss new findings about the ancient city of Ur.

SB: What are the most popular courses?

MB: Sneak Previews, which offers previews of upcoming or current films accompanied by discussions with directors, writers, and producers, is a consistent draw. We're selling out at about twelve to thirteen hundred people. The whole entertainment field—whether it's music, film, television, or theater, is burgeoning. There's a greater demand for language courses—particularly the Asian languages—which is driven by international trade and the growing immigrant population in Los Angeles. Interior and environmental design as a profession is a bit weak because of the economy, but there is an increasing interest in the hands-on courses, and the audience is very sophisticated. Computer graphics is strong, and so is accounting. There's growth in the areas of environmental science and fund-raising. There have been some very large psychology classes, but they are generally geared to professionals rather than lay people.

SB: *What can we expect to see in the future?*

MB: A change that is happening nationwide has to do with the format of courses. The traditional course offerings—which conformed to the degree credit system—met three hours a night and ran for twelve sessions. We were seeing a lot of attrition because it is so difficult for people to attend so many meetings without having scheduling conflicts. So we have also adopted shorter classes that run for four to eight sessions. These tend to be very popular. New York University and the New School have also offered shorter courses and lectures for some time. I suspect everyone will start adapting to this format.

EVERYWOMAN'S VILLAGE

"My mother, her sister, and a mutual friend were inspired to start Everywoman's Village in 1963 by a quote they read: 'Frustration is the shrieking of the potentialities,' " says Executive Director Laura Selwyn. "That kind of summed up how they felt. They were all homemakers. Their children were grown to the extent where they didn't need their moms at home all day long. So the three women joined forces and opened a center that offered courses that weren't available elsewhere. It was a grassroots organization, and it took off. In 1965, *Life* magazine did a feature story on them."

Today more than seven thousand people take classes at Everywoman's Village annually. Currently the most popular courses are in computer training; languages, including Spanish, French, Italian, Japanese, and Chinese; sign language; and the self-improvement areas. The village offers more than two hundred classes each semester in the arts, business/professional development, personal development, languages, and recreation.

"Many of our classes are geared toward opening doors that people just don't believe they can enter," says Selwyn, "particularly in the areas of artistic and creative expression. But we've always believed that a relaxed, informal atmosphere is most conducive to free expression and personal growth."

While Everywoman's Village is a nonprofit organization in Van Nuys, California, other programs throughout the country are offered through community colleges, high school night schools,

WHAT WE'VE GOT TIME FOR

■

"I'm a member of a book club that meets once a month. I also do the accounting for my husband's business as well as handle our personal finances. I have an M.B.A. and keep up with the latest business and financial information so that I can invest wisely."

■

"Not much. A preschool conference once a year. I wish I could use my college education. I feel as if I'm sliding backward."

■

"I read magazines and newspapers and take an active role in ongoing training with my business. It's a crapshoot, but I'm satisfied at this time."

■

and private organizations like the New School for Social Research in Manhattan, the Learning Tree in Manhattan, and the Learning Annex in Los Angeles.

Source: Laura Selwyn is the executive director of Everywoman's Village, 5650 Sepulveda Blvd., Van Nuys, CA 91411; 818-787-5100. She is the mother of one.

PARENTING RESEARCH
Written Sources

• **Books.** I am very much a book person, and I think that nothing—presently or on the horizon—is going to change the need for basic book reference. There's nothing that gives you the depth, the breadth, and the reliability of books. People shouldn't let all the bells and whistles delude them into thinking that there are better ways to get basic information. For that books are still the best.

• **Parenting magazines.** There are lots of choices including *Parent, Parenting, Child,* and *Working Mother,* among others. They will keep you up to date on a lot of things. You don't need to read them cover to cover. Read them in the bathroom. Cut out the articles that interest you. Use the magazines to glean important bits of information.

• **Government publications.** There are some very good consumer-oriented publications that many people don't know are available. *The FDA Consumer* (301-443-3220), which will keep you current on food news and health and safety issues, is so wonderful that we've bought a subscription for ourselves and five subscriptions as gifts for family and friends.

• **Specific parenting resources.** Parents who are looking for reviews of books, toys, videos, audiotapes, and computer programs should contact the Parents' Choice Foundation, Box 185, Waban, MA 02168; 617-965-5913.

• **Seek out hot lines and help lines.** The numbers change and go out of date, but there are some general numbers you can call to get help. If it's an 800 number you need, call 800-555-1212 and see if they have a listing. For government information, the Federal Information Center will refer you to the proper government agency; call 800-347-1997. For referral to the government organization dealing with specific health questions, call the National Institutes of Health at 301-496-4000. For referrals to other hot lines or help lines, call the National Health Information Clearinghouse at 800-336-4797.

Electronic Sources

There are lots of times when you want more information than you can find in a book—you've run into a problem, you want more current information, or you need urgent information. Since many parents these days are computer literate and have computers and modems in their homes, hooking up to an electronic database is not a problem.

Two electronic databases that are very consumer oriented and user friendly are the Prodigy Service and America Online. As long as you are familiar with the basic computer and the way it works with a modem, the programs are easy because you don't have to remember a lot of information. It's all point and choose. You can easily go into a menu and readily find a lot of information, which is highly varied. There are columns by recognized columnists, and these can be useful. Both services offer forums or chat clubs, where parents who have a particular problem can get advice in a public forum. It's different from e-mail (electronic mail) in that it's not a private communication—anyone can read your message—which is something to be aware of. Another important consideration when using electronic services is—apart from whatever is covered in basic services—time is money. You are paying for the time you use, although more and more the services have downloadable files that you can put in your own computer and read at your leisure.

• **The Prodigy Service.** Prodigy is available for a single flat fee per month, no matter how much usage. After start-up the only additional costs are for the telephone call to the nearest installation and for each electronic mail message over thirty. Among other services Prodigy offers parenting advice; a science center for kids, titled Nova and created by Boston's PBS station; a crafts center; stories; and games. For parents there is parenting advice, including articles from the National Parenting Center on topics like prenatal care and children's books. There is a *Parenting Guide*, loads of other information, and not surprisingly (because Prodigy is a joint venture of IBM and Sears and Roebuck), there are dozens of shopping services. For more information, contact Prodigy Services Company, 445 Hamilton Avenue, White Plains, NY 10601; 800-Prodigy (776-3449).

• **America Online.** Also charges a monthly fee. Its software and *Getting Started* guide are free. It provides a lot of services similar to those of Prodigy, and special ones such as a parent information network that has newsstand clippings on education, and parents'

"I'm an attorney, and I work three days a week. My older son is now in school, and the little one goes to day care. Working saves me. I also read in the evenings."

■

"I took and passed the American College of Sports Medicine Health Fitness Instructor certification after intensive studying. That was my goal, so I am satisfied for the moment. In time I know I will have the desire to take more courses and go for another certification."

■

"I'm a doctor, so I prepare medical lectures, read medical journals, and of course, I read the daily newspaper. There is never enough time to read or study or do pleasure reading. There is so much medical literature to keep up with that it's impossible."

■

libraries with downloadable software programs for children and for parents. It also has a *Parents R Us* newsletter. There is a wonderful service for school-age kids, including on-line classes, taught by professional teachers, and nightly on-line homework help for kids. For more information, contact America Online, 8619 Westwood Center Drive, Vienna, VA 22182; 800-827-6364.

• **CompuServe.** For parents who are more sophisticated computer users and have a wider and deeper need, CompuServe is the grandparent of all the electronic services. Nearly 1.4 million members can now access the service in most U.S. cities and in more than 120 countries. CompuServe members can choose from a selection of more than seventeen hundred databases, including information resources, communications, and transactional services. In the past CompuServe was more difficult for the layperson to use, but that is no longer the case. It has a new user-friendly program called the CompuServe Information Manager, which allows you to point and click. There is a monthly fee for basic services and there are special fees for special services. For anybody who is doing research beyond the minimum, CompuServe is really the place to go. For more information, contact CompuServe, 5000 Arlington Centre Blvd., Columbus, OH 43220; 614-457-8600 or 800-848-8199.

Source: Irene Franck is the coauthor with her husband, David Brownstone, of sixty reference books, including The Parent's Desk Reference, What's New for Parents, *and* The Women's Desk Reference. *She lives in Chappaqua, New York.*

KVETCHING

Kvetching *is Yiddish for "complaining." Its very tone connotes the word's essence. I've always hated people who complain; it isn't a very attractive quality. I used to believe that you either worked to resolve problems or you suffered them silently. I've never enjoyed being with people who whine.*

Now that I'm a mother, I realize that whining has its time and place. As much as I love motherhood, there are upsetting elements about it you just can't change, and the only real solace is a bit of complaining now and again. For example, my two biggest gripes about motherhood are increased housework and housewife-related chores and a lack of time for myself. I see no way to resolve either problem.

The first seems to come with motherhood. When I was in college and read The Feminine Mystique, *I snickered aloud when Betty Friedan said, "Housework expands to fit the time." In a discussion group for a women's history class, we uniformly condemned women who had nothing better to do with their day than housework and thus filled their entire day cooking and cleaning.*

Now that I'm a mother, I can't imagine I was ever so critical or so misinformed. I, who have far more interesting things to do with my day than housework and housewife-related chores—and am doing them neither for any sense of personal validation nor fulfillment—am amazed by how much time they take. Between grocery shopping, continuously tidying up after Alex, doing the laundry, preparing meals, and cleaning up after them, I could easily spend four hours a day engaged in these activities.

What's amazing is that I have only one child, a relatively small house, and a housekeeper who cleans once a week. If these chores are distasteful and repetitive for me, I can't imagine what it must be like for women with more children and no help.

Since the only two solutions I can think of are to hire someone to clean the house every day and to take over all housewife-related chores—a fantasy I can't afford—or to live in total sloth and go hungry (an unappealing solution at best), the only solution is to complain.

My second-biggest gripe—having no time for myself—had been partially resolved. When Alex was an infant, Vilma took care of him three days a week; now he goes to preschool. In a pinch, my mother, Claudia, and my sister took care of him as well, but there were still times when I wished I had the flexibility to be by myself, to go out to dinner spontaneously with friends, or to write late into the night without worry about the care and feeding of a small child in the morning.

There are ways I can resolve each situation on a short-term basis, but the larger issue, one of personal freedom, is not resolvable. I knew that when I decided to get pregnant. Ninety percent of the time I welcome my new responsibilities, then all of a sudden they make me crazy.

I've finally learned that the only way to feel better is to complain. Initially, my propensity to want to resort to this type of behavior bothered me. It is not in my gene pool. However, once I got comfortable with the concept, I realized I genuinely enjoy it. A critical element, though, is finding an attentive audience.

After much thought I determined that a good friend and colleague with a little girl six months older than Alex would be the perfect partner. She agreed. These days we schedule kvetching lunches once a week. She tells me about the annoyances in her life. I tell her about mine. We feel 100 percent better when we're done. It's a modern-day miracle. Had I known that whining would feel so good, I would have started years ago.

ॐ

A RABBI'S POINT OF VIEW

Rabbi Lennard Thal is the regional director of the Pacific Southwest Council of the Union of American Hebrew Congregations. He is married and the father of two and lives in Los Angeles.

SB: How would you define kvetching?
LT: The best English synonym is *complain*, but that just doesn't carry the same impact as *kvetch*. As is often the case in Yiddish—which is a language that is a combination of mostly German, some Polish, and a number of other European tongues—words seem far more colorful than they do in English. The color comes not only in the additional nuances but also in the sound of the language itself. Just as *chutzpa* carries much more punch than *nerve* or *gall*, *kvetching* is more onomatopoeic than *complaining*.

SB: In Leo Rosten's The Joys of Yiddish he says, "There is a prized lapel button that reads: 'Franz Kafka is a kvetch.' Who would you say are some of the most famous kvetchers and kvetcherkehs today? Why?
LT: In my opinion Joan Rivers is a good example, although in her case it may be an affected style. Richard Nixon, as president, was a world-class kvetch, always complaining how the press treated him so badly. John McEnroe has had his kvetching chronicled by national television—falling on his knees, banging his tennis racquet on the ground. In a sense John McEnroe could give kvetching a bad name because he crosses the boundary between kvetching and temper tantrums.

SB: Kvetching has become a fairly common expression among non-Jews as well as among Jews (at least in New York and Los Angeles). Why is this word so appealing?
LT: Aside from the word being colorful, there are very few words that begin with the letters *kv*. If Dan Quayle, who was certainly a kvetch, had changed his name to Dan Kvale, he might have been more popular.

SB: Why does kvetching make you feel better?
LT: I think that some people do it just to vent, and then they compose themselves and get on with what they're doing. Others simply cannot make it through a paragraph of dialogue without kvetching. These are the people who not only see the glass as half empty; but for them it's cracked as well, and the milk that was in it has gone sour because their child didn't put it in the refrigerator!

SB: For people who have yet to experience kvetching, how does one do it? Is there a particular tone, posture, or body language that conveys it best?
LT: I don't think you can take lessons; either you can do it or you can't. Maybe it comes with mother's milk. As far as posture and

OUR BIGGEST GRIPES

■

"Not having any time for myself. Feeling wholly responsible for two young lives. It's scary but not a real gripe."

■

"The chronic fatigue. Listening to other mothers complain about really minor difficulties or taking parenting so deadly seriously."

■

"Sibling rivalry, the routine of picking up, feeding, laundry. Too little discretionary personal time."

■

body language go, you don't have to look defiant to be a kvetch, but a whiny tone of voice certainly helps.

AN ALTERNATIVE TO KVETCHING: TIPS FOR HANDLING STRESS AND CHANGE

• **Acknowledge that motherhood is a time of stress and change.** This seems obvious, but some women may not realize how much change motherhood is going to cause, especially depending on the age and maturity of the woman. An unplanned pregnancy may be more difficult at any age. Women in their thirties and forties—who have well-established careers—may not be as well prepared for the different energy levels required, and the time and effort it may take away from their careers. On the other hand, some may feel that they had their younger years to do what they liked and are now more ready to devote themselves to being mothers, without feeling that they are "losing out."

There may also be a change in the sexual relations of the couple. Some women may not be interested in having sex in the first trimester or during the last month of pregnancy. Most doctors recommend abstinence during the first six to eight weeks after giving birth. This shift in sexual patterns has to be taken into account.

• **Recognize that there will be role adjustments.** Many women feel that the classic mothering role that includes all the tasks of child care has not changed for most families. Moms still change the diapers, prepare food, pick up toys, do laundry, and

---

ENGLISH KVETCHING EQUIVALENTS

• Beef	• Grouse	• Object to
• Bellyache	• Grumble	• Protest
• Bitch	• Kick up a fuss	• Snivel
• Complain	• Lament	• Squall
• Fret	• Make a fuss about	• Take exception to
• Fuss	• Moan	• Whine
• Gripe	• Mutter	• Whimper
• Groan		

feed the baby, especially if they are breastfeeding. In the modern house, where dads share some tasks, it doesn't always extend equally to cover baby-care needs. While moms may still be involved with work or a career, they may suddenly find themselves doing what seems to be an overwhelming amount of housewife-related tasks. How each mother chooses to deal with it may differ.

• **Set realistic expectations.** The best advice might be to limit expectations. Usually couples run into trouble when they expect duties to be shared equitably and life to return to prebaby conditions. But the baby's sleeping patterns may alter the energy level of both parents. Lack of sleep can aggravate all conflicts and needs to be taken into account. The parents' lives—socially and professionally—are going to be affected. There's also the superwoman expectation created by the media and advertising, which makes motherhood seem easy and satisfying when not all components of it are.

• **Talk with your spouse.** This is probably one of the most important elements of handling stress and change. Even though it's hard to find time to be alone with each other when you're not exhausted from loss of sleep, it's critical to talk about your lives, about the daily chores and trials, your feelings and fears, and your expectations and sharable pleasures. While you may not have the gamut of social activities you previously had—and as you learn to live with this new person in the house who doesn't always respect your schedules of sleeping and eating—many of the stresses may be reduced if you can talk and laugh with each other.

• **Develop a support system.** Whether it's a prenatal or postpartum exercise class at the YMCA, or a parent-child play group, meeting other moms of infants or toddlers, enjoying their company, and sharing experiences is very important. You don't want to become isolated. Many of these kinds of groups are replacing the old-fashioned community center of another generation and the close-knit extended families that are less and less part of the society in which we live. Observing other mothers and their babies will help you learn how to deal with the day-to-day problems you're having and to feel that you're not alone. This may be particularly important if your parents live in another city.

• **Allow yourself to kvetch a bit.** Unless it gets to be offensive and overpowering, there is certainly a value in kvetching; complaining (within reason) helps release some of the stresses, strains, worries, and concerns of motherhood. There are going to be bodily changes, schedule changes, energy changes that are part of having a child. There is also an overwhelming joy. If you have

"I work four and a half days a week and I don't have enough time to get things done, which is limited to evenings after our daughter's bedtime, nap time, or my two days off."

■

"That I am 'forced' into screaming and nagging and thinking ahead for every moment. Sometimes I don't smile enough."

■

"Dealing with my mother-in-law. Now that we live closer, and since our kids are her only grandchildren, every visit seems like an invasion into our lives. She competes with me. She competes with my mother. She makes suggestions I don't appreciate. It's awful."

■

WHAT WE MISS ABOUT PRE-CHILDREN LIFE

■

"Being able to sleep whenever I want to."

■

"Spontaneity. Being able to get tasks/projects completed. Getting up and going at will."

■

"I miss being able to go out to dinner with my women friends as often."

■

"Time, freedom to go anywhere—do anything. That lack of the frightening attachment that you have to your children."

■

a baby who smiles a lot, that's certainly going to be one of the bonuses, and babies who are loved abundantly will often smile a great deal. With all the adjustments that being a parent requires, it's important to remember that there are many rewards.

Source: Irv Berkovitz, M.D., is a clinical professor of child psychiatry at UCLA. He is a psychiatrist/psychoanalyst in private practice dealing with children, adolescents, and adults. He is the father of three and the grandfather of two.

ANOTHER ALTERNATIVE: OPENING UP

James W. Pennebaker, Ph.D., author of Opening Up: The Healing Power of Confiding in Others, *is a professor of psychology at Southern Methodist University in Dallas, Texas. He is the father of two.*

SB: Why is it healthy to disclose the private side of our lives?

JP: People naturally try to understand their world, and one of the best ways to understand something is to put it into language. Disclosure forces us to change the way we think and feel. If we have a unique or overwhelming experience, we may have a lot of emotions and thoughts jumbled together. By putting them into language we force some kind of structure or organization on them. The more potent the event is, the bigger the emotions, the more beneficial it is to put into words. But even talking about day-to-day experiences is helpful. Friends or a spouse can offer emotional support and advice or just listen as we organize our day in our own mind.

SB: In what ways can inhibiting our feelings affect our health?

JP: It seems to have two negative effects. First, the mere act of holding back is associated with increased bodily stress; we can actually measure changes when people are actively holding back. Second, when we don't resolve issues after having an upsetting experience, it impedes the cognitive process of organizing the event.

SB: How does all this relate to new moms?

JP: When you have a baby, you usually feel a great need to talk about it. I always found this quite annoying in friends until my wife and I had our first child. We talked about it so much, we started to bore our friends to death. Now I understand why. Having a baby is such a massive upheaval in your life—whether it is wonderfully positive as it was in our case or negative—that you can't help talking about it.

And did you notice when you were pregnant how people feel compelled to tell you the worst stories they've ever heard about pregnancy? They'll tell you about a pregnant friend who had a miscarriage in her eighth month. They also tell you awful stories about infants, fatigue, and the adjustment to parenthood. It's an interesting phenomenon and a bit difficult to understand. It's almost as if seeing a pregnant woman reminds people of all the unresolved stories in their own lives, so they start dumping out pregnancy-related stories without thinking of the consequences.

SB: *What are some tips for opening up to friends and loved ones?*

JB: Find somebody to confide in—and this may turn out to be more complicated than it sounds. The biggest problem when you confide in someone is finding a person who will accept you no matter what you say. And very often something you say might hurt the other person's feelings; it might change the nature of the relationship. On the other hand, if you can't be honest with the person you chose to confide in, or if you have to worry whether the person will be upset by what you have to say, then you are defeating the whole purpose of disclosure.

Writing is another way of opening up. When you find yourself thinking about something, dreaming about it, or worrying about it too much, set aside twenty minutes a day for three or four consecutive days and explore your very deepest emotions and thoughts associated with this topic. Write about what happened and how you feel about it. In many cases it is a good idea to keep what you have written to yourself. If you find writing difficult, consider talking into a tape recorder.

What is important to remember, whether you are writing or talking about your experiences, is that the purpose of disclosure is to help us integrate and organize our complicated lives. Good experiences and bad ones are often intertwined. Even positive events like marriage and childbirth greatly disrupt our lives and our self-image. Positive emotions and negative ones are most healthy when they are expressed openly.

"Time alone with my spouse, time alone, time with friends. Quiet, calm."

■

"Freedom. Travel. Quiet. Time to read a book."

■

"I miss my job with an architectural firm. I miss dealing with adults; a feeling of accomplishment; my independence."

■

"Being able to go to the bathroom by myself; going out with my husband; stimulating conversation with adults."

■

LAUNDRY

I once figured out that my paternal grandmother must have washed and ironed more than 21,900 shirts when my father and his three brothers were growing up. If you factor in my grandfather for that fifteen-year span (I'm estimating she ironed from the time the boys were three until they turned eighteen), you add 5,475 shirts.

When I used to hear my grandmother say with pride that everyone commented on how neat and clean her boys were, I never understood her sense of satisfaction and accomplishment. I couldn't imagine how anyone could find self-actualization doing the laundry.

My own mother does not know how to iron. Even when our family resources were slim, we always had weekly household help. It was from them that I learned how to iron, although my father's shirts were always sent out.

Having grown up in a family with an aversion to permanent-press fabrics, I developed certain standards. When I started college at Berkeley in 1968, I was undoubtedly the only person in the entire student body who left antiwar demonstrations early because I needed to do my laundry. I, too, wear only 100 percent cotton shirts, and they take hours to wash and press. Those days I couldn't afford to have them professionally laundered.

Once I began earning a decent salary, the first luxury I indulged in was sending my shirts out. When Bernie and I began dating, we were delighted to find out that we shared an appreciation for "real" fabrics. It may seem like a small and rather picky aesthetic, but it is reflective of an entire value system; it represents quality versus convenience. After we married, we were shocked to *find out how much our combined laundry and cleaning bills were, but we bit the bullet and continued to send our clothes out because it was important to us.*

Now that we've got Alexander, I am shocked to find that my priorities have changed. With all the other attendant chores of motherhood, I am absolutely unwilling to iron Alexander's clothes, and Claudia doesn't have the time. When Alex was an infant I spent one afternoon ironing a fancy cotton outfit and vowed I would never do it again. It was a surprisingly easy decision.

So Alexander is the first person in my entire family to wear cotton-polyester shirts and pants. What's amazing is that they don't look half bad. It has already had an impact on us. Recently, when I went shopping for a few items for myself, I tried on a cotton-polyester shirt for the first time in more than forty years. It looked great. I just couldn't bring myself to actually buy it; I didn't know how to tell Bernie. Maybe next time.

꒜

CLEAN CLOTHES TIPS

Sorting Secrets

Sort by color. Wash all whites separately, pastels and medium colors together, brights and darks by themselves. Pay special attention to white and lightly colored synthetics; they can pick up dark dyes from other fabrics. Check trimmings and decorations for colorfastness too.

Sort for soil. Separate those heavily soiled items from the lightly soiled ones since these items can pick up the extra soil from the wash water. Whites will slowly get grayer or yellower; colors will become duller and duller.

Consider specialty sorts.
• **The unmatched set.** Mix small and large items together in each load. This lets clothes move more freely, resulting in better washing.
• **The fabric types.** Consider the fabrics and how they are constructed. Separate loosely knitted garments and delicates from regular wash loads, then wash on the gentle cycle.
• **The lint losers.** Fuzzy sweatshirts, chenille robes, flannels, and new towels have a tendency to share their lint with other garments during washing. Wash them in a load by themselves—away from corduroys and permanent-press garments, which attract lint easily.

TIPS ON MANAGING LAUNDRY

■

"I do all the sheets on Monday, and the rest of the week I wait until the laundry basket is full and do it then. I try to keep up with it all week so that it never piles up."

■

"I wash clothes right away when I get home from work. My son thinks it's a fun game to fold towels and clothes. He helps me put things away. I also iron *faithfully* once a week so it's never more than a one-hour job."

■

"It's easier for me because I work at home and I can keep at it all day. I do a load in the morning and let it wash while I am cleaning the house. Sometimes I'll let it wash while I'm out doing errands. I never put clothes in the drier if I am going to be out, because once the cycle stops and the clothes sit for a long time, they get too wrinkled."

■

• **The fluorescents.** Hot pinks, bright greens, electric blues are often much less colorfast than other fabrics. Wash them separately or test them first before washing with other colors. For safety's sake, do not pretreat with stain removers unless you have tested them for colorfastness first on an inconspicuous area. Fluorescent colors may fade over time.

Laundry Products

Considerable diversity exists among laundry detergents. They are classified by general or light-duty performance and are available in granule or liquid forms.

General-purpose detergents.
• **Liquids** are especially effective on food, grease, and oily soils. They are good for pretreating spots and stains.
• **Powders** are good for general wash-day loads. They are especially effective for lifting out clay and ground-in dirt and thus are ideal for children's play clothes.
• **Super concentrates** are more compact and concentrated. Most liquid and powder detergents available today are concentrated. You often need only ¼ to ½ cup instead of the usual 1 to 1½ cups, so follow label instructions.

Light-duty detergents.
• **Laundry liquids and powders** are designed for hand or machine washing those lightly soiled items and delicate fabrics. They're ideal for baby clothes.
• **Dishwashing liquids** are designed for washing dishes, but some can be used for handwashing delicate fabrics. Read the label instructions. Do not use in automatic washers.

Laundry aids
• **Bleaches** convert soils into colorless, soluble particles that are easily removed by detergents, then carried away in the wash water. They brighten and whiten fabrics and help remove stubborn stains.
• **Enzyme presoaks** are especially effective in removing protein stains, like baby formula, blood, body fluids, dairy products, eggs, and grass. When added to the wash water, they also boost the cleaning power of the detergent.
• **Fabric softeners** decrease static cling, which is especially useful when washing permanent press and synthetic fibers,

make fabrics softer and fluffier, reduce drying time, reduce wrinkling, and make ironing easier.

- **Prewash soil and stain removers** are effective in pretreating heavily soiled and stained garments, especially those made from polyester fibers. They work well on oil-based stains like animal fats, body soils, cooking oils, cosmetics, and motor oils. Soap bars work well on fabric softener, perspiration, and tobacco stains.
- **Starches, fabric finishes, and sizings** give body to fabrics, make fabrics more soil-resistant, and make ironing easier.
- **Water softeners** help detergents do their job better by deactivating calcium and magnesium minerals, which make water hard.

Washing Away Spots and Stains

• **Identify the spot.** The more you know about what made the spot or stain, the more likely you are to treat it appropriately. That means you have a better chance to remove it and are less likely to set it further by using the wrong treatment. When in doubt, rinse or soak in cold water before treating or laundering.

• **Treat the spot immediately.** The sooner you attack the spot, the easier it will be to remove. Get into the habit of checking freshly washed wet clothes for stains that didn't wash away. Instead of drying them, pretreat the stains and wash them again. Drying can permanently set some stains.

• **Pretreat, plus . . .** Pretreating a stain before it is dried or set increases your chances for removing it. Use a prewash stain remover, liquid laundry detergent, or a paste made from a powdered laundry detergent and a little water. First, test for colorfastness by pretreating a seam or other inconspicuous area. Then launder the entire garment with a detergent—plus a bleach that's safe for the fabric.

• **Blot it out!** Sponge a stain—don't rub it. Rubbing only spreads it and may even damage the fabric.

• **Beverage stains: gone today, back tomorrow.** Beverages containing sugar, such as wine or ginger ale, may seem to disappear. But don't be fooled—they may still be there! Once the stain is exposed to the air, the sugar oxidizes and leaves an invisible stain, which ultimately turns yellow or brown. The stain never left, it was there all along. The remedy? Treat even those light stains you can't see immediately—before they dry.

"I do the laundry two to three times a week. I push myself to do it each time. I wash at night, dry in the A.M., and take the clothes out before they wrinkle."

■

"I wait until the laundry piles up so that I have enough whites and darks to do a full load. I do laundry in the evenings so my husband can at least fold things."

■

• **Using a bleach?** Prevent uneven color changes by bleaching the entire garment—not just the stain.

• **Old stains rarely fade away,** but it's possible. Try pretreating or soaking in a product containing enzymes, then launder.

• **Wash it away!** After treating a stain, launder the complete garment to remove any residue left from the stain or stain remover.

Source: Sorting It Out: Facts About Laundering, © *1991, The Soap and Detergent Association, 475 Park Avenue South, New York, NY 10016.*

MORE LAUNDRY TIPS

• I sort all my clothes. I separate whites and anything white enough to go with the whites. I wash dark clothes together. I wash blue and green clothes together because I wash them in cold water. With red clothes, I put them in the sink and test them to make sure the color doesn't come out. If it does, I wash them by hand.

• I spot the whites and wash them in hot water. When I find a spot, I take the article of clothing to the sink or to the bathroom and spread it out so I can spot it with 409 and scrub it with an old toothbrush.

• I wash all colored clothes in cold water.

• I turn all socks inside out to wash them. I turn them back when I dry them.

• If the instructions on an article of clothing say not to wring it or twist it, I usually wash it by hand or carefully put it in the washing machine in such a way that it doesn't wrinkle.

• I dry whites for the full cycle.

• I don't dry shirts too hard; I take them out of the drier before it stops. I hang them up even if I am going to fold them. They fold better and straighter when they're hot.

• If drying instructions say that a piece of clothing should be dried flat and not put in the drier, I still put it in the drier for a few minutes to get at least some of the water out. Otherwise it will never dry.

Source: Claudia Hudgens, mother of three, grandmother of five, and great-grandmother of five, has been a professional housekeeper for more than sixty years.

MALLS

I have always hated malls. Part of the reason is that I dislike shopping, so there has never been a good reason to frequent them. Part of it is that I believe if God had intended people to stay indoors in a temperature-controlled environment, She would never have created the sun and the sky.

With this type of attitude, it is not surprising that when a major mall was scheduled to be built within walking distance of our house, I wrote my political representative a harsh anti-mall diatribe. I suggested that the mall would not only destroy the quality of life in our neighborhood as we knew it, and create a traffic and parking nightmare, but also would attract an undesirable element of the population—shoppers.

It was built despite my protestations. And I am embarrassed to admit that once Alexander was born it became our home away from home. For the first six months of his life we walked there at least three days a week. It was convenient. It was a pleasant diversion. It was a meeting ground for new mothers. I had never seen so many infants in my life other than in the hospital.

The premier department store, Nordstrom, appeared to cater to mothers. Its ladies' lounge is so large and tastefully appointed; I could nurse Alex in comfort. It provides a changing table in the bathroom, a convenience I rarely find in other department stores. Staff members who used the bathroom and caught you in the act of nursing or changing your baby would smile warmly and murmur something complimentary about your infant. Nordstrom also has a lovely but casual café on the same floor as the ladies' lounge so that you can mosey back and forth as you eat your lunch, a helpful convenience.

On the days when Alex and I wanted a more business-oriented clientele, we would go to Century City, a lovely outdoor shopping center, which is five minutes away by car. Century City offers a far greater selection of places to eat, although the ladies' lounges of the two department stores are neither very attractive, convenient, nor child oriented.

So, suffice it to say that it was at Century City that I decided to breastfeed Alex outdoors in public for the first time in our respective lives. We had gone to lunch there with my mother. After we finished, she wanted to look at a sweater in a boutique. Alex and I sat on a bench outside one of the department stores waiting for her to return when he began to scream. This was one of the "Feed me immediately; I'm starving" screams that could be heard for a mile in any direction.

Unfortunately my mother didn't hear it. My debate was whether to push a screaming child in his stroller and try to find his grandmother to tell her we were going to make the trek to the third-floor ladies' lounge or to breastfeed Alex right where we sat.

It was the height of rush-hour lunch. Armani-suited, upwardly mobile professionals walked by us in droves. I quickly decided that I would probably never see any of these people again, nor did I think I knew anyone who worked in Century City, so I attached my kid to my breast, draped a receiving blanket over his head, and sighed with relief as he started sucking with abandon.

Two moments later my mother approached us, and while I thought no one could possibly know what was going on under the blanket, she audibly gasped. Much to her credit, she didn't say anything. Later, as we walked to the car, she did suggest that I walk in the sun so that the milk stain on my blouse could dry.

Now that Alex is older and I've gone back to work part-time, we've cut back dramatically on our mall visits. Recently, though, I did have to drop by Nordstrom to buy a present and then had to make a stop in the ladies' lounge. There was a new mother preparing to breastfeed. I murmured something complimentary about her child; she flashed a grateful smile.

I'm constantly amazed at how much I've changed.

A BRIEF HISTORY OF MALLS

Why they are so popular. Malls developed as a postwar phenomenon along with the spread of the population from the central city to the suburbs. As people increasingly were unable or unwilling to go to traditional central business districts, malls extended the retail distribution system to where people lived. Malls had significant advantages that central business districts didn't offer. First they provided parking. Second the stores were brand new. Third they were intelligently planned for convenience by having stores together on one site that was useful to visit, and they provided one-stop shopping opportunities.

What the mall building philosophy was in earlier years. The philosophy had several dimensions. One of the big mall developers was Sears. What it did was to build malls in areas before there was a population. From a real estate perspective that made sense because creating a shopping mall made the surrounding land valuable, and you did not need to depend simply on a retail income but could depend on substantial gains from the increase in the land value. In those early years the mall developers owned a lot of land in real estate around the malls they developed, particularly when those malls significantly led to residential construction.

But beyond the fact of the mall as a real estate phenomenon, the philosophy was that the site, in effect, would become the dominant business district for a population area. The developers would be able to bring to one site a substantial share of the retail income that those households or residences spent, and again in doing that would bring together stores in which people wanted to shop. This was facilitated by an increasing growth of national and regional chains, like Sears and some national speciality chains, like Radio Shack, The Limited, Foot Locker, Walgreens (which is almost a national drugstore chain), and Toys "R" Us.

What the current status of malls is. Now we're overmalled. There are more malls than are needed to provide retail services, so there are three fates that confront malls. The first group of malls are in prime locations that have significant tenants and important anchor stores, and those malls are, in fact, expanding and becoming an even stronger business district. There are not too many of those.

The second group includes malls that are having occupancy problems and are beginning to use their spaces in ways for which

MALLS: WHAT WE DO THERE

■

"My son enjoyed getting out in his stroller (and now running), and it's an air-conditioned environment in hot, humid Houston. It's easy to take him along, and he really likes looking at other people."

■

"Malls are great. It's a good controlled atmosphere. We have indoor and outdoor malls near our house. When's it's raining, we go and play in the toy stores and have lunch. There's a market in our mall, which makes it really convenient for me, especially when the weather is bad."

■

they were never built nor intended, such as libraries, drivers' license offices, various kinds of service facilities, senior citizen centers, and medical offices. These have become similar to what the old-fashioned traditional central business districts were—a central business district with secondary stores around it that offered many kinds of services and facilities you would never have found in malls. But with an overcrowding of malls, the people who own them or lease them are now willing to lower their economic investment return to have full occupancy.

The third group are malls that are going out of business, that are shutting down altogether. We're seeing malls that are closed down because they are redundant and there is no hope of turning them around.

What we can expect in the future. New malls are being built, and there are two kinds of malls that are popular. One is called the *power mall*, which is made up of stores that were never in the original malls. A typical power mall would be a Price Club, a Home Depot, a Toys "R" Us, and maybe a Circuit City. They are low-priced retailers that have big stores and huge selections, sometimes called *category killers*. In the past these stores tended to be outside of malls in much-lower-cost retail space. They are now being put into single-mall developments. They are not huge malls, they're not enclosed malls, but they're simply a combination of stores that a developer puts together.

The other development is the supermall. The prime example would be the Mall of America (which is detailed in the sidebar on page 217.) It can be described as a mall that's gone into festival retailing, thus becoming a tourist attraction. It has a theme park, an entertainment park, movie theaters, restaurants, and so many stores that it becomes as much of an event as going to Sea World or Disneyland. The mall has a drawing power that is almost national—certainly regional—in that only a share of its business comes from the local market. What these new malls have going for them is not only a modernity but also an entertainment dimension as well as a broad store selection that is designed to eclipse and crush lesser malls.

Source: George Rosenbaum is the chief executive officer of Leo J. Shapiro & Associates, a market research firm, in Chicago, Illinois. He is the father of three shoppers.

MALL OF AMERICA

Mall of America, which opened in Bloomington, Minnesota, on August 11, 1992, is the largest fully enclosed combination retail and family entertainment complex in the United States. At the center of the project is Knott's Camp Snoopy—a seven-acre indoor theme park with twenty-three rides and attractions. The thirty-one thousand trees, plants, and shrubs together with the streams, fountains, and ponds give the park a real Minnesota woods flavor. At night, 750,000 Tivoli lights produce a magical wonderland. For those who like rides, there's Paul Bunyan's Log Chute, which ends in a drop over a forty-foot waterfall, a sixty-foot roller coaster, a kite-eating tree, and Americana carousel, among others.

The mall is kid friendly, with rest rooms with diaper-changing area and family rooms designed for infant care. There's also a Knott's Camp Snoopy's Wilderness Theater, which hosts a variety of wildlife; a miniature golf course; an operating toy train display with more than thirty moving trains; and a seven-thousand-square-foot Lego Imagination Center that includes sixty large-scale Lego models and features flashing lights, animated motion, and a thirty-foot-tall crane.

Other interesting facts:

• Mall of America's 4.2 million square feet is five times larger than Red Square, which is eight-hundred thousand square feet.

• The forty acres of gardens surrounding Buckingham Palace would fit inside Mall of America.

• Mall of America's 13,300 short tons of steel is nearly twice the amount in the Eiffel Tower.

• There are 12,750 free parking spaces, forty-four public escalators, fifteen public elevators, ten sets of rest rooms, and 2.9 miles of hallways. An average of 8,340 strollers are checked out per week.

Source: Mall of America, 60 E. Broadway, Bloomington, MN 55425-5550; 612-883-8805.

"We go to look at new clothes and new toys. We also go because my daughter likes to look up at the bright colors and see the things there. It's a cheap way to entertain her."

■

"I don't go to the mall to entertain myself. I have a list, I know exactly what I want, and I do it fast so I don't give my kids time to drive me nuts."

■

"We don't live near one now, but when my son was little I'd take him there so he could practice walking in air-conditioned comfort. Alabama summers are real hot."

■

"Actually, I think I frequent them less—too much hassle. When we go, it's for a change of scenery and a trip to McDonald's to play with other children at their indoor playground."

■

"The food court at the mall is our favorite 'manageable' restaurant with kids."

■

"I went a lot when my oldest daughter was a baby. I would meet friends there and have lunch. As the kids got older, we'd go and play in the toy stores. It's harder now that I have two children, but it's definitely the place to go when it's raining."

■

MALL EVENTS

The purpose of mall events for children is to attract family shoppers. Mall events are always free, they are G-rated, and the trend is to have some sort of parental participation, according to Nancy Walters, president of Very Special Events in San Diego, California. "We're interested in using the mall as a destination for family outings, so we plan events where parents and their children can have a good time, whether it's a puppet show, a children's movie or new games to play." So what are some of Walter's most successful events?

"The Pamper Play-Offs was a national event in eighty malls across the country where moms and dads could bring their toddlers during the week for a preliminary 'race' (crawl) to be eligible to return on Saturday for the finals. The malls provided amenities, including diaper-changing areas and stroller-parking areas. It was an incredible promotion, and we had great media coverage."

"We do an annual event that's called 'The Sweetest Baby Face in the U.S.A.' It's not a beauty contest—because we're philosophically opposed to that—but it salutes the truism that every baby has a sweet face. Children are judged on personality and sweetness of expression. There's no entry fee. The winning babies and their parents from each mall win a trip to San Diego each year for the U.S. finals. The national champ wins a $5,000 mutual fund for future college expenses."

If you're interested in the upcoming mall events in your area, call the marketing department of your local mall, which will give you current children's event information.

Source: Nancy Walters is the president of Very Special Events, San Diego, California; 619-485-1171.

MARRIAGE

I love being married. Bernie and I lived together for four years before we said "I do." I was thirty-two; he was forty-four. I had grave reservations about marriage. My biggest concern was that our relationship would change. We had a strictly monogamous albeit highly flexible relationship. I didn't see any comparable role models among married people we knew.

The moment people married—even those who had lived together successfully for years—their previously harmonious households seemed to turn into War of the Roses. It was as if the whole institution of marriage had such a stultifying and restrictive tradition that even the healthiest of relationships couldn't survive it.

So it was no wonder I put off getting married as long as I could. Finally, after Bernie had repeatedly assured me that he was not looking for a Stepford Wife and I finally believed him—because, after all, he had been an absolute prince during the entire time we'd lived together—we decided there were no good reasons not to get married. And, in fact, there was one very good reason to marry: we loved each other.

Still, it was lucky we had resolved a number of issues before we set out on the marriage odyssey. Nothing is ever easy. When we went to see the judge (a family friend) who would marry us and he asked whether we wanted the long or short ceremony, he was very disturbed when I picked the short one. Oh, I was willing to love and honor Bernie, although certainly not to obey him. I was also willing to stick by him in sickness and in health, an important negotiation point since Bernie's older. But that was it. I would agree to very little else. The judge was quite concerned about the brevity of our *vows; Bernie wasn't. We stuck to the short ceremony. Any guest who sneezed during the nuptials missed our marriage vows.*

Once we were officially married, I am happy to report, nothing changed. Bernie didn't turn into Ralph Kramden (from "The Honeymooners"), and I didn't become Alice. The great thing about getting married was that the legality of it all did add the element of "future" to our relationship. When you've been living together, even if there's a strong commitment, and there was, it is more of a commitment to the present than to the future. Saying "I do" and "until death do us part" and meaning it is about as future oriented as it gets.

The biggest change in our marriage has been Alex's entry into our lives. He's altered every element of our relationship from sex to Saturday night dates. (We do both with less frequency.) The changes have not always been easy to adapt to, but we've managed fairly well because we established such a strong foundation before he came along.

Perhaps that's why I am always so amazed when I read magazine articles—mostly about celebrities—who have a child first and marry later. (Mick Jagger and Jerry Hall must have held the record until they married fifteen years later—after having two children— and then divorced.)

I am also surprised by my newfound disapproval of people who are living together. I think it's more than a case of middle-age latent Victorianism. It's that I know so many women who expected these relationships to evolve into marriage and were so sadly disappointed. Still, talk about the pot calling the kettle black . . .

It is quite unbelievable how people change, and of course I'm speaking from experience. These days my friends say I'm almost evangelical about marriage and children. I guess it's no worse a transition than Eldridge Cleaver selling jeans or Jerry Rubin operating a professional networking service.

Still, I am shocked when I begin sounding more like Phyllis Shlafly than Gloria Steinem. With all apologies to Ms. Steinem, I guess I'm just plain delighted that I've become a Mrs.

FROM MARRIAGE TO PARENTHOOD

Brad E. Sachs, Ph.D., author of Things Just Haven't Been the Same: Making the Transition from Marriage to Parenthood, *is a psychologist in private practice in Columbia, Maryland, founder and director of the Father Center, and the father of three.*

SB: What are the most difficult aspects of making the transition from marriage to parenthood?

BS: One of the most common problems is that couples often romanticize parenthood and imagine that having a child is automatically going to make their marriage better, but that rarely happens. Usually the addition of a child puts strains on a marriage, and couples react with disappointment. They assume either that they're doing something wrong or that their partner is. That becomes a self-fulfilling prophecy in which people begin to feel more alienated and polarized rather than coming together as a couple.

Another problem with parenthood is that many of the couple's resources begin to be compromised, whether it's time, sexual energy, sleep, spontaneity, or social life. They then start to feel frustrated and abandoned and begin turning to each other to satisfy all these unmet needs, which can sometimes make the marriage collapse under its own weight.

In addition, while most women, on the surface, say they want their husbands to be involved as parents, there is sometimes a conflict when a man begins to participate more fully. If a woman's primary source of her own self-esteem lies in caring for children and being the sole expert on child care, she may feel either threatened by or competitive with her husband once he starts to become more involved with child care.

On the flip side, of course, a lot of men may want to be more involved with their kids, but because their own fathers weren't involved with them, they don't know how. They don't have the road map that will guide them through this new territory and help them establish the kind of connection they'd really like to have.

SB: What are the most effective ways for dealing with these problems?

BS: First, couples need to allow themselves room to experience a range of emotions associated with parenthood. We're led to believe that we're supposed to feel only joyous, exhilarated, and delighted about having children, but we may also feel bored, irritable, angry, and exhausted. We shouldn't feel there is some-

HOW IT'S CHANGED WITH CHILDREN

∎

"Our oldest child is two and a half, and I don't remember life before him, although my husband and I have been married for fourteen years! There's definitely more stress, because we're both tired and rushed, but the flip side is that the children have produced an adhesive bond between us. We've created these great kids together, and we're both thrilled and proud of that."

∎

"We're almost always tired. But we were as ready for this as you can be, I guess. We like to watch the kids."

∎

"I miss the time we used to have alone with each other during the day on weekends. We get baby-sitters at night, but I miss long drives on Saturday, browsing together in bookstores, Sunday brunches, time to talk with each other without being interrupted, and hikes in the mountains."

∎

thing wrong with our partner (or ourselves) for feeling this way.

Second, it's important that men and women not rely solely on their spouses to work through these problems. They need to have relationships that are supportive and friendly outside the marriage. Again, the marriage shouldn't have to bear the full weight of all the problems attendant with parenthood. From my perspective as a therapist, I think it's healthy for couples to consider consulting with someone to give them some outside perspective and to help them rebalance or reequilibrate their marriage when there is a problem.

Finally, if I had to make one recommendation about the lines of parental responsibility and communication, it would be that men and women try to express their needs clearly rather than expect their partners to read their mind. So if a woman is feeling as if she needs more support, more involvement, and more participation from her husband, she should say "I need you to do the diapering in the morning because I don't have time to get ready for work" as opposed to "How come you don't do more around here?"

Likewise, a man should be specific about *his* needs. He may be feeling that whatever he does is criticized by his wife and so will just back off. Instead, he should say something like "It feels like whenever I give our baby a bath, you find something wrong. That makes me less likely to want to do more. Can we handle this differently?"

The more that men and women can be specific about what they want and need, the less room there is for error and misinterpretation. They can then develop the respectful compromises that are essential to any working family.

SB: In your book, you have a chapter "The Marriage of Sex and Parenthood." In what ways does sex change with parenthood?
BS: It changes dramatically, which is no surprise. I often encourage couples to find ways to broaden the way they define sexuality. For better or worse, couples usually define sex as going from point A to point Z, whatever that is. Once you have a child, you may not have the spontaneity, let alone time, and the sheer physical energy required for the previous kind of sexual interaction. Sex ultimately is a form of communication, and it needs to be treated as such. There are all kinds of ways to communicate, and the more ways that men and women can find to touch each other,

the more it will help their sexual relationship, even if the frequency of their lovemaking per se is less.

SB: As a husband, father, and therapist, what tips do you have for moms and dads who are trying to fit a baby into their relationship?

BS: The marriage has to be the priority; it is the keystone of a successful family. You can read all the parenting books you want, and spend all this time and energy with your child, but unless the marriage is a solid one, it's going to affect your child adversely. The marital relationship has to get as much care and nurturance as the children do. That may mean creating time together as a couple, finding ways to "date," scheduling time to talk on the phone, holding hands, or giving massages. Some parents feel guilty about leaving their child at home at night with a baby-sitter when they have left him or her during the day. I think it's a gift to children to display and model a healthy marriage.

WHEN COUPLES BECOME PARENTS

The Becoming a Family project was a ten-year study in which we recruited ninety-six couples comprising seventy-two expectant couples and twenty-four nonparent couples to find out what happens when partners become parents. Our study was unique in two ways. First, we tracked couples for seven years beginning at pregnancy and ending when the children completed kindergarten. Most other studies that detail the transition into parenthood stop somewhere in the first year or year and a half in the children's lives. Second, a randomly chosen set of parents in our study met once a week throughout the last three months of pregnancy and the first three months of parenthood in small groups led by couples who are trained mental health professionals. Some conclusions of the study follow.

Changes in identity and inner life. What we found about the women—over the first few months of pregnancy and beyond—was that the sense of themselves as mothers was, of course, increasing. The men, too, were developing their sense of identity as fathers, but when couples diagrammed these feelings using a pie as a symbol, the space was twice as big for women as it was for the men. How much of a woman's identity was based on motherhood

"Finally, after three and a half years, my husband is connecting with us as a family group by becoming more interested in family things—reading, playing, eating together, driving somewhere for burgers."

■

"Less sleep, less sex, more tired. My husband is more understanding of my time commitments."

■

"We really function as a team since we've had children. Things are definitely more stressful, but we work together really well, whether it's preparing meals or doing bath and bedtime. I love watching my husband play with the kids. He's so loving, such a nurturing father."

■

"Children redefine and expand on the word *love*, especially with a spouse who shares in the child care."

■

depended largely on the woman's sense of herself. What was diminishing was their sense of themselves as students or workers. For the men, even though the parent or father piece of the pie was getting bigger, the piece representing their perception of themselves as workers or students was staying the same size.

We think this is a pretty graphic, quick way of telling what happens to an awful lot of men and women during the transition to parenthood. She becomes more and more "mother," and she is very likely to give up her work or her studies at least for a time. His life doesn't change. That, in fact, becomes one of the new bones of contention between parents. Many of them have this new ideology that they are going to make a different kind of family from the one they grew up in—that it is going to be more egalitarian—but it is very difficult to pull off. The one aspect of their lives that did diminish for both women and men was the perception of themselves as partners or lovers.

Shifts in the roles and relationships within the marriage. Before their babies were born, we asked couples how they arranged the "who does what" of life, the household and family tasks, and how they predicted they would share the tasks specifically related to bringing up children: bathing them, feeding them, clothing them, and calling the doctor or the baby-sitter. When the children were six months old, eighteen months old, three and a half, and five and a half years old, we asked parents how the tasks were structured.

What we found was that they were predicting much more egalitarian relationships—not necessarily a fifty-fifty division of labor—than they actually were having once the children came along. As a group they were getting more traditional than they expected. She was doing more housework and baby care than he was; he was doing less than he expected he would. Their satisfaction with that aspect of life was going down, and their level of conflict and disagreement was going up. The number-one cause of dissension was the division of family labor.

Shifts in the three-generational roles and relationships. During the pregnancy most men and women made some attempt to connect with their parents even if they had not been in contact with their parents for quite some time. In some cases it was wonderful. Their families reconnected around a joyful event, the grandparents were excited, they had a lot to talk to their own kids about, and there seemed to be an avenue for reconciliation that was almost a new beginning. In other cases it opened up old wounds in ways that were obstacles to healing.

Changing roles and relationships outside the family. The men and women in the study wanted to be nurturing parents. What began to happen, though, was that the father felt it was extremely necessary to keep up with his work and his reputation at whatever he did because now he had a family to provide for. The mother was torn about staying home and going back to work. Her level of conflict depended on the kind of job and role she had as well as her image of what kids need.

A lot of the women did go back to work early. By the time the babies were a year and a half old, 49 percent of the women were back at work at least on a part-time basis. That meant a lot of pulls in different directions: harried, rushed days and nights trying to get everything done—the laundry, the kids, the meals, the work, and the car pool. However, the women who went back to work reported fewer symptoms of depression than the women who stayed home. It seemed as if they were saying that they were stressed but it was OK.

The pressures on families during the birth of a child are inordinate. The men in our study who could have taken paternity leave were hesitant to take it because they feared that they would be looked on as less serious workers. The women had even worse stories to tell about unsympathetic bosses or concerns and problems with work. The couples who met with us in groups began to realize this was a common problem, and knowing that made them feel better.

New parenting roles and relationships. What most men and women told us was that their friendship patterns were changing and that their friends who didn't have kids just didn't "get it." Their friends couldn't understand that the new parents couldn't be as spontaneous in arranging activities. The new parents couldn't understand it when their babies weren't included in group social activities. So the new parents began associating more with families with young children, who often were neighbors or acquaintances from the playground or the preschool. However, there is something about losing intimate long-term connections for a while that can leave parents feeling lost and vulnerable.

For many parents in the study, parenting roles were not changing as fast as they had hoped. There was some disappointment and disillusionment that our culture does not support families with young children. Even though people can read about it in any newspaper, couples seem to discover it on their own. At first they don't realize they are part of a bigger issue.

One of the dramatic results of the study was that the marital satisfaction of the couples who did not participate in our small groups (that met once a week for six months) went down in the first year of the study and went down even more steeply in the second. The couples who had been in our groups showed a slight dip in marital satisfaction from pregnancy to six months after the child's birth, but their relationships remained stable the second year. Until the children were three years old, there were no separations and divorces in this group, compared to 15 percent among the other parents in the study.

Source: Carolyn Pape Cowan, Ph.D., with her husband, Philip A. Cowan, is coauthor of When Partners Become Parents: The Big Life Changes for Couples. *They are codirectors of the Becoming a Family and the Schoolchildren and Their Families projects. She is a research psychologist and lecturer at the University of California at Berkeley and the mother of three grown children.*

MONEY

M oney has never been a motivating factor for me. I've always made career decisions based on interest rather than salary. I have never been willing to suffer boredom, dissatisfaction, or unhappiness at a job for the sake of money. I've been driven to accomplish things because of passion rather than economic return. I lived for many years with relatively few material things and was quite happy.

While I genuinely enjoy having money, I have never made enough on my own to support myself in the style in which I was brought up or in which I currently live. Without Bernie's salary I would undoubtedly live in genteel poverty. When we were a double-income family, we certainly earned enough to live comfortably if not extravagantly. We have always bought exactly what we've wanted and would rather do without than do with less.

We have never let money, or the lack of it, affect our lifestyle adversely. We know a number of people who make far more money than we ever have, and they don't seem to live half as well.

These days, with my part-time working situation, where I earn less than half of what I did when I worked full-time and have many more expenses, including child care, which is significant, we have little disposable income, and quite frankly, it's depressing. There is no impulse shopping. I don't know what I would do if I had to replace any of my good suits for work. We still eat out but much less frequently. We no longer buy any extravagant gifts, except for Alexander.

For someone who never thought that much about money, I genuinely miss my DINK (Double Income No Kids) status. It was great fun blowing a small fortune on a weekend getaway to Palm

227

Springs, buying Laura Biagiotti sunglasses and unlimited paper-
back mysteries without giving it all a second thought.

Now, when I contemplate all the attendant expenses of raising
a child these days—food, clothing, well-baby doctor visits, toys, child
care, haircuts, dental visits, and tennis shoes, to name a few—I
realize I may have made some ill-advised choices early on.

Maybe money should have been more important to me. Per-
haps passion is an overrated motivating factor. I wonder if it's too
late to apply to law school.

ڪ

MONEY-SAVING TIPS

Baby-Sitting

• Consider asking a family member—grandparent, sister-in-law, or
cousin—to take care of your children on a weeknight. Exchange
a service or chore. You or your spouse could offer to mow their
lawn on Saturday morning if they provide a few hours of care for
your kids. Bake an extra tray of lasagna, a ready-to-use dinner,
for their weeknight stay or for them to take home for a future
meal.

• Start a baby-sitting co-op or baby-sitting pool with a group of
parents. In many areas, established cooperatives are already in
operation. Ask around and you will probably find one. If not,
initiate one with a group of people who share your parenting
philosophies and values. The idea is to establish a baby-sitting
exchange for a group of families within a certain geographic
area. You can earn "credit" by baby-sitting for others in the co-
op. Other participants, in turn, watch your children when you
need to go out.

• Suggest to a neighbor, "One Friday night, we will watch all of
your kids from 6:00 P.M. to 9:00 P.M., and the next week it will be
your turn."

Coupons

• Get together for tea once a week and exchange coupons with
friends, a church group, or co-workers.

• Shop the stores that are offering case-lot sales or buy-one-get-one-free. Buy only if prices are reduced and you really can use the item. Let's face it, if sardines were available at five cents a can, it would be no bargain for my brood.

- File coupons alphabetically or by aisle if you always shop at the same store. As you write out your shopping list at home, note the items that you have coupons for by putting an asterisk next to the product on your list. When you get to the checkout booth, retrieve the appropriate coupon from your file and match it to the item in your cart.

Going Out with Your Spouse

- To celebrate a special occasion, go out for lunch instead of dinner. The meals are usually lower priced at this time of day. The decor is the same, the celebration is the same, but your check will probably be half the dinner price. Leave your children with a relative or friend; use the baby-sitting co-op.

- Keep your eyes open for the two-for-one specials that are often advertised in the paper. Restaurants offer these specials so that you will become familiar with the restaurant and thus become a full-paying customer in the future. Try not to go for the appetizers or drinks, or your bill will increase substantially.

- Another way to eat hearty and save simultaneously is to go to a "happy hour" that serves appetizers and a variety of snacks and hot and cold hors d'oeuvres. For the price of one drink or a soda and a tip you can engage in fun conversation with your spouse and sample the goodies from the "happy hour" buffet.

Grooming Items

- Make your own baby wipes. Place a small amount of baby oil and some soapy water in an empty baby-wipe container. Add folded damp paper towels to the container, and you have your own premoistened minitowels for necessary baby cleanups.

- For the kids' hair, buy the store-brand shampoo and dilute it with water, usually 50:50. The less expensive brands work just fine, and you won't get upset when the kids use more than the recommended portion.

- Save the little slivers and almost-finished bars of soap. Sew a

NOTABLE POST-CHILDREN CHANGES

■

"It used to be two incomes supporting two people. Now it's one income supporting four people. We've given up expensive vacations, restaurants, and new clothes. We drive older cars. We try to watch daily expenditures more closely."

■

"There's more planning, less on-the-spot spending. We set goals and have learned to be patient. We make more joint financial decisions."

■

washcloth on three sides. Put the soap in the three-sided pouch. When the kids wet the washcloth, the soap foams up and bubbles go all over them, getting them clean while they have fun.

Source: Patricia Gallagher, author of five books, including Raising Happy Kids on a Reasonable Budget *and* How to Entertain Children at Home or in Preschool, *is the mother of four and lives in Richboro, Pennsylvania; 215-364-1945.*

COMMON CENT$ BUDGETING

Setting financial goals. A key to gaining financial control is to set your financial goals. Each family's goals will be different depending on their value system and what their family wants to obtain. Immediate/short-range goals are those goals you want to reach immediately or within a year. Middle-range/long-range goals may extend from two years to retirement.

If you're thinking about getting pregnant—and you want to reduce your income from two salaries to one—you should plan for a few years. If you are pregnant, you may want to totally rethink your current budget to save a considerable amount of money in a short time. Ask yourself, "Where do we spend the most money? Can we adjust our lifestyle? In what ways can we substantially reduce our expenditures for food, entertainment, transportation, or clothes?" Your goal, in this case, would be to estimate how much money you need and to figure out how much you could put aside monthly.

If you are expecting a child, a long-term goal may be to begin saving money for college expenses when your child is eighteen years old. For long-term savings, remember the rule of 72, which is that you divide 72 by the rate of interest you're getting, and it will take you that many years to double your money. If you are investing $2,000 and you are getting a 6 percent interest rate, it will take you 12 years to make $4,000. The whole idea is that time and money will make an investment grow. Whether you can save $50 a month or $150, begin putting money away each month.

Goal savings record. Once you determine your goals, set priorities. Then decide when you need the money and estimate how much money you will need. If the goal is to save $2,000 to decorate a nursery, do some research to determine the estimated costs of buying a crib, a mattress, linens, a changing table, a lamp, a rocking chair, or whatever else you'll need. If you've got a year to save, divide the total amount by 12, and in this case you will need to save $167 a month. Keep track of what you actively save each month. Some months you will have major expenses and may save only a portion of what you need; you'll have other months to make it up. If your goal is to buy a car or to save money for private school or private lessons, the premise is the same. For longer-term goals, factor in the rates of inflation and interest. Consider working with a financial planner to examine your options with long-term investments.

Getting the money. When you know how much money you need, ask yourself where you're going to get it. Do you have to cut back or postpone some other purchases? Do you need to work overtime or add a part-time job? How will you realize your goals?

Yearly budget. The yearly budget is designed to give you an overall picture of all your yearly obligations at a glance. By detailing your yearly expenditures, you can see what you are spending, when you are spending it, which months will be heavy and which months will be light, and how you can budget for new debts or expenses. Begin with the fixed expenses, which may include mortgage payments, life insurance, and automobile expenses. Fixed estimated expenses are those you know will be due but you do not know the entire amount, whether it's tax preparation, utilities, or school tuition. Estimated expenses, including major medical and major automobile, home improvement, children's activities, holiday events, gifts, and vacations, are expenses that are not immediate but are important to try to manage within your budget.

When people are willing to do this exercise—and go item by item—they are always shocked by how quickly the amounts add up. When you can anticipate what expenses you project for the entire year and compare what you make with what you are spending, it suddenly becomes obvious why you're short, which months you need to save for, and where you might budget more effectively.

Monthly budget and expense record. The monthly budget is a more specific way of analyzing monthly expenditures. Cost out your fixed amounts, fixed variables, occasional expenses, and installments. Anticipate your expenses besides your bills. Over time you can see what groceries, children's expenses, telephone

"We spend more money, and we spend it on our daughter. We've moved since she was born and got a bigger place, which doubled our rent. Now there's a cleaning woman and a baby-sitter once a week. We haven't taken our daughter on a big vacation yet, but we go on many more weekend trips than we used to. So there's no savings and only one income since I'm not working these days. Money is definitely tighter for us now."

■

"We moved to a small town for a better quality of life. I had to give up my career. I work part-time and make about one-quarter of what I made before."

■

"We spend most of our money on the kids and very little on us. Health insurance costs have increased for us. We still take nice vacations, but it isn't as relaxing. We go out every Friday night, and my parents baby-sit. It is too expensive to go out to eat and pay a baby-sitter."

■

"We're much more conscious of money. I'm no longer working, and we feel that. We spend a lot on toys. We're more concerned with long-term savings, and I've told my husband he can never retire! We used to go out every weekend, but we don't because baby-sitting costs are so high on top of a movie and dinner. We'd rather go to parties at people's houses than go out alone, just the two of us."

■

"I don't buy business suits, and we have moved from Los Angeles to Idaho, where the cost of living is much less."

■

bills, clothes, and medical costs average each month. Determine which bills need to be paid in a given month and which ones can wait. Coordinate your bills and expenses with your take-home pay.

Designing a list of needs and wants. This is a way to acknowledge that your needs and wants and those of your children are valuable but that you may not have the money to buy *whatever* you want *whenever* you want it. As new needs and wants come along, jot them down, but don't buy items unless you can afford them. When you see something at the mall that you want, jot it down on your list to see if it's more or less important than the other items you've noted. When you do have an extra $50 or $100, refer to your list and choose what you'd like to get. Needs and wants are different from goals because they are smaller-ticket items and are ongoing. Keeping a list gives you more control, a better sense of focus, and a better sense of discipline than impulse shopping.

Source: Judy Lawrence, author of The Budget Kit: The Common Cent$ Money Management Workbook, *is a personal budget consultant. She can be reached at P.O. Box 13167, Albuquerque, NM 87192; 505-296-8792.*

AN INTERVIEW WITH THE FRUGAL ZEALOT

Amy Dacyczyn is the founder of The Tightwad Gazette *newsletter. She lives in Leeds, Maine, with her husband and six children.*

SB: You're the mother of six children, and you live in a hundred-year-old farmhouse on seven acres that you and your husband bought when your combined salary was $30,000 a year. You've said your kids lack for nothing. How have you done it?

AD: When we got married ten years ago, we were in our late twenties and early thirties. We were starting kind of late in life, and we had nothing in the bank. We didn't own anything of any value. We'd spent a lot of years working and wasting money. When we got married, it was evident to both of us that if we were going to make it we were going to have to change, because I really wanted to be a stay-at-home mother. We wanted to live on one income, have a big house, and a lot of children. So the only alternative was to learn how to save money better. For a period of about seven years we simply scrimped and saved and learned a lot on the way. We ultimately saved about $49,000 out of the $30,000-per-year income. In addition we spent $38,000 (not out of savings) on new vehicles, major appliances, and furniture.

SB: *Why did you start* The Tightwad Gazette, *a newsletter on how to live frugally?*

AD: We had selfish motivations. We were looking for a home-based mail-order business that we could do from a rural area. One day I had the idea for a newsletter for tightwads, and I realized I had all the basic skills to put it together. When I was in my twenties, I went to art school and worked as a graphic designer in the Boston area, so I come from a design background. I knew how to do a publication very inexpensively, I can illustrate, and I can write. I also knew I had a unique way of looking at money that no one else seemed to have. I was more precise. For example, conventional wisdom says if you use a lot of coupons, you'll save tons of money on your grocery bill. I said to myself, "How cheap does this item have to be for it to be less expensive than the same item I can make from scratch?" Yet time was a precious commodity for me. I routinely calculated how much time it would take to do a task. If it took me an hour, and I saved $10, then my time was worth $10 an hour. I developed a lot of ideas and ways of handling money that I had not really seen expressed on paper before, and that was incorporated into the newsletter.

SB: *You've now got sixty-thousand subscribers and employ six to eight full- and part-time employees. To what do you attribute the newsletter's success?*

AD: It's a combination of things. Somebody recently wrote to me and said that I had reinvented thrift. Someone else said that I'm giving advice our parents and grandparents knew a generation ago but that we've never learned or forgotten. When I started my newsletter, it was at the right time. We were struggling through a recession. There was and is a cultural shift where we're recognizing that bigger is not necessarily better. We're seeing baby boomers who started having children in their thirties and have changed their values. They are working hard but are scrambling to figure out how they can live on less money so they can spend more time with their families. Balancing family and work is so difficult. Something's got to give, and that's what I think we're all learning.

SB: *Now that your business has expanded, do you still have the time to continue looking for the least expensive option?*

AD: I'm in a unique situation because my business is frugality. I have to be continually searching on my own for new ways to do things so I can give good advice. Much of the newsletter comes from my own experience. My husband is now fully retired from the military, and he doesn't work in our business anymore. He takes care of our children and does all the shopping and diapering, gardening, canning, and pizza making. So that really frees up my time to concentrate on my two basic priorities, my family and my newsletter.

I feel very strongly that my children need to be raised in frugality, because if they're not—if I raise them in a style that I can afford to now—they wouldn't learn how to save or have any respect for this kind of life. They benefit tremendously in many different ways. For example, I've started making quilts from recycled materials. It's time consuming, but it's been really beneficial for the children to watch me do this. They're learning how to design a quilt, how to create it, and how to do the mathematics so the squares come out right. They iron, they clip, they watch the whole process of how the quilt is made. They may never make quilts when they grow up, but they may engineer some other projects. Our children have a tremendous appreciation for things that come from yard sales. They have no problem with second-hand clothes whatsoever. It's just become part of their lives.

SB: *What tightwad strategies can you recommend for new mothers?*

AD: • Breastfeed your children. You'll save about $500 a year. Aside from the health benefits, a lot of women don't fully comprehend how expensive formula feeding is until it's too late.

• Use cloth diapers. We have toddler twins, and we still spend less than an hour a week rinsing, washing, and folding diapers. If you're pregnant, and you anticipate that people will be giving you gifts at showers, let them know you plan to use cloth diapers. It's a big money saver.

• When you're introducing solid baby foods, never buy them. Many adult foods such as soft vegetables, potatoes, and applesauce—things you can mash—are good. You don't have to buy a food grinder. Use a fork. I've never bought baby food; it's just one of these recent inventions people think are necessities.

• Find baby equipment at yard sales. Borrow items. We had four children, and we didn't think we were going to have any more, so we gave everything away. Then the twins were born. We managed to reoutfit everything for under $50. A note of caution: make sure used cribs are safe—that the slats are not too far apart, that they don't have lead paint on them, and that they can be put together properly. The other items, like front carriers, strollers, and car seats, can be borrowed or bought cheaply. There are many items you don't need. I had six kids who hated the jumpers you hang in the doorway. The windup swings kept our babies happy for only a month.

• Improvise. I've never had a baby changing table. A towel on your bed and a little shoe box next to your bureau with the things you need works fine. A baby swing can work as a high chair. Bear in mind that children are infants for a short period of time. Suggest that your relatives give you diapers rather than those little baby outfits that the children will wear for six weeks. With a little creative borrowing and a lot of ingenuity, you can get most of the baby items you need for free.

• For a free sample copy of my newsletter, write to *The Tightwad Gazette*, RR 1, Box 3570, Leeds, ME 04263-9710. We'd also be happy to send my article called "Bringing Up Baby Cheap," which is a page and a half of ideas on equipment substitution and suggestions on what you can do without, what you don't need, and how to improvise.

MOTHERHOOD

When I was in kindergarten and my teacher wouldn't allow me to hammer with my left hand, my mother went to school and told the teacher not to try to change me into a right-hander (a common practice at the time). From that moment on, I knew my mother would always stick up for me. And so she has.

In elementary school my mother, as well as almost all my classmates' mothers, didn't work outside the home. While my mother was the Blue Bird leader several times, participated in school activities, took our Camp Fire girl troop on an overnight, wrote a column for a weekly neighborhood newspaper, volunteered at a home for disturbed children, played tennis, worked for political candidates, wrote poetry, had letters to the editor of the Los Angeles Times published with regularity, and spent her summers devising all sorts of fun and interesting activities for us, I always wondered what my friends' mothers did. Their level of activity seemed to pale in comparison.

In high school all my best friends' mothers worked. They were respectively a high school art teacher, a nurse, a staff member for the Social Security Administration, and the co-owner of a family-owned Chinese hand laundry. Two of them were divorced; I had never known anyone who was divorced. I vaguely remember feeling sorry for all of them because they had to work. In those days few middle-class women worked. My mother's life seemed so privileged in comparison.

When I came of age—with the advent of the women's movement—I not only wanted to work but also felt that it was the only way I could make an important contribution to society. For many *years I forsook marriage and motherhood, partially because of my burning desire to find a career that I loved.*

I never thought to ask my mother how she felt about my lifestyle. Luckily for me, she is not one to offer unsolicited advice. Luckily for her, I never positioned my choice as a rejection of hers; I said only that different times required different actions. In truth, I did believe that perhaps women of her economic background and circumstances—middle-class women who never worked—had a limited perspective. There were years when I felt that raising children, volunteerism, and even social activism weren't enough; at least not for me.

So I charted a new course. For twenty years I've had a succession of jobs—some very glamorous, others not. I learned what the working world is all about—and found it oddly dissatisfying. Either the work was exciting but not meaningful, or it was meaningful but boring, and I rarely worked for anyone I felt was a particularly good role model.

It has been only in the last few years, after many therapy sessions, that I could see that I had been unrealistic to think that the work environment—and the people I worked for—could satisfy my personal and professional expectations. And it suddenly became apparent to me that my mother's life choices were more satisfying for her than mine had been for me. The job of being a wife and mother, her writing, her causes, her friends, and her myriad cultural, educational, and social interests have made her life very rich.

Now that I'm a mother, I'm not sure I think any other calling is more important, and the "career" is as challenging as any I've had. The work is eminently more satisfying, and the payoffs are inestimable. It's a roller coaster of emotions. It brings out the best in me. I've never had a job where they cared if I was loving, patient, supportive, and flexible; but my son does care and seems to be thriving. And finally, I have a wonderful role model—my own mother—after whom to pattern my behavior.

I only hope that when Alexander is forty-something, he will love and admire me the way I love and admire my mother. Since he's already left-handed, at the very least he'll know that I won't let anyone try to change him. I'll stick up for him, always—as my mother has done for me.

ॐ

WHAT OUR RELATIONSHIPS WITH OUR MOTHERS ARE LIKE

■

"She is my best friend—I can tell her anything. She is very supportive but doesn't butt in unless asked. She is lots of fun to be with, whether it's just her and me or all of us together."

■

"It used to be that I was the person who made it all worthwhile for my mother. Now my daughter is that person. My mom and I have always been close. It's both wonderful and strange to see her so close with my child. I love watching them together, but I'm also a little jealous. What's been really interesting for me is that I view the choices my mother made as my parent in a much different light now that I'm a parent myself."

■

A LOOK AT THE ''PRONATALIST'' PERIOD

Judith D. Schwartz, author of The Mother Puzzle, *writes on women's health issues. She is married and lives in Evanston, Illinois.*

SB: *How has the popular culture affected our views of motherhood?*

JS: In recent decades alone, there have been times that were antimotherhood and times that were pro-motherhood. An obvious example is the postwar era, when there was so much support in the culture for having lots of children. Then things changed. We had the feminist movement, the sexual revolution, the Pill, and then the ecology movement and the Vietnam War. People were asking fundamental questions like ''Is this a society in which we want to bring children into the world?'' So the fertility rate went down, bottoming out in 1976.

In the last few years motherhood has come back in a very big way. We're in what we can refer to as a ''pronatalist'' period—suddenly, it's in to have children. If you look at the celebrity profiles in the women's magazines, they're all about who's pregnant, what they wear when they're pregnant, what they eat when they're pregnant, why they're better people since having children, and the litany goes on. Even in the tabloids it used to be ''Who's sleeping with whom?'' Now it's ''Who's having babies?''

Advertising has played into the trend. Advertisers have always told women we should be beautiful. Now we're supposed to be beautiful and have beautiful children who, of course, behave beautifully. Products that have nothing to do with children feature children in the ads. The perfume industry is a good example. In the 1980s perfume ads relied on images of sexual attraction, exotic landscapes, and enormous wealth. Now they're selling home, family, and children.

SB: *Why are some moms—particularly those who grew up in the late sixties and seventies—approaching motherhood with such ambivalence?*

JS: It has a lot to do with how we've been raised. Our generation is the first to have been raised to identify with our mothers domestically and with our fathers professionally. So the model of who we're supposed to be is in itself contradictory. We feel we should be the perfect stay-at-home full-time mothers that our mothers were (or at least the model of motherhood at the time), and at the same time we should be as successful as our fathers were (or as we wished them to be). We're ambivalent because to play both roles is a tremendous task, especially because we lack models that integrate the two.

SB: What are the most common fears that the mothers you interviewed had about motherhood, and how did they resolve them?
JS: Fears ran the gamut. A lot of women feared losing their identity, especially when work had played a large part of who they were. They were afraid of what would happen if they stopped working or even just shifted the balance. When you've gotten your confidence from your work and that's not going to be your main focus anymore, who are you?

Many women were also afraid about what would happen to their relationships with their husbands or partners. Many of us go into marriages today expecting a greater degree of equality. We expect our experiences within the marriage to be more alike than different. So our husbands marry us thinking they are getting ambitious career women, and suddenly they're not if we decide to have babies and we want to stop working. So the fear is whether our husbands will still care about us if we become full-time mothers and whether they will find us as exciting in our new roles as in our old ones.

SB: In your chapter "Sex, Babies, and Rock and Roll," you say that the sexual revolution drove fertility underground. How have things changed in the nineties?
JS: Everyone is talking about babies and about "making them." Whereas in the past having a child marked the end of sexiness (in society's eyes), today being fertile is seen as a badge of sexiness. Reproduction has replaced sex in the public imagination. We're jaded about sex, but reproduction has a kind of thrill. If I put a sign outside my door that said, "Do not disturb; we're fooling around," no one would think twice. If it read, "Do not disturb; I'm ovulating," that would be pretty provocative.

SB: In writing your book, did you solve "the mother puzzle"?
JS: The conclusion I came to is that it's not something you "solve"; it's a matter of evolving. I found it liberating to realize that what I and many women feel is a result of societal pressure. We have a right to our ambivalence. It is the price of our complexity and the complexity of our lives.

"Fair to good. I come from a dysfunctional family, so there is a lot to work out. We have come a long way, but there is still room for improvement, especially on my part."

■

"My mother still deals with me as a child. Our relationship isn't great."

■

"My mother and I have always been close. What's funny to me now that I'm a mother is that I understand my mother's side of our relationship more—that intense love that can move you to tears or anger."

■

"I'm more realistic about my mother's limitations. It's taken me a long time to learn how to tell her what my needs are. I find that I'm able to do that with greater ease when it's about my kids. She can be very critical, and I've seen her be that way with my older son. In response, I can't believe that I actually was able to say 'Maybe it would be better if you did this rather than that because you really hurt my son's feelings.' It was amazing. She felt terrible for weeks but has made an effort to change. I never could stick up for myself."

■

"I had a pretty good relationship with my mother before I had kids, but it's changed and gotten better. I love that she's as interested in my children as I am. When they were infants, she was interested in every burp and poop. It was wonderful to have someone care about them like that. She never tired of my stories about them, and now that they're older, she is still as interested. I understand her worries more now that I'm a mother. When you're the child, you just want to fly. As a mother I worry too."

■

MODERN MOTHERHOOD

Eleanor Morin Davis, Ph.D., is a psychoanalyst, a faculty member of the Center for Modern Psychoanalytic Studies, and codirector of the New Center for Modern Parenthood in New York City. She is the mother of two.

SB: *What is the New Center for Modern Parenthood? What services do you provide for moms?*

ED: We're a small private practice of psychoanalysts and psychotherapists who do special programs for parents, conduct parent education, and provide family therapy. We offer a pregnancy-to-parenthood education/therapeutic program that combines emotional and physical preparation for parenthood, including a parent education program for women during pregnancy where they talk about the whole issue of pregnancy and becoming a mother; a Lamaze-plus course that focuses on the physical preparation for childbirth and continues to deal with the emotional and psychological issues; a postpartum mother and/or father support group; and a series for parents of children one to six years old.

We developed our program because our psychoanalytic experience has taught us that women, couples, and babies need a lot of help during this period of their lives. It is a crucial, vulnerable period in which either positive emotional growth or severe psychological damage can occur. Our program helps parents learn how to help their children develop a positive sense of self that can enable them to grow, fulfill their potential, and contribute in today's world.

SB: *Why is it so difficult to be a mother today?*

ED: One of the major reasons is that women have such enormous conflict about it. They have so many options and so many choices these days. Today we demand more of women than ever before, and yet we give them less of what they need, particularly women who are mothers. On one hand we devalue the role of *mother* if a person is "just" a mother. If she's a working mother, we expect her to go back to work shortly after giving birth and breastfeed to boot. On the other hand, the structure of the workplace is such that many of the basic emotional and psychological needs a woman has related to mothering and motherhood are not met.

The primary need, of course, is for a mother to have time to be with her baby over an extended period. I strongly feel that women need a minimum of six months—preferably a year or two—before they go back to work. The idea of a six-week maternity leave is damaging to both the woman and the child in the long run. It doesn't allow them to develop the kind of close and empathic relationship that the baby and the mother both need. Women need time to heal from the exertion of giving birth, both the physical and the emotional exertion, and we don't give them that time either.

SB: *What are some of the most significant changes and/or realizations we can anticipate upon giving birth and assuming the responsibilities of motherhood?*

ED: Motherhood stimulates women to mature, to grow, and to discover parts of themselves that they consciously did not know were there. It allows them to get in touch with their deepest, most primal human feelings—feelings of dependency, longing, affection, love and caring, but also feelings of anger, hatred, resentment, and jealousy; many issues they thought they had resolved.

After all, people experience a wide range of emotions toward a baby, toward themselves, and toward their parents. When you're dealing with a new baby, you're dealing with many layers: the baby, yourself as a baby, your unconscious memories of yourself as a baby, the people who parented you, and yourself as a parent. When your needs as a baby are reawakened, you may also revive the disappointment and anger that you had at your own parents, who didn't meet all your needs. No parent ever does.

And, of course, your baby makes such great demands on you that these feelings are rekindled in you as well. If you learn that you *have* these feelings, and if you learn how to work through them, that will make you stronger within yourself, and you will be better able to help your child deal with these feelings when they arise.

Having a child may also allow you to become more forgiving toward your own parents. Once you understand more about the responsibilities and difficulties of parenting, you can see what they went through and how they either succeeded or failed. More often than not, you will have more tolerance toward them.

Another big change you can anticipate is that parenthood is full of surprises. No matter what anyone tells you about how it's going to be, you won't know until you get there. People often say "I am going to raise my child this way," and they are trying to give their child what they weren't given. They are then shocked when they hear their own parents' words coming from their mouths. All the things they vowed they would never say to their child—things they repudiated—start coming out, and it's often a big surprise.

HOW MOTHERHOOD HAS AFFECTED US

■

"It's just so real. It's exhausting but remarkably fulfilling. It isn't neat and tidy. It's anger and love and gratefulness."

■

"It is great! I never knew how intense the emotion would be. I feel so much love for my daughter. People told me it was different, but I didn't understand."

■

"The hassles, especially with infants and toddlers, are not the issue I thought they'd be before I was a mother, and the joy and love are fantastic. The challenges are huge, but I learn a lot about myself in the process."

■

"It's what I expected, only it's harder to be a good parent and have a career."

■

"The intensity of love is all-encompassing and wonderful. I am not as patient as I thought I was. I delight in my children's growth more than I could have imagined."

■

"It's better because it is a whole new dimension of feeling and worse for the same reason. There is so much to lose. I never felt that way before."

■

"I have a much broader sense of responsibility. It has helped me delight in the world of life versus concentration on professional accomplishments. It has brought a new dimension of love to my relationship with my husband."

■

SB: How can women best prepare themselves to become mothers, and what can they do on an ongoing basis so that they feel comfortable and confident in this new role?
ED: Keep talking. Talk to other mothers, join mothers' groups that are led by a professional or peer groups. Sometimes it helps just to talk even when you don't find a solution. In groups I've led, I've had women come in totally unable to deal with a particular issue, and after they've talked it out, and the group has talked it out, they feel better. When they come back a few weeks later, and someone in the group asks, "What happened with such and such?" they often answer, "Oh, I don't know. It just doesn't seem to bother me the way it used to."

ADVICE AND TIPS FOR NEW MOMS

Adjusting to motherhood is just a huge shock. It's really the first time any of us have had to put someone else's needs before our own on many different levels. That's the biggest change: to be responsible for someone else's life. It's not something you can prepare for.

Then there are the obvious other adjustments, such as being tired, not having any time to yourself, and having the relationship with your spouse change. If you've given up a job or have taken time off from work, that is a kind of wedge out of your identity and may affect your feelings of competence.

The range of feelings of new mothers is just extraordinary; joy, anger, sometimes despair, great feelings of love, and connection. It's like a roller coaster of emotions, but I don't believe in trying to overcome those feelings. Part of the process is learning to accept those feelings, knowing you're not alone. That's why it's so important to connect with other new mothers who are in the same boat. You should also try, as best you can, to carve out some time for yourself when you can take care of yourself and focus on your needs.

What advice and tips on the following issues do I have for mothers of newborns?
• **Crying.** Give yourself time to learn to interpret your baby's cries. It's trial and error at first for you *and* your baby. Crying is your baby's initial way of communicating as she learns to adjust better to the outside world. If you recognize early on that you can't be the magical-fix-it person all the time, you will be better off.

• **Spoiling babies.** With my first baby I thought holding her too much would spoil her; by the time I had the second one, I knew better. Holding babies reconnects them to the world they're most familiar with, which is the world inside your uterus. When you hold your baby, she is physically in touch with you; she feels your body, your warmth, and your movement.

• **Getting out of the house.** One of the keys is to get very organized ahead of time. Write a list of everything you'll need, but try not to take too much with you. Again it's a question of trial and error. The first time you'll undoubtedly take more diapers and pacifiers than you can use in a week. Then you'll realize you can eliminate them. It's important to practice; your first outing shouldn't be to your cousin's wedding. Keep your expectations in line with reality. Don't expect things to go perfectly whatever that may mean to you. Almost everybody in the world has had a baby, and people can be really accommodating. You will be much more conscious about this baby than they are. Other people really don't care if your baby cries in public; we just think they do. They're actually a lot more flexible and forgiving than we may think.

• **Establishing order in your life.** Recognize that as new mothers and fathers we need a period of adjustment when we let go of our previous expectations of ourselves. That's where the real conflict comes. We expect to be the competent, organized, get-things-done type of people we once were, and it's very frustrating when we can't be. The reality of having a baby is that the baby interrupts you all the time and takes a lot of your time. The key to keeping your self-esteem intact and feeling competent is to change your expectations. If you can say to yourself, "my main job right now is to rest and focus on my baby and try to get to know him or her," then just being with the baby will seem like an accomplishment.

Source: Frances Wells Burck, author of Babysense: A Practical and Supportive Guide to Baby Care *and* Mothers Talking: Sharing the Secret, *is the mother of three and lives in South Nyack, New York.*

"I've stopped doing a lot of things—flying airplanes, skiing, sailing, and photography—because of lack of money, time, and resources. Now I'm a mom, and I have completely changed, and I wouldn't want to change that for anything!"

■

"It's humbled me."

■

NAMES

I have always liked my first name. When I was in elementary school, there were five other Susans in my class; I thought that was "neat." I called myself Sue all through school. When I started working, I became Susan. I thought it was wonderful to have a name you could grow with.

I also liked having a straightforward name. In the fifties, when I was born, the names were somewhat synonymous with the times. My friends were Nancy, Barbara, Kathy, Ann, Bobby, Mark, and David. People with unusual names were considered a bit odd.

For twenty-seven years I was Susan Mary Schwartz. I always thought Mary was a rather Christian middle name for a Jewish person. But in Judaism, while you don't name children after living relatives, nor do you usually give them the same name as someone who has died, you do use the same initials of loved ones who have died. So I was named after my great grandparents, Sarah and Max. I was, at the very least, grateful my parents didn't pick Minnie or Maidel for my middle name.

My last name is another story. I have been ashamed—on a long-term basis—of only one thing I've done in my life. When I was twenty-seven, I changed my last name from Schwartz to Bernard. In retrospect I can't imagine why I did this. I still am not sure if it was because I wanted a less "Jewish-sounding" name or if I just wanted to reinvent myself. In either case, more than a decade later, I am still embarrassed by my decision. Still, for whatever it means, Susan Bernard is who I've become.

When it was time to pick a name for our unborn son, I knew I had some difficult decisions to make. My father was dying, my *hormones were raging, and I was concerned with not only our son's first name but his last one as well.*

Should it be Rotondo, Bernie's last name? Should I change my last name back to Schwartz out of respect for my father? Should our child have a hyphenated last name? What should be hyphenated? Schwartz-Rotondo? Bernard-Rotondo? This is further complicated since my father's first name was Berny, and my husband's first name is Bernard, although he calls himself Bernie.

In terms of a first name, I had always planned to name this child after my maternal grandmother, Anne. Now that my father was dying, I wanted to name the baby after my father and my grandmother. In Judaism they say that the spirit doesn't rest until someone is named after the person who has died. So we had only two letters of the alphabet we could use for naming our son, A for Anne and B for Berny.

After much thought, we chose the name Alexander Bernard Rotondo. The last name had become a fairly easy choice. I ultimately decided that since I was no longer a Schwartz, it was ridiculous to consider that as part of a hyphenated last name.

The process of choosing our son's first and middle names was much more difficult. It consumed the entire ten-month pregnancy. Given all the other variables, we also had to determine whether a half-Jewish, half-Catholic kid with an Italian last name should have a Jewish-sounding first and middle one to reflect his entire heritage. I thought that Aaron Benjamin Rotondo sounded ridiculous. Bernie liked it, but then his family has made some interesting name choices: his cousins are named Matthew, Mark, Luke, and John.

We picked Alexander because it was the name we both liked best. We picked Bernard for obvious reasons. When I think back on all this, it still gives me knots in my stomach, although I do love Alexander's name, and I am thrilled he is named after my father and grandmother. He couldn't be named after two better people; his name has great sentimental value for me.

I only hope when he turns twenty-seven, he doesn't change it.

NAMING NUANCES

How kids feel about popular names. Young kids really like having a popular name, except if things go to an extreme and they are one of five Ashleys in their class, which causes an identity problem. When they get to be older—early teens—they will probably love having an unusual name. But it depends on the environment they're growing up in. If it's someplace like Greenwich Village or Beverly Hills, where there is a certain cachet to having an unusual name, that's a positive. If they're in middle America, there's a good chance that they are going to be teased if their name is distinctive.

What psychologists say about offbeat names. This is more complicated than it sounds because it's not just offbeat names that create problems. Usually psychologists are dealing with unpleasant names; names with disagreeable connotations; names like Gertrude or Hester that are not currently in vogue. The research in the past seemed to show pretty conclusively that names do make a difference in terms of social acceptability and success. These days, that theory is not as prevalent. A name is only one factor out of many. If, for instance, someone is named Elmer and people hear the name, they might be put off. On the other hand, if they spend any time with Elmer and he has positive qualities, like good looks and a great personality, the name becomes irrelevant.

What to keep in mind about nicknames. Derogatory nicknames like Peewee, Shorty, and Curly are dying out. The use of diminutives isn't. A lot of parents these days want their children to be called by their full names, but they often aren't. So if a diminutive that parents absolutely detest is attached to a name they like, parents should think twice about the original name. Many parents are getting around this by deliberately picking names that don't have a short form, like Clare and Kyle. That's another solution.

What it's like for a boy to be a junior. This again is a double-edged sword. The positive element is the carrying on of the family name and identification with the father. The negatives are a loss of individual identity and the child feeling overshadowed by the father's image. It's also important, if you do make your son a junior, to avoid confusion by calling him a different name from his father. Usually, however, the child gets stuck with a shortened version of the name—in its juvenile mode, such as Bobby or Petey—for life. On the other hand, there are an inordinate number of "successful" men who are juniors, including Robert Redford, Clint Eastwood, Robert De Niro, Alec Baldwin, Marlon Brando, Tom Cruise (who is the fourth person in his family with that name), and virtually all the astronauts. So who knows?

Naming tips. Don't think of it as naming a baby; think of it as naming a person. The name you pick is, in some ways, the person's identity for life. I am totally against bizarre spellings of names and cuteness in general. Consider the last name carefully. Say it out loud. If there are older siblings, think of how the names sound together, because you'll be saying them together all the time. Think carefully before you pick a trendy name. Discuss it with your mate: men sometimes tell the woman to go ahead and pick any name and then resent it afterward.

Source: Linda Rosenkranz is the coauthor of four books on baby naming, including Beyond Jennifer and Jason: An Enlightened Guide to Naming Your Baby. *Her daughter's name is Chloe.*

MORE NAMING NUANCES

Cleveland Kent Evans, Ph.D., author of Unusual and Most Popular Baby Names, *is an associate professor of psychology at Bellevue College in Nebraska and a member of the American Name Society. His niece and nephew are named Ashleigh Marie and Charles Alexander Elliott.*

SB: How important are names?

CKE: They are important in determining a person's self-concept. One of the first ways a child is identified is by his or her name. But a name is not as important in social interaction as some of the research has suggested. If you force people to make judgments about hypothetical individuals on the basis of a name, they will resort to stereotypes. Then it looks like people with unusual names are at a disadvantage. However, when you start adding other information about the person, most of the effect of the name washes out. So names by themselves have an impact on prejudice in those situations only when the name precedes the person without a lot of extra information.

SB: How do we name our babies?

CKE: Most people spend a lot of time thinking about the child's name before he or she is born, but there are gender differences. A fairly common pattern is that of the wife coming up with a list of names and the husband vetoing the ones he doesn't want.

People from different educational backgrounds have different ideas about what names are appropriate. One of the ironies is that most children who get named after wealthy, glamorous characters on soap operas are children whose parents are less affluent and less educated. Stanley Lieberson, a sociologist at Harvard University, who studied birth certificates in New York State, found—when

WHY WE PICKED THE NAMES WE DID

■

"Our daughter's name is Whitney Marie. My dad climbed and loved Mt. Whitney, and he's passed away. My mother's name was Marie, and she's also deceased."

■

"We picked Nicholas because boys find it harder to have odd names. We wanted to name him Nicolo. We chose Gianina for our daughter because of its Italian style."

■

"Both our sons were named after relatives who passed away the week before they were born."

■

he had access to a mother's educational level—that during the seventies and eighties many less-educated mothers named their daughters Crystal (based on the character in "Dynasty"), while Emily was the choice of mothers with graduate degrees.

SB: *What are the trends?*
CKE: The biggest trend is simply that everybody seems to be looking for "different" names rather than more common ones. The top ten list of names accounts for a smaller percentage of all the children who are born.

People of different ethnic backgrounds tend to choose names differently. If one can generalize, within the African-American community there is a trend to pick names that are specifically African-American. Within the Asian community there is a trend to assimilate to the general Caucasian naming patterns. One of the ironies here is that children of recent immigrants often get so-called American names that are old-fashioned like Nolton or Gladys because the parents are not acculturated enough to know they should be naming their children Brittany and Joshua. Within the Latino community there are the traditional names like Jose and Maria, but there are other names, like Vanessa, which are popular because of Spanish television.

SB: *Are there regional differences?*
CKE: In the working-class South, you see more names like Eddie, Bobby, and Johnny on birth certificates. There are more Katies in the North than in the South. Other than that, you tend to get more East-West differences, not just on the West Coast but using the Mississippi River as the dividing line. The East Coast is more conservative, so names like Robert, William, Stephen, and Mary are more popular in the East than they are in the West. The Northeast has a lot of Irish-American names—Ryan, Sean, Patrick, and Shannon. Nebraska, more than all other places, seems to have even fewer "common" traditional names.

Utah—with the Mormons—is the other place that has some fairly unique names. Part of the reason may be that the birth rate is so much higher than in the rest of the country and there are more children to name. Whatever the reason, in Utah they pick up on fads very quickly. Ten or fifteen years ago they were the first people to widely use the name Brittany, which is big everywhere now. These days they're using names like McKenzie, Madison, and Sydney for girls and Colton, Tyson, Schuyler, and Colby for boys. There is a growing usage of these names elsewhere, but it started in Utah.

SB: In your most recent naming survey, what are the top twenty names for boys and girls?

CKE:

Girls		Boys	
Ashley	Emily	Michael	David
Brittany	Stephanie	Christopher	Joseph
Jessica	Rachel	Joshua	Ryan
Sarah	Chelsea	Matthew	Justin
Amanda	Elizabeth	James	Daniel
Megan	Jennifer	Andrew	Stephen
Samantha	Lauren	Brandon	Zachary
Caitlin	Nicole	Nicholas	Jonathan
Kayla	Courtney	John	Robert
Katherine	Amber	Tyler	Jacob

GUIDELINES FOR NAMING YOUR BABY

• **Namesakes.** Probably the greatest number of strange, weird names that are uncomfortable for the person who has them are foisted on children in loving memory of some namesake. Names that were appropriate in a previous generation or two or three often sound archaic, if not downright awkward, to contemporary ears. If you feel compelled to honor some friend or relative's memory, consider choosing a contemporary version of that name or simply starting your child's name with that initial.

• **Nationality.** I recently encountered the name Diego Goldberg. Names that cross ethnic and nationality boundaries are often not complementary and come across as a bad joke. Standard American names can easily go with most last names of almost any national origin. But when a highly ethnic name of one national origin is matched with a last name of another national origin, the result is often discordant rather than harmonious.

• **Religion.** It is possible to reflect your religious origins or beliefs in a name choice without making the name boring or stereotypical. You can show pride in your religion without naming a Jewish child Abraham, a Catholic child Mary, and a Muslim child Mohammed. Religious names can be a straitjacket; watch out.

• **Gender.** Psychological research indicates that it is a lot more uncomfortable for boys to have names that are commonly used for girls, such as Shirley or Carol or Leslie, than vice versa. Boys may be teased more readily about their masculinity. Girls, on the other hand, could actually benefit from the perception of being more

"We originally picked out a name that I loved, but when my husband told his co-workers what it was, they all said it was too common. So we bought several books of baby names and looked for a more unusual name, but one of substance as well. We chose Taylor."

■

"I picked a name from the book of 3,000 Christian names. We toyed with some others, but in the end we stayed with the name I'd always had in mind."

■

"We picked Bryce Ryan because we wanted a strong name. We didn't want diminutive nicknames. We also wanted to incorporate our Celtic heritage."

■

"We went through family names, and then, after looking through five different baby name books, we finally found one we liked. When my younger son was born, I thought we'd never find another boy's name we liked, but we did."

■

"We chose Damian from living in Honolulu for Friar Damian, who worked with the lepers. We picked Maggie (actually Cecilia Margaret) because we loved Maggie but wanted her to have a 'full' name for her adult years. We picked Brandon because I loved it from a leading character in a novel I'd read years before."

■

active, more competent, and more aggressive by having a name that is also commonly used for a boy.

• **Number of names.** Most people have three names. Most bureaucratic forms have space for three names. If you don't fill in one of the spaces, there could be a problem. If you have more names than there are spaces, there could be a problem. Enough said.

• **Sounds.** You don't have to be a poet to be able to hear the advantages of putting three-syllable first names together with one-syllable last names or vice versa.

• **Rhythms.** Test the rhythmic sound of any name combination you come up with by substituting the sound of "dah" for each syllable. That will help you make an informed rhythmic choice.

• **Pronunciation.** I would hate to be asked several times a day how to pronounce my name by people who see it written and are clueless. Wouldn't you?

• **Spelling.** I would hate to be asked several times a day how to spell my name by people who hear it. Wouldn't you?

• **Popularity.** I would hate to be the fifth boy named Michael or the fifth girl named Jessica in kindergarten. Wouldn't you?

• **Uniqueness.** Many parents hope their child develops unique personal characteristics and believe a unique name will spur them on their way. The problem is that many unique names come across as strange, are hard to spell, are hard to pronounce, and are confusing as to gender.

• **Stereotypes.** You'd be surprised to discover that just about any name you can think of creates an impression in people's minds. Before you settle on a name, definitely consider what impression it makes. Why saddle your child with a losing image or a weird one?

• **Initials.** Your child may not plan to monogram his or her initials on a shirt, but you can be sure he or she won't if the initials spell some awful word.

• **Nicknames.** Most names have common nicknames associated with them. If any of those nicknames are derogatory, you can bet your child's classmates in school will use them.

• **Meanings.** Every name has a meaning that you can look up. It is nice when the meaning seems appropriate, but that's not necessary.

Source: Bruce Lansky is the author of three books on baby naming, including 10,000 Baby Names *and* The Baby Name Personality Survey *(for which he surveyed 75,000 people). He lives in Wayzata, Minnesota, and is the father of two.*

NEIGHBORHOODS

I live in the same neighborhood in which I grew up. When I met Bernie, he owned a house that is five blocks away from my parents'. For years I have frequented the same cleaner, pharmacy, jeweler, hardware store, and stationery store that my mother does. In Los Angeles that's a bit of an anomaly.

Before Alex was born, we talked about moving across town to a wonderful neighborhood in Pasadena (home of the Rose Bowl), where the houses are known for their architecture and the lots are much bigger. The downside was that it's about fifteen degrees hotter in the summer, much less convenient for us because everything we like to do is on the west side of town, a longer commute for Bernie, and you can breathe there only from October to June. The rest of the year the smog is unbearable.

Besides, we like our crowded little neighborhood. We're centrally located: it's twenty minutes to the airport, downtown (if there's no traffic), and the beach; ten minutes to UCLA; and five to the closest park.

Our house is a half block north of a busy commercial street. While I wouldn't have picked this location, it turns out to be quite convenient. Alex and I do most of our errands on foot, and few people I know have so much so close.

There are two good public elementary schools in our neighborhood within walking distance—one that I attended. That is a terrific advantage for us. I believe in neighborhood schools, and I'm hoping that when Alex is older he can ride his bicycle to school.

There are also two parks, two golf courses, public tennis courts, a post office, and a neighborhood library within walking distance. There are three markets, two malls, dozens of neighborhood restau-

rants, and fifteen movie theaters we can drive to within minutes. There is a delicatessen, a church and a temple, a half dozen banks, a movie studio, and Starbucks.

It takes Bernie and me seven minutes to drive to work. Sometimes, when we wish we lived at the beach, in the mountains, or in a more rural area, we think again and delight in our proximity to everything.

For better or worse, this is the neighborhood in which we're raising our son. I know there are prettier neighborhoods and less crowded ones, neighborhoods with bigger houses on larger lots and more historic buildings. There are also neighborhoods with more kids, and I'd like that a lot.

But our neighborhood does have a history—mine and that of my family. When Alex is older, I can show him where I attended school, where the pollywog pond used to be, where his great grandparents played golf, and where his grandfather and I won tennis tournaments. We can go to the public pool where I learned how to swim, the library in which I learned how to read, and I can point out where the best hills are for bike riding.

Yes, there are better neighborhoods, but not many in which you can see where your mother grew up and walk to your grandmother's house in five minutes. It is for these reasons that I'm delighted that Alex is growing up in my neighborhood. I hope he likes it.

A REAL ESTATE BROKER'S VIEW

Kendall Rojas is the vice president/director of relocation for Fred Sands, 11611 San Vicente Blvd., Ninth floor, Los Angeles, CA; 800-292-2656 or 310-820-6811. She is the mother of three, and has moved fifteen times over the last twenty years.

SB: What elements define a neighborhood?
KR: In the past a neighborhood was a very small area of your immediate neighbors and the people you knew quite well. Today a neighborhood encompasses more of the area you live in because your friends are not necessarily your neighbors or your immediate living companions. Of course, today there is a big difference because so many of us are two-income families—everyone works, so you may not even know if your immediate neighbors are going to be home.

SB: What criteria make a neighborhood a "good" one?

KR: In their immediate neighborhood people usually look for homogeneity and a pleasant environment. If they have young children, their first priority is generally to determine the quality of the schools even if their children won't be in school for a few years. Second, parents are interested in a secure area where their children can play outdoors safely. They might ask if there are parks and sidewalks for their kids to ride bikes. They depend on us to tell them which areas are safe and which areas are good for young children. Our agents all live locally, so we refer prospective buyers to agents who live in the areas in which the buyers are interested.

SB: How is the definition of a "good neighborhood" affected by regional differences?

KR: In the South, neighborhoods tend to be more like the old-fashioned neighborhoods in which we all grew up—no matter what part of the country we lived in. In the Northeast there are larger properties, much bigger yards. But buyers are also looking at a totally different climate. I think they want to look for larger houses because they are indoors a great deal. In Southern California our outdoor area is more important to us although the properties tend to be smaller. A play area for children in Los Angeles may consist of a cement area with a basketball hoop and a place to ride bikes. The Midwest tends to be more like the Northeast. When you get into the Southwest, it becomes more like California because even though there is lots of land you are looking at smaller properties and again, more of an outdoor climate.

SB: Where are some of the best places to buy these days in terms of bang for your buck?

KR: Right now there are places in Missouri, South Dakota, and Utah where the cost of living is quite low and you can get an awful lot of house for your money. Actually, you can get a lot of house for your money almost anywhere in the Midwest compared to what you would pay for a house in Southern California. Texas is becoming a really big place for companies to move to because the cost of housing is not expensive and there are no state taxes.

SB: What advice do you have for families who are relocating?

KR: If you are brand-new to an area, talk with a good relocation department of a real estate firm. It's important to discuss your

WHAT'S BEST ABOUT OUR NEIGHBORHOODS

∎

"I know everyone on my block. There are lots of little children and also a fair number of kids who baby-sit. Everyone is friendly in the old-fashioned sense. Sometimes it seems a little too much, but it gives us a feeling of security. When we're going out of town, five people offer to bring in our paper or feed the dog. It's nice not to worry about our house or safety. My husband was out of town recently, and my son got sick. My neighbor told me to call her day or night if I needed anything. That's pretty great."

∎

"There's proximity to lots of amenities: a setting in the woods, schools, and a mix of people. It's centered around families and children. It's safe. Everyone keeps up their property. There's lot of space to walk and bicycle."

∎

needs with people who are familiar with the entire area. Then set up tours with agents who work a local area. What we do when people call us is to counsel them on where they'd like to live after they tell us what their needs are: How far are they willing to commute? Where are they going to be working? What is their price range? What are they looking for in the way of schools? Then we set them up with agents in however many areas we feel honestly fit that person's profile and suggest that they take a look at one or two houses in each neighborhood. Once you've found a neighborhood, you zero in on the house you like and can afford.

RATING METROPOLITAN AMERICA

• **Cost of living.** The difference between a high-cost area and a low-cost area really amounts to less than 2 percent of the household budget for consumer items like food, clothing, haircuts, and sporting goods. What you need to be concerned about is housing and taxes; they make up about 80 percent of the difference between the cost of living in any two areas, whether it's New York City or Joplin, Missouri.

• **Jobs.** The big reason why some seven million people move between states every year is that they are looking for work or being transferred by an employer. Be careful of places where too many workers get their paychecks from the Department of Defense, from construction work, or from low-tech manufacturing.

Be leery of high unemployment rates in growing places; job-seekers are likely to be newcomers rather than established residents. Look for places with federal or state government employers; these areas are less likely to be cut back and also represent some opportunity. Consider places where major employers are higher education or health care, preferably both. The cities don't have to be large: Albuquerque, New Mexico, Iowa City, Iowa, and Hanover, New Hampshire, are a few good examples.

• **Housing.** A family has seven basic housing options: buying a house, a condominium, or a mobile home or renting any of those three or an apartment. When you are looking for a place to live, look for areas that have all these alternatives, not just single-family detached houses. Renting is the main form of housing for newcomers for one good reason: you can cut your cost of living by at least half while you decide where you'd ultimately like to settle.

• **Education.** There are two sides to it; K–12 and higher education. Many parents shopping for public school quality are not aware that most states issue annual reports comparing their public school districts by valuable indicators, including pupil-teacher ratios, instructional dollars, and the percentage of teachers who have advanced degrees in the subjects they teach. These are among the most unread books in the country, yet you can get them for nothing.

You might also want to know what the alternatives to public schools are, whether private or parochial. A high proportion of students in nonpublic schools can mean the public schools in an area aren't seen by many parents as being the best places for children to learn.

Finally, colleges or universities in the area are assets. In some cities they are major employers. In others there is a connection between academic research and the local economy. Often college professors, researchers, and students participate in the local schools in some way. And colleges and universities offer evening and weekend classes as well as an array of cultural activities.

• **Recreation.** Good restaurants tend to go with resorts and large metro areas where dining is on expense accounts. Movie theaters tend to be located in suburban shopping malls where exhibitors think they're going to make a lot of money. Crowd pleasers like zoos and aquariums, family theme parks, and professional sports franchises can be found all over the map.

Outdoor recreational assets like coastlines and inland water, national forests, parks, and wildlife refuges are not fairly distributed throughout the country. Cincinnati, Kansas City, Wichita, and Pittsburgh, for example, are shortchanged. Seattle is blessed. Even Los Angeles has some great state and national parks. Outdoor recreational areas are not easily acquired by cities; once acquired, they don't disappear. They should be an important consideration for families.

• **Health care.** Pediatricians and family practitioners tend to congregate where there are populations with a lower median age than the national average and where people are covered by health insurance. They're looking for middle-class to affluent areas where they can set up a practice and be assured that, within a reasonable time, they're going to have an adequate number of patients. This won't necessarily happen in Sarasota or Palm Beach, where there are large populations of older adults; it also doesn't happen in smaller areas in the South, where large numbers of people aren't covered by health insurance.

• **Transportation.** For most newcomers public transportation

"There are great people. The swim and tennis club is where I meet most of my friends."

■

"There are theaters, shops, markets, and basically every essential is very close by. We can walk to the video store, the yogurt shop, or the video arcade. It's great."

■

"I like the location. Our street is very quiet, and we have a real sense of neighborhood. There are other children around. It's fun to go on walks with my daughter and run into other mothers with children. It's a good way to meet people, and the kids like it too."

■

"The playground next door has swings plus an open field of woods."

■

"I love my neighborhood. Most of the kids are older than my daughter, but they still come over to play with her. We spent almost every evening outside this summer. The sidewalk in front of my house was a huge drawing board. I keep a lot of sidewalk chalk available, and we draw. I take my daughter on a lot of walks. It takes us twenty minutes to walk to the beach, and there are some fun shops to look in along the way."

■

"We live in Manhattan. Culturally, there's no place that compares. Central Park is a remarkable asset. I worry about the crime and safety when my children are older. Maybe by then we'll move to Connecticut."

■

isn't a necessary option. Public transportation routes are designed for workers who don't have a car and for shoppers avoiding parking hassles in the central business district. However, a well-run transit system, like an established parks and recreation program, is a big line item on the municipal budget, a sign that the city provides a range of services for its customers.

There are other transportation considerations. Flying is second nature for just about everyone these days; not just for business travelers but for people visiting you or those you want to visit. The airport should be in a community that is classified as a "medium" or "large" hub; if it's not, you are going to pay a lot of money to reach most every destination.

• **The arts.** For most people the lack of performing arts in an area is no reason to move elsewhere. Indeed the tendency today is to move from cultured (i.e., older, larger) cities to low-brow (i.e., newer, smaller) cities. Still the arts are a positive dimension of a local economy. They bring people downtown in the evening. An art museum and a symphony provide educational opportunities for schoolchildren. Their presence indicates local philanthropy, arts appreciation, and alternative leisure-time activities. Moreover, if a city has a minimum level of cultural life, you know you will be able to have an intelligent conversation with at least someone in town.

• **Climate.** Rain, snow, heat, cold, drought, and wind can certainly make a physical difference in your life. For decades people have headed from north to south and from east to west because these destinations were perceived as warmer, drier, and milder. Yet it turns out that some migrants miss seasonal change and are bored out of their trees by "paradise" climates. There are other places in the country that lack extremes but nevertheless have a little snow, a little rain, a long spring, and a long fall. Asheville, North Carolina, Denver, Colorado, and Washington, D.C., are some good examples.

• **Crime.** There's no place so pristine that it has no crime. A large number of police per capita indicates a high-crime area rather than one where crime is being prevented. Bear in mind, too, that crime rates vary dramatically among neighborhoods as well as among cities. Violent crime is usually concentrated in certain places. Property crime, such as burglary, auto theft, and larceny, is everywhere.

A good choice of neighborhoods is some protection from property crimes. Look for some kind of stability in residents; these days that can mean as little as five years. Avoid neighborhoods near interstates, major highways, or arterials because they are getaways. If you are interested in the suburbs, you can go to the local police station and ask them to indicate where burglaries take place. If it's diffuse, take extra steps to protect your home.

Source: David Savageau, coauthor of Places Rated Almanac *and* Retirement Places Rated *has lived in Denver, St. Louis, Indianapolis, and Boston and now is home in Gloucester, Massachusetts.*

FINDING A NEW HOMETOWN

Before you start the five-step plan for finding a new hometown, you need to establish what your family is looking for so that you will know when you've found it. This sounds so fundamental, but it's not common practice. Put in writing what you need, what you hope to accomplish, and what you're looking for in terms of schools, shopping, neighborhoods, employment opportunities, access to medical care, acceptable living costs, and any other considerations. Then it's time to begin the search.

1. Round up suspects. Look at the information you're going to be gathering as intelligence that you will use to compare cities to each other. Once you begin collecting brochures on different cities, you will find that one of the most difficult tasks is to learn what's gloss and what's real, what's important and what's not. Part of the process is to get information; the second part is to be realistic about what you find. One of the biggest misconceptions about the prospect of relocating is that the final destination is going to be utopia. People think, My God, I've spent all this time and all this money; this place better be perfect. So they overlook the potential drawbacks because they're so excited about the prospect of changing their lifestyle and getting rid of the things that are problematic in their lives. What you should be looking for is to make a dramatic improvement in your lifestyle. If you have a lousy commute, if you're in a dead-end job, if you're in an area that doesn't have enough opportunity, if you live in a place where you can't afford a first home or the taxes are too high—whatever it is, that's what you want to improve. Don't look for nirvana; it doesn't exist.

2. Put on your detective hat. When you are interested in moving into an area, obviously one of the most important tasks is to gather information. While it may sound old-fashioned: telephone, telegraph, tell your mother. Get the word out that you're considering relocating and see if you can network. Find other people who have family or friends who live in the area you're considering. Talk to them and find out what it's like from their perspective. Write to the Chamber of Commerce, Visitors' Bureaus, and real estate offices. Contact the local school district. Subscribe to the Sunday edition of the local newspaper. Sometimes you're going to have to pay for the information, and people are taken aback by that. Realize that the search may be expensive, but it will cost you much more if you move to the wrong place.

3. Take inventory. Evaluate the material you're getting so that you can turn suspect cities into prospects. Compare the list of what you want and need with what you're learning about particular communities. And don't turn a deaf ear to the potential drawbacks. Sometimes people get so excited about an area that they begin compromising too early. They may be hearing or seeing things they don't like, but they just ignore them. This is the stage to pay attention, to ask questions, and to begin comparative shopping in earnest.

4. Search and destroy. Here's where you narrow your possibilities. You compare two cities and eliminate one. You look carefully at the merits and the drawbacks. What are the positives, and how important are they to you? What are the negatives? How does one city compare to the other? Which ones come closest to what you're looking for? Continue the process until you're down to three or four finalists.

5. The on-site inspection. This is the single most important step in the entire process. Again this is where families can get into a bind if they don't budget the costs of taking their entire family on site visits. You may want to go to one place several times or several places one time. You cannot realistically expect to move to an area without visiting it.

It may be love at first sight, or you won't want to spend a half hour there let alone the rest of your life. And these are the feelings that can't be gleaned from a brochure or picked up in an interview with a real estate agent who loves the place and wants to promote it. The on-site inspection may change everything. Some people have said that it has made them so excited they couldn't wait to move. For others a visit made them realize that they'd averted a disaster.

Places always look different in person from pictures or videos. When you arrive, it's important to spend time by yourself rather than spending all your time with a real estate salesperson. Go to the places you would if you actually lived there. See if you have a sense of whether you will fit in. Go to a mall. Look at the people.

Ask yourself whether you will be comfortable with the people you see. Look beyond the brochures. Be honest with yourself even if it means eliminating some place you had your heart set on.

Finally, realize that no matter how much money you've invested in the search, if a place is not right, the investment is minimal compared to what it would cost for you to move there. For some that means there's no place like home. For others the site visit will confirm their greatest expectations.

Source: Saralee H. Rosenberg is coauthor, with her husband, Lee, of 50 Fabulous Places to Raise Your Family. *They live in Long Island, New York, with their three children.*

NEWBORNS

Once Alexander was born, I suddenly realized that what little research I had done prebirth was all focused on my pregnancy and childbirth. I had absolutely no clue how to take care of a newborn. Upon seeing him for the first time, all I remember saying to Bernie was "Does he have all his fingers and toes?" When he assured me that Alex did, I vaguely remember saying "Don't let him out of your sight" before I fell asleep for two days because—as my hospital bill confirms—I was given enough drugs to supply a small community of pregnant women in some rural location.

In retrospect, I'm not sure what prompted my sudden concern for Alexander's safety. After all, we had picked a hospital we loved and where we felt we could both get top-rate medical care. Perhaps my unconscious self was afraid that Alex would be switched at birth (as in the film Twins) and I'd end up with Danny DeVito when I'd given birth to Arnold Schwarzenegger. Or were my instructions just an initial attempt to begin trying to manage and organize an experience that was so overwhelming?

The physical elements were difficult enough: recovery from the cesarean section with all the attendant bleeding. I had personally never seen so much blood coming out of someone who was alive. Why hadn't I read about lochia? What in the world does that word mean? Books describe it as a bloody vaginal discharge that's like a heavy *period*. For whom? To me it looked like the Red Sea. And the sanitary napkin they gave me was like a huge brick—albeit a soft one. The idea of having nurses help me change it and spritz some warm water over the perineal area (crotch) would have been enormously embarrassing had I retained any of my faculties.

The constant discussion of my bowel movements was amusing rather than irritating and certainly a portent of things to come with Alex. I could also deal with the breast engorgement; I'd always wondered what it would be like to have huge breasts and didn't find it particularly painful after all I'd been through. The fatigue wasn't a big problem either since a good friend had highly recommended that while we keep Alex in the room during the day we leave him in the nursery at night so that I could get some sleep. It was a great suggestion.

Dealing with Alexander was somewhat more mysterious. He was fine for the first few days before he got sick with a viral infection, and it was during that time that I continuously wondered why I had taken no child-care preparation classes or read any material on the subject. Not only had I no idea how Alexander was supposed to look and thus was a bit surprised by the size of his head and his penis, but I also realized that I had no idea what the doctors and nurses were doing to him and how I was supposed to respond.

When my pediatrician told us how well Alex checked out on all the initial tests, I had no means of comparison. When we learned that he was in the 95th percentile for height and the 75th percentile for weight, I had no idea that what was important was the relationship of the two numbers to each other.

The one decision Bernie and I had made in advance was to have him circumcised in the hospital by the doctor because—despite my Jewish heritage—the idea of a brit (party) eight days after his birth to celebrate cutting off his foreskin (actually it's a celebration of a covenant with God) has always seemed a bit off-putting to me. Besides, I was sure that when he got older and saw a videotape of the event he would hate me. As it turned out, his viral infection prevented his circumcision for two months, which ultimately was a nightmare.

Despite my ignorance Alexander survived—even flourished— once we left the hospital. And despite my lack of preparation it seemed that God gave me a whole lot of common sense, and that combined with my mother's expertise enabled us to deal successfully with the myriad new experiences we faced those first few weeks.

When I look at Alexander now, I can't imagine he was ever so tiny and helpless. When I discuss with friends whether a forty-something mother should consider having a second child, they ask with genuine amazement, "Do you really want to go through all that newborn stuff again?"

My gut-level emotional response is unequivocally "yes." I loved

DIFFICULTIES WE EXPERIENCED

■

"Waking up three to four times per night to breastfeed was my greatest difficulty. My son didn't sleep through the night until he was one year old. I also found the lack of freedom to plan my day around my needs to be a great adjustment."

■

"One of my problems with my second child is that she wants to be held all the time. I've learned to rotate her around. Sometimes I put her in the baby seat with stuff to look at. Then I'll move her to the swing, then to her crib. And I often sit in the rocking chair in my son's room and rock her while he plays on the floor."

■

every moment of Alexander's infancy. My more rational answer is that I am frequently tired, and I'm not sure if I have the stamina to take care of two young children.

Whatever I ultimately decide, I wouldn't trade the "newborn stuff" for all the tea in China.

჻

POSTPARTUM AND YOU

• **Vaginal discharge.** The normal discharge after delivery is a type of bleeding called lochia, which can be heavy at first before tapering off. It normally lasts up to six weeks. It's recommended that you use sanitary pads rather than tampons to handle the blood flow. There's a minimal risk of infection, especially if there's an episiotomy (an incision made in the perineum between the vagina and anus), so you will want to be gentle with the healing tissue and clean it thoroughly with water after a bowel movement or urination. Wipe from front to back.

• **The uterus.** Immediately after delivery the uterus is the size it was when you were about twenty weeks pregnant. It is roughly at about the level of your navel. If it's the first delivery, the uterus tends to be contracted rather well right after delivery and remains that way. In subsequent deliveries the uterus doesn't contract quite as strongly, and many women will have after-cramps, which are pains not unlike contractions, especially during nursing. Those tend to dissipate as the uterus shrinks further, and within a couple of weeks the uterus is back to the size it was when you were two months pregnant. In six weeks it's virtually back to its normal size.

• **Stitches or sutures.** By and large an ideal situation is when someone can deliver vaginally, without an episiotomy and without tear or laceration. If it's a matter of choosing between an episiotomy and a larger laceration, an episiotomy is far and away the better choice. They are almost always closed with absorbable sutures that dissolve on their own. Most of the stitches are buried, and there are few, if any, protruding through the skin. While there is some discomfort with an episiotomy, it is usually not a major problem. Sitz baths are recommended by some doctors to help ease discomfort.

• **Constipation.** Gastrointestinal motility, which is the contraction of the gastrointestinal tract that basically propels the food from the mouth to the anus, is slower during pregnancy. That's why constipation is so commonly seen in pregnancy and in the postpartum period. Sometimes there is also a reticence to have that first bowel movement after giving birth because there is tenderness near the rectum due to swelling from an episiotomy or from pushing, which sometimes causes hemorrhoids. The bowel movement is usually not as painful as most women think it will be and getting it over with sooner is better than putting it off.

• **Hormonal activity.** Hormones change a great deal during pregnancy, but it is a gradual change over time. Shortly after the baby is delivered, with the delivery of the placenta the source of all these hormones is gone. Although the hormones don't disappear immediately, the change is much more rapid and acute, which is probably the cause of some postpartum depression.

• **Breast engorgement.** There is a period of breast engorgement, which varies in intensity from woman to woman. It tends to be more intense before the milk starts to flow, which is typically during the fourth day postpartum. The breast engorgement will precede it by a day or a day and a half. If you are nursing for the first time, it is important to realize that the engorgement you feel is not something that will be there during the entire time you nurse. It will be there until the milk is flowing well, which usually happens fairly quickly.

• **Skin changes.** A common change and concern postpartum are the stria or stretch marks, which not all women have. They are related to weight gain, size of the baby, and size of the mother when the pregnancy began. There is also a very strong genetic component: women whose mothers did not have stretch marks often will not have stretch marks; the opposite is true as well.

Another common change has to do with the *linea nigra* (Latin for "black line"), which is a vertical brown line below the naval that typically appears during the pregnancy toward the end, often is darkened immediately postpartum, ultimately fades, and eventually disappears entirely.

• **Varicose veins.** Pregnancy is a risk factor for varicose veins. Not unlike stretch marks, there is a genetic predisposition; daughters tend to have them if their mothers did. The ones that appear during pregnancy generally get smaller postpartum. Whether or not they'll disappear varies from person to person.

• **Perspiration.** The hormonal changes that occur with nursing may initially include a period of night sweats in which you awaken with the sheets drenched. It doesn't last the entire time you nurse.

"Colic with both. What a nightmare! My son's was so awful and lasted so long that we almost decided not to have another child. With my daughter the Snugli ruined my back but saved my life. We went for a lot of car rides."

■

"My daughter was allergic to formula, both the milk and the soy formulas. We spent a lot of money trying different formulas until we finally found one that was completely hypoallergenic and predigested. When she was a year old and ready for milk, we had the same problem. We finally went to the health food store and bought liquid calcium. We mix it in her juice. It was a godsend."

■

"First, learning how to breastfeed. Then it was fighting criticism from others who felt I was breastfeeding too frequently."

■

"My baby doesn't sleep as much as I'd like. She sleeps for short stints rather than taking fewer, longer naps. I'm constantly trying to get her to go to sleep. I sometimes try to put her in a quiet part of the house. I keep on reminding myself that this too will pass and that it's OK if nothing else gets done besides taking care of the kids."

■

The hormonal situation for nursing mothers changes from the initial postpartum to the later postpartum period; things get easier.

• **Postpartum depression.** It's ironic that the time the new mom expects to be wonderful and enjoyable can be a depressing one. Yet postpartum depression, so called because it is limited to the postpartum period, is often "normal." Some women find themselves crying easily or becoming unusually upset over situations that wouldn't ordinarily bother them. Postpartum depression may be related in some way to hormonal change as well as to some of the psychological changes a mother encounters with the birth of a baby. During pregnancy the woman herself was the focus of attention. With birth the baby is the focus, and suddenly there are so many new responsibilities that often have a psychological impact.

Source: Edward Sigall, M.D., is an obstetrician-gynecologist in private practice at Cedars-Sinai Medical Center hospital in Los Angeles, California. He is the father of one.

YOUR NEWBORN

Height and weight. As with adults, there is a relationship between height and weight. Babies of a certain height are expected to have certain weights, and these are based on statistical comparisons of many babies. This is not of any particular significance, but we are concerned when babies are extremely large or extremely underweight for their gestational age. Overweight babies are usually more than 10 or 10½ pounds and can present a mechanical problem with delivery. Underweight babies, five pounds or less at term, frequently have problems with low blood sugar at birth. They have inadequate stores of energy, and when they lose their connection to the mother's placenta they can get reactive hypoglycemia.

Head. The head is the largest part of the newborn infant, and during the birth process the bones of the skull are designed to move to allow the head to pass through the vagina. As a result of this bone movement or due to intrauterine positioning, the head may be somewhat asymmetrical at birth or may be an unusual shape, which is called *molding*. It needn't be of concern, because it will generally resolve to a normal shape in several days.

Fontanel. There are actually two fontanels—the anterior and the posterior. These are openings between the various bones of the skull and are present to allow for the molding movement of the bones during the birth process and for the growth of the brain over a period of time. Normally the anterior fontanel is closed by a year or year and a half, the posterior by six months. These fontanels are covered by a fairly thick membrane, so a mother needn't be concerned about damaging the brain underneath; it's quite unlikely.

Eyes. At the time of birth there are lots of questions about variations in the appearance of the eyes. Most babies have a kind of dark grayish blue eye color, and it is not until six to twelve months of age that the final eye color can be determined.

Babies frequently look cross-eyed for the first six months, and the reason is that they have very prominent folds at the nasal portion of their eyes. These folds cover up the white of the eye in the nasal area and give the appearance of cross-eyes, which is really an optical illusion in most cases. It is something that pediatricians look at during the first visit.

Because of medication put in the baby's eyes at birth, there is frequently a yellowish crusty discharge from the eyes called *chemical conjunctivitis*. Depending on the medication used for prevention of eye infections, this can be a prominent irritation or a less prominent irritation, and these medications are required by state law.

Skin. Babies' skin color is variable because the nervous control of circulation to the skin is underdeveloped. Very often babies have a splotchy appearance (called *mottling*), especially if slightly chilled, and they frequently have blue hands and feet. This is not of any significance and shouldn't be of any concern.

Babies who are of Asian, African-American, or sometimes of Hispanic descent might have a black-and-blue mark on their buttocks, which may or may not disappear over time. It can be of some concern if you don't know about it, but it is usually found in the parents as well, although theirs may have faded with age.

Babies can have peely skin. Toward the end of pregnancy they lose their vernix, which is the greasy coating that protects the skin from the amniotic fluid. Toward term the vernix starts to disappear, and the amniotic fluid can saturate the skin with water, causing it to peel.

There are several kinds of common rashes. One is milia, which is little cysts that appear on the chin, the nose, and the forehead. They are due to an accumulation of normal skin oil that cannot be released from oil glands that have tiny ducts and get

OUR TIPS FOR NEW MOTHERS

■

"Leave your compulsiveness at the hospital when you check out. There isn't time to be perfect, look great, have a clean house, and a sweet, adorable baby. The less you expect of yourself, the more relaxed you'll be. What's most important is to hold and love your newborn."

"Call your doctor as much as you want. They don't charge for phone calls, and the peace of mind is immediate. I called at least twice a week for the first few months."

"Ask your friends for help, both for advice and for picking up stuff at the store. Talking with other moms keeps you from feeling isolated, and it's great to find out that they've gone through whatever you're going through."

"Get out. My daughter loved to go on errands. The first week, we did the drive-through teller at the bank because I didn't want her to be around strangers with germs. She loved the car, and it was great for me to get out of the house."

plugged easily. They usually go away in a couple of weeks.

Erythema toxicum, another common rash, consists of small areas of redness up to a half inch in diameter in the center of which is a yellowish white bump that looks like an insect bite. These usually are not found at birth but show up in the first twenty-four hours and can last for up to two weeks. Nobody knows what causes them; they may represent the sensitivity of newborn skin to an environmental substance or environmental chemical.

Breasts and sex organs. Breasts are frequently subject to the same hormonal influences that cause the mother's breasts to enlarge during pregnancy, and it is not uncommon for both boy babies and girl babies to be born with either prominent breasts or breasts that actually have lumps beneath them. This is normal breast tissue that has been stimulated by the hormones in pregnancy, and after birth the effect of these hormones disappears and the breast tissue shrinks over a period of weeks.

As far as sex organs are concerned, girl babies frequently have a clear or milky vaginal discharge with a very mucusy characteristic to it for a couple of weeks after birth. This is also due to the maternal hormonal effect and will disappear.

Bowel movements. Most babies have bowel movements in the first twenty-four hours of life, and the pediatrician should be informed if they don't. The initial bowel movements are very dark and sticky. This material is called *meconium* and actually represents the normal turnover of tissues in the intestinal tissues that have broken down in utero. The stool will change to a more yellow or greenish loose movement within a couple of days of life.

The normal breastfed baby may have a bowel movement with every feeding or as infrequently as once every several days. The real concern should be with the consistency of the bowel movement. Constipation in babies is diagnosed when the bowel movement has a form and shape. Most babies have shapeless bowel movements that resemble mashed potatoes at the hardest consistency. The color depends to a large extent on the transit time. The bile from the liver that's put into the bowel movement gives the bowel movement a yellow color. Normal babies pass their bowel movements through fast enough so that the color remains quite yellow. If the bowel movement is taking a longer time to be passed, it will change from yellow to green and then to a darker color. The concern is not so much with the color of the bowel movement, however, as it is with the consistency.

Source: Stephen Fernbach, M.D., is the director of nurseries for Kaiser Permanente Medical Center in Santa Clara, California. He is a clinical associate professor at Stanford University Medical School and the father of two.

NEWBORN TESTS AND EXAMS

• **Apgar score.** Virginia Apgar, the person who devised this score, was interested in looking at a baby in a very specific way rather than generalizing. She felt you should be able to evaluate the way the baby was adapting to birth, by looking at five vital functions: heart rate, breathing, general body tone, reactions to stimuli, and color. In evaluating the heart rate you need to determine whether it's absent, low, or normal. Is the baby's breathing absent, does it require a little effort, or is it vigorous? Does the baby have muscle tone? He could be limp, have some tone, or be very active. Does the baby respond if you touch her or manipulate her in some way? Is he unable to respond, does he just move his face a little bit and grimace, or does he cry? What is the baby's color? Is she blue all over? Is she blue just on her hands and feet and pink elsewhere? Is she pink all over?

The baby is assessed one minute after birth and five minutes after birth, and the score should rise as he adapts to the air-breathing independent environment. He can get a zero, one, or two rating on each of the five items, depending on the pediatrician's evaluation. The Apgar scores enable all the health professionals in the delivery room to have a common set of items for evaluation of the baby's condition. Most doctors don't tell the parents the Apgar score because it is just a transient moment in the baby's life.

• **PKU screening.** PKU screening, thyroid function screening, and a number of other metabolic tests are done in every state, but the panel of tests varies from state to state due to health department regulations. These tests are done on a drop of blood that is taken from the baby's heel or finger, put on a filter pad, and sent by mail to the state laboratory, where they do thousands of analyses every year. The tests are used to screen for diseases detectable at birth with a fair degree of accuracy and for which treatments are

"Consider starting your day with a walk in the morning. The fresh air put my baby to sleep, and I loved the exercise."

"A Snugli is a wonderful way to feel close to your baby, and yet it leaves your hands free. I didn't get a stroller until my daughter was three months old. I think we both benefited from my holding her so much."

"Take naps when the baby naps! Forget the housework."

"Relax. Nervousness and anxiety seriously get in the way of good, enjoyable parenting. When I am relaxed, I am not only better able to listen to my own intuition but also more open to listening to my child."

"Expect to feel overwhelmed some of the time."

available that can prevent permanent damage to the child. The most common disease—which occurs about one in two or three thousand cases—is hypothyroidism, which causes slow mental development or retardation if it's diagnosed later. If detected immediately at birth, it can be treated and the child will be normal.

• **Hearing tests.** Hearing tests are controversial. Some people believe every child should be tested for hearing at the time of birth because, again, if a hearing loss is not diagnosed until later, developmental problems in speech and language may occur. On the other hand, congenital hearing loss is rare, so most doctors screen for it only if a baby is considered to be at risk.

• **Bilirubin check.** If the baby turns yellow, an indication of jaundice, the pediatrician will check the bilirubin to see how high it is and whether the baby's liver is making the adjustment from fetal life to extrauterine life, where it has to cope with the normal breakdown of red blood cells. Our red blood cells die and are replenished about every four months, so the liver has to adjust to that. Probably about 15 percent of babies have some kind of bilirubin problem. The most common way of treating high bilirubin is to use phototherapy (lights) or, if it's extensive, to do an exchange blood transfusion.

• **General evaluation.** When a baby is born, generally three evaluation periods are important. The first one is in the delivery room; that's where the Apgar score is done. Again, it's meant to determine whether the baby's lungs which have never breathed before, can breathe on their own and whether the circulatory system, which has generally depended on the placenta rather than on the heart and lungs, can adapt and function in an efficient and normal fashion.

The next day the pediatrician examines the baby again, looking for birth defects. Has the baby had any development problems that could have consequences now and in the future? The pediatrician also assesses the baby's growth to see if the baby is well grown. He or she looks at the way the baby who as a fetus was dependent on the placenta, is adapting to having to start swallowing and using the stomach, esophagus, and intestines. The pediatrician is looking to see if the baby can eat and move food through the body and whether the kidneys—which used to depend on the placenta—are functioning properly.

Right before the baby goes home, the pediatrician checks once again to see if the baby is growing and has made the successful adaptation to extrauterine life. With early discharge, the final check is sometimes done in a pediatrician's office.

Source: Marilyn Escobedo, M.D., is a professor of pediatrics and neonatology at the University of Texas Health Science Center in San Antonio, Texas. She is the mother of two.

FURTHER READING

Caring for Your Baby and Young Child: Birth to Age 5, by Steven P. Shelov and Robert E. Hannemann. New York: Bantam Books, 1993.

The Baby Book: Everything You Need to Know About Your Baby from Birth to Age Two, by William Sears and Martha Sears. Boston: Little, Brown and Company, 1993.

The Complete Mothercare Manual, by consultants Rosalind Y. Ting, Herbert Brant, and Kenneth Holt. New York: Prentice Hall, 1987.

Dr. Spock's Baby and Child Care, by Benjamin Spock and Michael B. Rothenberg. New York: Dutton, 1992.

The Good Housekeeping Illustrated Book of Pregnancy & Babycare. London: Dorling Kindersley Limited, 1990.

Your Child's Health, by Barton D. Schmitt. New York: Bantam Books, 1991.

ORGANIZING OUR TIME

I am one of the most task-oriented people I know. Given any project, whether I have a background in the field or not, I am instinctively able to break down the elements into a sequential order and figure out how to complete the job efficiently and effectively.

Until recently I never realized that this is a skill some people don't have although I have always felt that an ability to organize things is of great importance to the social order. I have sometimes thought my to-do lists were poetry in motion. I have enjoyed my fairly narrow but intense focus. I have always found it crazy-making to deal with people who cannot understand the components of a project, prioritize them, and complete the task.

Imagine my surprise when a few months after Alex's birth I suddenly realized that I had become what can be described only as disorganized. On a daily and weekly basis I was finding that few tasks were getting done. I would start something, the baby would cry, and I would leave it unfinished for hours. The cumulative progression of putting things off or delaying them was leading to chaos.

Initially I approached my problem logically and systematically. I took out my Day-Timer notebook, began writing to-do lists, and started accounting for my time in fifteen-minute intervals the way I used to do at work.

I quit after one day. First of all, the tasks I listed were so mundane and housewifey to begin with that even looking at the list of what I hoped to accomplish in a day nauseated me. Then, when I started counting how many times I changed Alex, picked him up because he was crying, got him something to eat or drink, found

270

him something to play with, or just picked him up to cuddle, I could see why nothing got done.

I decided it was better to live in chaos than to make us both crazy. Slowly I became more philosophical about the importance of "accomplishing" tasks each day as opposed to just living one's life. My resolution was that I would learn to live with disorganization.

At a meeting later that week, when a client who lacked any understanding of systems and logic made a totally ridiculous suggestion for accomplishing a particular project, I assumed an almost Zenlike posture and said, "What an interesting approach." He later complimented me on my openness.

That night I stared at myself in the mirror for a long time. The meeting had made me sick. I couldn't believe how stupid the client was. I was furious at myself for responding like such a "wimp." I was offended by his compliment.

When Bernie came into the room and asked me what the problem was, I told him what the guy had said. He laughed heartily. "It's clearly a case of mistaken identity," he responded. "You're absolutely rigid and inflexible."

I sighed an enormous sigh of relief and began writing my to-do list for the next day. There are some things you never want to change.

~

TIPS FOR LIST MAKING

- The key to a well-organized system is a master list. You write down tasks as they come up without organizing them. You simply list everything you have to do—whether it's ironing, cleaning a closet, or doing the laundry. Some people separate business tasks from personal ones.

- The daily list is your working daily action guide. Every morning or evening, depending on your biological rhythm and energy cycle, you should make a to-do list—compiled mostly from your master list—of the ten items you want to accomplish that day.

- To-do's should be specific and limited. Rather than writing down that you need to "clean your house," you will want to differentiate between everyday tasks, like making the beds, washing dishes, and dusting lightly, and "deep cleaning" tasks, including scrubbing floors, waxing and polishing furniture, and cleaning walls and woodwork, which are once-a-week operations.

HOW WE ORIGANIZE OUR TIME

∎

"I write everything down: personal, professional, family, and social obligations. I figure targets for long- and short-term projects. I weigh each task's importance. I know that when I'm motivated I can accomplish what I want to. If I don't hit the bull's-eye, it's OK to hit the target."

∎

"Laundry and housecleaning are done on the same day weekly. My daughters go to a sitter once a week. During this time I run errands— schedule doctor appointments for myself and make quick stops—so that I don't have to haul my daughters in and out of the car seats."

∎

"Lists, lists, lists for home and work. I do work-related and personal calls at my desk while I'm eating lunch. I dictate letters in the car sometimes."

∎

- Rank each item in order of importance—one for high priority, two for medium priority, three for least urgent. A task is a high priority if it has an immediate deadline, if it is very difficult, intellectually challenging and makes heavy demands on your creativity, or if it is very stressful.

- Schedule your tasks in terms of the practical factor, the biological factor, and the deadline factor. The practical factor might mean that you drive a car pool three afternoons a week at a certain time or that you like to grocery-shop in the morning, before the supermarket is crowded. The concept of biological rhythm is defined by whether you are a "morning" person or a "night" person. While the deadline itself may be obvious, some people require pressure to work at top capacity; for others it is better to complete the job with time to spare.

- Cross off each item on the list as you complete it and transfer unfinished items to the next day's list.

More Organizing Tips

- Be efficient. Barter. Use cooperative arrangements. If a task is inconvenient or unmanageable, consider asking a friend to take it on in exchange for a service from you. Consider cooperative arrangements with other parents, whether it is carpooling or baby-sitting.

- Make use of bits of time. Recognize that there are tasks that take only five, ten, or fifteen minutes. List them accordingly and do them in "bits." If they pile up, keep a "fifteener" list. Set aside fifteen minutes once or twice a day, steadily working your way down the list, and do all those pesky tasks that drive you nuts.

Source: Stephanie Winston is the author of Getting Organized *and* The Organized Executive. *She lectures extensively throughout the country and conducts workshops and classes on the subject of organization. She lives in New York.*

THE BEST THREE-BY-FIVE SYSTEM

How it evolved. Our system for organizing your life has evolved over sixteen years. When my sister and I thought it up, she had three kids under three years of age and my three were a little bit spread out, but it was basically a three-by-five card file tickler system we developed to keep our houses organized. We first wrote about it in 1977, when our first book, *Sidetracked Home Executives*, came out. The book has ultimately sold over a million copies. (We think the sales are that high because those who buy it are so disorganized, they lose their copies and have to buy more.)

What it is. Our system for your home is really a system for your life because your home is the center of life. If your home is organized well, you'll be that much better off in the world. The backbone of the system is the weekly plan. The thought behind it was to balance everything in your life by working on it every day of the week in the following ways:

1. **Free day.** Every week you have to have some free time. That doesn't mean you have twenty-four hours to do nothing, but at least one day a week you'll have time to do what you love to do.
2. **Family working day.** This is the day you and your family do housework, vacuum, dust, wash floors and windows.
3. **Desk day.** That doesn't mean you are strapped to your desk for twelve hours. But at least once a week you need to sit down someplace where you have a pen, stamps, and a calculator and attend to all your paperwork. You do planning and organizing and work with your card file.
4. **Gofer day.** This is an errand day. This doesn't mean you can't go on errands any other day, but at least one day a week you do lots of errands and pick up things.
5. **Highly effective day.** This is the day when you work like Ordell Daily, a mystical person we made up, who died when she was thirty because she worked so hard and didn't have any play days. On this day you need to be just like a compulsive person who is driven. You need to memorize a routine for that day. You won't have time for people or for pets. What we've found is that when you do this you're surprised at your ability to get things done, but then you have to do it only once a week.
6. **Minimally effective day.** This is when you catch up on things. Water some plants that didn't get water on the day you were supposed to water them, take care of any "piles" that have started, clean out the refrigerator—things like that.
7. **Family play day.** This a day of shared recreation with your family.

The inspiration. We were inspired to stick to a weekly plan because of the Amish. There are no disorganized Amish. They have a high suicide rate, but they are not disorganized.

"I wake up early, shower, and start the day. If you wait until after your children are awake, it is more difficult to break away to shower. I start errands early or plan around lunch and nap times. I put my children to bed early to spend private time with my husband. I have a sitter/cleaning lady once a week to help so I can get out of the house alone."

■

"I do two grocery shopping trips a week—one large one and one small one. I make all the sandwiches that day and clean all the fruits and vegetables and cut up everything. It takes about two to three hours. Then it's easy all week."

■

"I have a weekly planner. Before a month starts, I go through and write down what I know I have to do each day, which includes daily exercise. Then I'm prepared to add things as they come."

■

The card system. Our new card system, which we've changed recently, is a method for organizing your life. We have fun cards, reason-for-living cards, indulgence cards, a twenty-second kiss card—which was inspired by a psychologist we met who said that this tip helped more marriages than all his marriage counseling combined—work cards outlining tasks in each room in your house, cards for self-improvement, home improvement, and community outreach.

Our goal. Our end goal now is to help people streamline their lives so that they can get organized. If you have too much stuff (and most of us do) and you aren't using it, it's really not you—it's somebody else, or it used to be you, or you think it will be you someday—you need to dejunk. Once you've done that, you can use the weekly plan and the cards—you can use ours or make up your own—to organize your life.

You will need to make a list of everything that has to be done, decide how often it has to be done, and then determine what kind of focus you need to give it. Should it be in your minimally effective day, your highly effective day, or your family work day? You just put the cards where they should be. We work only one day at a time. We don't worry about what's coming down the line. You already know if Christmas is four months away. But as far as your everyday living is concerned, we just look at a week at a time.

Source: Pam Young's most recent book, which she coauthored with her sister Peggy Jones, is Get Your Act Together, a Seven-day Program for the Overworked, Overbooked and Overwhelmed. *She is the mother of three and lives in Vancouver, Washington.*

ORGANIZING YOUR PREGNANCY

• **Start preparing as soon as you know you're pregnant.** See what can be accomplished during the first and second trimesters so that you can have more free time in your last one. Confirm your health insurance. Start budgeting for the baby. Buy or borrow some books and or videos on pregnancy. Stay away from people with contagious diseases. Identify and avoid domestic and occupational hazards.

• **Buy a workbook or notebook that you'll carry around all the time.** Treat your pregnancy as a research project. Include information on everything, including questions for your office visits with your OB-GYN, criteria for choosing where to have your baby, places to acquire maternity clothes, information on childbirth classes, and dozens of other topics relating to your pregnancy.

• **Keep a monthly calendar.** Record deadlines for things that need to be done in a timely manner. Note all important dates and appointments for the duration of your pregnancy, including dates for visiting hospitals or birthing centers, meetings with birth attendants, birth attendant visits, prenatal exercise classes, anticipated arrival date for your baby furniture and equipment, child-care or day-care interviews, and pediatrician interviews, among others.

• **Make lists and refine them.** Outline all the things you need to get done such as travel necessities, a second trimester dental visit, layette and furniture to buy or borrow, calls to make, items needed for the hospital bag, arrangements to be finalized after the baby is born. Enjoy checking them off when you've accomplished them.

• **Pay attention to your body.** Give yourself a little more time to get things done during the first trimester and last month of pregnancy. Try to get a lot of your to-do's accomplished in the middle months.

• **Create your own support system.** Put together a group of people who will be there for you: your partner, friends, family, health professionals, support groups, and hired help. Delegate responsibility whenever possible.

• **Plan for things that will need to be done after the birth.** Preaddress baby announcement envelopes, premake and freeze meals, find out about postpartum exercise, plan to make a new will, arrange for a religious ceremony. The more you get done before the baby is born, the more time you'll have afterward for rest, recuperation, and getting to know your baby.

Source: Louise Edeiken is the coauthor of Now That You're Pregnant. *She is the mother of one and a professional organizer and lecturer based in New Rochelle, New York; 914-654-8285.*

OUR BODIES

I was participating in a university-affiliated diet clinic when I got pregnant. I was about twenty pounds over-weight, and I wanted to get back in shape as well as look good in my pregnancy photographs. I didn't think I would get pregnant so quickly. I figured it would take me six months.

The problem with the diet clinic was that I have never done well in support groups—they make me hostile. I also tend to dislike the people who lead them; they're too perky and nice. Suffice it to say that I almost dropped out when the nutritionist, who reminded me of Betty White's Sue Ellen on the old "Mary Tyler Moore Show," said with all seriousness that a baked potato with mustard tastes as good as one with butter and sour cream. "To whom?" I muttered sarcastically.

Luckily for me, I got pregnant in two weeks and was able to leave the program gracefully before they asked me to. The downside was that I was not thin going into my pregnancy. While a friend at work was almost five months pregnant before anyone noticed, it was obvious after three months that either I was denying myself nothing foodwise or I was pregnant. I was forced to disclose my situation before I had intended.

At seven months I began wearing my husband's summer shorts. Bernie is six feet tall; I am five feet six inches. He weighs 170. While I will never reveal my pregnancy weight, suffice it to say I outgrew his shorts by my eighth month.

After Alexander was born, weighing in at eight pounds six ounces, I was horrified to find that there was no discernible change in my physical condition. My stomach was still distended, my rear end (not small to begin with) was Rubenesque, and my thighs were *sumo wrestler material. Worse yet, my once firm and well-proportioned breasts had seemingly overnight blossomed into earth-goddess primitive-sculpture material.*

Within the first month, possibly because of breastfeeding, I lost twenty-five pounds. The problem was I had gained fifty. Perhaps I should have found something I liked besides milk shakes to satisfy my calcium requirement.

In any event, when I couldn't stand looking at myself in a full-length mirror one more minute, I joined Weight Watchers as a last-ditch measure. As much as I disliked the group leader, who reminded me of a high school cheerleader who had attended too many Est seminars in the seventies, the method is foolproof. And while I absolutely detested listening to other overweight people discuss their lack of willpower (which seems hypocritical even to me), the system does work.

While my figure may never be what it was prechild, at least not without the aid of a topflight plastic surgeon, I can live with it. There is something almost gratifying about knowing that the reason your stomach may never be as flat as it was and your breasts will always sag a bit is that you gave birth. Thank God, Bernie agrees.

෴

WEIGHT GAIN AND LOSS DURING PREGNANCY

How much weight we should gain. The current recommendations for total weight gain for women of normal weight is 25 to 35 pounds; women who are underweight (more than 10 percent under ideal weight), 28 to 40 pounds; and women who are overweight, 15 to 25 pounds.

There is a correlation between the maternal weight gain in pregnancy and birth weight, so that in general the greater the weight gain, the larger the baby. Beyond that, does weight gain make a difference? Probably not, at least directly. Indirectly, it might. For example, if a woman does not gain enough weight, it is usually because the energy, or caloric, content in her diet is too low. If the caloric content is too low, other nutrients may be low as well. The woman may not get enough protein, enough vitamins, and so on, and there may be some damage in that, but it's an indirect one.

The caution against gaining too much weight is actually a

holdover from a former time. Thirty years ago it was generally believed that excessive weight gain led to a lot of complications, principally toxemia. There was folklore that suggested that whatever went wrong came from gaining too much weight. When those relationships are examined with modern scientific scrutiny, however, they don't really hold up. There probably isn't any complication that comes from excessive weight gain during pregnancy except that it may lead to obesity in the long run. Since pregnancy weight gain does correlate with fetal size, theoretically you could make a baby so big there would be difficulties in delivery. However, that really happens quite infrequently.

What a good pregnancy diet is. It's the same as a good non-pregnancy diet except you have an increased need for calories and protein. You need vitamins, both fat soluble and water soluble, and the richest source of these is fruit and vegetables. You need minerals; two that are particularly important in pregnancy are iron and calcium. You need iron because both you and the baby have to make blood. You need calcium because the baby has to get calcium, along with everything else, from you. As a general rule all nutrients are needed in increased amounts during pregnancy.

How to lose weight after giving birth. There are no secrets. Weight loss after pregnancy is fairly gradual, although many women mistakenly assume it's going to be rapid. That's not likely if they've gained an appropriate amount of weight. In fact, on average, it probably takes about six months to return to the lowest level, and some women never return to that level. In any event, it's unrealistic to expect weight loss to happen quickly.

Weight loss after delivery is like weight loss anytime. It's a balancing of intake and output. If you are breastfeeding, you need to take in 500 more calories daily to support lactation; that's a substantial amount. The output is the basal expenditure plus physical activity. To lose weight faster than the usual rate over the first six months a woman must either take in less or expend more from physical activity or both. A woman who eats more than she expends in physical activity will lose at a slower rate or maybe not lose at all.

So how do you lose weight after pregnancy? As we said earlier, you eat less, exercise more, or do both. If you eat less, it shouldn't be a marked degree of caloric restriction. You should aim at a gradual loss, but that's true anytime. Rather than going on a starvation diet and losing ten pounds in two weeks, which you are not likely to keep off, it's probably better to lose ten pounds in two months.

If you're nursing, your caloric and nutritional intake will determine, to some extent, your ability to produce milk. You'll need to make sure you're getting enough calcium because you're putting out more calcium. Your needs for iron become a little less because nursing women don't have menstrual periods. Some women may need iron supplements because they have depleted their store during pregnancy, but the actual needs of iron are less.

Source: Roy Pitkin, M.D., is a professor and chair of the UCLA Department of Obstetrics and Gynecology. He is the father of four and the grandfather of two. He says that, had he known grandchildren were so much fun, he would have had them first.

PREPARATION AND REPARATION DURING THE CHILDBEARING YEAR

Elizabeth Noble, P.T., author of seven books, including Essential Exercises for the Childbearing Year, *is director of Women's Health Resources in Harwich, Massachusetts. She is the mother of two.*

SB: What happens to our bodies during pregnancy that makes exercise so important?

EN: There are enormous physical changes: weight gain, stretching of muscles, softening of ligaments, and loosening of joints. In pregnancy the abdominal muscles become lengthened. They feel fine because they're stretched taut against the uterus, and the belly feels firm. They have a sort of stimulus to their tone and elasticity because the uterus is giving them resistance.

At the end of nine months, when the baby is born, the muscles are suddenly not stretched taut over the uterus; they are just lengthened like a semicircle. If you do isometrics from the first few days after birth—every time you sit down you just suck your belly button to your backbone while you breathe out forcefully and slowly—you can catch those muscles on the rebound while they are still elastic. If you wait a couple of weeks, a couple of months, or a couple of years to exercise, you most probably will be left with lengthened muscles. So it's really helpful if women can learn some exercises to do before pregnancy and then re-member to begin exercising again after the baby is born.

BIGGEST CHANGES AFTER PREGNANCY

■

"Fat! Percentage of body fat is higher. I will tackle that after I stop having kids. I'm about fifteen to twenty pounds heavier than I'd like to be, and I'm still nursing. After my next child I'll have everything redone."

■

"I'm ten pounds heavier, and my body (bones) seems to have stretched. My shoulders and hips are broader. My hair is no longer blond now, either. It's brown. I hate to exercise, so I just think about it. I haven't done anything about my hair color yet."

■

"My breasts have become smaller; my bladder, weaker; and my legs, flabbier. I began a diet/exercise program after I couldn't stand it another moment. Before that I cried a lot."

■

SB: What are the goals of a good prenatal exercise program?

EN: A key goal is to strengthen muscles that are challenged by pregnancy. You'll need to stretch out the muscles that tend to get tight from a sedentary lifestyle and also those that shorten during the adjustment to pregnancy. For example, because the abdominal muscles stretch, the back muscles tend to get tight just to counterbalance that. It's what we call the *bowstring effect* and can cause backache and fatigue. A comprehensive exercise program can alleviate that. Research has shown that the prevailing cause of lower back pain during pregnancy is lack of physical exercise.

And the *kind* of exercise you'll want to do in the childbearing year is very important. This is why I teach very slow classes where everybody does a variety of calisthenics and stretches with a lot of precision and supervision so that they understand how to perform the exercise properly without holding their breath, jerking, or straining. While a lot of people think exercise should be aerobic to have any benefit, aerobics is not my priority during the childbearing year. Throughout pregnancy there is added stress from the enlarging uterus, which the pelvic floor must uphold. I don't see the point in running just to keep your heart and lungs fit if you're ruining your pelvic floor. Besides, being pregnant itself is aerobic; your resting ventilation is up 50 percent. I do recommend recreational aerobics like walking and especially swimming. It's important to get out in the fresh air and do something that's relaxing, that takes you away from your routine and stress.

It is also important in a good prenatal class that the background music be soft and rhythmic, which allows everybody to talk and share. With all the women I've taught over the years, I would say that half come not only because they feel good about moving and stretching but because of meeting the other women and sharing fears and expectations. So you need a class that facilitates these meaningful exchanges.

A good prenatal class prepares women for labor. In my classes women do a hamstring stretch with their partners, which really helps them focus on their limits, working with the edge of pain, and it gives them tremendous courage for dealing with contractions later. We spend twenty minutes each hour and a half on relaxation; that can also include meditation or a guided visualization. Sometimes the moms pair off and do a foot massage, a back massage, a face massage, or sing. The relaxation component is always different and unexpected and helps them feel happy and relaxed.

SB: *What are the goals of a good postpartum program?*

EN: The main goal, as we talked about earlier, is to get the abdominal muscles very early, on the rebound, so they can bounce back to their former length. If you miss that opportunity, you may be stuck with lengthened muscles that are a challenge to strengthen or shorten because they atrophy. The pelvic floor doesn't get stretched during pregnancy, although toward the end of pregnancy it does descend about an inch. It is stretched during the birth, and there is often some nerve damage. Many women have weak pelvic floors and incontinence after birth because the nerve fibers are pulled apart from the muscle fibers they supply. The way you regenerate peripheral nerves is through exercise, so it's very important to exercise these key muscles.

GETTING BACK IN SHAPE

"The key to a postpartum fitness program is a combination of aerobic exercise, muscle strengthening, flexibility, relaxation, and proper nutrition," according to Julie Tupler, founder and director of Maternal Fitness in New York. "While pelvic floor exercises and simple isometric abdominal exercises may be done shortly after delivery, you can start a more comprehensive program after six weeks. Our B.A.K.S BASICS, an appropriate acronym since backaches are the largest complaint both during and after pregnancy, can be incorporated into your daily activities."

B

Belly breathing

Purpose: To provide more oxygen during aerobic exercise; to help you use the abdominal muscles correctly; for relaxation.

Exercise: Take air in through the nose and expand the belly. Exhale through the mouth and bring the belly back to the spine.

Belly dancing (pelvic tilts)

Purpose: To shorten the rectus abdominus (outermost abdominal muscles) and lengthen the lower back muscles; to prevent and help lower back pain.

Exercise: Start with a flat back and knees bent. Bring pelvis forward, hold for five counts, and bring back to flat back.

Positions: Standing, hands above knees, on all fours, and on back. Do ten repetitions in each position.

"Varicose veins; worse PMS. I've gotten to the point where I don't worry about the things I can't change. If I did, I would really make myself crazy."

■

"My breasts sagged, my tummy bulged, and I have a scar after my second pregnancy from the C-section. I've signed up for an exercise class twice a week. The changes don't bother me that much. My weight is about the same, and I can fit into a size six, so I don't care."

■

"No big changes. Everything came back very quickly. In fact I was thinner and lighter six weeks after the baby than before. So that felt good."

■

A

Aerobic exercise

Purpose: To strengthen the heart; to enhance endurance; to elevate one's mood due to a production of endorphins.

Exercise: Walking, swimming, stationary bike, treadmill, prenatal aerobic classes.

Precautions: Be able to carry on a conversation while exercising. Drink water before, during, and after exercise. Do safe exercises that won't put you at risk of falling. Listen to your body; if anything is painful, don't do it.

Abdominals

Purpose: To support the lower back. To get the abdominals back in shape after pregnancy. To bring diastasis together. Diastasis, a separation of the rectus abdominus around the navel, may happen during pregnancy with the stress of the enlarging uterus on this muscle.

- **Transverse muscle** (the innermost abdominal muscle, which wraps around like a corset, whose action is forward and backward; used in breathing and helpful during labor with pushing).

Exercise: Sit with back supported against a wall. Take a breath and bring navel to spine, release a little, and repeat. Do this isometric squeeze-release exercise one hundred times three times a day.

Tips: Only the navel moves. The emphasis is on backward movements. This will be felt in the back if done correctly. Count aloud when doing it so you will breathe.

- **Obliques** (the muscles that run diagonally down each side of the body).

Exercise: Squat with straight arms, heels on floor, and weight on outside of feet. Do one to five times a day. Read the newspaper each morning in this position. Hold onto an immovable object. Work your way up to five minutes per day.

- **Rectus abdominus** (outermost abdominal muscles that run vertically in front of the body).

Exercise: Head lifts. Lying on back with knees bent, expand belly, bring transverse to spine, hold it there, and then do pelvic tilt as you bring the chin to the chest. When you are lifting the head, bring the transverse out the back of the spine.

Tips: Before doing head lifts, check to see if you have a diastasis. If you have one of three fingers' width or more, put a sheet around your waist to bring the diastasis together when doing the head lifts. The transverse muscle needs to be strengthened first. Make sure you can do one hundred contractions easily at one time.

K

Kegels
Purpose: To strengthen the pelvic floor muscles.
Exercise: Squeeze or hold the muscle that starts and stops the flow of urine. One repetition is a ten-second hold. Do twenty repetitions five times a day. Do not do while urinating.

S

Squatting
Purpose: To strengthen oblique abdominal muscles and pelvic floor muscles. To stretch lower back muscles.
Exercise: Hold on to an immovable object and sit in a squatting position. Arms are straight, heels on floor, and weight on outside of feet. Work your way up to five minutes a day.

Stretching
Purpose: To lengthen muscles that have shortened during and after pregnancy in the chest, lower back, inner thighs, and back of legs.
Exercise: Stretch chest with a towel behind the head. Stretch inner thigh muscles with legs on wall. Stretch back of leg with one leg straight and one leg bent.
Tips: Before stretching any muscle, make sure you relax it. Breathe through the stretch, seeing the muscle lengthen.

Strengthening
Purpose: To shorten muscles that have been stretched out during pregnancy in the upper back, abdomen, pelvic floor, and legs.
Exercise: • Upper back. Hold a dyna band (a device for resistance) in front of you with straight arms. Pull the band out further and hold it there and then do little pulses for the count of ten. Do not bend the wrists.

- Legs. Do sitting knee press for inner and outer thighs. Have your partner or friend be your machine and give you resistance.

Abdominals (as described earlier).

Pelvic floor (as described earlier).

Tips: All exercises start with belly breath so that transverse will be IN on the part of all exercises.

Source: Julie Tupler, R.N., is a certified childbirth educator, certified personal trainer, and the founder and president of Maternal Fitness in New York, 4 Park Avenue 18-J, New York, NY 10016; 212-213-6949. B.A.K.S BASICS program © 1993, Maternal Fitness, Inc.

PEDIATRICIANS

When it was time to pick a pediatrician, I got some recommendations from my OB-GYN and called a few friends with children. By the time I was ready to begin interviewing doctors, I had a list of a half dozen people. Los Angeles is such a big city and there are so many doctors that you can be quite picky. It makes the choice that much more difficult.

Still, I had an ace in the hole. I asked my OB-GYN's wife, who is also his office manager, the name of their pediatrician. I figured whomever a doctor would pick for his own child would be a pretty safe bet.

However, before I interviewed their pediatrician, I set up an appointment with a friend's doctor. I wanted some means of comparison. This pediatrician was in a group practice of four. Their offices occupied half of a small building. Their waiting room was as big as my living room. There was another waiting room for sick children. We met in a special consultation office. There must have been a dozen examining rooms. I wondered how many office visits it took to pay the monthly rent.

The pediatrician, as it turned out, was quite nice. He reminded me of Robert Young in "Marcus Welby, M.D." One of his associates would have given James Brolin some competition in the looks department. I asked my prepared questions, and he answered them with dispatch. There was nothing specific about him that I didn't like. I just knew that he wasn't the right person.

The interview with my OB-GYN's pediatrician was quite different. He's a sole practitioner. His waiting room is quite small; sick children are scheduled in the afternoons. Bernie and I interviewed

WHAT WE LIKE ABOUT PEDIATRICIANS

■

"He's fantastic; he's also African-American. When my children were little, they thought all African-American men were doctors. I think it has given them a color-blind view of people."

■

"Very competent. He explains the facts, then allows us to decide what we think is best for our son. He is available readily and never makes me feel stupid."

■

"I've changed doctors three times and have learned what questions to ask. I like a doctor who doesn't rush me out of his office, doesn't prescribe drugs too freely, and respects me as a person."

■

with him at 6:00 P.M. after his last office visit. He was quite relaxed; we weren't.

Although my entire orientation toward life is to do research and ask questions, I had very few questions prepared. I did want to know what his philosophy toward his profession was, what he felt the role of a good pediatrician was, and how he dealt with emergencies. Other than that, I just wanted to make sure I felt comfortable with him and that he was a caring person who was good at what he did.

There are no questions you can ask to determine whether you like someone and feel good about him. That's a gut-level reaction. I knew I could check his professional reputation through the network of doctors who are my mother's friends. I did. He got rave reviews.

What seemed like a fairly effortless decision quickly became a critical one. Once Alex developed a fairly high temperature when he was two days old, his life, as far as I was concerned, was in the pediatrician's hands. I was greatly impressed by the way the doctor handled the whole situation. Not only did he take quick action when Alex became ill—he immediately put him into an incubator and scheduled a series of tests—but he also visited him at all hours. Since I was staying in a guest room in the hospital and came down to visit Alex throughout the day and night, I was always surprised and reassured to find that my doctor had been there before me. Once he had determined it was only a viral infection, he was still attentive, cautious, and watchful.

When things returned to normal, I was even more delighted by my choice. Over the years, the good doctor has given me plenty of sound advice. He has prepared me for each developmental stage. He always asks what Alexander is doing and what problems, if any, I'm having. He is genuinely interested in our collective progress, and he's got entertaining anecdotes to reinforce his advice.

What I didn't ask in our initial interview, and probably should have, was to meet his nurse. She has played an integral role in keeping Alex healthy. For the first year we talked on the phone a great deal. I called her when I was concerned about Alex's bowel movements. I called her when he got a rash. I called about his sleeping patterns, his eating habits, his teething problems, his colds, and his two bouts with the flu. She was always helpful, returned my calls quickly, referred questions to the doctor when appropriate, and generally kept both patient and mother in good shape.

As time has passed, I feel so lucky that even when Bernie and I knew absolutely nothing about how to pick a doctor for Alex, we made such a terrific choice. Thank God for small favors, and for big ones too.

ॐ

PEDIATRIC ISSUES

Richard J. Sagall, M.D., FAAFP, a board-certified family practitioner, is the editor of Pediatrics for Parents, *P.O. Box 1069 Bangor, ME 04402-1069, 207-942-6212, and the father of two.*

SB: What are the key pediatric issues for parents of a newborn?

RJS: The most important issue is feeling comfortable with the baby and comfortable with what you're doing. You hear all sorts of scary stories about things that have happened to other people, and you worry that they will happen to you. The reality is that most babies do well and most medical problems can be handled easily.

Deciding whether to breastfeed or bottlefeed your baby is one of the most important decisions parents should make *before* the baby is born. Every study has shown that breastfeeding conveys many advantages to the infant: less illness, better growth, fewer bowel problems, less colic, better sleeping. Human breast milk is the best nutrition available. Breastfeeding is important for the bonding between mother and child, and it helps the mother lose weight after childbirth and get back into shape.

Bedtime is another common issue. Parents need to understand that a baby who cries or fusses at bedtime is not a reflection of poor parenting skills; it's just the nature of that baby. Getting babies to sleep is difficult, and parents have to find a method that works best for them. Babies are remarkably resilient and varied. There are very few things within the general range of normal behavior that will hurt the baby. So you can either mold the baby to fit your lifestyle or mold your lifestyle to meet the baby's demands.

A word of advice to new parents: comparing babies is dangerous. There is a wide variation of normal. Much of what babies do is not predictive of what's going to happen later in their life. Whether a baby walks early or talks late doesn't mean anything. Some geniuses didn't talk until they were three or four. There are certainly some cognitive milestones that we want to see all babies reaching, but they will reach them at different times.

"He's very gentle with the kids and calm about the way he handles problems. Our first child was quite sick his first couple of months, so we know how lucky we are."

■

"I like his down-to-earth approach to child care and child rearing. His bedside manner is exceptional. He is very knowledgeable in children's medicine, and he has a good reputation."

■

"It's an association of male and female doctors. I like going to people who are my contemporaries."

■

"I like his availability for questions and visits. He's responsive to me and gentle with the baby."

■

WHAT WE DON'T LIKE

■

"He is sometimes short on empathy; too cut-and-dried."

■

"He isn't available enough, and we often see a nurse-practitioner. Occasionally the doctor is running behind schedule and rushes us through."

■

"Other pediatricians rotate weekend calls with him, and I don't like any of them nearly as well."

■

SB: *How should parents choose a doctor for their child?*
RJS: There are a number of variables to consider. It's a difficult decision because there is no hard-and-fast set of rules. Somebody who has completed the best residency and training in the world may have a very poor bedside manner or may not want to spend time talking with you. Find someone you feel comfortable with and who meets certain academic standards. Past training lessens in importance the longer someone is in practice. As they tell you in medical school, "Fifty percent of what we teach you won't apply to what you do within five years. The trouble is we don't know which 50 percent."

Find someone who has hospital privileges if that's a standard in the community. That means the physician has met a certain level of scrutiny by his or her colleagues. In larger cities where there are dozens of hospitals, make sure the doctor you select goes to a hospital you want to use. Obviously, if you're part of an HMO or PPO, that would influence your choice.

What I recommend for new parents-to-be is that, before you have the baby, you set up a visit with the physician to get acquainted, to find out about his or her background and philosophy, and to determine if you feel comfortable with each other.

Ask about coverage and availability. No doctor can be available all the time, but you want to make sure the doctor has a good coverage system, that the backup doctors are people you feel comfortable with. Sometimes you can't tell about their level of competence and your level of comfort with them because you won't meet them unless there is an emergency, but you should know who they are. Make sure that after-hours coverage is not just a visit to the emergency room.

Ask about fees. That's not a primary consideration, but it's definitely a concern. If you were to survey your community, you would probably find that the fees of most doctors who care for infants fit well within a standard range and there is not going to be much variation.

Find out who the office staff is, what their backgrounds are, and what functions they perform. Many times routine questions are answered by nurses rather than by the physician.

Talk to your friends who take their children to a prospective doctor. Realize that people have their own likes and dislikes and that some problems are purely ones of communication. It's amazing how one unpleasant experience can turn the greatest doctor in the world into the biggest villain.

SB: How can parents help their doctor give their children the best medical care?

RJS: Learn what's going on medically. Be alert to your child and how the child is feeling. Be aware of symptoms and what they mean. Common sense is important, and it's also important to be wary of all the information you get because there is so much misinformation floating around.

You have to become a partner in your child's medical care. I don't want patients of any age who want me to tell them what to do, because that takes them out of the process. Ultimately parents are responsible for their child's health. A doctor can make recommendations for treatment, but a parent makes the final decision. It is important to recognize that medicine is an art and not a science, particularly when you're dealing with children. There is no *one* right way to do most things, and there's controversy about what we might think is a simple procedure like treating an ear infection.

Finally, it's important for parents to have expectations as to what they hope to get out of a visit with the doctor. When you come in—particularly with a sick child—you should have some thoughts about what you want to walk away with in terms of advice and treatment. Be forthright.

VISITING THE PEDIATRICIAN WITH YOUR INFANT

Every doctor does an examination differently. Some doctors start at the toes and work their way up. Some start at the head and work their way down. Some start with the heart—especially when the baby is not crying, so that the doctor can get a chance to listen to it before any crying begins. Not every doctor or even the same doctor will necessarily use the same system to examine each baby, but a good examination is going to include a total overall appraisal.

• **Growth.** Grandparents like to brag about how heavy an infant is. Parents like to use the child's growth pattern as a means of evaluating how well they, the parents, are doing. The doctor, however, is concerned only about whether the growth pattern is normal. That, of course, is where the problem lies. What is normal and what isn't? What might be normal for one child may not be normal for another of exactly the same age. Basically the doctor uses the growth measurements of the head circumference, the weight, and

"I do have to wait an hour to see him. This gets tiresome when our son no longer finds the waiting room interesting."

■

"The practice is doing so well it's difficult to get appointments."

■

"Passive toward me—not proactive—which I would prefer as a first-time parent."

■

289

the body length as a basis for evaluating the baby's status at any given time. There are conventional statistics available that have been put into graph form, and this is what most pediatricians use. A so-called normal pattern usually implies that the baby has good health and good nutrition.

• **Ear.** The doctor will look at the ear to check for the presence of an auditory canal and the recognizable anatomical landmarks of the eardrum. The doctor will look at the way the ear is shaped and how high or how low it is in relation to a line drawn from the corner of the eye toward the back of the head. Low-set ears (ears that fall below the line) are sometimes a clue to look for genetic abnormalities. Ears are very frequently involved in genetic syndromes because they form early and genetic problems develop in early gestation. One of the most common problems with the ears are little pits that can occur in the front of the upper part of the ear and within or behind the structure of the ear. They are usually harmless, although they may have some potential for infection or may be part of a genetic syndrome.

• **Eyes.** The doctor looks for the movement of the eyes. Are they moving together or separately? Do they tend to deviate in or out? The doctor will use the ophthalmoscope to see if the baby has what is called a *red reflex*, the absence of which may indicate a cataract or other ocular pathology.

• **Nose.** Most babies must breathe through their nose because breathing through the mouth is usually a learned process. Therefore, the doctor checks for patency (lack of obstruction). If the baby is breathing through the mouth, the doctor will have to determine whether the nose is obstructed—not common, but it does occur.

• **Throat.** The doctor observes whether the baby's facial expression is symmetric when crying and not crying. Does the mouth droop when the baby cries? One side drooping could indicate facial paralysis caused by pressure in the birth canal, although that is rarely a problem. When the doctor opens the mouth, he or she is looking for clefts of the gum borders and the palate, any flaws in the uvula, and the presence of natal teeth. Every so often, a baby will be born with a natal tooth. Some are normal, but the vast majority are not well formed and are frequently removed.

• **Neck.** The doctor checks the neck, looking for swellings that may represent lymph glands or cysts. The doctor is looking for sinus tracts, any little pits or holes in the neck, especially in the front of the neck or in the anterior-lateral area, which may represent abnormalities in the development of the ears or the thyroid. In utero the thyroid starts way up on the back of the floor of the mouth and migrates down into the neck, where sometimes it gets misplaced. The doctor will check the clavicles (the collarbones). He or she will check to see if the baby's arms can be extended or abducted (when you raise the arms up) and the baby's response to these movements.

• **Chest.** When listening to the chest, the doctor is listening primarily for breath sounds throughout both sides of the chest, in the front and back. The doctor checks the heart for the rhythm of the heartbeat and for the heart sounds. Are there any abnormalities that may suggest a heart murmur, which in itself may or may not be normal but may suggest that other studies are necessary?

• **Abdomen.** The doctor will generally look at the contour. Is it bloated, soft, or depressed? Then the doctor will palpate it to see if any of the organs are enlarged. Sometimes, in a very young baby, the doctor will feel the kidneys to see if they are normal size. Of course, at the same time, the doctor is always looking for an abnormal mass that will represent a tumor. These are rare, but certain tumors can be present in the newborn period.

• **Hips.** Hips are very important because hip dislocation can be corrected. The doctor is going to check the hips for their stability, their symmetry, and flexibility. The doctor is going to check at some point to see if he or she can feel the femoral pulses, which when absent can be due to obstruction of the aorta or a blockage of the heart valve.

• **Genitals.** The doctor will make sure that the genitals look reasonably normal. If it's a boy and he has been circumcised, the doctor will want to make sure that the circumcision is clean and that the parents are taking care of it. If it's a noncircumcised boy, nothing has to be done about retracting the foreskin at the baby age. But the doctor will ask the parents if they can see the baby urinate to make sure the urine is coming out. The doctor will check the testicles.

With a girl the doctor checks for the general shape of the labia. The doctor will want to make sure the clitoris is present, the baby can urinate, and there is an opening in the vaginal area. Every so often the baby has an obstruction that has to be opened at some point.

• **Extremities.** The doctor checks the shape of the legs. Are they bowed? Are there any abnormalities? Is there an extra toe or finger or a rudimentary extra toe or finger? Once in a while dead skin forms around the distal part of the big toe, and the nail gets caught in it. Sometimes the doctor has to help free up the nail before the baby gets an infection or a hangnail.

• **Other assessments.** While the doctor is playing with and checking the baby, he or she is also doing a neurological assessment. Is the baby floppy? Does he or she feel normal? When you hold the arms, do they snap back or fall down? When you hold the baby upright, does the baby extend the legs or not? How much head lag is there if you put the baby down and pull the baby up? What kinds of postural attitudes does the baby take when in the mother's arms?

Some doctors examine the reflexes, and others don't. When examining the baby's back, the doctor is looking for sinus tracts, little pits or dimples that indicate there may be a leak from the spinal cord to the outside that would have to be removed surgically. The doctor is looking at the skin for birthmarks or other marks that shouldn't be present. The inspection of the baby goes on simultaneously with each part of the examination.

• **Questions for parents.** Asking the parents what they have observed is one of the most important parts of the examination. Has the baby smiled? Does the baby respond to your voice? Does he or she turn the head toward the origin of sounds? Does the baby startle? Does he or she suck vigorously? How does the baby sleep? The answers to these questions are the way the doctor determines developmental milestones. The parents handle the baby much more than the pediatrician does. Even though the doctor shouldn't miss anything major in the examination, the parents may find a little gland, or bump, or something on the back of the scalp, or a lymph node that the doctor hasn't noticed. They should feel very free to ask about it. I would encourage parents to write their questions down and bring them to every examination.

Source: Harvey Shipper, M.D., is a practitioner of pediatrics in Santa Monica, California. He is the father of one.

AMERICAN ACADEMY OF PEDIATRICS IMMUNIZATION SCHEDULE

Age	DTP[1]	Polio[2]	MMR	Hepatitis B[3]	Haemophilus[1]	Tetanus-Diphtheria
Birth				✓		
1–2 months				✓		
2 months	✓	✓			◆	
4 months	✓	✓			◆	
6 months	✓				◆	
6–18 months				✓		
12–15 months					◆	
15 months			✓			
15–18 months	●	✓				
4–6 years	●	✓				
11–12 years			*	#		
14–16 years				#		✓

[1] The Hboc-DTP combination vaccine may be substituted for separate vaccinations for Haemophilus and DTP.

[2] Children in close contact with immunosuppressed individuals should receive inactivated polio vaccine.

[3] Infants of mothers who tested seropositive for hepatitis B surface antigen (HBsAg+) should also receive hepatitis B immune globulin (HBIG) at or shortly after the first dose. These infants also will require a second hepatitis B vaccine dose at 1 month and a third hepatitis B vaccine injection at 6 months of age.

◆ Depends on which Haemophilus influenzae type b vaccine was given previously.

● For the fourth and fifth dose, the acellular (DTaP) pertussis vaccine may be substituted for the DTP vaccine.

* Except where public health authorities require otherwise.

Where resources permit, the hepatitis B vaccine series of three immunizations should be given to previously unimmunized preadolescents or adolescents.

Source: Used with permission of the American Academy of Pediatrics, 141 Northwest Point Blvd., P.O. Box 927, Elk Grove Village, IL 60009-0927; 708-228-5005

PETS

My sister and brother-in-law are pet people. I am not. I like dogs in a global sort of way but I hate having dog hair all over my clothes. I dislike big dogs who jump up on you, lick you in the face, and slobber all over your car windows. I can't stand small, yappy dogs who nip at your feet, run around furiously, and squeal constantly. I grew up with two dachshunds whom I loved, so I guess you can say that I like short-haired hot dogs with feet.

I detest cats of all kinds. They are imperious, willful, and disloyal. When I moved in with Bernie, he had a cat, Toby, whom he'd raised from a kitten and who was then fifteen years old. Because I loved Bernie so much, I vowed to try and develop a relationship with his long-time companion. Besides, he assured me that Toby was very old in cat years.

My relationship with Toby never worked out. Since cats are one of the few species in creation that love people who loathe them, Toby became my best friend. It was a one-sided love affair. He died when he was eighteen years old—surely a Guinness world record. I am convinced that it was my lack of affection that propelled him on.

Needless to say, Alexander does not have any pets, although we did make a go of it briefly. We won him a goldfish at a local fair. It cost $7 for us to alternate trying to toss a Ping-Pong ball into a small goldfish bowl.

Alex was ecstatic as he carried "Sally" home in a plastic bag. I assumed he named her Sally because his favorite book that week was The Cat in the Hat (and the little boy in the book doesn't seem to have a name). Once we got home, we had to go out and buy a *real goldfish bowl, food, and a small net to take Sally out when we cleaned her bowl.*

When I told an animal-loving friend about our new boarder, she reminded me how short-lived goldfish are and suggested I begin reading about what to tell Alex when Sally died. I couldn't believe it. We'd just spent $20 on the fish and her living environment. I had bought enough food for Sally to live to a ripe old age. I was sure my friend was overreacting.

Two days later, Sally was floating at the top of the bowl. I didn't know what to do. Alex was playing at a friend's house; I called Bernie at work.

"Sally's dead," I moaned.

"Oh, no," he responded with enormous sadness in his voice. "I can't believe it!" He sounded devastated. I thought he was over-reacting a bit. We'd had the fish for only two days. It was not long enough to develop a relationship. But I didn't want to appear unfeeling.

"What will I tell Alex?" I asked.

"Nothing. He doesn't know Sally. Why tell him anything?" Suddenly, everything became perfectly clear. Bernie and I had a mutual acquaintance—whom we both liked quite well—named Sally. He must have thought she *had died.*

"Oh my God," I said. "Not that Sally."

"What?" he asked with genuine confusion in his voice.

"Not Sally the woman; Sally the fish." After a moment's pause we both burst into uncontrollable laughter, which was somewhat inappropriate but a great relief as well.

As it turned out, Alex handled Sally's death in a much more mature manner than we did. When we told him Sally had died, he shrugged his shoulders, looked sad for a few moments, and then went back to playing with his Legos.

He never mentioned a word about having another pet until recently, and suddenly he's begun talking about it a lot. When I think about all the different types of pets he's suggested—birds, cats, hamsters, snakes, and bunnies—a dog sounds quite appealing in comparison. In fact, lately I have been wondering if our yard is too small for a short-haired hot dog with feet.

ॐ

THE UPSIDE AND DOWNSIDE OF HAVING PETS

∎

"Our tortoise is practically care-free. We can't have pets with hair due to allergies. The kids get sad when the fish die."

∎

"Our son loves the cats, is very gentle with them, and respects them. The downside is the hair."

∎

"Our daughter and the puppy play well together. She will grow up unafraid of animals. The dog requires a lot of attention. Puppies are more difficult than babies."

∎

"Having pets teaches the kids to be kind and gentle. The downside is that the pets are jealous of the kids."

∎

WHY PETS ARE GOOD FOR KIDS

"There is a great proviso in saying that pets are good for kids," explains Dr. Robert Poresky, associate professor of human development and family studies at Kansas State University. "They are good only if the parents handle them properly. There is nothing automatic about animals becoming 'good' pets."

Some of the research Poresky has done at Kansas State University—in which he has studied the impact of pets in forty-five families with children aged three to six—does show benefits in terms of the children's social development and increased evidence of empathy and cooperation. "We even had an IQ effect, which I didn't quite believe," he says with a laugh.

"But companion animals do help build trust—which is a key element in self-confidence," Poresky explains. "They also help kids become less egocentric—and this is based on Jean Piaget's theory that kids become less egocentric by interacting with others. To interact, you need feedback," Poresky says, "and animals can provide that. If the cat is fed up with the way a child is holding it, the cat is going to leave. So the animal is telling the child how to work with him. He is giving the child another point of view.

"But I think one of the key factors in all this is how the parent oversees and monitors the child's relationship with the companion animal," Poresky says. "And we're talking basically about responsive animals, which are pretty much dogs and cats rather than snakes and turtles." Poresky recommends that before a family buys a new animal the parents ask themselves whether they are ready to have both an animal and a child.

"The pet is a big additional responsibility," he cautions. "And the child—especially if he or she is only three or four—can assume only part of it. Toddlers can feed the animal, spend time with the animal, hold the animal, and learn to interact with the animal. But you wouldn't really want a three-year-old to change a litter box, would you?" he asks.

Before buying an animal, he suggests you make sure its temperament or nature is appropriate for your child. "If you're talking about young kids, you need an animal that is pretty well behaved and self-controlled. It's partly maturity. With a puppy that is bouncing all over the place, the toddler is going to get knocked over. Not because the puppy is nasty, just because puppies bounce. A more mature animal can interact quite nicely with a young child," he says.

Finally, Poresky explains why pets *can* be good for kids. "The child can talk to the animal if the child isn't great on verbalization. One of the really nice things about companion animals is that they are almost always there for you. They are very good at listening. They are very good at loving and attending, and they usually don't give you much static. They provide a lot of emotional support. If you have a problem, they are sympathetic. If nobody else loves you that day, generally your companion animal will. In that way, owning a pet builds on the idea of Dr. Eric Ericson's (renowned child psychoanalyst and educator) definition of basic trust, which Ericson says comes from a warm, responsive environment. As long as the animal is such that it can provide that kind of feedback, it will work out very nicely."

Source: Dr. Robert Poresky is an associate professor of human development and family studies at Kansas State University, and the father of two.

TIPS FOR FINDING AND CARING FOR THE RIGHT PET

1. The entire family should decide whether they really want a pet. Everyone must be a part of the conversation. Then you need to address the first issue, which is "Let's learn a little bit in general about dogs or cats or rabbits and see whether this is a responsibility we want to take on." If it is, you should decide whether you want a pet that requires high, low, or no maintenance.

2. The next question is whether you want a puppy, a kitten, a bunny or a little anything or whether you are better off with a full-grown pet. All baby animals require a lot more maintenance. The advantage of any baby pet is that it's cute and small. The disadvantage is that raising it is a full-time job.

3. If you want a dog, pick one from a breed known to be mild tempered, rather than a high strung and neurotic breed. Even if Pongo and Purdy are "in," a Dalmatian may not be the best pet for your family. You need to research the breed. Of course the ASPCA recommends going to a shelter. If you know you want a particular breed, you can also go through rescue clubs. If you don't care about the pedigree, you are better off with a mixed breed. There is less chance of genetic disease and high-strung temperament.

4. When you're thinking about cats, consider an older cat or a mellow cat. A declawed cat might be a safer bet for little kids.

"My children love their pets. Since we've got four kids, we've had a number of different pets throughout the years. We've now got two dogs and three cats, although we've had birds, hamsters, and gerbils. What's remained consistent is that all the kids fight over who's going to take care of the pets during the first week. After that, I become the primary caretaker."

■

"Our dog loves the children unconditionally. Cats and kittens teach the kids limits. Animals don't put up with mistreatment."

■

"The kids study the pets. They see the demands of caretaking and eventually will do it themselves. It teaches them responsibility and provides companionship. Since my kids are young, I do most of the cleaning and feeding."

■

The ASPCA doesn't advocate declawing, but some cats available at the animal shelter may already be declawed. (If you adopt a declawed cat, you are not sanctioning declawing; you are saving the cat's life.)

5. Birds can be very fragile. They are not very huggable. The smaller birds—that children like to pick up—can easily have their necks broken. The bigger birds that are a lot of fun, like the macaws, bite. You have to watch the weather with birds. They don't respond well to drafts. A bird can have a heart attack during an earthquake or a thunderstorm. Birds can be quite messy.

6. Bunnies are a popular pet, but they are very high maintenance. Contrary to what the media show us, they don't like to be held. They will sit next to you if you're nice to them. Their necks and backs are very fragile. Bunnies groom themselves like cats do but they don't know how to vomit, so they require once-a-week treatment for fur balls; otherwise they'll die. They can be litter box trained and make wonderful house pets.

7. Another popular category includes guinea pigs, hamsters, rats, gerbils, and mice. Rats are great. They are low maintenance, easy to take care of. They tend not to bite like hamsters and guinea pigs. They keep themselves clean. They're very intelligent. They live a long time, and they will develop a personality. All these animals are nocturnal so they are more active at night than during the day.

8. Snakes are not great pets for young children. They tend to bond with one person.

9. Some tortoises are on the endangered species list, so you need a permit to buy them. Little turtles—like the kind we grew up with—are not legal anymore and there is a high rate of disease. Lizards and iguanas require care. They are not appropriate for young children.

10. For whatever animal you buy—particularly ones that are not as common as dogs and cats—you need to find a veterinarian. If you just let a pet die when it is sick, you need to think about the message you are giving to your children. The subliminal message is that things that are alive are disposable; children might assume that if they should become sick or inconvenient you might get rid of them. A lot of research is being done that recognizes the correlation between the desensitization of children toward animals and future criminal behavior.

It's important to remember, then, that a family pet not

only is a major commitment but can also give children some of the most positive lessons life has to offer, such as self-respect, sharing, caring, and a reverence for living things.

Source: Madeleine Bernstein, the mother of two, is an attorney and the regional vice president of the ASPCA in Southern California; 212-876-7700. Check your local phone book for an ASPCA or humane society in your area.

DOGS AND KIDS

When you are choosing a dog, you need to realize that no matter how humane you are, if you have children, the dog is going to be whacked. The dog's meals are going to be interrupted. He's going to have peanut butter put in his hair. Your child may try to ride him, pull his tail, or step on his paws. So it's very important to select a dog with a sweet temperament. You don't want a dog who demonstrates guarding behavior or gets very upset if you take something away.

Once you choose "the right breed," it is a good idea—if your children are old enough—for everyone in the family to go for dog training. Everyone needs to learn to communicate with the dog, and the dog needs to learn what behavior is acceptable.

If you're pregnant and you have a dog that precedes your baby, you have to be very careful. The fact that your dog is already good with you or an older child doesn't matter in the least. If you have gotten your dog from a shelter, you won't necessarily know everything there is to know about the dog, so you can't determine how he will be with a newborn.

A problem we see frequently—particularly in a house where the dog is treated well or where there are no children—is that when you introduce the baby to the dog, the dog does not like the baby. He may think the baby is a rabbit and try to eat him, a toy and try to play with him, or a rival for your attention and try to hurt him.

What we recommend is preparation. Look at your dog's behavior and deal with it before your baby comes home from the hospital. If your dog snaps, recognize that a snap is just an unconnected bite and train him not to snap. If your dog is used to eating without interruption, start taking food out of his mouth and begin interrupting his meal. Once you're home with a newborn, you are not going to want to begin a dog obedience class.

The key is selecting the right dog and preparing him in advance. Take home the baby's T-shirt from the hospital with the baby's scent on it. If the dog is attached to one parent, be sure that parent shows the dog attention when you come home from the hospital. When you coo at the baby, mention the dog's name and say, "Oh, you're going to have this wonderful dog, Benjamin, to play with."

Never introduce the dog to the baby without having someone hold the dog. Let him sniff the baby. Show the dog some of the baby's toys. Don't let go of the dog until he is able to walk alongside the baby and not growl or try to charge it. No matter how sweet your dog is, *never* leave him alone with your baby. That is when fatalities occur. It is said that a child under seven should not be left alone with a dog, but some breeds should never be left alone with a child.

Source: Madeleine Bernstein has produced Baby Training Your Other Baby, *a brochure that is available through the ASPCA; 212-876-7700.*

NAMING YOUR PET

"The number one priority for naming your pet should be a name that appeals to you," says Dr. Wayne Bryant Eldridge, author of *The Best Pet Name Book Ever.* "People who try to impress other people with their pet's name are probably as uninspiring as people who try to impress others with their pet's unique breed or heritage. Naming a pet is not a contest of who can come up with the cutest name.

"It's like naming a child. You want to find a name that fits your pet that you're not going to regret later. A lot of names from the sixties and seventies are not as appealing today. I doubt that Cher is really glad she named her child Chastity."

Dr. Eldridge, who has been asked to name many pets in his career as a doctor of veterinary medicine, has chronicled more than three thousand names in twenty-two categories in his book. Some of the most popular categories include:

- **Appearance**, which is the most common way to name a pet. More dogs are named after their appearance than anything;
- **Personality**, a way to relate to your pet in a personal way. People who name their pet by personality rather than appearance tend to be closer to their pets;
- **Terms of endearment**, which also imply a very personal rela-

tionship. Lovey, Sweetie Pie, Patty Cake are all somewhat self-explanatory, and they certainly suggest affection;

- **Historical names**, which are usually picked by people who are intelligent and tend to look beyond the obvious. Half the people name pets this way to impress other people; the other half are genuine history buffs;

- **Unusual names and nicknames**, which provide an opportunity for the owner to express his or her creativity. Names like Jenni-purr, Purrsnickidy, and Sir Pent, are usually spontaneous choices; and

- **Just for fun** names that encompass a lot of celebrity names like Madonna, Willie Nelson, or Ringo Starr. These names are usually an indicator that the owner likes the entertainment industry. I don't think people are trying to make a statement. On the other hand, people who name their animals after expensive cars usually wear big gold chains and try to impress others with whom they know or where they've been.

Source: Wayne Bryant Eldridge, D.V.M., author of The Best Pet Name Book Ever, *is a veterinarian as well as the owner of the Pet Place Veterinary Center, 1806 NW Military Highway, San Antonio, TX 78213; 210-349-9393. He is the father of three.*

PHOTOGRAPHS AND HOME VIDEOS

ince Bernie is an art director, he knows all about photography. I don't, so it was only fitting that I become the official family photographer. On our first Christmas together Bernie bought me a new camera because it was so easy to use.

Our photo albums reflect my picture-taking philosophy: "Candid shots are unattractive. Picturesque sights were created to stand in front of and be photographed. A phony smile is better than none at all."

In the first seven years of our marriage we shot three albums full of pictures. In the first eighteen months of Alexander's life, we also filled three albums. During the first few months of his life we were shooting two rolls of twenty-four exposures a month.

The pictures I treasure most are the ones we took in the hospital. We didn't record Alex's birth, but we do have a few precious photographs of his first few days of life. He seems so tiny and helpless. The look on Bernie's face as he is holding him reflects such love and pride it still brings tears to my eyes. The photograph of my mother and the baby is one I'll always treasure.

I, on the other hand, should have had a hairstylist, manicurist, and makeup person visit me on the second day of my stay. I looked just the way I felt. And it's amazing how one's pregnancy weight doesn't disappear with the birth. So my pictures look more like the "before" version of the before-and-after photographs used by weight-loss clinics. It's not my best moment; we keep them in the album only so that Alexander knows that I participated in the birthing process.

When Alex was eighteen months old our picture taking tapered *off. Once we bought a video camera, shooting videos seemed a better way to record his life. Besides, it wasn't that easy to get a toddler in focus for still shots. And I think our camera had run its course. The photos were all right, but we didn't have a zoom or a wide-angle lens, and when we got too close to Alex he knew he was being photographed and ran away.*

When I took a roll of film to be developed for the first time in months, and the proprietor of the camera store asked me where I'd been. "Well, we're just not taking as many photographs these days," I answered apologetically. "We've been using the video camera more often."

He shook his head. "You'll be sorry," he admonished. "How many times do you think you'll play back the videos?" I shrugged.

"Take it from experience. Not very often. But photographs last a lifetime."

I knew he was right. We'd played back the videos only a couple of times; I looked at the photo album at least once a month.

"Besides," he went on, whetting my appetite, "there are some terrific new cameras on the market. Let me show you. They're easy. They shoot great photographs. You can buy additional lenses." I left with five rolls of film, and a brochure for the new thirty-five-millimeter camera I wanted for Christmas.

When I showed the brochure to Bernie, he said he thought that buying a new thirty-five-millimeter camera was a bit excessive for a family who had just bought a video camera. I disagreed. "Photographs last a lifetime," I intoned.

He smiled weakly. Sometimes a phony smile is better than none at all.

꒰

PHOTO TIPS

• **Steady as she goes.** A nervous shutter finger equals fuzzy pictures. Hold the camera steady with both hands. Keep your arms close to your body. Press the shutter button smoothly.

• **Move close.** When in doubt, get close. Getting close to your baby is probably the most important step to better pictures. Make sure your photo says "This is my son/daughter." The subject (your child) should fill a third or more of the photo area.

• **Keep the background plain.** Look through your viewfinder and inspect the scene before you press the shutter button. Move

WHAT WE DO

■

"I have had a professional photo taken of the baby every four months of his life (he's fifteen months old), but the most priceless photos are the candid photos I've taken of him with his dad, grandmas, and grandpas."

■

"Marry someone who's organized. That's what I did. All our home videos are cataloged and up to date. All the photographs are organized in photo albums. We never let pictures pile up. We've kept baby books on the kids, and they're fun to look at as the children get older."

■

around until you eliminate distractions in the background. Try using the sky or the grass as a background.

• **Watch the light.** The light in your scene can change your photo dramatically. Study the light before you take your photo; see how the direction of the light affects your child—front light (the sun behind you) always works well, back light (sun behind the child) will create a silhouette, and side light (sun at the side of the child) will show form and texture.

• **Change your view.** Try experimenting with viewpoint. While children are fun to photograph because they are generally more animated than adults, they seldom hold still. You need to perfect some of your photographic skills to capture them on film. Move close to get a full image in your photo. Stoop down for an eye-level view. Let them act naturally—doing the things they enjoy. Use a fast shutter speed or flash if they are on the go.

Source: Adapted from HOTSHOTS with Any Camera. *Rochester, New York: Eastman Kodak Company,* © *1991; 800-242-2424.*

A PHOTOGRAPHER'S VIEW

• Spontaneity is probably the best thing to go after. Keep a camera loaded at all times. That's the best way to get the extraordinary picture.

• If you don't want to bother with a lot of lenses, buy a camera that goes from a wide angle to a medium-length lens. A twenty-millimeter to an eighty-five-millimeter is a great camera to have because it affords you a wide angle and a longer lens. All cameras are fairly high quality now, so there are a lot of choices. The only difference between a professional camera and an amateur camera is how durable it is going to be. You might want to lean more toward the bigger thirty-five-millimeter cameras that have auto-focusing and auto-zoom lenses. I think the quality is much better than the smaller ones like the Sure Shot and the One Step.

• Use a higher-speed film like a 400 ASA if you're just starting out. The quality of this film is much better now, so it won't look very grainy. As you get more comfortable, the higher-quality film has a lower ASA. The 200 or 100 ASA is preferable.

• Consider using a flash all the time—indoors and outdoors. A little strobe light is great. It's more difficult to use because it requires some practice, but if you cut back the power of the flash so that it's almost not there, you get a prettier, saturated picture. That's what they do in motion pictures.

- A little warming filter—like an 81—is great. That would be more for color slides. One of the nicest places to photograph kids is in open shade. That means where there is no direct sunlight. You're on the side of a building or in a north-light window. You get a beautiful quality of light, and it's very easy to find this. But when you're in the shade, the light becomes more blue, so you use the filter to warm up the photograph.

- An overcast day is wonderful if you're shooting color film. You can get a beautiful soft light. People think that photographs won't come out well when it's not sunny, but that's just not true.

- Find a good color laboratory. A lot of these labs that process one-hour photos are terrible. You should try a few different labs before you settle on one because these are your once-in-your-lifetime shots and there's a lot to be said for the processing. That's where the film usually gets damaged.

Source: Peter Darley Miller, a professional photographer and director of music videos, is the father of two and lives in Santa Monica, California.

HAVING YOUR CHILDREN PHOTOGRAPHED PROFESSIONALLY

Many people have their children photographed at milestones in their lives, but as long as the parents do not have great expectations, you can photograph children at any age. To get a *great* baby shot, the child needs to be able to lift his or her head. If parents want a photograph taken earlier, the mother or father can hold the baby, and you can get a great shot if you crop the parents out. There are other ways to photograph babies: you can put them on a blanket or lay them on their side. But if you want an "energy" shot, where they show personality, it's usually better to wait a few months.

If I photograph a one- or a two-year-old, it's important that the child has a good time. We play lots of games like peekaboo. When they "peekaboo," I get the shot. With a little one, we sometimes play with the pacifier. We'll take it out of the baby's mouth and say, "Here it comes," and they'll laugh. You really have to get down on your knees and play with children to make it work.

If I develop a rapport with the child right away, I'll get good

"We take loads of photographs during the year. My favorites are of my son and daughter a half hour after their births and one of both of them kissing with bubbles covering them from head to toe in the bathtub. We have a professional photograph of our family taken for the holidays. It's a good way to let friends and relatives across the country see how we've changed."

■

"We don't have a video camera, but luckily my sister does, and we have borrowed it on occasion. I loved watching the home movies my parents took of us when we were children. I'm afraid I haven't been as conscientious, but each year I put together a photo calendar of the grandkids for our parents. They love it, and it's a great keepsake."

■

"We have videotaped our children's births. We take short videos of each child every month for their first year to track their development. Our children love watching these tapes."

■

pictures. I let the children get involved in the process. I'll let them use my camera and push the button. To get their attention I use puppets, toys that make noise, musical instruments, or two pieces of metal that clang together. Sometimes you can make funny noises, and that makes them laugh; a mother or father will make a sneezing sound, and the child will smile and giggle.

A regular session with a child usually takes an hour or less, and it's nice to have two people per child. One of them can help get reactions from the child. The other person may have to help tell the child where to stand. Children always do better with people they know. If a child is having fun, we can take our time and go for a number of good shots. If he or she is antsy—and I know I'll have a half hour at best—I shoot quickly.

I ask the parents to take home a child who is unhappy or starts crying and to come back to the studio another time. If you're doing a clothing change, and the child doesn't want to, you stop. Most young children like to be outdoors better than in the studio. Many parents like the studio shots better. If I can get a few good studio shots and then go outside, everyone is happy. When the parents are willing to let children be themselves—and not worry about whether or not they smile or laugh—it's always easier, and you end up with some wonderful shots.

I shoot primarily in black and white because it's a timeless medium; it's permanent and archival. I like to capture what's inside the children. Usually that shows in their eyes, so color is more distracting. For a special photograph I hand-tint the prints in color. I like it better than photographing in color because it's more subtle. I'll either hand-tint the whole photograph, tint it in sepia and black and white, or hand-tint particular areas. It's quite beautiful.

Source: Ronna Mendelson Photography, LAPA, 626 Broadway, Santa Monica, CA 90402; 310-395-3300.

VIDEO TIPS

- As with still photography, keep a plain background. There is a feature called *standby* that you can engage. Count to three and see if you like what you see before you record.

- Be careful of the light, because most video cameras adjust for an overall lighting situation. They won't be specific. That means if you get a child in a window that's too big, the camera will adjust for the larger picture. So you have a dark foreground and the window will be lit. A lot of shots are blown that way.

- Go in for the close shot. People don't want to see everything. They want to see the little nuances of your children: their feet, their toes, their hands, their nose, their lips. Those are the things that are very interesting, and with a lot of the video cameras you're able to do almost a macro-shot. You don't want to do this all the time, but you do get a real sense of your children when you go in close. You get less of a sense when they are running around and doing things.

- Go for the "firsts," whether it's riding the bike for the first time, the first day of school, or the first trip to Disneyland. You'll appreciate having a record of those important events.

- Try to shoot in the early morning or in the late afternoon. These are the best times with videotape because it's very sensitive to contrast. It doesn't have a broad range. It's very complicated to light things for video.

- If you're really a fanatic and want great videos, then use a different tape each time, try to think about what you're going to shoot in advance, and try to do in-camera sequential editing. But that takes a lot of planning.

- Don't shoot for long periods of time. Later on you won't care about most of it. You'll end up wanting to fast-forward through it; it's a waste of film. Take little snippets of everything. It's much more interesting.

- The best thing you can ever do is go to Disneyland and videotape the rides with your children. You will get zillions of miles out of that. If you videotape the whole experience—from leaving in the car through the entire afternoon—your children will want to watch it all the time. It's better than Barney.

Source: Peter Darley Miller, a professional photographer and director of music videos, is the father of two and lives in Santa Monica, California.

CAPTURING COMICAL GESTURES

Since most babies—even very young ones—are natural mimics, it usually doesn't take much effort to lure them into a spell of silliness. Make a silly face and you'll likely get a sillier one back. Meal and bath times are especially promising opportunities for funny pictures since such adventurous situations (for baby and parent) lend themselves well to lively behavior.

Because it's hard to be both entertainer and photographer simultaneously, it's usually best to have someone else— a parent or sibling—keep the baby amused while you snap pictures. Indoors, a flash is a good idea because it will provide extra lighting and its short duration will freeze those prize-winning reactions. If you prefer to use existing light, use a very-high-speed film for color prints.

Source: Winning Pictures: 100 Ideas for Outstanding Photographs. *Rochester, New York: Eastman Kodak Company,* © *1988; 800-242-2424.*

PREGNANCY

When Bernie and I decided we wanted to have a baby, we went on a weekend getaway to the Sonoma Mission Inn, a great spa resort in Northern California. I had a massage and a facial, we made love, and Alexander was conceived. It was easy and pleasurable, and so was my entire pregnancy for the most part.

There were some rough moments I've tried to forget. The amniocentesis was extraordinarily nerve-wracking. Actually the test itself was quite amazing. I will never forget seeing the first sonogram; learning we were going to have a boy, that he was progressing as he should be, and seeing his heart flutter for the first time. The three-week wait to find out whether the results were normal seemed like eternity. I, who have always been pro-choice, was suddenly struck by the enormous magnitude of the decision we'd have to make should there be a problem. When I learned everything was fine, I started sobbing.

Once I knew I was having a boy, and we'd agreed we'd probably call him Alexander, he became that much more real to me. I'd say we bonded from the start if the word didn't make me want to gag. What I felt was the most intense sort of love for him and a wonderful sense of well-being. I spent ten months dreaming of the things we'd do together when he arrived. When he was still the size of a peanut, I was thinking about the mixed-doubles matches we'd play, the walks we'd take at the beach, the bicycle rides we'd go on, and the trips we'd take.

It seemed as if each and every step in the pregnancy was a milestone. Once the first trimester was over, and I could manage to come home from work without falling asleep during dinner, I charted his progress with great interest. When I heard his heartbeat with a fetal stethoscope for the first time, I couldn't believe how thrilling it was. When he started kicking so that I could feel it, I was sure it was an indicator of athletic prowess.

Throughout the pregnancy, he and I seemed to share similar tastes and sensibilities. We both loved Japanese food, and I inwardly praised him for the sophistication of his palate. When total strangers came up and patted my stomach, I was sure he joined me in thinking this was the oddest and most presumptuous behavior we could imagine. When friends and acquaintances started telling me their worst pregnancy stories, I was sure I could feel him shaking his head in disbelief. When I went to buy maternity clothes, I wondered—when he saw my pregnancy pictures years later—if he would share my intense dislike of the pastel polyester floral fluff that seemed to abound. Would he ask, as I did, where the Land's End clothes for pregnant women were?

For all the years when I thought that pregnancy must be so uncomfortable, I was amazed at how wonderful I felt throughout mine. Other than a seemingly constant need to urinate, I suffered no discomfort. Most of all, I finally understood what a miracle it is to create life.

THE DEVELOPMENT OF THE BABY

Your baby starts out as a fertilized egg, no bigger than the period at the end of this sentence. The baby will change and grow almost every single day, and your body will change and grow too. It will take 280 days or 40 weeks before the baby is fully developed and is ready to live outside your uterus (womb). This is about $9\frac{1}{3}$ calendar months. Pregnancy is often divided into three periods called *trimesters*. Each is about three months long.

The First Trimester

During the first trimester you may find it difficult to believe you are pregnant. You may experience few signs of pregnancy and gain only three to four pounds. Yet the first three months of pregnancy are critical to your baby's health. During this time the baby will grow to three inches long and will have developed all the major organs. Untreated illness or disease, radiation, or the use of tobacco, drugs, or alcohol during this time may harm your baby for life. Make sure you eat well, rest, and don't take any medication that has not been prescribed by your doctor. Tell any doctor, nurse, or dentist you visit that you are pregnant. Prenatal care, good nutrition, and adequate rest should be started immediately.

Your first month. For the first six weeks the baby is called an *embryo*. The heart, lungs, and brain are beginning to develop, and the tiny heart will beat by the twenty-fifth day. The embryo is enclosed in a sac of fluid to protect it from bumps and pressure. The baby will grow in this sac until birth. Your baby's umbilical cord is also developing. The cord is made up of blood vessels that carry nourishment from your body to feed the baby and carry away the baby's wastes.

During this time you may not notice a weight gain, but your breasts may be larger and may feel tender. You may also have some "morning sickness" or nausea. Consumption of alcohol and smoking of cigarettes should be stopped as soon as you think you might be pregnant. Take only those drugs prescribed by a physician who knows you are pregnant. You should schedule your first prenatal exam.

Your second month. During this month the embryo becomes a fetus, which means "young one." Arms with tiny hands and fingers and legs with the beginning knees, ankles, and toes are starting to form. Organs such as the stomach and liver have also begun to develop. The head now seems very large compared to the rest of the body because the brain is growing so fast. Tiny ears and the beginnings of hair are forming on the head. You may still not have a weight gain but may tire more easily and need to urinate more frequently. Also, you still may experience some nausea. It is very important to eat the right foods, because you and your baby are changing and growing every day, and you both need proper nourishment.

Your third month. Your baby is now about three inches long, weighs about one ounce, and signs of the baby's sex are beginning to appear. Fingernails and toenails are developing. The mouth opens and closes, and the baby is now starting to move the hands, legs, and head. At this point, though, you will not feel this movement. You may have gained about three to four pounds, and your clothes will begin to feel a little tight. You may also feel warmer than usual.

WHAT IT WAS LIKE

■

"My pregnancy was easy. I wish I had concentrated less on the labor and delivery aspect during pregnancy and more on how this baby was going to change my life. I swam every day and felt good and fit. I wish I had eaten less, but I know that for the next time."

■

"I loved being pregnant. I read a lot of books and felt very well informed. We took lots of pictures of my pregnant body, and I love looking back on them. I took yoga during my pregnancy, and a lot of the women in the class, including me, had easy deliveries."

■

The Second Trimester

The second trimester begins with your fifteenth week of pregnancy. Many of the minor discomforts of the first trimester will disappear, and you will begin to feel especially good. You can feel the baby move, and you will start to look pregnant. Your baby starts to gain weight and is clearly a boy or a girl. Good nutrition will help you and your baby gain at the right rate. Your doctor will now begin listening to your abdomen for the baby's heartbeat with a special instrument called a *fetoscope*.

Your fourth month. Your baby, now weighing about six ounces, is growing very fast and is about eight to ten inches long by the end of this month. The umbilical cord continues to grow and thicken to carry enough blood and nourishment. During the fourth month you will gain three to four pounds and start to "show." Maternity clothes and a maternity bra may now be more comfortable. You may start to feel a slight sensation of movement in your lower abdomen. This feeling is like "bubbles" or fluttering. When you first feel this movement, called "quickening," write down the date. This date will help the doctor determine when your baby is due.

Your fifth month. By the end of this month your baby will weigh about one pound and be about twelve inches long. The doctor will now be able to hear the baby's heartbeat, and you will begin to feel more definite movements. This month you may gain three or four pounds and begin to breathe more deeply and more frequently. The area around your nipples may look darker and wider as your breasts prepare to make milk.

Your sixth month. You are now carrying a fully formed miniature baby except that the skin is wrinkled and red and there is practically no fat under the skin. The baby still needs to grow, being only about fourteen inches long and weighing only about 1½ pounds. The baby cries and sucks on the thumb, and you regularly feel the baby's movement. You may gain three or more pounds. You may experience some backache, but wearing low-heeled shoes will give you a better sense of balance and comfort.

The Third Trimester

You have now completed twenty-four weeks of pregnancy. During these last three months your baby will continue to grow and gain weight. As the baby grows larger, you may experience some discomfort from the pressure on your stomach or bladder. You will feel the baby's stronger and more frequent movements. This is the time to start preparing yourself and your home for the baby's arrival.

Your seventh month. Your baby is now about fifteen inches long and weighs about 2 to 2½ pounds. The baby exercises by kicking and stretching and changing position from side to side. You might even be able to see the movement when one of the tiny heels pokes you. You may gain another three or four pounds this month and may also notice some swelling in your ankles. A slight amount of swelling is normal. You may feel better if you lie down or prop your feet up during the day.

Your eighth month. Your baby has grown to about sixteen inches and weighs about four pounds. The eyes are open, and the baby changes position in the uterus. This position is maintained until the baby is born. During this month you may gain three to five pounds. Continue your daily activities, with rest periods, but stop doing any heavy lifting or work that causes strain.

Your ninth month. At thirty-six weeks your baby is about nineteen inches long and weighs about six pounds. The baby's weight gain is about ½ pound per week. At forty weeks the baby is "full-term" and weighs from six to nine pounds. Your baby settles farther down into your pelvis, and people will say that your baby has "dropped." You may feel more comfortable, and your breathing will be easier, although you may need to urinate more frequently. You will be visiting your doctor every week until your baby is born.

Source: U.S. Department of Health and Human Services, Bureau of Health Care Delivery and Assistance, Division of Maternal and Child Health and Prenatal Care, Rockville, Maryland © 1983; 703-524-7802.

CHOOSING A DOCTOR

You want to judge whether a doctor is a good match for both you and your husband—emotionally, intellectually, and philosophically. Before interviewing the doctor, talk to friends and to friends of friends about their obstetrical experiences. That's one way to vet out a doctor without wasting time. Ask someone who has had a baby within the last five years, because if it's longer than that, a doctor may have changed his or her techniques.

"My first pregnancy was horrible. I was sick and terrified the whole time. I was really scared of being a mother, and I felt very uncomfortable with my body. I was ambivalent about the whole thing and pretty resentful. My son turned out to be this easy, sweet baby. I think that's why my second pregnancy was better. I wasn't sick at all, although the last three months were difficult because my younger son was breech, and he never turned."

■

"With my first pregnancy I read a lot of books, and they made me crazy. I knew about every possible disease. I was way less neurotic with my second pregnancy. I knew what to expect. I also figured that since I had one healthy, normal baby, it was very likely I'd have another, so I calmed down a bit."

■

"With my first pregnancy I got gestational diabetes. I was really angry because my OB-GYN just had a nurse call me on the telephone to tell me. He didn't take into account how I might feel upon hearing the news. The last three months were really hard. I had to give up sugar, which was hard for me. But then I realized that it wasn't about me; it was for my baby. If I wasn't ready to make sacrifices for my baby, then maybe I wasn't ready to be a mother. Needless to say, I gave up sugar—no problem."

■

Questions for Friends and Acquaintances

- During prenatal care, did you think the doctor and/or office staff made time to answer your questions and respond to your concerns?

- When during labor did the doctor get there, and for how long did she/he stay? Did you feel comfortable with that? If not, did you express your needs, and how did the doctor respond?

- Once you were in labor, what was her/his attitude toward childbirth techniques or to prescribing medication?

- Did you get the support, compassion, or medical intervention you felt you needed?

- What would be your main complaint, if any, about the doctor?

- Would you or did you have another baby under the care of the same doctor and why?

Questions for a Father Who Participated in the Childbirth Experience

- How would you rate the doctor's attitude and supportiveness during prenatal care?

- How was her/his bedside manner during office visits and labor?

- What about the way she/he handled any problems?

- What was her/his attitude toward your involvement or lack of it in the childbirth experience?

- Was there any interaction after birth?

Questions for the Doctor

Once you've found a doctor, the way you ask questions is highly important. Recognize that doctors are usually deferred to; that's the nature of being a doctor. Be as polite as you would be at a cocktail party, but get the information you need to make an informed decision. Ask the questions you need answered—three might suffice—to personally address your greatest concerns, hopes, and fears.

- Do many of your patients take childbirth classes? What percentage wind up giving birth without medication?

- Do the other doctors in your practice share your views on most aspects of childbearing? When would I get to meet them?

- How often do you induce labor and under what circumstances?

- I'm a worry wart (don't worry, all pregnant women are) and might have a lot of neurotic questions during my pregnancy that I need answered. Do you have a time of day set aside for those kinds of phone calls, or do you have a nurse I could call for reassurance?

- If a cesarean section is necessary, how do you feel about the father being present?

- Would you consider eliminating any of the routine hospital procedures for labor and delivery?

- Do you always do an episiotomy?

Questions for the Office Staff

You can ask these questions—regarding office policy—on the telephone or in person. They're not the best use of the doctor's time.

- **Office visits.** How often are office visits scheduled? How many appointments do you book per hour? What tests are standard?
- **Payment.** What is the fee? When is full payment required? What does it cover? What is extra?
- **Hospital affiliation.** Does the doctor use more than one hospital? If so, what are the differences between them? Where do women seem to have a better experience?
- **Labor and delivery.** When does the doctor arrive at the hospital? If labor is slow, does she/he go back to the office and return later? What is the likelihood that one of the other doctors in the practice will deliver my baby?
- **Diet.** What recommendations do you make about nutrition and weight gain?
- **Breastfeeding.** Do you have a support system for breastfeeding?

Source: Tracie Hotchner is the author of Pregnancy & Childbirth, Childbirth & Marriage, The Pregnancy Diary, *and* Pregnancy, Pure and Simple. *She is the godmother of ten (FYI: she is not accepting any new godchildren) and lives in New York.*

"When I was pregnant with our oldest daughter, I was putting my husband through graduate school by working as a waitress and giving music lessons. I wasn't sick. I felt good, and I walked miles and miles each day. With my second I wasn't working, but my daughter wasn't napping, so I was pretty tired. During that pregnancy I went to Jazzercise every day until my daughter was born. For my third I had bronchitis during the last two months and lost nine pounds. I was coughing all the time and broke two ribs. It was most unpleasant. The last one was tiring because I had three small kids. But all in all, I loved being pregnant. I always felt I looked better when I was pregnant. I loved the feeling of having the baby inside."

■

PREGNANCY TESTS

Ultrasound scan. This is a diagnostic method of visualizing the fetus. In fact it's a method of visualizing any structure inside the body that is not solid bone or filled with gas, like the bowels or lungs. It's a very good method for imaging tissues that are primarily fluid; the human body is about 70 percent fluid, while the pregnant uterus is actually about 90 percent fluid. Ultrasound is used to measure the fetus to determine its age and to correlate information—based on the patient's calculated gestational age from her last menstrual period—with the size of the fetus. It is also done to screen for structural fetal abnormalities such as open neural tube defects like spina bifida, heart defects, abdominal wall defects, and many—but not all—of the structural abnormalities. Another common and very important use of the ultrasound is to guide what we call *invasive diagnostic procedures* such as amniocentesis, chorionic villus sampling, and fetal blood sampling.

For patients who are concerned about the risk of diagnostic ultrasound, there are no reproducible studies that have shown any harmful effects. That doesn't mean there is absolutely no risk. We don't know. The general recommendation is that if there is a valid indication for doing the ultrasound, there should be no hesitation on the part of the doctor or the patient.

Alpha-fetoprotein (AFP). AFP is a blood protein that is found in the fetal body fluid and manufactured in the fetal liver. It is evident in high concentrations in the fetal body fluid, very low concentrations in the amniotic fluid, and even lower concentrations in the maternal bloodstream. If there is an open defect in the skin of the fetus, that will allow the AFP to leak into the amniotic fluid and to cross the membrane into the mother's bloodstream, elevating the AFP level in her blood. Using that as a screening test, one can detect open neural tube defects such as anencephaly, spina bifida, and encephalocele (defects in the skull), as well as abdominal wall defects. A patient with a low AFP is at risk for a chromosome abnormality, particularly Down's syndrome. The test is administered between fifteen and twenty weeks from the last menstrual period. It is now changing over nationwide to a multiple marker test with AFP being just one of the markers.

Amniocentesis. This is a procedure by which a needle is inserted, usually through the abdominal wall and through the wall of the uterus, into the amnion, or inner of the two sacs that surround the fetus. Once the needle is in place, a small amount of amniotic fluid is withdrawn, and that fluid can be used to analyze more than two hundred chromosome and genetic abnormalities, including Down's syndrome. Genetic amniocentesis—which is the most common amniocentesis procedure—is generally done between sixteen and eighteen weeks dated from the first day of the last period. It is a procedure that is recommended for women who are considered to be of advanced maternal age, which by most definitions in this country is thirty-five or older; patients who have had a previous child with an abnormality that can be diagnosed prenatally; or those couples who have been identified as carriers of inherited genetic diseases such as cystic fibrosis, Duchenne muscular dystrophy, sickle-cell anemia, or Tay-Sachs disease. The other indication for amniocentesis is when labor is going be induced prior to the pregnancy's reaching full term, and the fetus needs to be tested for pulmonary surfactant, a substance that indicates whether its lungs are ready to breathe air.

There is a risk of miscarriage associated with genetic amniocentesis, but there is also a risk of miscarriage among patients who don't have prenatal diagnostic procedures. The background risk—for patients to miscarry in pregnancy between fifteen and twenty weeks—is approximately one in three hundred. In the hands of experienced people doing the amniocentesis, the risk is between one in three hundred to one in five hundred.

Chorionic villus sampling (CVS). This procedure is an alternative to amniocentesis. Its major advantage is that it can be performed much earlier in pregnancy, as early as the end of the ninth week, although it's typically done between ten and twelve weeks. Instead of a needle or catheter being inserted into the amniotic sac, the device remains outside the pregnancy sac and samples tissue growing from the outer membrane called the *chorion*. The procedure can be done either transcervically—by going through the cervix with a flexible catheter—or by a method similar to amniocentesis in which a needle is placed through the abdominal wall and the wall of the uterus to get to the chorionic villi. In either case, once the device is in place, with gentle suction, a small amount of the tissue growing on the outer membrane of the pregnancy sac is sampled. The CVS can test for all the same disorders that amniocentesis tests for with one major exception—the group of neural tube defects. The main reason that CVS doesn't detect neural tube defects is that they are found by measuring AFP in the amniotic fluid. Amniotic fluid is not obtained with CVS. The risk for a neural tube defect does not change with age: a forty-year-old has no greater risk than a twenty-year-old.

There has been a tendency to reserve CVS for patients who are at higher risk because of a widely held perception that CVS carries a higher risk than amniocentesis. In fact, recent data suggest that in the hands of experienced operators the risk of CVS is no greater than the risk of amniocentesis. You must take into account, how-ever, the background risk of pregnancy loss, which is one in three hundred at the time of amniocentesis. The earlier you intervene in pregnancy, the higher the risk is. The background risk at ten or eleven weeks is 2 percent; the risk for pregnancy loss with CVS is 2 percent.

Source: John Williams, M.D., is the medical director of the Prenatal Diagnostic Center of Southern California, 8641 Wilshire Blvd. Suite 200, Beverly Hills, CA 90211; 310-652-5884.

PRESCHOOLS

When Alexander was two years old, I began researching preschools. An acquaintance told me I was already in big trouble. She assured me that all the other parents in the entire city had put their children on multiple waiting lists as soon as they were born. A friend with two older children, who I always thought was somewhat laid-back, had said a few months earlier, "You really should move on the preschool thing. If you don't, Alexander will be left out in the cold."

The visual image of Alex being left in the cold—even though the weather in Los Angeles in September is in the seventies—brought tears to my eyes. Not only had I done nothing about finding a preschool, but I was also having a difficult time adjusting to the idea of it.

Sometimes I worry about my pervasive unwillingness to anticipate Alexander's developmental stages and take an aggressive approach. I think one of the reasons I don't constantly anticipate what's next in his life is that I don't want to miss out on what he's currently doing.

With all that said and done, I did have some thoughts on what I wanted in a preschool for Alex. Most important, I wanted the teachers to be loving and warm. I wanted their participation in the preschool to be a calling, not just a job. I wanted them to feel as passionately about what they do as I feel about what I do.

I wanted the teachers to have good common sense and a good sense of humor—which is not always the case even in the best of schools. I wanted the teachers to love music and art. I was looking for a preschool where they believe that small children should play rather than be taught preacademics. I don't want Alexander to be

319

bored in kindergarten because he learned everything in preschool. I didn't want him to feel pressured to learn things before he was ready.

I wanted a place that encouraged parents to visit anytime. I was considering a cooperative-type situation where the parents volunteer a few times a month. I didn't want a school where all the kids are rich. I wasn't interested in spending $500 on a birthday party so that Alex could compete with his classmates. I didn't plan to begin buying him designer clothes because his friends were wearing them.

I didn't want a school that was a training ground for private schools. I didn't even want anyone to discuss private schools with me. I've heard all the arguments and remain a public school devotee.

I was looking for a school where the tuition was reasonable so that I wouldn't have to return to work full-time to pay for Alex's early childhood education. I wanted a preschool that was located in a safe neighborhood. I wanted it to be clean, but I didn't want the teachers to be obsessed with cleanliness. I wanted the school to have a safe environment. I don't ever want to worry about Alexander's well-being at school.

I wanted to find a school where Alexander would like the other children. I wanted to find a school where I liked the other parents. I wanted a school that offered flexibility in scheduling so that Alex could attend three full days a week but not go on Tuesdays and Thursdays—the days I've always spent with him.

When I finally felt ready to look at schools, I talked to other moms and picked six schools that seemed to meet at least some of my criteria. I quickly realized, once again, that so much of the decision would be based on a gut-level reaction rather than on a lot of facts and figures. I always came to visit with a list of questions I rarely asked. What became so very clear to me was that you could tell a lot about a school by pure observation.

There were schools where I liked the director but didn't like the teachers. They didn't seem happy, and neither did the children. There wasn't enough laughter, hugging, talking, and energy in the air. There were schools that seemed too big; I thought Alex would get lost. There were others where there wasn't enough supervision; I thought he might feel lonely and abandoned. There were a few schools I liked that weren't really geared to working mothers; there was a morning-only schedule and two months off in the summer.

And then I fell in love. I loved the director, I loved the teachers, I loved the atmosphere, and I loved the feeling I got when I went there. Although I had a list of questions to ask, I put them aside and watched the kids. While I talked in great depth to the director, and liked her better than any director anywhere, on a gut level I just liked the feel of the place. I sensed that Alex would be happy there.

And so he has.

ॐ

TIPS FOR CHOOSING A PRESCHOOL

• **Identify your own philosophy.** What do you think a preschool experience should be? What do you want for your child? Do you want a traditional academic setting or a more developmental program that moves with your child's individual needs? There are church schools, traditional academic schools, schools based on a particular philosophy (Montessori, Waldorf, Summerhillian, Carden, etc.), and open or humanistic schools. Remember to consider your child's abilities, interests, and needs. What program will best meet your son's or daughter's needs, intellectually, physically, socially, and emotionally?

• **Keep your ears open.** Actively take part in discussions about other children's schools. Word of mouth is a powerful source.

• **Keep your eyes open.** Look for schools within your vicinity— be it close to home or to work. Convenience is a big factor.

• **Call schools.** Find out their hours: is there a part-time program as well as a full-time one? What about fees? Is there an application fee or a deposit? What are their holidays? Are the schools open year-round? At what age do they take children? Do they need to be toilet trained? Is there a waiting list? Ask the schools for a brief description of their philosophy or have them mail you an information packet. This is the beginning of the selection process.

• **Set up appointments to visit.** See for yourself. Follow your instincts on this one. You may not think you know what you're looking for, but take note of what you feel when you enter these environments. Do the children seem happy? How do they relate to their peers/teachers? How do the teachers relate to the children and to each other? What kind of artwork is displayed? Is the art from the children or the teachers? Is it creative? Is there a childlike environment with colors, natural light, and low furniture? Do you hear music? A cheery, stimulating setting allows for creativity and expression. Are there many toys? Are they age appropriate? Do they look like they are being used? Are they clean? Inside, is there a variety of centers openly available for the child (books areas,

WHY WE SEND OUR CHILDREN TO PRESCHOOLS

■

"We have never lived in a neighborhood with many playmates, so preschool was primarily social. I also found preschool was a good source of new friends for me. My husband was a Marine for eight years, and we moved frequently."

■

"We send our children to school because they need their friends. My daughter does things at school that I can't give her at home— dress-up, social interaction, great art projects, and learning to cope without Mommy's help."

■

housekeeping areas, science areas, art areas, block areas)? Outside, do they have swings, sandboxes, painting easels, safe climbing structures, and tricycles? Are activities available at the tables? Is there adequate supervision? Is there good security? Does the school look and feel safe?

• **Compile a list of questions you want to ask the director.** What is the teacher-child ratio? What are the teachers' qualifications? What is the teacher turnover? How many children are in the school? What is their policy on discipline? Are they prepared for emergencies? Do they go on field trips? Are extracurricular activities available (music, dance, gymnastics)? Is there an extra fee for these? Is there parental involvement? Parent workshops? Any fundraisers? Does the school provide lunch? Snacks? While you are asking these questions, remember that the director sets the tone for the school. Take note on how comfortable he or she makes you feel.

• **Do your homework.** Make comparisons, recheck your priorities, and try as much as possible to match your needs as well as your child's to the school of your choice. Remember, nothing will be perfect, so prioritizing is a must.

Once you've made your final choice, check one more time to see how your child's needs will be met:

Intellectually: Will the school stimulate your child with hands-on learning activities, allowing questions and answers through exploration? Is the curriculum set up for individual development? Remember that everyone does not grow at the same pace.

Physically: Is there enough outdoor space to allow for adequate motor development? Children have to be encouraged to try new things and to know the feeling of accomplishment when conquering a new challenge. They must run and play. Remember, their play is their work.

Socially: Will your child be encouraged to problem-solve, have play experiences with children of different ages and backgrounds, and develop communication skills?

Emotionally: Will your child be loved and respected? Will the school listen and respond to the child's needs and yours?

Source: Roleen Heimann is the co-owner/director of The New School West, 12731 Venice Blvd., Los Angeles, CA 90066; 310-313-4444. She is the mother of one.

SIGNS OF QUALITY IN EARLY CHILDHOOD PROGRAMS

Staff-Child Interaction

• **Conversation.** Adults spend the major share of their time talking to, listening to, and closely observing the children. Adults engage children in conversation, at their eye level, that encourages them to express their feelings and ideas.

• **Activity.** The environment is marked primarily by pleasant conversation, spontaneous laughter, and exclamations of excitement rather than harsh, stressful noise or enforced quiet.

• **Involved children.** Children and adults are involved actively with each other and with materials. Adults help children play cooperatively. Aimless wandering, fighting, and withdrawn behavior are kept to a minimum.

• **Accessible teachers.** Children show no hesitation to approach adults with questions, bids for affection, and requests for help. Adults liberally provide individual attention when they are asked or when it is needed. Adults do not spend long periods talking to other adults or involved in housekeeping chores that don't include children.

• **Affection.** Affection is expressed spontaneously and frequently, and children in distress are comforted.

Curriculum

• **Variety.** A wide variety of materials geared to young children's interests is available, such as picture books, records, puppets, blocks, puzzles, paints, climbing equipment, and props for make-believe play.

• **Involvement.** Hands-on activity is encouraged. Materials are readily accessible to the children; for example, toys are on low shelves, not in toy boxes. Children are busy and actively involved with the materials rather than passively watching or following rote instructions.

• **Child-directed activities.** The planned, daily schedule balances indoor and outdoor activities, quiet time and active time, periods when individual children choose their own activities and periods for group activities, and child-initiated and adult-initiated activities.

• **Teacher-guided activities.** The teachers' roles are to plan and arrange the learning environment. It's important to see adults

"Our son was in a family day-care setting with a woman who used to be an assistant teacher at a preschool. It was terrific, and I would have kept him there for at least six more months, but we moved across the country, and the only comparable environment was a preschool. It's been all right, although he went from a group of six kids playing in a house to a more institutional setting. He made the initial adjustment better than I did."

■

"I felt my daughter was ready for nursery school at around two and a half. She became very interested in her friends, thrived on the days when we had play dates, and also needed help learning to share and to use language instead of pushing and grabbing."

■

"Our daughters outgrew their family day-care situation. They needed more intellectual stimulation, more kids their own ages, more creative play, and more structured activities."

■

"I think my son needs the company of other children. He needs to learn social skills. I didn't go to preschool, and I think the transition to school was especially difficult because I'd never been away from my mother. I was already five when I started school for the first time."

■

asking questions of children, reading to children, making suggestions for "next steps," setting up new experiences, and observing and recording children's progress.

• **Cultural diversity.** Multiracial, multicultural, nonsexist, nonstereotyping pictures, dolls, books, and materials are fully part of the classroom to teach children the value of diversity and to ensure that all children's backgrounds are respected.

• **Responsibilities.** Daily, routine activities are part of the learning process. For example, children are given responsibility for setting tables at mealtime and helping with cleanup during the day.

Communication with Parents

• **Informed parents.** Parents are given written information about what to expect from the program and what the program expects from them. They have opportunities to communicate with the staff about their child's individual needs and progress. They are made to feel welcome at any time.

• **Home-school communication.** Parents have opportunities to communicate with the staff about their individual child's needs and progress through notes, phone calls, conferences, and face-to-face conversations at arrival and pickup.

• **Welcome access.** Parents are welcome to visit at any time and are encouraged to participate in a variety of ways, such as eating lunch with the children, observing during the day, volunteering to help, and attending parent meetings.

Staff Hiring and Qualifications

• **Careful hiring.** Hiring procedures include careful checking of personal references of all potential employees. New staff members serve a probationary employment period during which the director makes a professional judgment of their suitability for working with children.

• **Trained teachers.** Entry requirements for director and teachers include training in early childhood education and child development. The training must include specific instruction in the age groups for which the adult is responsible. The director has also received training or has experience in business administration.

The amount of training required varies with the level of professional responsibility of the position.

• **In-service training.** The program provides regular in-service training for staff to improve and expand skills in working with children and their families.

Staffing Structure

• **Supervision.** There is a sufficient number of adults for the number of children in the program to ensure adequate supervision, frequent personal contact, and time for individual instruction as needed. Recommendations vary by age.

• **Continuity.** Staffing patterns are planned so that the same adults have primary responsibility for the same children each day. This allows for greater consistency in the daily experience of children and enables the staff to be highly familiar with the child's needs, interests, and background.

• **Small groups.** The number of children in a group is limited to facilitate constructive interaction and activity. Group size will vary with age. It is suggested that two- and three-year-olds be in groups of no more than fourteen with at least two adults; four- and five-year-old children in groups of no more than twenty with at least two adults.

Physical Environment

• The indoor and outdoor physical environments should be designed to promote involvement in the daily activities and easy, constructive interactions among adults and children.

Health and Safety

• The health and safety of children and adults are protected and enhanced. Good programs act to prevent illness and accidents, are prepared to deal with emergencies should they occur, and also educate children concerning safe and healthy practices.

Source: Adapted by permission from the National Academy of Early Childhood Programs, 1509 16th Street, N.W., Washington, D.C. 20036-1426; 800-424-2460 or 202-232-8777.

"I send my child to a preschool to learn social behavior, negotiations, and conflict resolution. I was really affected by a child abuse case at a local preschool. I chose my son's preschool because I liked that there were always parents around but that the teachers were professionals. I thought it was a good balance. I also like that it meets every day."

■

CRITERIA FOR CHOOSING ONE

■

"No structured curriculum, lots of play and discovery, size of the class, the environment, attitude of teachers and directors, and proximity to home."

■

"I looked at a couple of schools but chose the one I did because it was highly recommended. I had a great meeting with the director and I liked their philosophy, which is that love cures a lot. The price was right, and we got in. We're all happy with the decision."

■

"I always chose church-affiliated schools. I was looking for a preschool that was not too structured or too academic and where there were warm and caring teachers."

■

SCHOOL READINESS

Diana Townsend-Butterworth, M.A., is the author of Your Child's First School: A Handbook for Parents. *She has over twenty years of experience as a teacher, school administrator, and educational consultant. She is the mother of two children and lives in New York.*

SB: How do you know when your child is ready to go to preschool?

DTB: It's important for parents to realize that readiness is a global concept; it is not just a list of skills that your child needs to know. It is social, emotional, and physical. It is also important for parents to know that readiness for preschool is not related in any way to intelligence. A smart child—a child who will later have a very high IQ—might not be ready, while a child of average intelligence might be ready. Readiness is relative; you need to know what you are asking your child to be ready for. You need to know what is going to be expected of your child at school.

SB: What are the major differences in sending a two-, three-, or four-year-old to school?

DTB: First of all, let's set the parameters. What we're talking about is a child-centered preschool, one where they are aware of the child's social, emotional, and physical needs as well as their cognitive needs. We are talking about a preschool where the director and teachers understand the needs of young children, where they are knowledgeable about child development, and where they understand that children learn through play. We're talking about an appropriate-quality preschool.

Most children are ready for this kind of a preschool at age three because they are ready to begin to separate from their parents. They are also ready to begin to relate to other children and adults. They are able to communicate their needs verbally; they can tell you their likes and dislikes. They also are more physically able to deal with their environment. They can drink from a cup, dress themselves, and do what they need to do to be comfortable in an environment outside their home. Also, three-year-olds are very eager to reach out and explore; they are very curious. They are more able than younger children to concentrate on a task, whether it is building a tower out of blocks or making a simple collage. They have a sense of independence.

Two-year-olds, on the other hand, don't really need to be in school. Going to school before the age of three is usually a response to the social and economic needs of the family rather than the needs of the child. If you are going to send a child to school at age two, the program should be geared specifically to the needs of a two-year-old; it shouldn't be a watered-down version of a program for three- or four-year-olds. Again, you should be aware that children learn through play and that children at this age shouldn't be expected to share; they're not ready. They should be treated as two-year-olds.

That being said, some children will benefit from being in a toddler program; by this I mean one that meets for a few hours a couple of days a week. These children are the ones who seem hungry for new experiences that may not be available within their home environments. Also, children who don't have access to other children or a safe outdoor play area can benefit from being in a toddler program. Children who come from two-career families—and are not being taken care of by caregivers who are knowledgeable about child development and are not being encouraged to verbalize and explore their thoughts—benefit from being in a toddler program. The other children who can benefit are those who are living in a home where English is not the main language. If one wants them to be fluent in English, being in a toddler program can help. Children with special needs can also benefit from a toddler program; the earlier a child with special needs is identified and given the specialized help needed, the better.

Basically, all four-year-olds would benefit from being in an appropriate early childhood school because they like to share and make friends and they are ready to work in a group. They are ready to begin to discover and define their world.

SB: What is the importance of parent readiness?
DTB: Just as important as the child's readiness is the parents' readiness. Before you send your child to preschool, it's important to come to terms with your own school memories so you don't send your children to school with the emotional baggage of either the good or the bad things that happened to you when you were in school. It's important to come to terms with your own fears of separation from your child and to realize that these fears are quite natural. When a child starts preschool, for most parents this is the first time their child is leaving home and going off into the big world, and parents need to come to terms with it.

SB: What are some tips for making the transition to pre-school a positive experience for your child?
DTB: The transition, of course, is much easier when you pick a

"I visited four different schools, two cooperatives and two that were privately owned. I watched how the teachers related to the children, and I talked to the directors. I chose a co-op because I wanted to be involved. Also, the cost was much less. We got into the school that was my first choice, and our whole family is really happy with it."

■

"Good word of mouth, proximity to work, flexible, fabulous staff, safety, cleanliness, racial diversity, state licensed, and good management."

■

"I chose my son's nursery school because of my neighbor's experience. Her kids went there and loved it, and they're really nice kids. I also liked that it was a part-time school. I figured I would meet other mothers who were doing what I was doing, mothering full-time."

■

quality program. It should be a place where you feel safe sending your child, because your child will sense your fear. Don't talk to your child about how much you are going to miss him or her. This is something that parents tend to do without realizing the effect it could have on their child. Instead, talk about the exciting things or interesting things the child is going to be doing and how much you are going to look forward to hearing about them when he or she comes home from school. Don't linger over good-byes. So many parents keep saying good-bye, again and again, when the child is ready to go off and play, and the parents can't drag themselves away from the door. A child who senses that you're uncomfortable leaving is going to think, Is it safe to leave Mommy and Daddy? The other fear is if Mommy or Daddy are so nervous, am I going into a place that is dangerous?

Finally, remember that a preschool experience should be a wonderful one for you and your child. Your child will make friends and learn how to work together with other children in a group. He or she will also discover the excitement and joy of learning. And you will learn what it means to be part of a school community and how to work as a partner in your child's school experience.

RELIGION

'm Jewish. Bernie is Catholic. When we were dating, the differences in our religious backgrounds didn't present a problem. When we decided to marry, the interfaith nature of our relationship didn't seem to bother our parents, either. They were probably so relieved we were finally getting married—I was thirty-two and Bernie was forty-four—that religion was the least of their concerns.

While I consider myself a fairly religious person, I go to temple only a half-dozen times a year. I do know all the words to Fiddler on the Roof. I am embarrassed by Jackie Mason's borscht-belt humor, distressed that Michael Milken is one of our fold, and dismayed by Roseanne Arnold's antics.

Other than that I don't think very much about Judaism on a daily basis, unless something comes up. When Bernie and I got married, it became an issue only in terms of who should marry us. He didn't care. I felt it was unfair to have a rabbi, in deference to his parents, so we were married by a family friend who is a judge. It was short, sweet, and totally unmemorable. It lacked a certain spirituality that I've since decided is important. At the time I thought it was just fine.

It was only when I was pregnant with Alex that the religion issue seemed to come up over and over for me. "Would it bother you if Alex had a bar mitzvah?" I asked one night out of the blue.

"I've never thought about it," Bernie answered honestly. "We can certainly talk about it when the time comes."

"It's very important," I responded. "He needs to know about his heritage."

"Then he should probably be baptized," he said.

"You've got to be kidding," I responded weakly. "I can't let him get baptized. I don't believe in original sin."

"Neither do I," Bernie said laughingly. "I was just testing you. When you said he needs to know about his heritage, I wondered which heritage you were talking about."

"Uh . . . his entire heritage," I explained after some hesitation. "You can take him to church for Midnight Mass. We'll celebrate Christmas."

"I'm never awake for Midnight Mass, although I do appreciate the sentiment," he replied. "You have celebrated Christmas your entire life, so I just want you to know I don't consider this a concession."

He was, of course, right. I was embarrassed. I decided to drop all discussions about religion until there was a reason to bring it up. Alex wasn't baptized, although he was delivered in a Catholic hospital. But I made Bernie promise he wouldn't sprinkle any water over Alex's head when I was asleep. He said he didn't, and I believed him.

Alex was named in temple, and Bernie agreed that he could be. When I told him that Alex's Hebrew name was Hannan Dov, his only comment was that he found it odd that I was naming our child after a DoveBar.

My sense is that we'll deal with religion the way we've dealt with everything else—honestly and openly. Bernie thinks there are great similarities between Jews and Catholics. I don't see it. I do know that he and I share fundamental values and that we have very similar views of what's right, what's good, and what's moral. I know many people who have the same religious backgrounds and don't share any of the same values. I think we're far better off.

I'm hoping that Alexander will have the best of both worlds. Judaism and Catholicism have such wonderful rituals that his religious life should be rich and full. I think there might be some problems. I imagine he will be the only boy in his bar mitzvah class with the last name of Rotondo. I would guess he will be the only person in church who's got a Hebrew name as well.

When my sister was young, she had a friend whose mother had converted from Catholicism to Judaism, and the child described it by saying "My mother was a Catholic, and now she's a Jewish." I laughed for years every time I heard the story, and now my son is a Catholic and a Jewish. There is something to be said for a kid who will get presents for both Christmas and Hanukkah. Whatever the problems, I know the compensations will outweigh them.

$\backsim$

THE IMPORTANCE OF RELIGION

Obviously it depends on the individuals: how religious they consider themselves to be and how they define religion. A lot of Americans identify religion with belonging to a particular institution like a synagogue or church. The importance of religion, to them, depends on how actively they are involved in that institution.

But Americans also define religion in terms of a kind of inner spirituality that comes out of the eighteenth- and nineteenth-century pietist movements. There's a strong understanding that you can have religious belief without being part of an institution, that religion can be important in a kind of interior way without institutional commitments. Those people would say that religion is very important to them but would have a hard time defining what it is and would have a harder time talking about it. They are much more likely to identify religion and spirituality with nature, with being outdoors, with a kind of creationist ethic.

I think there are very few people in America—other than a few atheists—who would absolutely deny that spirituality is important to them. Most people who are antireligion are actually anti-institutional, and that, of course, is a deep strand in American thinking.

For most people religion defines a set of values, a set of ethics, and a sense of morality. In more traditional communities religious institutions are tied to strong social definition and social boundaries. For these people, whom one worships with defines the community they belong to, whom they will have relationships with, and how these relationships are structured. Because religion is so central to their lives, people are willing to work very hard to keep those boundaries intact, especially if they feel that they're threatened in any sort of way. Defending those central beliefs is one reason religion and violence are so often associated.

There are a lot of sociological theories about this. But I think religion—for most Americans—establishes a sphere of social activity and defines the most important kinds of interior values and sensibilities. In some ways it provides a venue that enables them to explore the mysterious and transcendental issues that they would ordinarily talk about only with intimate contacts.

Source: Karen King, Ph.D., is an associate professor of religious studies at Occidental College in Los Angeles, California.

HOW WE FEEL ABOUT RELIGIOUS EDUCATION

■

"Neither my husband nor I have a real firm belief in 'organized' religion—we believe it comes from within."

■

"I believe children should be given some religious education to lay a foundation. If they choose to change churches later, at least I've given them the basics."

■

"I haven't decided yet. Neither my husband nor I were raised religiously, although I feel very culturally Jewish."

■

A RABBI'S VIEW

Rabbi Sanford Ragins, the senior rabbi of Leo Baeck Temple in Los Angeles, has lectured at Hebrew Union College in Los Angeles, Waseda University in Tokyo, Institut Kirche und Judentum in Berlin, and currently teaches at Occidental College in Los Angeles. He is the father of three.

SB: *What does it mean to raise your child as a Jew?*
SR: It means to give that child a clear sense of his or her roots in an ancient people. To be a Jew is to be a member of a vast family in the world today, global in scope, and also an ancient family. Alongside the Chinese, we are the oldest surviving family from ancient times, but that's only part of it. We're not just a people. We are a people who have had a specific kind of history, certain kinds of experiences, and certain kinds of values that we have slowly hammered out over the centuries, often as a result of suffering.

And that's not just in modern times, when one thinks of the holocaust, but even in ancient times. The Bible is, in part, the record of human suffering as a result of which people formulated certain trenchant values having to do with social responsibility, justice, the sacredness of human life, the unity of God and creation, and the unity of the human family. I think these values are vital for our culture today, for the world in which we live. For Jews who practice their religion in this sense, and who are focused and centered on these values and what they mean, there's a tremendous sense of sustenance and strength.

But there is a challenge as well, because these values are not always terribly comforting. They can be guilt inducing, and there is something to the old tradition of Jewish guilt. We expect a lot of people, and we tell them they have to behave in certain ways to make society and the world a humane place in which to live. If they fail to behave that way, they should feel guilty about it, so it's a tough religion—a demanding religion—and I think that's good.

SB: *What is the importance of ritual?*
SR: I love ritual, and I think people often love it if it's presented properly. Some of the things that religion deals with are so intangible, so difficult to articulate, that these insights and values have to be dramatized. And that's where the wonderful powerful dramatic poetry of ritual—and only something like ritual—can be effective. When I say ritual, I mean the usage of certain words, poetry, music, silence. I think human beings are ritualistic by nature, although language is very important to us. But there are

certain events in the life cycle—birth, coming of age, marriage, death—that require ritual.

SB: *What advice do you give to people who want to inter-marry?*

SR: If you're planning to marry someone outside your culture, your religion, or your race—and I did all three—you need to be clear about what you're doing. You should know yourself fairly well. You have to be sensitive to family issues because such a marriage often creates tension in extended families.

My wife was born and raised in Japan, completed her university training there, and we met in graduate school in this country, where she had come to study Judaism. She converted, and we raised our children as Jews. When we were engaged to be married, I think the best advice of all was given to me by one of my professors, Jacob Marcus, at Hebrew Union College.

We had lunch together one day, and, because he had a bad back, he was pacing up and down in his kitchen while I was eating. All of a sudden he wheeled around, turned to me, looked me right in the eye, and said, "Son, do you love her?"

And I replied, "Yes, Professor Marcus."

"Good," he nodded, "because if you do, it's a lot easier."

While I am often suspicious of a romanticization of love, a deep caring for the person of that other culture, race, or religion is critical. Because then your trust in each other, and hopefully a sense of humor about what you're doing, can smooth over and help you deal with some of the cultural and religious issues. And don't pretend problems won't arise, because they will. In some marriages the diversity makes it more difficult, and in others it is enriching.

There's something else I want to say about intermarriage. Of course, as a rabbi I'm committed to Jewish survival, and I am most interested in encouraging Jews who intermarry to become part of the Jewish community and to raise their children as Jews. We know that intermarriage is going to happen, and there's very little we can do to stop it or to slow it down. My own vision of the Jewish community, which is not shared by all rabbis, is that our posture should be one of embrace and encouragement for those families who want to raise their children as Jews.

Before we end, let me tell you a story I think you'll enjoy. Once a month we have an early service on Friday night for families with young children. Usually my associate rabbi, who is a woman, and I conduct this service together. But right after the High Holi-

---

"We aren't sending our kids to religious school. I was brought up Roman Catholic. I personally have a conflict with organized religion that I can't seem to resolve enough to be able to have my children participate."

■

"My husband was brought up Jewish and hated it. I was brought up Catholic and hated it. If our son wants religion, he can choose his own."

■

"I feel it is important for our son to learn to develop his own beliefs and faith and to learn about God."

■

"I want to expose our son to Christianity and Judaism but let him ultimately decide what to do."

■

"My husband and I feel that the way we live our daily lives is much more important than which church we attend on Sundays."

■

"I would like our daughter to have a better understanding of the Jewish religion than I did and do and participate more in religious holidays."

■

"I'll send my daughter to religious school so that she can get good values and associate with WASPS and find out why our family is the way we are. I want her to know Jesus Christ and to develop and nurture a faith in Him that will sustain her through life's hardships. I want her to become a good and just person in a world that is increasingly violent, greedy, and uncaring."

■

days we were both fatigued, so I said to her, "Let's split it. I'll take the adult late service, and you take the children's service. Then you can go home early, and I'll come a little bit later."

When I arrived at the end of the children's service, one of the mothers who always attends with her three-and-a-half-year-old said that when her daughter noticed my absence, she asked her mother, "Where is the boy God tonight?"

A PASTOR'S VIEW

The Very Reverend Mary June Nestler is dean of the Episcopal Theological School at Claremont in Claremont, California. She is married to an Anglican priest and is the mother of one.

SB: What does it mean to raise a child as a Christian?
MJN: For me, it is to have a child who participates in a tradition, who feels part of a family that's two thousand years old, and who by virtue of learning about Christianity feels an interconnection to other people, whoever they may be. It means to raise a child who does not feel alone, who has a grounding in being, in having God present, in feeling sustained by God, and who has faith in God. Specifically it means to raise a child with the knowledge and love of Jesus and what His life was about as a pattern for what her life can be.

SB: The concept of God and Jesus are fairly abstract for children. How do you talk to children about this?
MJN: Children seem to understand God. They don't have a problem with someone who loves them, a presence. A lot of people in children's lives are physically absent. They know that Grandma (or whoever) can love them but lives far away. It is more difficult to explain Jesus to them. It's harder to talk to them about a person who lived a long time ago yet who is concerned about them and loves them. I haven't had to explain Jesus to my own daughter yet, because she's only thirteen months old. But when I was a chaplain in schools, I taught children about Jesus by telling them stories. We'd read Bible stories, Hebrew scriptures, and Christian scriptures, so they would know the lay of the land, as it were, the tradition. Later they'd learn how to interpret the tradition.

SB: What is the importance of ritual in Christianity?
MJN: It's critical. It provides us hangers to hang our hats on. It gives us stability in the midst of a changing life. It is poetry. It's a

way of escaping the mundane, if you will, and it provides us a basic outline for responding to what happens in the world.

While there are different rituals in Christianity, all Christians, of course, would recognize baptism. It is usually the first ritual in which children participate; it may be the first time they are brought to church. My child was baptized when she was four months old, although she had been in church before that. We celebrate her baptismal anniversary. We will keep reminding her of something that happened when she was small, and we have pictures to show her.

Another important part of ritual in the Christian church is the communion. Because our daughter has been baptized, she now receives bread and wine with everyone at church. She is brought to the altar, sips from the cup, has her piece of bread, and has done this ever since she was able to. Some Christians don't allow infants to take communion; Episcopalians do. I think it's very important.

As a priest, when I am giving out communion, I'm always saddened when parents don't allow their children to participate. You see them pull the children's hands back when they reach out for bread because the tradition has been—within some churches—to allow only older children to take communion. So you still see adults who are not sure whether to allow their children to participate. I always want to stop, give them a lecture, and say, "Why would you exclude this child?" Children see the bread going to everybody but them, and it's very important that they feel included in the ritual.

SB: *What advice do you have for couples who want to intermarry?*

MJN: You would find very few Christians who would say it's not possible to intermarry with a non-Christian. I think most of them would say it is difficult if the other person is at all devout. The advice I would give is to learn as much as possible about each other's faith, to decide about the religious education of the children before you have children, and let your families know how you plan to handle religion. I probably would not advise conversion for the sake of having one happy household. I believe you need to stick to your religious beliefs, but you need to think them out. I don't believe in raising kids by letting them choose the religion they want to practice. It doesn't work. The parents need to make the choice, and the children should be given a grounding in whichever religion the parents choose.

SB: As a pastor and a mother, how are you teaching your child about religion, and what advice can you give to other parents?

MJN: Of course, we have a special challenge with our daughter. Both my husband and I are priests. Since so much of her life with us revolves around going to church, we need to make sure we don't overdo it. We want her to love going to church, and we certainly hope it's not something she is going to rebel against when she gets older.

In terms of teaching other children about religion, it's important that parents set an example in the home. They can pray together as a family. I've already mentioned celebrating a child's baptism. We also celebrate our daughter's feast day; she was named Clare after Saint Clare of Assisi, and on that day we celebrate that there was someone she was named for. Parents should try to keep the holidays holy. That's difficult at Christmastime, but it's a bit easier at Easter and at other big Christian festivals like Pentecost. It's nice to tell your children the holiday stories, plan a special meal, and have a family celebration.

FOR FURTHER READING

Dovetail: A Newsletter by and for Jewish-Christian Families, Joan Hawxhurst, editor. 3014 A Folsom Street, Boulder, CO 80304.

Mixed Blessings: Overcoming the Stumbling Blocks in an Interfaith Marriage, by Paul Cowan with Rachel Cowan. New York: Penguin Books, 1987.

Talking to Your Child About God, by David Heller. New York: Bantam Books, 1988.

SIBLINGS

From listening to friends talk about growing up, I think my brother, sister, and I must have been the only children in the universe who weren't at one another's throat for our entire childhood. In fact I rarely remember fighting with my siblings. For good reason, I suspect. First, I can't imagine my parents tolerating constant bickering. In our "Father Knows Best" household, it wouldn't have been acceptable behavior.

Second—as corny as this seems—we have always liked each other. My brother Jim, who is three and a half years older than I am, let me play touch football with him and the boys in the neighborhood when we were children. True, I was a splendid athlete (for a girl), but still, he always picked me first on his teams. Yes, I was somewhat of a shill: we endlessly practiced complicated maneuvers in the secrecy of our backyard and then flawlessly executed them publicly. But from what I've been told—these things considered— my brother's loyalty to me in those early years should have exceeded all my expectations.

When my sister Jane was born, five and a half years after I was, my mom tells me I wept for joy. I'm not sure if it was because she was much more fun than dolls or because my parents bought me a new Annie Oakley cowgirl suit complete with a holster and guns. Whatever the reason, I never remember being jealous of her replacing me as the youngest and relegating me to a middle-child position—about which psychologists have written volumes.

What I do remember is that when she came home from the hospital I fell in love. My mom immediately put her in my arms, and I was allowed to hold her a lot. When people came by to see her and brought her presents, my parents gave me presents too, in case our

337

visitors didn't think to do it. By the time Jane was four months old, I had almost every toy I ever wanted. And as an adult I still believe that gift giving enhances most relationships.

As my siblings and I grew older, our relationships have evolved. Once my brother entered junior high school, he dropped me as a sports companion only to retrieve me years later for occasional mixed-doubles matches with my parents. Then, when I was fourteen and a half, Jim moved to Berkeley for college and later law school. He has spent the last thirty years over six hundred miles away. We see him a couple of times a year, frequently talk with him on the telephone, and delight in his children—my niece and nephew—whom I adore.

My sister, Jane, lives three miles away, and we have always been close. I like to think I have been an exemplary older sister. I certainly have tried. When we were younger, I let her sit in my room and listen to me and my friends gossip—if she promised not to talk. In high school I occasionally took her on group outings to a local pizza parlor. When she was in college, I flew to San Francisco to extricate her from a roommate she abhorred. For most of my life I have cherished my role as older sister.

As the mother of an only child, I can't help feeling saddened over what Alexander will miss if Bernie and I don't provide him with a sibling. The things that come to mind seem somewhat cornball, but I've always described myself as a "Pollyanna with an attitude." So here it goes.

Without siblings, Alex will miss unique bonds of love and affection. He'll also miss sharing a room, holding a small baby who's related to him, and cuddling in bed, giggling together uncontrollably late into the night, the group fear and anticipation of being caught sneaking downstairs on Christmas morning, and seeing other children with the same gene pool.

If Alexander remains an only child, I worry that his life will be less full, that he'll be lonely, that he won't have anyone to test himself against, that he'll be worried about having sole responsibility for two older parents, that he won't have peers to teach him about loyalty and friendship, that he won't have anyone but us at his side for his bar mitzvah and his wedding, and that he'll feel abandoned when Bernie and I die when he's middle-aged (I apologize for seeming so maudlin, but this is a real concern for older parents).

Bernie doesn't agree. He feels we were both mature—i.e., old (thirty-nine and fifty-one respectively)—when I gave birth and that if he ever wants to retire (and become a full-time artist—his pas-

*sion), we should stop with one. He worries about money for ortho-
dontia and college tuition. He has known some very happy only
children who don't at all regret the travel opportunities, discretionary income, attention, and—at the risk of sounding crass—inher-
itance potential that being an only child engenders.*

*On bad days I have an entire range of concerns myself. I worry
about being pregnant in my early forties and about the higher risk
of birth defects. I also worry about having the energy to take care of
two children, having the money to offer them the security and
privileges that I've enjoyed for the last fifteen years, whether I could
ever love a second child as much as I love Alexander, whether our
house, which seems to be bulging at the seams can accommodate a
fourth person, and whether my husband could ever retire with the
added financial burden of a second child.*

*On good days I don't feel any of these concerns should over-
ride my firmly held conviction that only children are lonely children. Since Bernie disagrees, we're still negotiating.*

ॐ

SIBLINGS

Adele Faber, the coauthor of Siblings Without Rivalry *and*
Between Brothers and Sisters, *is the mother of three. She lives in
Long Island, New York.*

SB: *Why is sibling rivalry such a problem?*
AF: Because siblings have to share a very scarce natural resource,
which is Mom and Dad, and food, laps, smiles, and time alone—all
the things they need to grow and thrive. The minute a second
child is born, there is less of everything.

**SB: *Does the age-span between siblings have an influence
on possible dissension?***
AF: Experts say it is easier to tolerate the mother's total obsession
with an infant when the first child is older—a little freer of the
parents—and has his or her interests, activities, and life outside
the home. But in my own experience I've found a lot of the
adjustment has to do with the specific child. There are some
children who can just accept a new baby more easily than others.
Some have a much harder time no matter what the age difference.
Some find it unbearable.

PREPARING OUR CHILDREN FOR SIBLINGS

■

"We read a lot of books. *Baby Sister for Frances* and *Berenstain Bears' New Baby* were our favorites, and we must have read them eighteen-thousand times. Our kids got new presents. My oldest daughter came to the hospital to see me when her sister was born, but I'm not convinced that is a good idea. She had to leave and go home with her dad, and that's a very difficult separation. Since most mothers are in the hospital for only twenty-four hours these days, it's almost better just to say that mom and the new sibling will be home the next day."

■

SB: *Are there personality traits that contribute to this?*
AF: There are personality traits that make some children gravitate toward each other and enjoy each other enormously from day one. And there are other children who just rub each other the wrong way. Sometimes you get a combination of kids where everything works; other times it's just a disaster. Here you brought another child into the world to increase the love and affection quotient and the support system of both children, and all they're doing is destroying each other. It can be very painful. So we need to teach children how to get along. Parents can't mandate love, but they can teach children how to relate to each other in civilized ways.

SB: *What are some tips for doing that?*
AF: First, you have to allow for the natural expression of hostility. When your older child says, "Send him back; we don't want him here anymore," instead of saying "Oh, you don't mean that," let the hostility come. Let it out into the light of day where it loses its power to do harm.

One parent who read my book told me that when she came home from the hospital with a second daughter her older daughter said to her, "I don't want her here."

"Normally," she told me, "I would have said 'That's ridiculous.' Instead I told her, 'I can understand how you might feel that way because, after all, there used to be just the three of us. Whenever you wanted me or needed me, I was there. But now I'm busy diapering the baby, feeding her, burping her, and cleaning her. I could see how you'd think it was better before the baby came. Why wouldn't you feel that way?' "

Her daughter listened to her and said, "Yeah . . . I guess." That conversation was repeated in that fashion several times over a few months, and now those two girls are terrific together.

It was permitting the negative feelings to air that made it safer for everyone. When negative feelings aren't allowed, they don't vanish. Either they go underground and get expressed symptomatically as asthma, bed-wetting, headaches, nightmares, or stomachaches, or they get acted out with punches and pinches. If your child says, "Mommy loves the new baby and doesn't love me anymore," it helps to acknowledge her unhappy feelings. You might respond by saying, "Honey, if you ever feel that way again, you come and tell me right away so I can give you an extrahard hug and let you know how much I love you and how precious you are to me."

I'm very much in favor of not interfering in the sibling relationship, trying to let the children "own" their own relationship. But I don't permit hurting, and that means verbal hurting or physical hurting. We've got to teach our children alternative behavior. We can say to them, "If you're angry, tell your sister with words, not with kicks or punches, not with bites or hair pulling." If your child is young and doesn't have the words to express his anger, give him the words. Say "Tell your brother, 'That's mine!' Tell your sister, 'I don't like that!' " Explain to your children that you can't let them hurt each other because they are both so precious to you.

As a parent you stand for something. You can't just abdicate and say, "Oh, well, boys will be boys" or "Kids fight." There have been too many instances of siblings who have been permitted to hurt each other in the name of "kids will be kids" and who grew up with a legacy of such hatred and resentment that they have no relationship with each other as adults because they will never forgive what was done to them.

SB: How should a parent prepare a child for a new sibling?

AF: There is not a lot you can prepare for. If you think there is anything you're going to say that isn't going to provoke some anxiety, you're mistaken. And to paint a beautiful picture of ideal love and the perfect playmate is not going to do it either. The truth is best. You can tell the older child, "I'm excited about the new baby. It will be fun. There will be a new person in the house. We won't know who it is. It will just be this tiny new baby, and we'll wonder who he or she is going to be. It will be a brand-new person who's never been in the world before. We will get to know him or her slowly. That's the good and exciting part.

"The hard part is that he or she requires so much care. Are we going to be busy! All of us. And when you can, I am going to ask you if you want to help. That would be great. But boy, it's going to be a lot of work. And you may even feel sometimes that I'm so busy with the baby that I don't care about you anymore. If you ever feel that way, you come and tell me." That's a little bit of protection. It is hard when there's a new person in the house. Giving a realistic picture helps.

It also helps to talk about and show pictures of uncles and aunts—especially when they are little. Talk about the positive and negative aspect of your relationship with your siblings. You can say, "I remember when I was so mad at your uncle Tim because he

"We talked about the baby a lot before she was born. After she arrived, our older son got a lot of attention from us and his grandparents. We made sure that he never felt left out. Now that the kids are a little older, we still make sure he gets his own attention. He hates it when his sister cries and helps by getting her a bottle or a cookie."

■

"I got my daughter books, and we talked. I brought lots of little presents so she would always get something special when people came to visit the baby. We bought her one special present that was from the baby. For the first month after the birth of her sibling, she was very angry at me but nice to the baby. Now, ten months later, she's starting to be rough with the baby. She wants to be a baby herself and wear a diaper and have a bottle. It's hard, but this too will pass."

■

"We did a lot of preparation before the baby arrived. I took my son to all of my doctor's appointments and read books to him about siblings. He was a part of the entire pregnancy. Then, when our daughter was born, we had the children exchange gifts. I've made a conscientious effort to give him the time he needs with me alone. We've worked hard at not disrupting his routines."

■

"Even though we talked a lot about what to expect and read books, my son had a lot of questions, and I was totally unprepared for their depth. After the baby was born, he got very angry with me, but he was sweet to the baby. He had trouble watching me nurse. He wanted to do it too. I said no, but I did let him try a bottle. He got bored with that pretty quickly."

■

did this. Or Aunt Clare took my doll, and I was ready to kill her. But now, when I think about not having him or her in my life, oh, that would be terrible."

That's preferable to "Oh, you're so wonderful, we decided to have another baby." It helps the only child to hear, "When I think of what it has meant in my life to have a brother or sister, I know I don't want you to grow up without one. I suppose some people do. But it was so special to me."

Finally, treat your children as unique individuals. Don't put them in roles. Give them the freedom to explore all aspects of their personalities. Be aware of favoritism. You do damage to each child—the one who is favored and the one who is not.

Don't compare, even favorably. If you say "You're a big boy! You can dress yourself better than your sister," what does that say to the "big boy"? As long as he is better than the baby, you will like him better. So when the baby starts to walk, he will have to push her down, because the way he gets approval is to be better than she is. Kids naturally compare themselves and can use each other to inspire each other. That's tolerable. What's intolerable is when the parents do it. We want each child to be valued for himself or herself.

BIRTH ORDER

Why birth order is important. It's another piece of the puzzle of personality and who you are. It's not an all-encompassing piece, maybe not even a primary piece. But it gives some helpful information on how we behave in various kinds of relationships like marriage, parenting, our workplace, and our social relationships. It suggests a kind of style we might bring to those relationships. It's a way to understand ourselves and to understand others and how they function in a relationship.

The general characteristics of first children. These are the ones who are most commonly studied and best understood. We have a long tradition of primogeniture in which the first child is the one who is most privileged. Some people look at the oldest child as getting a lot. Eldest children themselves experience that they have to work hard at being good, they become perfectionists, they become worriers, and they develop leadership skills. Eldest children tend to be more conservative within the family group. They tend to be the guardians of the status quo, and that's because, generally speaking, they identify more with parental values than their siblings. Eldest children tend to have better verbal and thinking skills. Some of their siblings will find them bossy. Jimmy and Billy Carter are great examples of this. More than half the presidents were eldest children; twenty-one of the first twenty-three astronauts were either eldest or only children (who share many of the same qualities). In one study of twenty-five successful businesswomen, all of them were either eldest or only children. None of them had brothers. All the energy that might have been invested in a male child was probably given to them.

Middle children. There's no specific way to pin down a middle child. There are some characteristics that tend to go with the middle position, but it depends somewhat on whether the child is closer to the older or younger sibling. For example, if a middle child is closer to an older brother, she may have more "younger sister of an older brother" characteristics; if she is closer to a younger sister, she is going to have more "older sister of a sister" characteristics. But the advantage of children in the middle is that they get both those characteristics if they have equal contact with both siblings in the growing-up years. Middles develop more diversity of role characteristics; they're more flexible. This often makes middle children relatively good in marriage, because they can negotiate. Often middles become mediators, sometimes professionally, mediation being a basic skill that goes with the middle position.

The negative for middle children is that they can feel shortchanged. There is always the focus on the oldest and the youngest. Parents will say "This is my oldest, and this is my youngest, and this is my other child." Of anyone, the middle ones are the most likely to drop out and disappear, because they just don't get enough of a sense of identity within the family. They are most likely to move away or be more separate in search of finding their identity; this is particularly true for siblings of the same sex.

Youngest. Dick Clark is the quintessential youngest child. Youngest children tend to act "young" all their lives. They can be long-lived. They usually have a sense of being special, and that's because they have always been referred to as the "baby" in the family. They get taken care of; as a consequence they tend to be more dependent. Often they are seen as incapable, so subjectively they feel as though their capabilities are not recognized. Sometimes they don't see the ways they are dependent. They are used to getting a lot of attention. Some of them become quite shy and

"I always let all the older children hold the new baby, but a friend of mine said something I think is really true. You don't want to endanger the new baby's life just for the older kids' mental health. I never let them carry the baby. They knew from the first second that I would never tolerate any jealousy that worked its way out physically. So it never happened. Once we had the third child, there was always competition for who got to hold him and feed him. The older kids usually like the younger ones until they're about four. By five they hate them."

■

uncertain about that. I would venture that most comedians are youngest children. Youngest children approach life with a lot of spontaneity; they pay attention to what gets a response. They tend to be more fun loving, lighthearted, and playful than older siblings. That is usually because parents are much more relaxed; they're less strict and less anxious than they were with their older children. So youngest children get away with more. They often become adventurous and daring. Jacques Cousteau was the youngest child in his family.

The unique problems and advantages of only children. Because only children are the first and the last, they can have qualities of both eldest and youngest children, or one side can dominate. Until recently only children had a bad image; they were considered spoiled and selfish. There's less of that kind of stereotyping today. Research data show that only children tend to be pretty well adjusted. They usually excel in their workplace and in life in general. On one hand, they can act like overachieving, responsible eldest children. On the other hand, depending on the family situation, they can be pampered, helpless youngest children. If they grow up in a family where the parents are devoted to them and focus all their energy on them, they are going to be more like youngest children. If they grow up in a family where the parents have a life of their own, where they are not looking to the child to make life better or more satisfying for them, and where the parents provide the correct amount of nurturance and protection, they will do fine. What's unique about only children is that they never have to defend their position with other siblings. They tend to assume that attention is going to come to them. They may do better in one-on-one relationships; they may drop out in groups. Only children may have to work at developing social skills necessary for friendships.

Source: *Dr. Ronald Richardson, the coauthor with his wife, Lois, of* Birth Order and You, *is a marriage and family therapist, a pastoral counselor, and the director of training at the North Shore Counseling Center in Vancouver, British Columbia.*

Further Reading for Your Children

Angelina's Baby Sister, by Katharine Holabird. New York: Random House, 1991.

Arthur's Baby, by Marc Brown. Boston: Little Brown & Company, 1987.

Baby Sister for Frances, by Russell Hoban. New York: Harper Collins, 1964.

Berenstain Bears' New Baby, by Stan and Jan Berenstain. New York: Random House, 1974.

How to Be an Older Brother or Sister (What to Expect When It Happens to You), by Mike Venizia. Chicago: Children's Press, 1986.

Source: Cathy MacLaggan, the mother of three, works part-time at The Baobab Tree, 3640 Bee Caves Road, Austin, TX 78746; 512-328-7636.

TELEVISION

n my first job, right out of college, I was an NBC page, which meant that I gave studio tours and worked as an usher and a gofer for the "Tonight Show," "Sanford and Son," and "Hollywood Squares," among other shows.

It was a difficult position to get. There was enormous competition for relatively few openings each year. I think every communications major in the country applies. The job itself allowed you the ability to be somewhat of a servant to a lot of rich, important, and well-known people. It was a terrific way to get your foot in the door if you were interested in moving up in the industry. Once I quit, I vowed that television would never play a major role in my life.

For many years following, I had a love-hate relationship with television. I was still attracted to the glamour. It had been fun seeing so many celebrities up close night after night, but I was still repelled by the medium's lack of social or educational value. In trying to rectify that, years later I went to work for the local public broadcasting station. While its purpose was loftier, the internal politics were equally intense.

In any event, once I was removed from it all, television became an important mental health barometer for me. There is an inverse proportional relationship between the amount of TV I watch and how I feel. When I am feeling happy and fulfilled, I watch next to nothing. When I have been dissatisfied and depressed, I have watched as much as four hours a night. In the worst of times I have never watched daytime soap operas or game shows. I can't even imagine being friends with people who do.

When I was pregnant, I became an antitelevision zealot. One night Bernie made the mistake of talking about "Sesame Street." I *responded with such venom that it was frightening. "Alexander will never watch 'Sesame Street,'" I raged. "I don't care how educational it's supposed to be. Television is a passive medium. I will not have my child hopelessly glued to such an addictive pastime."*

Bernie laughed. So did I. He asked me if we needed to discuss this further since the intensity of my response was so inappropriate. I said no, but later I thought about it. One of my problems was that I knew a number of mothers who used television as a baby-sitting device. I also knew parents who bought their children videos and let them watch them endlessly—even in the daytime.

We agreed that neither of us believed this was a good use of the medium. Bernie also pointed out that when you are unnecessarily restrictive about something, it becomes that much more appealing. So I relented. When Alex was two, he began watching "Sesame Street" and "Mister Rogers' Neighborhood."

The good news is that Alex's foray into the world of television has not detracted from his love of reading. The bad news is that Bernie and I have had some major battles about what is acceptable programming for a child. And I have once again become an anti-TV zealot, and this time I don't think the intensity of my response is unwarranted.

I find much of commercial television for children to be an abomination. I think it affects the way children play, how they act, and how they talk. Not only are the shows violent, the role models deplorable, and the language unacceptable, but the commercials must advertise every violent toy that has ever been invented and every unhealthy food item that has ever been manufactured. I sometimes just sit and wonder about the morality of the people who create the shows and advertisements and who broadcast them. Don't any of them have children? Don't they see there's a problem?

During these moments of rage I vow Alex will never watch commmercial television again. Then, after a busy day, when Bernie and I are both exhausted, we relent and let Alex watch some program that I don't detest but that I also don't find terribly entertaining, educational, or uplifting.

It's a constant battle.

OUR TELEVISION-VIEWING PHILOSOPHY

■

"We let our son watch 'Sesame Street' and 'Mister Rogers'. Otherwise we prefer videos because we have more control over them. Once our second child was born, videos became a godsend. There are times when the baby is crying, and I can put on a tape for my son and he's happy, and I'm able to take care of the baby."

■

"I try to keep it to one hour a day. In the beginning I didn't have any rules, and I noticed that if the TV was on for a long time, my kids started having behavior problems. They weren't playing outside or using up enough energy. I don't like them to watch robot monster violence, but I'm not too strict on what they see—mainly Looney Tunes."

■

A TREATISE ON TV

For the first time in human history a child is born into a home in which television is on an average of seven hours and forty-one minutes daily. This has never happened before. For the first time most of the stories our children hear most of the time are told not by the parent, school, church, community, or anyone who has something to tell but rather by a shrinking group of global conglomerates that have something to sell. This represents a major transformation in the way our children grow up, in the cultural environment into which they are born, and in their vision of the world, themselves, and other people.

This transformation has many implications for children, whether they're rich or poor, white, or people of color. What I would like to focus on is the influence of television on language development and reading and how it affects school achievement. My conclusions are based on studies of the relationship between the amount of television watched, and grades, IQ tests, and other methods of testing scholarly ability.

The interesting part of this analysis is that television affects different groups of children differently. If a child comes from a lower-income home of little education where people didn't have books before, they don't have books now, they are not book-reading people, and they don't participate in a variety of cultural activities, the more the child watches television, the better the child will do in school compared to his or her parents. So in terms of generational change, television viewing enriches the cultural horizons of people who have had very narrow, provincial, and in many ways impoverished cultural backgrounds.

On the other hand, a heavy television-viewing child from a highly educated home will do less well than his or her parents. Television depresses the top of the curve; it brings up the bottom of the curve. It manifests itself in what we call *mainstreaming*: namely, a kind of homogenizing influence in which people who come from very poor backgrounds do better while people who come from more privileged backgrounds are limited by the relatively narrow, highly organizing, and homogenizing influence of television.

Following is my advice for parents who are developing a television philosophy for their children. Parents basically act in three roles: as parents, as members of communities, and as citizens. In the home parents should not use television as a tool for

348

punishment or reward. This behavior suggests that indiscriminate television viewing is all right, that it doesn't matter what children watch but how much they watch. That is the wrong message. The right message is one of analytical, critical detachment, one of selective viewing. The best way to encourage selectivity is to watch programs with your children and express your point of view about the program content. Studies have shown that when children learn there is another perspective, a different way of seeing things, it has a powerful immunizing effect. It's important that children learn not to absorb in an unquestioning and unwitting way whatever they see on television.

As members of communities, parents should insist that their schools teach media analysis, media literacy. This new discipline that is being taught in our schools at every level is as important as history, math, English, or social studies. In many ways it is even more important because what's the use of learning methods of analysis or understanding if you don't put that learning to use in the everyday cultural environment in which we live?

Finally, as citizens parents should realize that it's not only a question of choosing from available dishes in the cultural cafeteria but also of asking the question "Is this the kind of cafeteria we want?" As citizens we make choices. A citizen should say "This is no longer just a medium. Our children have little or no choice when they grow up with television." Turning television off is not the solution, because even if you do, 999 out of 1,000 people won't. The solution is to begin participating as members of a diverse public—in various citizen groups and in professional groups—in media and cultural decision making. This is done in most other democratic countries, although we in the United States are way behind. Parents should join a coalition for cultural diversity and in each community throughout the nation begin to develop ways of participating in decision making at the networks, in the local stations, and wherever major cultural decisions are made.

Source: George Gerbner, Ph.D., is a professor of communication and dean emeritus at the Annenberg School of Communication, University of Pennsylvania. His field of research is media analysis. He is the father of two and the grandfather of four.

"Before my daughter was born, I said I'd never let her watch television. Then a friend asked if she watched 'Sesame Street' and I said we didn't have cable. She laughed and said it was on PBS. Recently, my daughter had a horrible cold and I let her watch 'Sesame Street' every morning for at least two hours. Funny how we change our opinions."

■

"I think television and videos promote imaginative play. My son watches 'Sesame Street' and 'Mister Rogers.' I let him watch an hour in the morning. In the evening I'll let him watch a video or a special show like *The Wizard of Oz*. I don't ever plan to let him watch cartoons."

■

"SESAME STREET" FACT SHEET: TWENTY-FIFTH SEASON

The Television Series

- Educational program for preschoolers designed to help children make a successful transition from home to school.
- The most heavily researched series on television.
- Every segment written with a specific learning goal, teaching basic cognitive and social skills.

Audience

- Aimed at 2 to 5-year-olds, with an emphasis on the needs of children from minority and low-income families.
- Viewership approaches saturation in the U.S.; more than 700 million child viewers outside the U.S.
- English-language version, now seen in 38 countries, has been aired in 90 nations over the past 25 years.

The Producer

Children's Television Workshop (CTW), a not-for-profit company founded in 1968 to explore television's capabilities as an educational medium. Today CTW has grown into a multimedia educational institution encompassing television, home video, software, and magazine products and reaches children in nearly one hundred countries.

Curriculum Goals

Based on ongoing research, subjects have evolved to include prereading, prewriting, and prescience fundamentals, geography, environmental awareness, social interaction, family relationships, and human and cultural diversity.

Awards

- Since 1970, won 85 awards, including 51 Emmy Awards, the Prix Jeunesse International, 2 George Foster Peabody Awards, a Clio, 4 Parents' Choice Awards, and an Action for Children's Television Special Achievement Award.

Source: Children's Television Workshop, One Lincoln Plaza, New York, NY 10023; 212-595-3456.

TV TIPS FOR PARENTS

• You, not the child, control the TV set. You should turn it on only under very special circumstances. With really young children a better step is to buy carefully selected videos. The kids will watch them over and over again so you don't have to invest in too many. Let your child watch only selected programs.

• There is no programming that is appropriate for infants. I strongly discourage parents from allowing any infants to watch TV. I would allow toddlers to watch it only as they near the age of two because there is already so much they need to grasp with their own eyes and ears directly and physically. TV can capture children and distract them from doing the necessary, fundamental things they need to do.

• Beyond the age of two, for the next year or two, I would say that you never want to have kids watch more than an hour a day and not necessarily that much. You want them to be playing more, to be actively doing things.

• If you want children to like books, read to them. Tell them stories. Let them see you read.

• There are only two shows I would recommend for toddlers: "Mr. Rogers' Neighborhood" and "Barney." Anything else could prove more harmful than valuable. These programs make children feel good. Mr. Rogers and Barney and the other kids on the show are positive and upbeat. They make children feel secure and happy. Mr. Rogers discusses children's fears and explains simple social behavior that is important, like helping others and cooperating. Barney emphasizes those as well but also throws in cognitive material like shapes, colors, and numbers.

• If children see commercials when you are watching a program, there has to be parental explanation. Say "These are commercials. They are trying to lure you into buying things. Some of them are not good. You don't have to believe everything you see on TV." Your children won't always understand what you are saying, but parents need to take a firm stand.

• What television viewing primarily teaches toddlers is that it is OK to watch television, and that's the problem. Children are getting hooked on TV. It becomes a substitute for doing anything on their own. As parents you want to be sure that your children have begun to play by themselves or have begun to engage in imaginative games and have their own world before you turn them loose with television.

• Television is in nearly every home. It is almost like a member of the family, but it is a stranger, not a member of the family. As parents you have to decide whether you want a stranger in your home, under what circumstances, and what kinds of things you want that stranger to tell your children.

Source: Jerome L. Singer is a professor of psychology at Yale University and codirector of the Yale University Family Television Research and Consultation Center. He is the father of three grown children and the grandfather of five.

TOILET TRAINING

When a friend of mine bragged that her daughter was toilet trained at eighteen months, I ran to our neighborhood children's bookstore, sought advice on the best books in the field, and bought two of them—one for Alex and one for me.

I religiously read mine, Toilet Learning, *by Alison Mack. It was very helpful. The first section explains the concept of toilet learning and basically suggests that you wait until your child is ready and that you prepare yourself and your child for the process. In the second section, which is for children, there is a story about a little girl who doesn't like her sticky and wet diapers and eventually learns how to go to the potty. We see pictures of a fireman, doctor, grandma, and baby-sitter, among others, sitting on the toilet.*

Alex listened to the story over and over. His favorite picture showed a little boy peeing in the park. Every time he saw it, he laughed gleefully and said, "He shouldn't do that." I nodded and agreed. The book became a bedtime favorite along with Once upon a Potty, *although neither book enhanced his interest in using the toilet.*

At Alex's second-year checkup I asked his pediatrician when I should consider training him in earnest. "When he shows interest," he replied sensibly. "Have him watch you and Bernie go, but don't make a big deal of it. Different children are ready at different times. Don't rush him."

That made sense to me. Alex became a steady companion in the bathroom. Bernie and I both learned how to urinate while someone watched us and asked questions. I drew the line when I had to do a "bm." Somehow I found endless questions by an inquiring mind caused constipation. Another six months passed. We

353

HOW WE DID IT

■

"I was overwhelmed by the whole concept of toilet training. I bought my daughter a potty when she was only a year and a half. She loved sitting on it but never actually used it. When she was two, I bought a book on toilet training. We read it a lot, particularly while she was sitting on the potty. At two and a half she seemed more ready. It took three weeks. We started by buying her big-girl underpants. We never used Pull-Ups, not even at night. She still occasionally has accidents, but we don't make a big deal out of it. She's really proud of herself, and so am I."

■

thought of putting a plant in Alex's potty seat and using it as a vase. I called the pediatrician again.

"He's showing absolutely no interest in potty training," I said, "and he's two and a half."

"He still has time," the pediatrician replied patiently.

I was embarrassed to mention that I was getting tired of changing diapers with bowel movements that were almost as big as my own. Alex's third birthday approached, and I was in a panic. We now owned seven books and one video relating to toilet training. We talked endlessly about peepee and poop. Alex had begun sitting on his potty seat with regularity, but he never actually considered doing anything in it. If I read about Joshua and his potty that wasn't a hat, a milk bowl, a flowerpot, or a birdbath one more time, I was going to scream. And the preschool Alex was going to start in three months required him to be potty trained. I called my pediatrician again.

"There are only two things that small children have real control over," he replied calmly. "Their food intake and their bowels. If you pay too much attention to either, you begin creating a big problem." Since Alex was a miserable eater who was clearly not going to be able to attend preschool because he wasn't potty trained, I felt like a total failure.

"But they won't take him in preschool until he's potty trained," I said with an audible groan.

"Then find another school," he responded, "and stop reading all the potty books to him. Each time you make a big deal out of it you probably delay the entire process for an additional two months."

I mumbled some rejoinder, hung up, and frantically called Bernie at work. "He won't be potty trained for another year," I screamed. "This is making me crazy. I visited six preschools before picking this one, and I need him to be toilet trained in three months. I don't know what to do."

"Honey, it's all right. He'll learn. He's a smart kid."

"Of course he's smart, but he's totally uninterested in toilet training. We have been letting him watch us pee for one bleeping year, and he's gone in his pot only once. He'll be wearing Pampers to college."

"No, he won't," he said, "and I thought we philosophically agreed that we shouldn't push him on this."

Because Bernie was handling this so calmly and in such an adult manner, I had no recourse but to hang up on him. Once I regained my sanity, I apologized and again agreed to ignore the *entire issue. Three months later the preschool teacher said that Alex could start school without being potty trained as long as he wore Pull-Ups.*

Within two weeks of starting school, he was completely toilet trained. Peer pressure can be a wonderful incentive. Alex simply came home the first day of school, told me that the other kids went potty in the toilet, and so did he. After a week he asked to wear his "underpants like Daddy's" to school. Within a month he was an old pro and asked us to leave the bathroom when he went.

Weeks later, as I loaned a friend with a three-year-old our seven potty-training books and the video, I felt a great surge of satisfaction. "It's driving me crazy," she said frantically. "Michael is smart enough to be potty trained, but he shows absolutely no interest whatsoever. How did you teach Alex?"

"With great patience and understanding," I replied calmly. "Don't make an issue of it. He'll learn in due time."

ॐ

A LOOK AT TOILET TRAINING

Louise Bates Ames, Ph.D., is cofounder and associate director of the Gesell Institute of Human Development in New Haven, Connecticut. She is a lecturer and professor emeritus at the Yale Child Study Center and the coauthor of a series of books, including Your One-Year-Old *through* Your Ten- to Fourteen-Year-Old.

SB: Why are there so many different philosophies about toilet training? Is there one "right" way?
LBA: For some reason toilet training used to be highly competitive. People lied. Parents would say "Why, he's only eight months old, and he is already toilet trained." Fortunately, in the last twenty years parents have calmed down. There's less pressure, and parents tend to be more relaxed about it.

There aren't that many toilet-training philosophies. There is no *right* way to toilet-train your children. You mostly have to wait. It's a very natural procedure. Children want to be grown-up. They also want to please. In our book on two-year-olds we say, "Many parents find that if they can hold off vigorous efforts to get their child to stay dry, sometime about two or two and a half, most children can and do stay mostly dry during the daytime, largely of their own accord." Certainly we believe in praise. That's normal

"We were forced into toilet training when our son learned to take his diaper off himself and was peeing in the crib. My husband has been instrumental in teaching him to use the potty, both by example and by constant reminders."

■

"Our oldest daughter was really easy to teach. But she was too busy to stop and go to the bathroom, so she had a lot of little accidents. Our younger daughter took much longer to get the concept. She'd sit on the potty for a half hour or more, and I got impatient. As the weeks rolled by, I got more and more concerned. Eventually she got over it and has never had an accident, and she's only two and a half."

■

"My younger son basically trained himself. My older son was much harder. He figured out the peeing part pretty quickly but wouldn't poop in the potty. It got so bad, he wouldn't poop at all. It turned into a major power struggle between us and him. Finally we took him to the doctor, who basically told us to mellow out. Things improved, but he wasn't completely trained until months later, when we went on holiday with another family who had a son his age. Peer pressure worked where we couldn't."

■

and reasonable, but making a big fuss about it is very foolish.

The main mistake that parents make is to start too soon. If the child is not dry after his nap, he is usually not ready to be toilet trained. I would say that 70 percent of the time, if parents didn't make a big issue out of toilet training, they wouldn't have any problems.

SB: How do you prepare a child for toilet training? Do books and videos help?
LBA: I personally don't favor books and tapes. I think that makes it too big an issue. As far as urination goes, most children do not have much emotional problem with it. It's the bowel movement that bothers them. People believe that some children actually think that their bowel movement is an important part of them that they're losing, and they really are scared to have one in a toilet.

Some children at two or two and a half, if they are having a battle with you over power—which is normal—may not want to do anything you want them to do. Since you do want them to use the bathroom in the usual way, they will notice—even if you are a patient person—that you have some emotional involvement in this, and it is one area where children may want to play out the battle.

In feeding, people have known for quite a long while that the less emphasis you put on what children eat, the more likely they are to eat a normal diet. You can set up a real fight over the dining table. Most parents have learned not to. With bowel movements, if you're really determined that your child use the toilet, and the child is determined not to, whether it's a battle with you, the child is scared, or is just not ready, you absolutely back off.

The same thing happens when bed-wetting continues. There are kids who are nine and ten who still wet the bed. If the pediatrician says there isn't anything physically wrong with them, it's important to back off. It is very safe to say that we virtually have never known a person who went to college, or to junior high school for that matter, who couldn't master this rather modest achievement.

HOW TO TOILET-TRAIN YOUR CHILD

Determining signs of readiness. Start trying to potty train your child when he or she is ready. Physiological readiness means that your child is able to walk and to use words that have a common meaning to both of you, such as *peepee, poopoo,* or *potty.* Your child must be able to hold his or her urine for at least three or four hours. He or she must be able to sit and stand, pull the pants up and down, and differentiate between being wet and being dry.

On a cognitive level the child must understand what it means to urinate and defecate. The child needs to be able to cooperate and must understand that potty training is something you want him or her to do. Children love pleasing their parents, although potty training may occur during a time when they are going through a negative stage.

Preparing your child. Buy a potty chair ahead of time. Put it in the bathroom and associate it with the big potty that Mommy and Daddy use. Allow your child to come into the bathroom with you and let the child know what goes on in there. Explain that everybody goes to the potty: siblings, aunts and uncles, and grandparents. There are two good books on the subject: *Toilet Learning* by Alison Mack and *Once Upon a Potty* by Alana Frankel. Let your child sit on the potty with diapers on. The child may want to carry the potty around the house. Children need to be friends with the potty. They need to know it has a name—that it's called a *potty—* and that *pee* and *poop* are associated with the potty.

How you talk about potty training with your child. It's a matter-of-fact kind of thing. You do it slowly over time. It gets incorporated into the day. Parents start taking their cues from their children. It's easy to notice when children have to poop. They get a funny look on their face. They usually stand still and start grunting. When parents ask if they need to poop, many times the child will answer no even when they are in the midst of going. Then you might say "Let's try." Sometimes you make it to the bathroom in time, and sometimes you don't. You put the poop in the potty, and say, "Yay! This is where the poop wants to be." You clean up, wash hands, and go back to the rest of the day.

It's a little bit harder to determine when a child has to urinate. It helps to ask your child every few hours if he or she has to pee. Sometimes you can catch them. Then you say, "Yay!" Give big claps and big hugs. That's usually the way it works. If it seems too

"Our son resisted every effort at potty training. It was making me crazy. He was almost four. We tried everything—books, bribes, videos, positive reinforcement, cajoling him, ignoring it—to no avail. Suddenly, one day he announced that we should stop bothering him and that he would start using the potty on his fourth birthday. The day after his party, he used the toilet for the first time, and I was ecstatic. When I finished praising him, he turned to me and said, "Mom, you're really making too big a deal of this."

stressful or your child has a temper tantrum, leave the child alone. This should not be an emotionally traumatic experience. It should be led by the child. It will be much easier for your child and you if you wait until the child is ready. Some kids can learn in a week or two, for other kids it takes months.

How you handle success and failure. You handle success with praise and love. Kids will always work for their parents' approval. There isn't any failure; it's just that your child hasn't mastered it yet. When the child has an accident, say, "Next time we'll try again." Look at potty training as an incredibly complex sequence of behaviors that the child has to buy into. Think of it in the child's terms. Realize that the child who becomes potty trained is giving up something of babyhood. Your child is probably thinking, Oh, you want me to do what? It used to be fine to go in my pants. Now all of a sudden you're changing the program? Why?

If you praise children along the way with the little steps, they will eventually master the whole process. It's important to realize that the little steps are part of the whole and that they will all fit together. At some point your child will get it and say to himself, Oh, is this what they want? That's no big deal. Why didn't they say so in the first place?

Source: Karen Fond, R.N., M.S.N., P.N.P., is a certified pediatric nurse-practitioner. She is on the faculty for general pediatrics and an assistant clinical professor for the School of Nursing at UCLA.

TOILET TRAINING IN A CHILD-CARE CENTER

How We Do It

- I talk a lot with the parents, making sure we are using the same words and techniques that they are using at home. You can't do toilet learning without this type of communication. I try to keep in close contact with the parents by means of written records describing how the children are doing at home and at school.

- We always offer the opportunity for children to go to the bathroom when they want to. I try to give them as much choice about when, where, how, which potty, and with whom.

- I take them into the bathroom in groups of two or three so they can learn from each other and get support from each other.

- I read them a lot of books about toilet learning. We take pictures of them all day: at nap time, when they're playing, and going to the toilet. We talk about the day through photographs.

- There's lots of doll and toilet dramatic play. We have a toy potty, or we build one with blocks and talk about the dolly using the potty.

- I let them explore in the bathroom and try to make it a fun place to be. I let them flush again and again within reason. I let them try to get their own toilet paper and let them wash their hands for ten minutes if that's what they need to do.

- I try to keep the bathroom as safe and clean as I can. We keep water off the floor. I personally don't like potty chairs in a child-care center because they are hard to keep clean. We have child-size toilets.

- We make sure the children have plenty of clean underwear at school. We let them choose whether they want to wear underwear or diapers. I don't go for Pull-Ups because I think they offer an ambiguous choice.

- I encourage parents to dress the children in clothes that are easy to take off. Instead of overalls, we recommend sweatpants.

What We Don't Do

- I never force children to go into the bathroom.

- I never compare children to each other or humiliate them if they have an accident.

- I never flush the toilet for them unless they can't do it or want me to do it. I think they need to be in control of the process.

- I always keep in my mind that toileting is a process that takes a lot of time and that there is no hurry. This is my message to parents who are anxious to get their kids out of diapers. You can't expect children to be trained overnight or at the same time that their cousin was trained. Children develop at different rates.

Source: Mary Ellis is the head teacher for two- and three-year-olds at the Bank Street College Family Center in New York. She has been teaching toddlers for twelve years.

TOYS

In anticipation of Alexander's birth, Bernie and I had periodic arguments about toys. We would walk by a toy store, he would want to go in, and then he would begin showing me all the great gifts he wanted to buy for his then-unborn son. There were electric trains, Lincoln Logs, chemistry sets, art supplies, books, musical instruments, sports equipment, and a host of educational toys.

While I liked some of the items better than others, by the time he was done pointing out the "necessities," I was always overwhelmed. The sheer volume inevitably prompted me to say angrily, "I don't want Alex to have a lot of things. I think too many toys spoil a child. He'll need just a few books and a few toys."

Bernie usually retreated immediately because he and I both knew that while he would never win the argument, he would ultimately do what he wanted and buy what he wanted.

Bernie also knew that I wouldn't be swayed. When I was a little girl, albeit a tomboy, I hated girl's toys. I have never liked dolls, which are certainly a market staple. While my sister, Jane, had dozens of dolls, my least favorite of hers was a doll that talked when you pulled a string and peed when you gave it water. This was supposed to be a magnificent innovation; I thought it was repulsive. And Jane and her friends literally spent hours on end playing with Barbie, Ken, and their insipid friends. While I am sure Ivana Trump used Barbie as a role model, Barbie represented everything I dislike.

So it was no surprise to Bernie when I didn't buy Alex any toys at all for the first few months of his life. At my baby showers, and upon Alex's birth, he had already received dozens of stuffed ani-

mals. Other than a few teddy bears, which I thought were quite wonderful, I politely grimaced upon opening each and every one. We stuck them in a corner of Alex's room, and to everyone else's surprise and my delight, he hated them.

But suddenly, when Alex was about three months old, everything changed. I went to the Imaginarium, a local toy store, and experienced an epiphany. It was just girl's toys I had hated when I was growing up, and even those were now different and less sexist. And when I saw the variety of trucks, cars, trains, sports equipment, tools, blocks, bikes, puzzles, and balls, I was amazed.

I quickly went to the section for infants and bought a mobile, a few nesting and stacking toys, a wonderful push/pull toy, and an array of tub toys. When Bernie came home that night, he was justifiably taken aback. On the weekend when we went to a toy store together, he almost had to physically restrain me because I was consuming so recklessly.

Perhaps as a counterbalance, he staunchly retreated. A few weeks later, when I bought Alex a few vinyl books, some teething toys, a crib gym, some sand toys, and a xylophone, he had the nerve to suggest that this might be excessive.

"Excessive?" I replied haughtily, "No way. He needs toys for his developmental growth. Don't you want him to learn how to grasp small objects, push, drop and retrieve?"

"Of course, but—"

"Well, there are no buts about it," I said. "We've got to teach him to develop spatial relationships, encourage mobility, and stimulate his senses. Toys are the vehicle for that."

Bernie shrugged and shook his head. After a bit of self-reflection, I decided I could scale back a bit. It's not that I had rediscovered my values. It was just that my freelance income could not support weekly toy buying sprees.

Still, every now and then there are occasional glimpses of a latent compulsive toy buyer hidden beneath my nonconsumer exterior. It's only January, and I have already begun thinking about what new toys to buy Alex for his birthday in June. There are so many wonderful items to choose from. Lately I've begun contemplating taking on a few additional clients so that I'll have more money to spend.

OUR TOY-BUYING PHILOSOPHY

∎

"The only rule on toys is that they need to be nonviolent. We try to get our daughter a few new things every three months. She's got a roomful, but I've seen kids with more. She loves her baby dolls the best."

∎

"We've never bought a lot of toys, although we do have a lot of books. Our daughter has friends who have closets filled with stuff, and she loves playing at their houses. She can keep herself occupied at home with her blocks and her dolls."

∎

TIPS ON TOYS

Joanne Oppenheim, coauthor of The Best Toys, Books & Videos for Kids, *is a former teacher, a child development specialist, and the mother of three. She is the cofounder of the* Oppenheim Toy Portfolio, *a consumer guide to toys, games, books, and videos, published quarterly, 40 East 9th St., New York, NY 10003; 212-598-0502.*

SB: Are toys good for children?
JO: It depends on the toy. Toys are classically called the *tools of children's play.* They can help children develop skills, including dexterity, imagination, and intellectual problem solving. They can also help with physical and social development. For infants and toddlers, well-chosen toys need to fit the young child's sensory style of learning. Toys that have interesting sounds, sight, textures, and chewability make a good fit. Toys should be easy to activate and foster your baby's sense of making things happen.

SB: Are there toys parents should avoid?
JO: Yes. A lot of people have lovely heirlooms that should stay in the heirloom chest because they don't meet today's safety standards. Old wooden toys may have lead paint on them, and toys from craft fairs may be made of materials that are not meant to be ingested. Soft, fuzzy animals may seem to be age-appropriate for infants, but if they have bells or ribbons on them or long-haired plush, they are inappropriate. Velour and terry cloth are safer for young babies. The rattles that come with flowers as decorations for new babies are not intended to be put in a child's mouth.

If you're talking about children under three, you won't want anything with small parts. Some parents read toy labels and buy their children more advanced toys because they think their children are so smart. The toy labels that recommend which toys are appropriate for children of different ages have nothing to do with a child's intellectual ability. They are based on developmental stages. No matter how smart you think your one-year-old or two-year-old is, you don't want any toys that have small parts. Choking is a real hazard.

People assume that if a toy is in the toy market, it has been tested like food and drugs, but that is erroneous. The toy industry is self-regulating. Manufacturers voluntarily test products, but when we hear about toys being withdrawn from the market, it generally doesn't happen until there is an accident. That's important information for parents to have. The buyer had better beware.

SB: *Can a child have too many toys?*

JO: I'm not sure there is any research to substantiate it, but it is common sense that when you walk through a house where children are simply drowning in toys, you can usually tell they are overstimulated. Toys have become one of the disposables in our society. When my children were growing up, we bought one toy at a time. Today, people load shopping carts with toys the same way we shop for food.

Just because toys are designed in multiples doesn't mean we have to buy that way. I recommend that parents rotate toys because even a little baby stops seeing things when they're always in sight. It's better to change what's in view, put toys away, and bring them back for a renewed life.

SB: *How do you find the right toys for a child's age group?*

JO: You need to know where your child is developmentally. You want to find toys that are a good match, that are challenging without being frustrating. Buying *up* often doesn't build confidence or competence; it just builds frustration. Use the toy box label as a guide, but recognize that labels are very broad because their purpose is to sell products. A product that is geared to children from six months to three years old may not really appeal to the youngest or the oldest children in that category.

Many items found in your home will be of interest to younger children, including the boxes toys come in, other boxes for nesting, kitchen ware, and plastic cups and spoons for the bathtub. A shopping bag with empty plastic bottles is wonderful fun for a toddler. Children can spend many hours playing with materials from your house that they can tote and carry, dump and fill. Remember, you don't have to buy everything.

ADVICE FROM THE TOY MANUFACTURERS OF AMERICA

Why Toys Are Labeled

Labels on toy packages make choosing safe, appropriate toys much easier. However, no package label can tell you exactly which toys are right for your child, and not all toys are appropriate for every youngster. On the other hand, child development experts agree that children develop in a sequence of stages, and toy makers use this information to indicate which types of toys are safe and appropriate for children of various ages. Product labels help con-

"We don't really have a lot, although it looks like we do because we don't put them away. Our den is one big toy room. On son loves trains, so we do have a lot of wooden, plastic, and metal trains in many sizes. Toy buying has gotten easier as our son has gotten older because we really have a sense of what he likes."

■

"No guns. I refuse to buy them, although my boys make them out of sticks and bats. I try to limit the number of noisy toys for my own sanity, except for musical instruments. We try to buy sports-related toys or blocks or things that make them think. I tend to shy away from battery-operated toys. I also like toys with interchangeable parts."

■

"The toys my daughters want—dolls, lipstick, kitchen stuff, and household appliances—defy everything I've tried to accomplish in trying to raise them in a nonsexist way. They also play with arts and crafts materials, blocks, Duplos, and balls, but they have never asked for a truck, a train, a garage, or any other typically 'boy' toys. We don't understand it."

■

"We had a no gun philosophy for a long time. It was easy since our first two children were girls. It's pretty useless, though. The boys make guns out of bamboo, yardsticks, plant stems, and seaweed."

■

sumers distinguish among the vast number of toys on the market to make the most appropriate purchases.

Remember, each child is unique and develops at his or her own pace. The best thing adults can do when purchasing toys is to know the maturity, skill level, and interests of the child, read the age labels carefully and use them as guides, and, above all, use common sense. Nobody knows your child better than you do.

How Toys Are Labeled

Toy makers follow the age-grading guidelines of the Consumer Product Safety Commission (CPSC), which consist of four main criteria:

1. the physical ability of a child to manipulate and play with the features of a toy
2. the mental ability of a child to understand how to use a toy
3. the play needs and interests applicable at various levels of child development
4. the safety aspects of the toy itself

A child's abilities, interests, and play needs will, of course, vary at each level of development. New toys are tested frequently by children in play settings to determine durability, age-appropriateness, and play patterns. At least one large toy manufacturer maintains an in-house, year-round nursery school for this purpose, while others establish relationships with universities and other educational facilities. Manufacturers also may involve parents, teachers, and others who care for children for their firsthand knowledge and valuable insights. In addition, a toy maker may have a child development specialist, psychologist, or physician on staff or working as a consultant.

Cautionary Labeling

Some manufacturers may also add cautionary information to the age label on a toy's package. This alerts parents that a toy may not be safe if it is misused or if the particular toy is in reach of children outside the recommended age group. For example, the manufacturer of a construction set labeled for six years and older may include a statement on the packaging that the toy contains small parts. This way, parents are reminded that if another child in the household is still putting objects into his or her mouth, ears, or nose, this toy should be kept out of the younger child's reach.

Cautionary labels simply advise parents that special care must be taken to use a toy properly, not that the toy is unsafe. Sometimes manufacturers wish to emphasize that children may need help understanding the instructions or that adult supervision may be required during playtime.

Source: The TMA Guide to Toys & Play, *Toy Manufacturers of America. For a free copy of this safety booklet, send a postcard with your name, address, and zip code to Toy Booklet, P.O. Box 866, Madison Square Station, New York, NY 10159-0866, or call 800-851-9955.*

GUIDELINES FOR CHOOSING TOYS

What Toys Are For

The purpose of toys is to help children through their developmental stages. Toys help children learn, whether they are at the stage of chewing, improving their vision, or learning language. At the same time, people say "But I thought toys were supposed to be fun." Well, learning is supposed to be fun. Somewhere along the line, we got the message that learning wasn't supposed to be fun. So we think play—which is fun—must have nothing to do with learning. In fact play is a process for development, learning, and growing. It's important to have things and people around to facilitate the best development possible.

What Toys Are Best for What Age?

Birth to two months. At this developmental stage children are able to see close up but not far. Hearing is good; it's already setting the stage for language learning. Select toys like mobiles and colorful toys that can be attached safely and securely to the side of the crib.

Three to six months. Children have improved vision, continued interest in sounds as they prepare for language learning; they can grasp small objects and lift their heads. Select toys like rattles, music boxes and song tapes, brightly colored objects or pictures safely placed within babies' views, pictures of people and animals, especially faces.

Seven months to one year. At this developmental phase children are able to sit up, crawl, and even walk. They have a concentrated interest in their environment. Select toys that make pleasing

"At first, when we had two kids, everyone got unbirthday presents, birthday presents, and Christmas presents. When I bought a new toy for one, I bought them for everybody. But somewhere around three kids, you just have to realize that you can't buy everyone new toys at the same time. And all the children can't get the most expensive presents during the same year. When we have to buy new bikes—which are a major expense—we need to spread it out, and they understand that. None of them are deprived, but they do get jealous in a normal sort of way."

■

365

sounds when touched. Balls, nesting cups, blocks and various geometric objects, all kinds of textures for the child to experience, and simple books are good choices.

One to two years. Children are able to walk. They have a sensitivity to tiny things, like watching ants. They climb and push objects. They are still concentrating on and practicing language. They're learning to trust and to experience themselves as separate beings. Select toys that subtly stimulate the senses. Extremely bright colored objects and jarring sounds are *not* helpful to the child's learning sensory discrimination. Simple puzzles, geometric designs that fit into shaped boxes, push/pull toys, musical toys such as a xylophone, and ride-on toys are appropriate.

Two to four years. At this age children have a great need for order. They also are curious about how things work. They are beginning to pretend, to solve problems, and to make things. They enjoy repetition. The child at this age is ready to learn good manners. Select toys such as Peg-Boards, shape sorters, dolls, cars, toy phones, trains, simple building blocks, and other materials to make playhouses. Puzzles help children learn space orientation and hand-eye coordination, as well as deal with colors and shapes. Musical instruments, crayons, paper, books, and art materials are always good choices.

Criteria for Choosing Toys

• Is the toy safe?

• Does the toy give your child a sense of competence and confidence?

• Does the toy allow your child to develop a sense of delight and wonder in the world?

• Does the toy enhance creativity?

• Does the toy help a child feel good about himself or herself?

• Does the toy foster independent thought?

A Few Caveats

No matter what the age, I don't encourage toys with batteries because that doesn't help the child gain a sense of his own competence. All children learn to do is push a button. Adults may like the ride-on batteried toys that children can drive somewhere, but children need to learn to push and pull themselves. Anytime you have a battery in the toy, the battery and the technology are doing the work and the child isn't.

The simpler the toys, the better. When small children get presents, they are often more interested in the bows and the wrappings than the gifts. That should tell you something. As parents we are often unnecessarily influenced by Madison Avenue. We feel guilty if we don't buy our children what is advertised. Yet why get your child a windup, pushbutton, or battery-mobilized toy when he would rather play with a wooden spoon?

I don't recommend guns for any age group. When I talk to children, I say "When you're shooting a gun, you're acting like you want to hurt somebody else. Do you want to hurt other people, or do you learn how to help them?" Whenever parents ask me about buying guns for their children, I say "Why spend time and have your child concentrate on something that is disruptive for them and can hurt other people?" Parents say "I played with a gun when I was small, and it didn't hurt me." So did I, but I think that all of us who did may have some unlearning to do. Guns are not horrible, but isn't it better to expose your children to the wonders of the world and teach them to cope in a very positive life-giving way?

Source: Karen Shanor, Ph.D., a psychologist and author, has developed seminars on choosing toys for children. She lives in Washington, D.C., and is the mother of one; 202-291-6222.

VACATIONS

One of the advantages of being a DINK (double income no kids) is that you take great vacations. In the years Bernie and I were married before Alexander came along, we went on some fabulous trips. When I was one month pregnant and we were traveling to Washington, D.C., we couldn't stop talking about how much we wanted to return with our son-to-be.

"Won't he love this?" Bernie asked when we were walking around the National Air and Space Museum.

"I'm sure he will," I responded, hoping he'd like the Hirshhorn more.

"How old do you think he'll be before we can begin taking him on driving trips?" Bernie asked as we admired the surrounding Virginia countryside.

"Immediately, I should think," I said with total ignorance. "Babies just sleep. I don't see any problem."

"What about Europe?" he continued blithely.

"I think he should be eight so that he can really enjoy it," I answered after giving it some thought. I had found that it was quite easy to be an expert on traveling with children since I knew absolutely nothing about it. Thus I made the following pronouncements. During the first three years we would take Alex on driving trips because, after all, small children can't do a lot and they're probably fine in the car. By four he would be ready to begin fishing trips with his father. At six we could consider a cross-country driving trip. And at eight we could begin traveling abroad. After that, our imagination and finances would be the only limitations.

With these goals in mind you can imagine our surprise when we took Alex on a weekend getaway when he was a few months old

368

and found it was a total disaster. It was a seven-hour drive, and he hated every minute of it. Not only did we have to take almost everything he owned and rent a portable crib at the destination, but we also suddenly realized that, without help along, traveling with an infant was exhausting. On the drive home, during which Alexander not only cried for hours but also threw up all over me, we revised our traveling schedule.

"Can you imagine what a two-week vacation would be like?" I said, returning to the car after giving myself a sponge bath in a restaurant bathroom.

"I think we'll stay home until he's ten," Bernie replied sadly. "I guess we won't make it back to Europe until we're retired," he continued with tears in his eyes. I shrugged dejectedly.

Despite that initial disaster, we've continued to take our son on vacations, and we've had some wonderful times. When Alex was eighteen months old, we flew to Austin, Texas, to visit relatives, and it was terrific. They were not only hospitable, but there were also six adults and three children who entertained Alex and took care of him.

On the flight home Bernie asked when I thought they'd like us back. I said that I felt our limit would be once every few years. "What about your aunt and cousins in Ohio?" I asked. "They should be good for alternate years."

Bernie hadn't been back to Ohio since he'd moved away at fifteen. Still, I didn't feel that four decades was too long a time span to renew acquaintances. I thought that they could be real contenders in the future.

Before Alex was born, we always wondered why, when people could travel anywhere in the entire world, they would visit relatives in ordinary places. Now we know. And I'm thinking that I'll call Bernie's aunt Dora in Wooster, Ohio, next week—just to say hello.

HOW TO TRAVEL WITH KIDS

- Plan according to the needs of your family and your child. At home, if you've got a play group, equipment, and support services, figure out which of these you want to replicate on vacation.

- Develop a structure for your child. Again, if at home your child naps and eats at specified times, you need to re-create this schedule as much as possible.

HOW OUR VACATIONS HAVE CHANGED

■

"Our big vacation is our ski vacation. When our boys were small, we would book a nanny beforehand to come to the condo. This cut down on our privacy but gave us lots of flexibility. We could have our kids with us, and yet we could ski all day and go out in the evening."

■

"Packing is now a major consideration. We take along familiar toys, a favorite blanket and pillow, the car seat, portable crib, bottles, favorite food, and a lightweight stroller in addition to all our son's clothes and diapers. I write everything down, and it seems to take forever to pack. But it's all worth it because our son feels comfortable and is entertained."

■

- Determine how to get a baby-sitter for your child in advance. Have the person come early so that you can make sure he or she is capable and you feel comfortable leaving.

- Plan to travel when your children are asleep. They won't miss anything, you will feel more comfortable, and it's easier.

- Communicate with your child. They need details about the trip. How long will it take? How often might you stop? Where are you going? What will you pass? When will you arrive? All this can be explained in terms that even a small child can understand. The length of a trip might be described as watching two "Sesame Street" episodes back to back or likened to driving back and forth from school several times.

- Make sure your child is physically comfortable. It's a given under the law that children under forty pounds and forty inches will be secured in a car seat when traveling in the car. But can they see outdoors? Can they quickly access their toys and games? Can they nap readily and comfortably?

- Help your children feel as if they are in control. Encourage them to pack travel toys, games, and food they like—even little children can do this. With each successive trip the toys and/or games your children select will become more appropriate.

- Bring lots of snacks. Freeze juice in the box the night before so it stays cold and will keep other food cold. While using some parental guidelines about how thirsty certain snacks will make them feel, let the children help determine what they want—and let them bring some special items.

- Make your cassette player "family friendly." Kids can listen to music for hours and hours and not necessarily the same music parents want to hear. Fortunately help is at hand. Sony, for example, has come out with a series of tapes entitled *Sony Kids' Music*. These tapes were designed specifically for an "educated, entertainment-savvy group [of parents] to share with their children."

- Pay no heed to the contingent that suggests that a museum visit with a child is something to be approached with trepidation. When taking your children to a museum, as always, common sense is your best support. Remember, strollers are not always permitted. Some museums limit them to midweek visits; others ban them altogether. Bring a backpack if you're not certain. Visit the museum gift shop at the start of a visit. Not only do you learn what appeals to your child, but he or she will have a focus and will less likely be bored or bewildered.

- If there is one certainty on a family vacation, it's that something will go wrong. There will be traffic when you least expect it; someone will get carsick; the lunch break will take longer than you allowed time for. It's OK. You're on vacation. There should be time to make an extra stop at the county fair you just passed or to stop the car and throw around a Frisbee.

- Limiting your expectations of distance to be covered and places that just "must" be seen brings a newfound freedom—a freedom that allows you to turn what might be perceived as a negative experience into a positive one.

Source: Dorothy Jordon is the publisher of Family Travel Times *newsletter, the coauthor of* Great Vacations with Your Kids, *and the mother of two.* Family Travel Times *newsletter is available from* Travel with Your Children, *45 W. 18th Street, 7th Floor Tower, New York, NY 10011; 212-206-0688.*

WHAT A FAMILY TRAVEL AGENT DOES

SB: *Why did you start Rascals in Paradise?*
TD: I started having kids and taking them on vacation, and my clients (from my travel agency) were asking me to do similar programs. My partner and I—she has two children and I have three—looked around and saw that nobody was addressing the family travel market.

SB: *What specific services do you provide when planning trips for families with infants and toddlers?*
TD: We organize vacations for families in places that can accommodate infants and toddlers. Most family programs start with kids of age five. What do you do if you have a five-year-old and a six-month-old child? Our programs go to places that are safe for infants and toddlers and where parents can feel comfortable going with young children. We offer a baby-sitter for each family so that if you do have an older child you can go snorkeling with her while someone watches the baby. The baby-sitters are provided by the hotels, but we tell them what American families want and require. The sitters are screened by the hotel staff, and they know how to take care of infants and toddlers whether they're in Fiji, the Bahamas, or Mexico.

"We go only to resorts that cater to families with children. It's much more relaxing for us. There are baby-sitting services, full-day programs for older children, and restaurants where you're not embarrassed when your kids throw their food on the floor and begin screaming. We never thought we'd go to these places, but we love them."

■

"We take much more luggage, eat earlier, schedule some touring each day but never a full day's worth, stop at all rest areas when driving, and plan trips that are fun but reasonable."

■

"We go to one place and take day trips rather than moving sleeping quarters. We visit family on virtually all vacations so that cousins can see one another and their grandparents. Since we don't have family nearby, it's our only opportunity to see our relatives. The kids love it."

■

TIPS

■

"Don't be overly ambitious. Realize that your kids will do the same things on a trip as they do at home. If they spend hours digging in the mud, don't spend a lot of money going to Europe."

■

"Motels with refrigerators are a big plus. It's great for formula, milk, and string cheese. We always pack a hot plate to warm things. The old saying 'An army travels best on its stomach' sure applies to infants and toddlers."

■

"We always bring a baby-sitter with us. We bring sitters our children are used to. I tell them in advance what I expect them to do. I pay them a flat rate. They get up early and feed the kids breakfast so that I can sleep in. I explain that this is my vacation—not theirs. But I do give them an hour off during the day and a few nights off during the week so that they can be with other kids their own age."

■

SB: How is the travel industry changing to accommodate families with small children?

TD: Since we started Rascals in Paradise in 1987, there has been a huge change in the industry. Before, they ignored the family market; now they are marketing their services to families. In some hotels, like the Four Seasons, they will have bottle-warming facilities in your suite and provide Pampers and pacifiers. Club Med now has locations that not only have miniclubs for older children but also baby clubs that are geared specifically for infants and toddlers. The Sand Piper in Florida and Ixtapa in Mexico are two good choices.

Some of the airlines will provide baby food if you request it. Another good place for infants as well as mixed-age kids is Franklin D. Resort in Jamaica. All the accommodations there are suites. Each family gets its own Girl Friday. Your Girl Friday can baby-sit for your children during the day or the night so that you can go out alone with your spouse for a candlelight dinner.

SB: What are some of the best trips you've planned for families with infants and toddlers?

TD: What we do is have special weeks, which are noted in our brochure, that are family weeks. In those weeks we have a teacher escort who goes along with the group. She will organize activities for toddlers as well as older kids. You can just lie under a palm tree and take a snooze, read a book, or go snorkeling or golfing while your child is having a good time with other children.

A good first Rascals trip for families is to Akumal, Mexico, accessed by flights to Cancun. We feature about ten to twelve family weeks there per year, plus we send numerous individual families there on their own. It is easy to get to, and the facilities, service, food, and child care are consistently good. For farther away, Fiji is a perfect, slightly exotic destination for families traveling with children. Our best trips perhaps are those that we have hand-tailored for individual families with more time, which would include some around-the-world sabbatical trips.

SB: What tips do you have for parents traveling with infants and toddlers?

TD: Years ago, when I was traveling to Fiji with my children, who were then three years old and three months old, I got cold feet the week before we were ready to leave. I thought, What if this little baby gets colicky on the plane? I don't want to be the person no one wants to sit next to. The flight was delayed for an hour. I had planned to nurse my baby when we were seated so she would fall asleep. I didn't want to nurse her in the waiting room, because I knew she would be awake on the plane. So I walked her around, she cried, and everyone glared at us. When we finally got on the plane, both my kids fell asleep and slept through the entire flight. People kept on coming up to me and saying, "What kind of drugs did you give those children?" Well, I hadn't given them anything. But the decision I had to make, once I knew there was a delay, was where it would be better for my baby to cry, in the waiting room or on the airplane.

So my best advice to new parents is to expect the unexpected. Be prepared and be flexible. After all, whether you are driving an hour to Grandma's or flying to Tahiti, everything isn't going to go as you planned. If you are calm and relaxed, the kids will pick up on it.

Source: Theresa C. Detchemendy, CTC, is the president/co-owner of Rascals in Paradise, 650 Fifth St., Suite 505, San Francisco, CA 94107; 800-U-RASCAL or 415-978-9800. She is the mother of three.

BARGAIN FAMILY VACATIONS

How You Plan Them

Consider the age of your child, what you like to do, and what you find relaxing, because one person's vacation pleasure is another person's vacation nightmare. The easiest time to travel with children is when they are between four and six months old, before they've started moving around too much. At that age you can go just about anywhere. As the kids get older, it is better to stay in one or two places rather than hop around a lot.

If you want to get the best deals in the best places, plan as far in advance as you can. Start doing research early. The best family resorts that are the most affordable fill up a year in advance with people who've gone the summer before. If you can't plan a full year in advance, you can often get cancellations, but the farther ahead you can plan, the more likely you are to get what you want.

If you have an infant or a toddler, you may not be constrained by a school schedule. If you travel off-season, whether it's spring or fall, you can get better prices and more available accommodations. Early June is also a good time to travel since most people with schoolchildren wait until July or August to take vacations.

A good source of travel information is the travel book section of any bookstore. You can also peruse parenting and travel magazines, look up specific magazine articles in the *Reader's Guide to*

"Let the airlines know you're traveling with a baby. Remember that it's as important for a baby to drink a bottle on descent as it is on takeoff."

■

"Buy new toys your kids have never seen before, especially for the airplane. This works, even for infants. Try a Walkman with a new tape. Toys 'R' Us has a whole wall of toys for a couple of dollars each. I stock up, and it works wonders."

■

Periodicals, or contact the chamber of commerce or local and regional tourist offices for information.

In terms of budgeting, the major vacation costs when you have infants and toddlers are accommodations and transportation. With older children, activity and meal costs can add up. With younger children who take naps and who are difficult in restaurants, comfortable accommodations with kitchenettes are key.

Accommodations

If you stay in condos, cabins, motels, or hotels with kitchens or kitchenettes, you can save a lot on food. Many family resorts, dude ranches, and family camps offer the "American plan," where your meals are included in the price of your accommodations. While these places often look more expensive at first glance because everything is included, if you add up all of the individual items, the American plan rate can be a bargain.

Home exchanges are a great way for families to save money on vacations, especially if you're exchanging with a family who has young children and a house full of toys. A source for home exchanges is the Vacation Exchange Club, which you can reach by calling 800-638-3841. It publishes catalogs and if you join, your home is listed in each one. Intervac U.S. is another option; the phone number is 800-756-HOME. Both charge a fee. I know a number of people who have exchanged homes, and it's been successful for them.

Apartment or condo rentals offer more space and kitchens. People traveling with infants and toddlers find the additional space that these accommodations afford to be more convenient than a hotel room, particularly if you spend more time inside because of naps. To find a condo or an apartment, contact the local tourist office and ask for a list of such accommodations.

Family camps are becoming more and more popular. A family camp is usually a youth camp that has added family camping times. Some of them have been designed exclusively for families. Many are simple and rustic and will remind you of the camps you went to in your youth. The accommodations are usually a cabin; often the bathrooms are a short walk away, and the meals are served in a cafeteria-type situation. They have the recreational amenities of a camp, so there are often boating, riding, arts and crafts, and other family activities. Many of them have a child-care component so that the parents can get a break.

Budget motels are usually plain and simple; you get one big room and a couple of double beds. Infants and toddlers are usually free. There are budget motel directories and 800 numbers for all of the chains.

Transportation

Cars are the least expensive way to travel. But if your time is limited, you'll spend more valuable vacation time in transit, not to mention that many infants and toddlers don't do well on very long car rides. You've got to gauge your own child.

For infants and toddlers long train trips can be difficult. On one hand, trains allow toddlers to get up and move around, but they are a nightmare if you have to chase your child all over the train.

If you're traveling a long distance, fly. Children ages two and under can fly free if they sit in their parent's lap. It's often advisable to bring an infant car seat in case the seat next to you is empty. Then you can actually strap your child in the seat; you'll feel safer, and it gives you more space.

Planning in advance as far as you can will allow you the greatest savings on airfares. Don't always trust a travel agent to get you the best deal; do some of the research yourself. Certain air routes have reduced rates at night if your children will sleep on a plane. Reduced fares often require midweek flights, and many weekly family resort reservations start on weekends.

Source: Laura Sutherland is the coauthor with Valerie Wolf Deutsch of The Best Bargain Family Vacations in the U.S.A. *and* Innocents Abroad, Traveling with Kids in Europe. *She is the mother of two and lives in Santa Cruz, California.*

WORKING

When I was pregnant and people asked me what my work schedule would be after the baby was born, I said I thought I would be coming back to work full-time but I really wasn't sure. My schedule was such that I left the house at 8:00 A.M. and returned home at 7:00 P.M. I felt that I would miss not only the major part of Alex's day but his entire life. Once I gave birth and had three months left of my maternity leave (part of it unpaid), I decided that while I would like to keep my job as director of corporation and foundation relations (fund-raising) for a small liberal arts college in Los Angeles, I would want to work only three days a week until I could figure out what was best for Alex and me.

Two months after I committed to this relationship, I quit. It had immediately become clear that I couldn't do a full-time job on a part-time basis. I also felt that even the three days of leaving home early and returning after Alex was asleep at night was heartrending.

Bernie and I discussed my decision at great length. We decided that, yes, the loss of my salary would be a financial hardship. We also knew that we would still be able to pay the mortgage, car and house insurance, and eat.

Perhaps because I was forty and had long since realized that my life was not my job, or perhaps because I'd changed careers a number of times and had worked as a freelance writer for a couple of years, I knew the marketplace had enough flexibility to reabsorb me when I was ready to return.

When working friends incredulously asked me, "What are you going to do all day as a full-time mother?" I replied that I suspected Alex and I would do a lot of lunches and go to the park with some regularity. I also knew that as an infant Alex would sleep a lot of the time and that I would either do housework, a never-ending task, catch up on my reading, or nap.

During the going-away party at work, a number of women colleagues with children came up to me and whispered that they wished they had the financial resources to quit. They hated leaving their children in child care all day every day, no matter how old the kids were. Other colleagues—men and women—couldn't seem to understand how much I had changed. Worse, they were shocked by my apparent satisfaction with the situation.

When I cleaned out my office that day, I didn't feel one twinge of regret. Two months later, when the college offered me a part-time grant-writing position, I was thrilled. I must admit that I wasn't happy being home full-time. I liked the intellectual stimulation of working. I missed the camaraderie of talking to peers about subjects other than nursing, baby poop, and child rearing. I liked having some money of my own.

It was a perfect schedule for me until I sold The Mommy Guide. I had written the first draft on my own time. Suddenly I had a deadline for a major rewrite and was working many more hours than I had ever intended. In retrospect, I don't know how I thought I could do it. At first I kept my three-day-a-week schedule so I could still have time with Alex, but since I was still working for the college because I needed the money, it didn't work out. I kept on missing deadlines for the book, so I tried a four-day-a-week schedule. By now Alex was in preschool, so I put him in for an extra day a week. But as the director of the school confirmed, he didn't like going the extra day. He was miserable, and so was I; we reverted to his original schedule.

When it finally appeared as though the book was in jeopardy, I took a leave of absence from the college, and for three months I worked solely on the book five days a week as well as on some weekends. My mother took Alex every Thursday, and between our housekeeper, Claudia, and play dates with other children, I tried to come up with a viable plan for him. It was awful. Alex was getting shuffled from pillar to post. I was miserable. I still missed deadlines, but ultimately the book was completed.

It was a very painful experience, and for the first time in my life my values were all askew. The irony was that while Alex was the most important person in my life, I was spending all my time writing a book on motherhood rather than being with him.

It had also become clear to me that work—and how we deal with it—is a universal problem. Other mothers have very strong *feelings about working full-time, part-time, or not at all. I'm just grateful that my life has finally gotten back on track and that I have the financial resources and the flexibility to make a choice.*

✥

WOMEN AND WORK

Ellen Galinsky is the copresident of the Families and Work Institute in New York. She is the coauthor of The Preschool Years, *author of* The Six Stages of Parenthood, *and the mother of two.*

SB: Does maternal employment have a good effect on infants and toddlers?

EG: It depends on the mother's attitude—whether or not she believes she should be working. It depends on whether the father or other people in the family support her work. It depends on the stress or satisfaction she derives from her job. It depends on the quality of child care that she has.

SB: Are there any studies that show whether child care—even quality child care—is really good for children?

EG: There are numerous studies showing that for children who are more at risk, born into poverty or with developmental delays, high-quality child care is quite beneficial. There are also studies that show that low-quality child care can be harmful to all children, low income and high income alike. Because the quality of child care in this country is typically barely adequate, this is of great concern. There are several new studies that should begin to disentangle the answer to this question.

SB: What are the key factors facing working moms with kids?

EG: Time, energy, guilt, and handling logistics. We found in our national study of the U.S. workforce that 66 percent of parents feel they don't have enough time with their children. That's not decreasing as companies downsize and as global competition increases. Parents are going to continue to be asked to work long hours in demanding and hectic jobs. So the issue of time is certainly a critical one.

In terms of energy our researchers have looked at how people come home from work. Depending on the nature of their job, they may come home feeling really stressed out because they have had a fight with a co-worker or their supervisor has been treating them badly. You can also work very long hours and come home feeling fine. Our research shows that certain aspects of work affect one's mood and energy level at home, including how hectic and demanding your job is and the kind of relationships you have with the people at work. Sometimes parents come home depleted. Sometimes they come home energized. It's how parents switch off the "work self" and switch on the "family self" when they may be feeling exhausted or depleted that makes a difference.

The third issue is the societal ambivalence about working. There is still an assumption that there is one right way to do things and a wrong way to do them. As a consequence, both mothers at home and mothers at work feel judged. The result for employed mothers is frequently guilt.

Another issue is the conflict between responsibilities at home and responsibilities at work. What if you work for a company that tells you to stay over Saturday nights on business trips to get cheaper airfares? Or what if your boss schedules a weekly departmental meeting at 5:30 P.M. but the child care center closes at 5:00 P.M.? Then there are the logistics of the teacher's conferences, the school plays, the days when your kids ask you to go on a school trip or make costumes for Halloween. Eighteen percent of parents feel highly conflicted between their work and family life, and another 40 percent feel "somewhat" torn between work and family life.

SB: In what ways is the workplace changing to accommodate mothers with children?

EG: I think it's important to say that the workplace is changing to accommodate mothers *and* fathers with children. Initially companies may see this as a women's issue. It's not a women's issue, although women, by and large, take the greater responsibility for managing these issues. Increasingly fathers are feeling more constrained and becoming somewhat more involved in raising their children. They are spending 60 to 70 percent of the time that women are taking care of their family and doing housework, although by and large women remain in charge.

Companies are changing in that 62 percent of large companies are now beginning to help families with child care while 10 percent of small companies are helping with child care. Overall, more advantaged workers—those who earn more money—have greater access to these programs and policies, and less advantaged workers have less access. If you ask parents what workplace changes will help most, they typically answer "more time flexibil-

HOW IT'S WORKING OUT

■

"I'm working part-time out of my home. I'm happy. I'm successful. I'm enjoying my children. I take time for me and for my husband. It allows for great flexibility."

■

"I work full-time. There are long hours in my work, so I don't have as much time for my son as I would like. On the other hand, being home with him and not working makes me totally crazy."

■

"I have a stable part-time practice as a psychotherapist. I plan my own hours. I share space with a colleague who has a young child. I get good support from my supervisor and my colleagues, and I am totally comfortable with my child-care helper."

■

"I own my company and have for six years. My income is important to me and to my family. So is the welfare of the twenty people I employ. What's right for me may not be for everyone."

ity." Only 29 percent of workers can set their arrival and departure times. Sixty percent have access to parental leave to have a baby or care for sick children, but there may be a price they pay for using these policies in terms of being seen as less committed.

Workplaces are beginning to respond to family needs by implementing programs and policies that offer parents some flexibility. But they may not be attacking the biggest issues of removing the constraints for using these programs and making the workplace more family friendly in terms of the way supervisors treat employees. If you look at our research in balancing work and family life, having access to a program and policy, in and of itself, doesn't reduce work-family conflict; having a supportive supervisor does. The way that workplaces can be the most supportive is by training supervisors how to problem-solve when employees have work-family problems and to work out win-win solutions with employees.

SB: *What advice do you have for mothers who are trying to integrate their jobs with their kids?*
EG: If you can, look for a boss who's supportive. If you go to your boss needing a family accommodation, come in with a plan for how your work can be managed while you're away. That way the company will be more likely to respond positively to your need. For example, if you need to stay home with a sick child, present a plan for how your work is going to be done, whether by you or someone else. Finally, to the extent that you can, give yourself the five-year test in regard to the decisions you are making. In five years, how will you feel about yourself if you do or don't stay home with this sick child today?

INTEGRATING MARRIAGE, CAREER, AND FAMILY

Arlene Rossen Cardozo, Ph.D., the author of Sequencing, *three other books, and numerous articles, teaches at the university level, produces a children's radio program, and is editor and publisher of the* Read Aloud Review. *She is the mother of three and lives in Stillwater, Minnesota.*

SB: *What is sequencing?*
ARC: Essentially, sequencing is a three-part lifestyle in which women start by having full-time careers, then concentrate on full-

time motherhood, and finally reintegrate their work and their lives. I coined the expression when my book came out in 1986. I interviewed more than three hundred women and found that many of them who had predicated their lives on the masculine success ethic found great fault with it. Those who had tried living the superwoman model of the seventies and early eighties were dissatisfied. They were finding it was impossible to work full-time at high-powered careers and take care of their children. What these forefront women were trying to do was to restructure the workplace so that they could integrate their work with their lives.

The women I sought to interview were primarily those who were among the first generation to *enter* previously male-dominated fields, and many of them were now leaving for full-time motherhood. At that time there was a big concern that once you left the marketplace you were out for good. These women wanted to have children, and they wanted to work, but they didn't necessarily want to do it simultaneously. They weren't interested in returning to work if it meant working fifty- and sixty-hour workweeks; they wanted more flexibility.

SB: *What were some of the new work options they pioneered?*

ARC: • **Entrepreneuring.** This was and still is a popular choice for sequencers. It is a terrific option for women whose husband's salary provides the family with a base income. It allows women great flexibility. They can determine their own schedules and be their own bosses. Many women view entrepreneuring as a window of opportunity to grow professionally and add money to the family income while their children are growing. Others plan to continue working as entrepreneurs throughout their lives.

What surprises me is that I didn't find the same reasons for entrepreneuring in women that I've found in men. Many men who are entrepreneurs are attracted to it because they want to pursue a career in business rather than in fields like medicine, law, or engineering. The women I've talked to may be lawyers, doctors, or engineers but are going off on their own because they need more flexibility than these work environments have allowed.

• **Flextime and flexplace options.** They have certainly burgeoned over the last ten years. Many companies now offer employees flexible arrival and departure time schedules; they can choose work modules from 7:00 A.M. to 3:00 P.M. or 10:00 A.M. to 6:00 P.M. Flexplace schedules, in which you can work wherever you want to, are increasingly popular. Computers, faxes, and

"I work part-time, and usually it's at home. When I have the kids at day care and I'm home and having trouble writing, I think, What the hell am I doing? Why aren't the kids here, where I can play with them? Then, when I go and pick them up and they want my constant attention, I think, How can I get anything done?"

■

"I'm very pleased by how work and baby have comingled. I didn't go back to work until my daughter was six months old. I love my job and love being with my daughter. I'm very lucky in that I have a schedule that allows me to have my cake and eat it too."

■

"I had to go back to work because my husband is out of work and doing a 'Mr. Mom' arrangement. I feel torn. I know I have to work, but I truly miss all the extras I used to do with the girls."

■

WHEN WE'VE STOPPED WORKING

■

"I have reached my career goal. My idea of parenthood did not mean putting our child in day care for twelve hours a day. We gave up a fast-paced lifestyle of travel and eating out often because we *wanted* this child and we want to provide a stable, loving environment for him."

■

"I was a CPA. Now that I'm a full-time mother, I work harder than I did when I worked full-time. I balance more balls—finances, home remodel, preschool, self-maintenance, and correspondence."

■

"My child is my life. I'm raising him the way I want to; between my husband and me there is enough change and difference without a third person being brought in to raise my child. I will not have to look back in twenty years and say I wish I could have spent more time with my child."

■

teleconferencing provide the technology. The flexplace work model is an academic one rather than a corporate one. You're paid to do a job, and you do it. How and where it's done is up to you. In an academic environment the number of hours professors spend in the classroom may be only a quarter of their total work time. They also have office hours and committee meetings on campus, but the rest of their time—where they do research, preparation, and grading—is their own. If they want to go fishing in the afternoon and work until midnight, they can as long as they get the job done.

• **Part-time professionalism.** There has been enormous growth here. Because of the economic situation and the white-collar layoffs, this is how some people are probably going to spend a number of years in the workplace. Companies are increasingly hiring professionals for a job or a project (although some projects may last for months or years) rather than putting them on the full-time payroll. For women with small children, whose health care and other benefits are being taken care of by their spouses' companies, it may be a good match. You are able to do professional work without putting in the long hours. Many professional women have been able to convince their former full-time employers to allow them this flexibility.

SB: How has sequencing evolved since 1986, when you wrote your book?
ARC: I find that there is a great deal more dissatisfaction among women who are now in their thirties than there was in those forefront women ten years ago. The forefront women almost didn't know what hit them. They did what they were programmed to do, which was to be like the men in their work environments. Then they found out that this was not what they wanted. They wanted to have their children, and they did. They were in a hurry to get back to work because they were afraid that if they waited too long the workplace wouldn't reabsorb them.

What I'm finding now is that women at all levels are saying that if they had their druthers they wouldn't work at all. They love taking care of their children. They are very interested in community involvement. They want to use their professional backgrounds but perhaps in new ways. They are certainly not in a hurry to get back to work. They have seen sequencers who have been able to reenter the workplace after an absence. They have other role models who are negotiating very flexible work arrangements. So they are no longer scared about whether the workplace can reabsorb them; they know that it can. Most have absolutely no desire to return to work full-time, and depending on their economic situation, they are opting to stay home.

MOTHERS WHOSE WORK IS AT HOME

Marian Gormley is the public relations director of Mothers at Home and lives in Falls Church, Virginia, with her husband and twin children. For information about Mothers at Home and Welcome Home, *write Mothers at Home, 8310-A Old Courthouse Rd., Vienna, VA or call 800-783-4MOM.*

SB: *How many mothers are staying at home?*

MG: Possibly the most reliable indicator of the child-care trends across the nation is the 1990 Bureau of the Census Report, *Who's Minding the Kids?* It tells us that 60 percent of preschool children under five years of age are cared for by their own parents: 47 percent have a mother at home, 5 percent are cared for by mothers earning income at home, and 8 percent are cared for by tag-team parents. In addition to that 11 percent are cared for by relatives, bringing to 71 percent the number of young children cared for by their families. Department of Labor statistics indicate that full-time homemakers still represent the largest single occupation category among American adults.

SB: *What is Mothers at Home?*

MG: Mothers at Home is a nonprofit organization devoted to the support of mothers across the country who choose to devote their exceptional skills and good minds to nurturing their families. It was founded in 1984 with a three-fold purpose: first, to help mothers at home realize that they have made a great choice, one made by many smart women today; second, to help mothers excel at their job, for which no one feels fully prepared; and third, to correct society's misconceptions about mothering.

Mothers at Home publishes *Welcome Home*, a monthly journal with a readership of more than thirty thousand. Our journal puts mothers at home across the country in touch with each other and is written almost entirely by its readers. Mothers at Home has also published two books, *Discovering Motherhood* and *What's a Smart Woman Like You Doing at Home?*

Mothers at Home also serves as an educational and communications resource by researching, writing, and speaking out about

"I was a producer, and I quit working to stay home with the twins. I'm really not sure what I'd like to do if I did go back to work. It's working out pretty well. It can be frustrating and confining at times, though."

■

"I worked for an advertising agency and quit working when our oldest child was born. We could use more money, but I am committed to being with the children as much as possible. I didn't have them to let someone else raise them. I really see a difference between my kids and those in day care or being raised by a sitter."

■

the needs of families and communicating with mothers' groups, the media, public policy organizations, government officials, and others.

SB: *How is full-time motherhood perceived?*

MG: Motherhood may well be the most controversial profession a woman can enter today. For at least a couple of decades our major cultural institutions, education, television, and publishing have driven home the message that capable women don't stay home. American women have in grassroots fashion confronted this myth and discovered what millions of mothers and their families already know. Mothers at home enrich and enhance the quality of their families' lives. Parents in the workforce today are experimenting with family-friendly work opportunities, participating in the labor force in creative and nontraditional ways in an effort to increase the amount of time they can have with their families.

There is no question that the challenges of parenthood are taken seriously, and it is unfortunate that the media and our culture still at times portray an image of today's mother at home rife with demeaning, negative, and inaccurate stereotypes. Being home is not about choosing a set of activities. It is a focused mental effort, a vision of family life unique to the persons who do it. With grassroots efforts, such as those of Mothers at Home, society is beginning to discover three very important facts: one, that the business of trying to guide childish innocence into adult wisdom is an art worthy of extraordinary effort and time; two, that rich home life requires persistent personal investment; three, that there is a measurable value in the rewarding, stimulating, and self-fulfilling work of full-time parenthood.

SB: *What are the advantages of being a mother at home?*

MG: Full-time motherhood offers a unique and rewarding opportunity for fulfillment. It's the rare career that offers a woman the satisfaction of using all of her talents, interests, education, and life experiences to benefit people now and generations yet unknown. A mother has the benefit of being valued for who she is, not only for what she does. She is genuinely irreplaceable, and the reward lies in the reciprocal permanent investment relationship with her children. Opportunity for advancement comes when she meets the next developmental hurdle from nurturing a baby to handling the challenge of teenagers to granting the graduate his wings.

Job security is assured for a mother; in fact retirement can be postponed indefinitely because children of all ages value continued contributions from mothers. Mothers create the job description, which is as diverse as the women themselves. Self-employment offers her the opportunity to educate herself for aspects of her profession, such as psychology, medicine, art, ethics, government, and management.

A full-time mother has extraordinary incentive to perform well. She consistently witnesses that what she is willing to devote to the job is returned exponentially. There is gratification in making a contribution to society as she teaches a child positive values and instills in him a social conscience thereby influencing generations.

ZEN OF MOTHERHOOD

I was recently at a retirement party for someone I'd once worked with, and an acquaintance I hadn't seen in five years said, "How do you like being a mother?"

"If I had known how wonderful it is," I responded, "I would have become one twenty years ago."

"If you had become one twenty years ago," she said with a smile, "it might not have been this wonderful."

Of course she was right, and perhaps I was as well. I am convinced, though, that one of the negatives of growing up during the height of the women's movement—at least for me—was that motherhood seemed to represent everything we disliked. Having children was certainly considered a less worthy goal than finding a good job and making your mark in the world.

In those formative years at college, when I read Kate Millet, Betty Friedan (who although a mother herself was obviously looking for her identity elsewhere), Germaine Greer, and Gloria Steinem, I thought they were saying that women who were solely mothers were missing out on something important. Perhaps they were, or maybe the key word was solely, and I somehow missed that.

Twenty-five years later, I can't remember what these authors said. I just know that as a young woman trying to figure out how I could make my mark and contribute, I felt very strongly that being a mother wasn't a way to realize one's potential or contribute anything meaningful to society. In those days motherhood—at least to me—seemed like just an easy way to avoid making difficult decisions and testing oneself against one's peers. It seemed antithetical to pursuing one's own dreams that were independent of the *demands of husbands and children, who were—at the very least—weighty responsibilities.*

For better or worse, many of us who grew up during these times steered clear of motherhood and marriage with a vengeance. The Pill, of course, helped us chart our course through untroubled waters. They were heady times and frightening times. There were so few role models to follow. Most of our own mothers had embraced marriage and motherhood. While some of them may later have wished they'd had more options, my own mother felt she had the best of all worlds.

In retrospect, while I deeply appreciate the opportunities and the freedom I had (which other women fought for), I only wish now that I hadn't seen it as an either/or situation. I wish that I had felt more comfortable about having a fully integrated life—one in which marriage and motherhood could be as important as my career and personal freedom.

Be that as it may, at forty-something I have finally had a taste of what motherhood has to offer, and it is better than I ever anticipated. Perhaps because I was so ready to be a mother and had been independent for so long, the dependency of a small child and the sense of responsibility feel good. Maybe I'm so happy because I had already established myself in a career and felt good about who I was and what I had accomplished before I became a mother.

Whatever the reasons, when Alex looks at me and says "Mama," my heart melts. When he cuddles with me and I kiss and hug him, I feel as if I have never known such love. When he laughs my laugh and smiles until his eyes twinkle, I feel I could burst with joy.

I guess that responsibility, love, and joy are what motherhood has always been about. I wonder how I almost lost sight of that and am eminently grateful that I caught on before it was too late.

ॐ

BIBLIOGRAPHY

Aldrich, Robert A., and Glenn Austin. *Grandparenting for the 90s.* Escondido, CA: Robert Erdmann Publishing, 1991.

American College of Obstetricians and Gynecologists. *Pain Relief During Labor and Delivery.* Washington, D.C., 1989.

———. *Exercise During Pregnancy and the Postnatal Period.* Washington, D.C., 1985.

American Sleep Disorders Association. *Sleep Problems in Children: A Parents Guide.* Rochester, MN, 1992.

Ames, Louise Bates, and Frances L. Ilg. *Your One-Year-Old: The Fun-Loving Fussy 12- to 24-Month Old.* New York: Delacorte Press, 1983.

———. *Your Two-Year Old: Terrible or Tender.* New York: Delacorte Press, 1980.

———. *Your Three-Year-Old: Friend or Enemy.* New York: Delacorte Press, 1980.

———. *Your Four-Year-Old: Wild and Wonderful.* New York: Delacorte Press, 1980.

Artal, Raul. *Pregnancy & Exercise: A Complete Program for Women Before and After Giving Birth.* New York: Delacorte Press, 1992.

Balter, Lawrence, and Peggy Donahue. *"Not in Front of the Children . . ." Helping Your Child Handle Tough Family Matters.* New York: Viking Penguin, 1993.

Balter, Lawrence, with Anita Shreve. *Who's in Control? Dr. Balter's Guide to Discipline Without Combat.* New York: Poseidon Press, 1989.

Berezin, Judith. *The Complete Guide to Choosing Child Care.* New York: Random House, 1990.

Boston Children's Hospital with Susan Baker and Roberta R. Henry. *Parents' Guide to Nutrition: Healthy Eating from Birth Through Adolescence.* Reading, MA: Addison-Wesley Publishing Company, 1987.

Boyer, Richard, and David Savageau. *Places Rated Almanac: Your Guide to Finding the Best Places to Live in America.* New York: Prentice Hall Travel, 1993.

Brazelton, T. Berry. *Touchpoints: Your Child's Emotional and Behavioral Development, The Essential Reference.* Reading, MA: Addison-Wesley Publishing Company, 1992.

Bright, Deborah. *Criticism in Your Life: How to Give It, How to Take It, How to Make It Work for You.* New York: Master Media, 1988.

———. *The Official Criticism Manual: Perfecting the Art of Giving and Receiving Criticism.* New York: Bright Enterprises, 1991.

Brokaw, Meredith, and Annie Gilbar. *The Penny Whistle Birthday Party Book.* New York: Simon & Schuster, 1992.

Burck, Frances Wells. *Babysense: A Practical and Supportive Guide to Baby Care.* 2nd ed. New York: St. Martin's Press, 1991.

———. *Mother Talking: Sharing the Secret.* New York: St. Martin's Press, 1987.

Campbell, Jeff, and The Clean Team. *Speed Cleaning.* 2nd ed. New York: Dell Books, 1991.

Cardozo, Arlene Rossen. *Sequencing.* New York: MacMillan Publishing Company, 1989.

Catchpole, Terry, and Catherine Catchpole. *The Family Video Guide: Over 300 Movies to Share with Your Children.* Charlotte, VT: Williamson Publishing Company, 1992.

Chapman, Eugenia, and Jill C. Major. *Clean Your Home & Everything in It*. New York: The Putnam Publishing Group, 1991.

Cowan, Carolyn Pape, and Philip A. Cowan. *When Partners Become Parents: The Big Life Changes for Couples*. New York: Basic Books, 1992.

Cowan, Paul, with Rachel Cowan. *Mixed Blessings: Overcoming the Stumbling Blocks in an Interfaith Marriage*. New York: Penguin Books, 1987.

Cullinan, Bernice E. *Read to Me: Raising Kids Who Love to Read*. New York: Scholastic, Inc., 1992.

Culp, Stephanie. *How to Conquer Clutter*. Cincinnati: Writer's Digest Books, 1989.

————.*How to Get Organized When You Don't Have the Time*. Cincinnati: Writer's Digest Books, 1986.

Deutsch, Valerie Wolf, and Laura Sutherland. *Innocents Abroad: Traveling with Kids in Europe*. New York: N.A.L.-Dutton, 1991.

Docents of Nursery Nature Walks. *Trails, Tails & Tidepools in Pails*. Los Angeles: Nursery Nature Walks, 1993.

Donkersloot, Mary. *The Fast Food Diet: Quick and Healthy Eating at Home and on the Go*. New York: Simon & Schuster, 1992.

Edeiken, Louise, and Johanna Antar. *Now That You're Pregnant*. New York: Macmillan Publishing Company, 1992.

Editors of Sunset Books. *Children's Rooms & Play Yards*. Menlo Park, CA: Lane Publishing Company, 1988.

Eisenberg, Arlene, Heidi Eisenberg Murkoff, and Sandee Eisenberg Hathaway. *What to Expect When You're Expecting*. New York: Workman Publishing, 1991.

Eisenberg, Ronnie, and Kate Kelly. *Organize Your Family: Simple Routines for You and Your Kids*. New York: Hyperion, 1993.

————.*Organize Your Home: Simple Routines for Managing Your Household*. New York: Hyperion, 1994.

Eldridge, Wayne Bryant. *The Best Pet Name Book Ever.* Hauppauge, NY: Barron's Educational Series, Inc., 1990.

Exercise During Pregnancy and the Postnatal Period. Washington, D.C.: The American College of Obstetricians and Gynecologists, 1985.

Evans, Cleveland Kent. *Unusual and Most Popular Baby Names.* Lincolnwood, IL: Publications International, 1992.

Faber, Adele, and Elaine Mazlish. *Between Brothers and Sisters.* New York: Avon Books, 1991.

———.*Siblings Without Rivalry: How to Help Your Children Live Together So You Can Live Too.* New York: Avon Books, 1988.

Ferber, Richard. *Solve Your Child's Sleep Problems.* New York: Simon & Schuster, 1986.

Franck, Irene, and David Brownstone. *The Parent's Desk Reference: The Ultimate Family Encyclopedia—from Conception to College.* New York: Prentice Hall General Reference, 1991.

———. *What's New for Parents: The Essential Resource to Products, Services, Programs, and Information for the 90s.* New York: Prentice Hall General Reference, 1993.

———.*The Women's Desk Reference: An A–Z Sourcebook.* New York: Viking Penguin, 1993.

Frankel, Alona. *Once Upon a Potty.* Hauppauge, NY: Barron's Educational Series, Inc., 1987.

Galinsky, Ellen. *The Six Stages of Parenthood.* Reading, MA: Addison-Wesley Publishing Company, 1987.

Galinsky, Ellen, and Judy David. *The Preschool Years: Family Strategies That Work from Experts and Parents.* New York: Random House, 1988.

Gallagher, Patricia. *How to Entertain Children at Home or in Preschool.* Worcester, PA: Young Sparrow Press, 1994.

———.*Raising Happy Kids on a Reasonable Budget.* Cincinnati: Better Way Books, 1993.

Gilleran, Susan. *Kids Dine Out: Attracting the Family Foodservice Market with Children's Menus and Pint-Sized Promotions.* New York: John Wiley & Sons, 1993.

Gilliat, Mary. *Designing Rooms for Children.* Boston: Little Brown and Company, 1991.

Gillis, Jack, and Mary Ellen R. Fise. *The Childwise Catalog: A Consumer Guide to Buying the Safest and Best Products and Services for Your Children.* New York: HarperCollins, 1993.

Goldstein, Sue. *Great Buys for Kids: How to Save Money on Everything for Children and Teens.* New York: Viking Penguin, 1992.

The Goodhousekeeping Illustrated Book of Pregnancy & Baby Care. London: Dorling Kindersley Limited, 1990.

Gordon, Thomas. *Discipline That Works: Promoting Self-Discipline in Children at Home and at School.* New York: N.A.L.-Dutton, 1991.

————.*P.E.T. (Parent Effectiveness Training).* New York: N.A.L.-Dutton, 1975.

Green, Diana Huss. *Parent's Choice: A Sourcebook of the Very Best Products to Educate, Inform, and Entertain Children of all Ages.* Kansas City, MO: Andrews and McMeel, 1993.

Greenberg, Martin. *The Birth of a Father.* New York: Avon Books, 1986.

Hawxhurst, Joan C., editor. *Dovetail: A Newsletter by and for Jewish-Christian Families.* Boulder, Colorado.

Hearne, Betsy. *Choosing Books for Children: A Commonsense Guide.* New York: Delacorte Press, 1991.

Heller, David. *Talking to Your Child About God.* New York: Bantam Books, 1988.

Hotchner, Tracie. *Childbirth & Marriage: The Transition to Parenthood.* New York: Avon Books, 1988.

————.*Pregnancy & Childbirth: The Complete Guide for a New Life.* New York: Avon Books, 1990.

————.*The Pregnancy Diary.* New York: Avon Books, 1992.

Hot Shots with Any Camera. Rochester, NY: Eastman Kodak Company, 1991.

Huggins, Kathleen. *The Nursing Mother's Companion.* Boston: The Harvard Common Press, 1991.

Huntley, Rebecca. *The Sleep Book for Tired Parents: A Practical Guide to Solving Children's Sleep Problems.* Seattle, WA: Parenting Press, 1991.

Jones, Sandy, with Werner Freitag, et al. *Guide to Baby Products.* 3rd ed. Yonkers, NY: Consumer Reports Books, 1991.

Jordon, Dorothy, publisher. *Family Travel Times* newsletter. New York: Travel with Your Children (TWYCH).

Jordon, Dorothy, and Marjorie A. Cohen. *Great Vacations with Your Kids: The Complete Guide for Family Vacations in the U.S. for Infants to Teenagers.* Rev. ed. Dutton, 1990.

Kitzinger, Sheila. *The Complete Book of Pregnancy and Childbirth.* New York: Alfred A. Knopf, 1989.

Klaus, Marshall H., et al. *Mothering the Mother: How a Doula Can Help You Have a Shorter, Easier, Healthier Birth.* Reading, MA: Addison-Wesley, 1992.

Lansky, Bruce. *10,000 Baby Names.* Deephaven, MN: Meadowbrook Press, 1985.

Lansky, Bruce, and Barry Sinrod. *The Baby Name Personality Survey.* Deephaven, MN: Meadowbrook Press, 1990.

Lawrence, Judy. *The Budget Kit: The Common Cent$ Money Management Workbook.* Chicago: Dearborn Financial Publishing, 1993.

Mack, Alison. *Toilet Learning: The Picture Book Technique for Children and Parents.* Boston: Little, Brown and Company, 1983.

Miller, Jeanne. *The Perfectly Safe Home.* New York: Simon & Schuster, 1991.

Mothers at Home. *Welcome Home* journal. Vienna, VA: Mothers at Home.

———.*Discovering Motherhood.* Vienna, VA: Mothers at Home, 1991.

———. *What's a Smart Woman Like You Doing at Home?*
Vienna, VA: Mothers at Home, 1992.

National Association for the Education of Young Children
(NAEYC). *Developmentally Appropriate Practice in Early
Childhood Programs Serving Infants.* Washington, D.C.:
NAEYC, 1989.

———.*Developmentally Appropriate Practice in Early
Childhood Programs Serving Toddlers.* Washington, D.C.:
NAEYC, 1989.

———.*Developmentally Appropriate Practice in Early
Childhood Programs Serving Younger Preschoolers.*
Washington, D.C.: NAEYC, 1992.

———.Ready or Not . . . What Parents Should Know About
School Readiness. Washington, D.C.: NAEYC, 1992.

Neifert, Marianne. *Dr. Mom's Parenting Guide.* New York:
N.A.L.-Dutton, 1993.

Neifert, Marianne, with Anne Price and Nancy Dana. *Dr. Mom.*
New York: N.A.L.-Dutton, 1986.

Noble, Elizabeth. *Essential Exercises for the Childbearing Year:
A Guide to Health and Comfort Before and After Your
Baby is Born.* 3rd ed. Boston: Houghton Mifflin Company,
1988.

O'Brien, Tim. *The Amusement Park Guide: Fun for the Whole
Family at More than 250 Amusement Parks from Coast to
Coast.* Old Saybrook, CT: The Globe Pequot Press, 1991.

———. *Where the Animals Are: A Guide to the Best Zoos,
Aquariums & Wildlife Attractions in North America.* Old
Saybrook, CT: The Globe Pequot Press, 1993.

Oppenheim, Joanne, and Stephanie Oppenheim. *The Best
Toys, Books & Videos for Kids: The 1994 Guide to over
1,000 Kid-Tested Classic and New Products—for ages 0–
10.* New York: HarperCollins, 1993.

Pain Relief During Labor. Washington, D.C.: The American
College of Obstetricians and Gynecologists, 1989.

Prenatal Care. Rockville, MD: Prepared for the Public Health Service by the Health Resources and Services Administration, Bureau of Health Care Delivery and Assistance, Division of Maternal and Child Health, 1989.

Pennebaker, James W. *Opening Up: The Healing Power of Confiding in Others*. New York: Avon Books, 1990.

Richardson, Ron, with Lois A. Richardson. *Birth Order and You: How Your Sex and Position in the Family Affects Your Personality and Relationships*. North Vancouver, B.C.: Self-Counsel Press, 1990.

Rosenberg, Lee, and Saralee H. Rosenberg. *50 Fabulous Places to Raise Your Family*. Hawthorne, NJ: Career Press, 1993.

Rosenkranz, Linda, and Pamela R. Satran. *Beyond Jennifer and Jason: An Enlightened Guide to Naming Your Baby*. New York: St. Martin's Press, 1988.

Sachs, Brad E. *Things Just Haven't Been the Same: Making the Transition from Marriage to Parenthood*. New York: William Morrow and Company, 1992.

Sagall, Richard J., editor. *Pediatrics for Parents* newsletter. Bangor, ME: Pediatrics for Parents, Inc.

Satter, Ellyn. *Child of Mine: Feeding with Love and Good Sense*. Palo Alto, CA: Bull Publishing Company, 1991.

Savage, Beverly, and Diana Simpkin. *Preparation for Birth: The Complete Guide to the Lamaze Method*. New York: Ballantine Books, 1987.

Schmitt, Barton D. *Your Child's Health*. New York: Bantam Books, 1991.

Schwartz, Judith D. *The Mother Puzzle: A New Generation Reckons with Motherhood*. New York: Simon & Schuster, 1993.

Sears, William, and Martha Sears. *The Baby Book: Everything You Need to Know About Your Baby from Birth to Age Two*. Boston: Little Brown and Company, 1993.

Shelov, Steven P., and Robert E. Hannemann, editors. *Caring for Your Baby and Young Child: Birth to Age 5*. New York: Bantam Books, 1993.

Soap and Detergent Association. *Sorting It Out: Facts About Laundering*. New York, 1991.

Spock, Benjamin, and Michael B. Rothenberg. *Dr. Spock's Baby and Child Care*. New York: Dutton, 1992.

Stoddard, Alexandra. *Living Beautifully Together*. New York: Avon Books, 1991.

———. *Making Choices: The Joy of a Courageous Life*. New York: William Morrow and Company, 1994.

Sullivan, S. Adams. *The Father's Almanac*. New York: Doubleday, 1992.

Sutherland, Laura, and Valerie Wolf Deutsch. *The Best Bargain Family Vacations in the U.S.A.* New York: St. Martin's Press, 1993.

Ting, Rosalind Y., Herbert Brant, and Kenneth S. Holt, consultants. *The Complete Mothercare Manual*. New York: Prentice Hall Press, 1987.

Townsend-Butterworth, Diana. *Your Child's First School: A Handbook for Parents*. New York: Walker and Company, 1992.

Toy Manufacturers of America. *The TMA Guide to Toys & Play*. New York, 1993.

Trelease, Jim. *Hey! Listen to This*. New York: Viking Penguin, 1992.

———. *The New Read-Aloud Handbook*. New York: Viking Penguin, 1989.

Varni, James W., and Donna G. Corwin. *Time Out for Toddlers: Positive Solutions to Typical Problems in Children*. New York: Berkeley Books, 1991.

Wiley, Kim Wright. *Disneyland and Southern California with Kids: The Indispensable Guide for a Wonderful Family Vacation*. Rocklin, CA: Prima Publishing, annual.

———. *Walt Disney World with Kids: The Unofficial Guide*. Rocklin, CA: Prima Publishing, annual.

Wilton Yearbook. *Cake Decorating*. Woodridge, IL: Wilton Enterprises, annual.

Windell, James. *Discipline: A Sourcebook of 50 Failsafe Techniques for Parents.* New York: MacMillian Publishing Company, 1991.

Winston, Stephanie. *Getting Organized: The Easy Way to Put Your Life in Order.* New York: Warner Books, Inc., 1991.

———.*The Organized Executive: A Program for Productivity— New Ways to Manage Time, Paper, and People.* New York: W.W. Norton, 1994.

Wolper, Sheila, and Beth Levine. *Playgroups: From Eighteen Months to Kindergarten—a Complete Guide for Parents.* New York: Pocket Books, 1988.

Young, Pam, and Peggy Jones. *Get Your Act Together: A Seven-Day Program for the Overworked, Overbooked, and Overwhelmed.* New York: HarperCollins, 1993.

———.*Sidetracked Home Executives.* New York: Warner Books, 1981.

INDEX